MAINE IN THE EARLY REPUBLIC

1. *A Map of the District of Maine*, 1795. Osgood Carleton (1742–1816), cartographer; Amos Doolittle (1754–1832), engraver.
(Courtesy of the John Carter Brown Library at Brown University)

MAINE IN THE EARLY REPUBLIC

From Revolution to Statehood

EDITED BY

Charles E. Clark, James S. Leamon,
& Karen Bowden

PUBLISHED FOR
Maine Historical Society   Maine Humanities Council
BY
University Press of New England
Hanover and London, 1988

University Press of New England

Brandeis University   University of Connecticut   University of Rhode Island
Brown University   Dartmouth College   Tufts University
Clark University   University of New Hampshire University of Vermont

© 1988 by Maine Historical Society and Maine Humanities Council

All rights reserved. Except for brief quotation in critical articles or reviews, this book, or parts thereof, must not be reproduced in any form without permission in writing from the publisher. For further information contact University Press of New England, Hanover, NH 03755.

Printed in the United States of America

Library of Congress Cataloging in Publication Data

Maine in the early republic.

"Published for the Maine Historical Society, Maine Humanities Council."
  Includes index.
  1. Maine—History—1775–1865.   I. Clark, Charles E., 1929–   .   II. Leamon, James S.   III. Bowden, Karen.
IV. Maine Historical Society.   V. Maine Humanities Council.
F24.M25   1988   974.1′03   87-40510
ISBN 0-87451-424-X

∞

5   4   3   2   1

This project has been supported by the National Endowment for the Humanities, a federal agency that supports the study of such fields as history, philosophy, literature, and the languages.

In Memory of
RONALD F. BANKS

CONTENTS

LIST OF ILLUSTRATIONS	ix
LIST OF PLATES	xiii
LIST OF TABLES AND CHARTS	xv
PREFACE, *Karen Bowden*	xvii

	Introduction *Maine in the New Nation* Charles E. Clark and James S. Leamon	1
1	Maine's Changing Landscape to 1820 David C. Smith	13
2	Maine Towns, Maine People *Architecture and the Community, 1783–1820* Richard M. Candee	26
3	"Bordering on Magnificence" *Urban Domestic Planning in the Maine Woods* Carolyn S. Parsons	62
4	Revolution and Separation *Maine's First Efforts at Statehood* James S. Leamon	83
5	Nathan Barlow's Journey *Mysticism and Popular Protest on the Northeastern Frontier* Alan S. Taylor	100
6	Religious Revolution in the District of Maine, 1780–1820 Stephen A. Marini	118
7	Cochranism Delineated *A Twentieth-Century Study* Joyce Butler	146
8	Martha Moore Ballard and the Medical Challenge to Midwifery Laurel Thatcher Ulrich	165

9	James Sullivan's History of Maine and the Romance of Statehood *Charles E. Clark*	184
10	Jonathan Fisher's Emblematic Mind *Dorsey R. Kleitz*	198
11	Jonathan Fisher and the "Universe of Being" *Richard Moss*	214
12	Maine at Statehood *The Search for a National Style* *David H. Watters*	228
INDEX		247

ILLUSTRATIONS

1. *A Map of the District of Maine,* 1795	ii
2. Samuel Melcher III. Dove weathervane	xix
3. a. Maine 1790, Population Density	3
b. Maine 1820, Population Density	5
4. *INDEPENDENCE!!* Broadside	9
5. *A Map of the District of Maine,* 1798	27
6. Raising a meeting house, detail of an overmantel from the Lazarus Hathaway House	28
7. "A Design for a Meeting House" from *The Country Builder's Assistant*	30
8. Maps of Sturbridge, Massachusetts, 1775, 1805, 1815 and 1825	31
9. Proprietors' map of Bethel	33
10. Chester Harding. *Moses Mason*	33
11. Madawaska farmlots	35
12. Log houses along the St. John River, New Brunswick	36
13. Shaker Meeting House, Sabbathday Lake	37
14. The Pepperrellborough Meeting House, Saco	39
15. Maps of Brunswick and Topsham, 1780 and 1802	40
16. *A Plan of the Villages of Brunswick and Topsham,* 1828	42
17. Interior of the Hapgood Carding Mill	43
18. Shipbuilding, detail from *A Morning View of Blue Hill Village,* by Jonathan Fisher	43
19. Interior of the Nash Cooperage	44
20. a. Lincoln County Courthouse	46
b. Cumberland County Courthouse	46
21. *Sketch of the Peninsula of Castine in the Bay of Penobscot and District of Maine in New England,* 1814	47
22. Norridgewock Common, Meeting House, and Somerset County Courthouse	49
23. *Falmouth, Now Portland, in Casco Bay,* 1786	50
24. Constantine Brumidi. *The Reverend Benjamin Titcomb, Jr.*	51
25. Commercial Portland	
a. Central pavilion of the Maine Marine Fire and Insurance Company	52
b. The Fox Store, Middle Street	52

26. Elevation, door, and section of the Portland Bank — 53
27. Charles Codman. *Billy Hans* — 54
28. Jacques Gerard Milbert. *View of Hallowell* — 56
29. Gothic Cottage, Bath — 57
30. Gilbert Stuart. *General Henry Knox* — 63
31. Montpelier and farmhouse — 64
32. Pleasant Hill, Charlestown, Massachusetts — 67
33. Sketch of Montpelier floor plan — 68
34. Two balusters from the stair hall, Montpelier — 69
35. Knox receipt for "4 Seasons paper" and "11 figures" — 71
36. Knox account for wallpapers and borders purchased from Moses Grant — 72
37. Appleton Prentiss billhead — 73
38. Cox armchair, Montpelier — 74
39. Square looking glass, Montpelier — 74
40. Chocolate pot and cups, Chinese export porcelain, Montpelier — 75
41. Frothingham bedstead, Montpelier — 76
42. Detail of post and cleat, Frothingham bedstead — 76
43. Robert Feke. *Brigadier General Samuel Waldo* — 77
44. Ashton demi-lune table, Montpelier — 78
45. Bookcase with looking glass, Montpelier — 79
46. *A Southeast View of Fort George with the Peninsula and Harbor of Majabigwaduce, 1780* — 85
47. "THE TOWN of FALMOUTH ... 1775" from *An Impartial History of the War in America* — 86
48. First issue of *The Falmouth Gazette and Weekly Advertiser,* 1785 — 89
49. John Brewster, Jr. *The Reverend Samuel Deane* — 121
50. Gilbert Stuart. *William King* — 139
51. Title page, *Cochranism Delineated* ... by a Watchman — 147
52. Medicine chest and bottles — 166
53. *View of AUGUSTA ...,* ca. 1825 — 169
54. Eighteenth-century maternity dress — 180
55. John Christian Rauschner. *James Sullivan* — 187
56. "HIEROGLIPH. X." from *Hieroglyphikes* by Francis Quarles — 200
57. Emblematic alphabet from *The New England Primer* — 201
58. Jonathan Fisher. "FAITH" from *Youth's Primer* — 202
59. Jonathan Fisher. "Our HEART" from *Youth's Primer* — 203
60. Heart emblem from *A Collection of Emblems* by George Wither — 204

61. Jonathan Fisher. "SATAN'S GREAT DEVICE" from *Short Poems* — 205
62. Jonathan Fisher. Title page, *Scripture Animals* — 206
63. Jonathan Fisher. "ANT" from *Scripture Animals* — 207
64. Jonathan Fisher. "PEACOCK" from *Scripture Animals* — 208
65. Jonathan Fisher. Woodcut from the last page of *Scripture Animals* — 209
66. "Tempus omnia terminat" from *Choice of Emblems* by Geoffrey Whitney — 209
67. Jonathan Fisher. *Self-Portrait* — 211
68. Jonathan Fisher. "LOUSE" from *Scripture Animals* — 218
69. Jonathan Fisher. *Larkspur* — 225
70. Tombstones:
    a. William Titcomb, Falmouth. b. Mrs. Anna Pote, Falmouth. c. Mrs. Mary Freeman, Portland.
    d. Brigadier General Francis Osgood, Portland — 234–235
71. Ralph Earl. *Chief Justice Oliver Ellsworth and his wife, Abigail Wolcott* — 239
72. John Brewster, Jr.
    a. *Mr. James Eldredge* — 240
    b. *Mrs. James Eldredge* — 241
73. John Brewster, Jr. *James Prince and William Henry Prince* — 242

PLATES

following page 106

I. *Map of the Proprietors of the Kennebeck Purchase,* 1785
II. *A View of Paris Hill,* overmantel from the Lazarus Hathaway House, Paris Hill
III. *Denny Soccabeson*
IV. Jeremiah Pearson Hardy. *Sarah Mollasses*
V. Elder Joshua Bussell. *A Plan of Alfred Maine*
VI. William Stoodley Gookin. *View of Saco Falls*
VII. John G. Brown. *The Bowdoin College Campus*
VIII. John S. Blunt. *The Launching of the U.S.S. Washington*

following page 170

IX. Lemuel Moody. *The Signals at Portland Lighthouse*
X. Montpelier wallpapers
   a. "Festoon" border
   b. "Festoon" border with yellow ground paper
   c. Mica paper
   d. Fruit paper
   e. "Chinoiserie"
   f. Lozenge paper
XI. Jonathan Fisher. *The Latter Harvest*
XII. Jonathan Fisher. *Four Birds*
XIII. Jonathan Fisher. *A Morning View of Blue Hill Village*
XIV. John Brewster Jr. *Francis O. Watts With Bird*
XV. Charles Codman. *The Old State House, Augusta*

TABLES AND CHARTS

TABLE 1. Population Growth, 1784–1820   15
TABLE 2. Forest-Related Activities on Isaac Hasey's Farm in Lebanon, Maine, 1768–1787   21
TABLE 3. Religious Bodies in the District of Maine, 1780–1820   120
TABLE 4. Maine Population by County, 1772–1820   129
TABLE 5. Geographical and Chronological Growth of Major Denominations by County, 1780–1820   135
TABLE 6. Religious Composition of Maine Counties, 1780–1820   137
TABLE 7. Maine Separation Elections by County   138

CHART 1. Martha Ballard's Obstetrical Practice (1785–1812)—Number of Deliveries   173

PREFACE

The collection of writings in this volume emerges from "Maine at Statehood: The Forgotten Years, 1783–1820," a project conducted from 1982 to 1984 by the Maine Humanities Council and cosponsored by more than fifty institutions statewide. The project was funded by an Exemplary Award from the National Endowment for the Humanities.

Organized in 1975 as a local grant-making affiliate of the Endowment, the Maine Humanities Council soon recognized the appropriateness of local and regional history projects to its effort to engage Maine's people in the study of the humanities. A number of obstacles to the development of substantive public programs in Maine history soon became apparent, however. Despite the survival of a rich written and material record, large and important areas of Maine history had received little attention from scholars. Work in local history also suffered from a pronounced gap between local and professional historians. Despite the growing interest of scholars in the local experience of larger events, professional historians were often not welcome in local history projects; those who did become involved sometimes misjudged their audiences and left their scholarship behind.

When the Exemplary Award program offered state councils an opportunity to identify and conduct their own projects, the Maine Council proposed "Maine at Statehood," a project that would encourage scholarship in Maine history, draw on and integrate the written and material record, and bring that work to the public. In so doing, the Council felt that scholarship at its best often combines the conceptual and the concrete in ways that make it exciting and accessible to professionals and laypersons alike.

With the advice of scholars, teachers, and historical societies, the Council proposed to work on the years between the Revolution and Maine's statehood, that is, between American independence from England and Maine's "independence" from Massachusetts. This was a period of spectacular growth and the establishment of political, economic, and demographic patterns that were to influence the state throughout its history. In his classic study *Maine Becomes a State* (1970), the late Ronald Banks had provided a definitive political history of Maine's fitful progress to statehood, but little had been published on other aspects of Maine's history in the period. Accordingly, the Council and its scholarly advisers identified several areas of study which might complement and set in context Banks' political analysis: patterns of community and economic development; religious ferment occasioned by the emergence of evangelical and other dissenting denominations; the life of women and families in new and changing communities; and reflections of stability and change in style and taste.

The research phase of "Maine at Statehood" began in December 1982 with a conference on the state of scholarship. It concluded in December 1983 with "Maine in the Early Republic," the symposium from which the writings in this volume are drawn. In the interim, scholars participated in a range of public activities: the development of "From Revolution to Statehood, Maine Towns, Maine People, 1783–1820," a major traveling exhibition of Federal-period artifacts; a successful community lecture series; day-long consultancies in schools and historical societies; library reading programs. In these activities, scholars encountered a large and eager audience: More than 25,000 people visited the exhibition, and some 6,000 children and adults were involved in the school, community, gallery, and library events.

The writings and illustrations collected here reflect the project's interest in bringing diverse scholarly perspectives and methods to bear on a critical period of Maine and national history. They combine broad analyses of town development, stylistic trends, and religious dissent with detailed studies of local and personal experience of a society and culture in transition. We hope that in its diversity and depth this volume serves as both contrast and complement to Banks' seminal work.

The traveling exhibition, "Maine Towns, Maine People," constituted a central and public element of the project's effort to integrate the study of the written and material records of the Federal period in Maine. Recognizing this effort, the Museums Program of the NEH has awarded the Maine Historical Society—one of the most active cosponsors of the Maine at Statehood project—a grant to support the production of this volume, which documents the exhibition and the project of which it was part.

The editors and contributors to this book were centrally involved in "Maine at Statehood." Many others—scholars, teachers, archivists, and museum staffs and volunteers—deserve recognition for their contribution to the project, and through it to this completed work. William Barry, curator of the "Maine People" section of the exhibition, merits particular thanks. Barry brought to the project extensive knowledge of Maine's archives and museums, and many of the most striking illustrations in both the exhibition and this volume were made available through his efforts.

During the production of this volume, the Maine Historical Society and the Maine Humanities Council have enjoyed the continued cooperation of the staffs and boards of many institutions from which the

2. Dove weathervane, ca. 1806, from the First Congregational Meeting House, Brunswick, site of the 1816 Separation Convention, by Samuel Melcher III (1775–1862). (White pine with a trace of gilding. The Pejepscot Historical Society, Brunswick)

illustrations were obtained. David Bohl provided valuable advice on photography. As reviewers of the symposium papers, Alice Stewart, Thomas Gaffney, and Jere Daniell contributed to our thinking about individual chapters and the book as a whole. Special thanks go to Bates College for contributing the preparation of the manuscript.

KAREN BOWDEN
Project Director,
"Maine at Statehood"

MAINE IN THE EARLY REPUBLIC

Charles E. Clark & James S. Leamon

INTRODUCTION
Maine in the New Nation

By the Treaty of Paris of September 3, 1783, the independent United States joined the family of nations. Britain relinquished control of her thirteen North American colonies, bringing a grim eight-year war for American independence officially to a close. Yet for these newly independent Americans, the forty years that followed the Revolutionary conflict were as demanding and dynamic as the war years themselves.

The years 1783 to 1820 were the formative years of the new nation and each of its states. The war had ended and independence had been achieved, but the "Revolution" in its most complete sense was far from over in 1783. Americans now had to confront complex and potentially divisive questions about what the Revolution really meant for reordering and rebuilding their society and finding cultural forms that would express the nature and values of the new republic. By the end of the second decade of the nineteenth century, Americans had resolved the most pressing of their postwar issues except the gravest and most divisive one of all: the question of slavery. Americans faced the world with self-confidence, tempered by an undercurrent of lingering tensions and contradictions. Not the least of these were the conflicts among loyalties—local, regional, and national—in a rapidly expanding country. This struggle was not only for an identity, but also for the reconciliation of multiple and at times conflicting identities.

The history of Maine during this period provides a case in point. It entered the period as an outpost of Massachusetts, an outpost in every imaginable sense from political and military to demographic and social. A significant part of its own identity-seeking involved the quest for political status distinct from that of Massachusetts. There had always been a geographic and historical logic to separation, but only since the Revolution had it begun to appear to make practical sense.

The settlements of Maine had begun quite apart from those of Massachusetts Bay, but as early as the 1650s they had been subsumed by their much more populous and powerful neighbor. The Bay Colony had purchased the region as a propriety in 1677 and retained jurisdiction over it under the new province charter of 1691. Independence and the formation of the Federal Union had changed nothing in that relationship; the towns and counties of Maine simply continued to function in every legal respect as towns and counties of Massachusetts. The coastal portion of New Hampshire, however, intruded inconveniently between Massachusetts Bay proper and her great eastern extension. That meant that the "easternmost counties" of provincial Massachusetts, or the "District of Maine," as the region was called after American independence, remained geographically detached from the government on which it depended.

For more than a century after the purchase, the region had remained only tenuously occupied and often embattled. Physically isolated from the more thickly populated parts of English America and located on the very fringe of settlement, the Maine hamlets had taken the brunt of almost constant warfare with the Indians and the French. These conditions had increased rather than reduced Maine's dependence upon Massachusetts while at the same time the more heavily settled areas of the Bay Colony had counted on the frontier townships that they sponsored and helped to provision and fortify to keep the enemy far from Boston. When the enemy became the British instead of the French and Indians, Maine's strategic role was altered somewhat, but warfare continued to retard its growth and economic development—and to encourage continued political dependence upon Massachusetts. Then, when the American victory at Yorktown and the Treaty of Paris ended more than a century of almost continual conflict in North America, the vast empty spaces of Maine suddenly became much more attractive. From 1783 to 1820, the population of Maine exploded from 56,000 to 300,000, an increase of 450 percent,[1] and instead of comprising only 15 percent of the population of Massachusetts, the inhabitants of Maine now made up 36 percent of its population.[2] This dramatic demographic change alone lent new urgency to the logic of separation, but there was much more.

The great Maine population explosion, remarkable as it was, reflected a national phenomenon unleashed by the Revolution. Many Americans interpreted independence from Britain as the right to secure land of their own. The British had tried to prevent the American population, doubling every twenty-five years, from advancing into the trans-Appalachian west. Once freed from British restrictions, Americans swarmed across the mountains, creating tensions with the Indians and problems of political control for the new government. By 1820, ten new states had joined the Union, some made from newly settled territories in the West and some, like Maine, Kentucky, and Tennessee, from the former back settlements within older states.

The rapid settlement of post-Revolutionary Maine occurred in much the same way as the settlement of new lands in the West. Companies of speculators obtained huge grants of land in the expectation of selling at a profit. As in the West, the losers were the settlers, who paid high prices for the speculators' best land, and the Indians, who were excluded from it altogether. By treaties in 1794, 1796, and 1818,

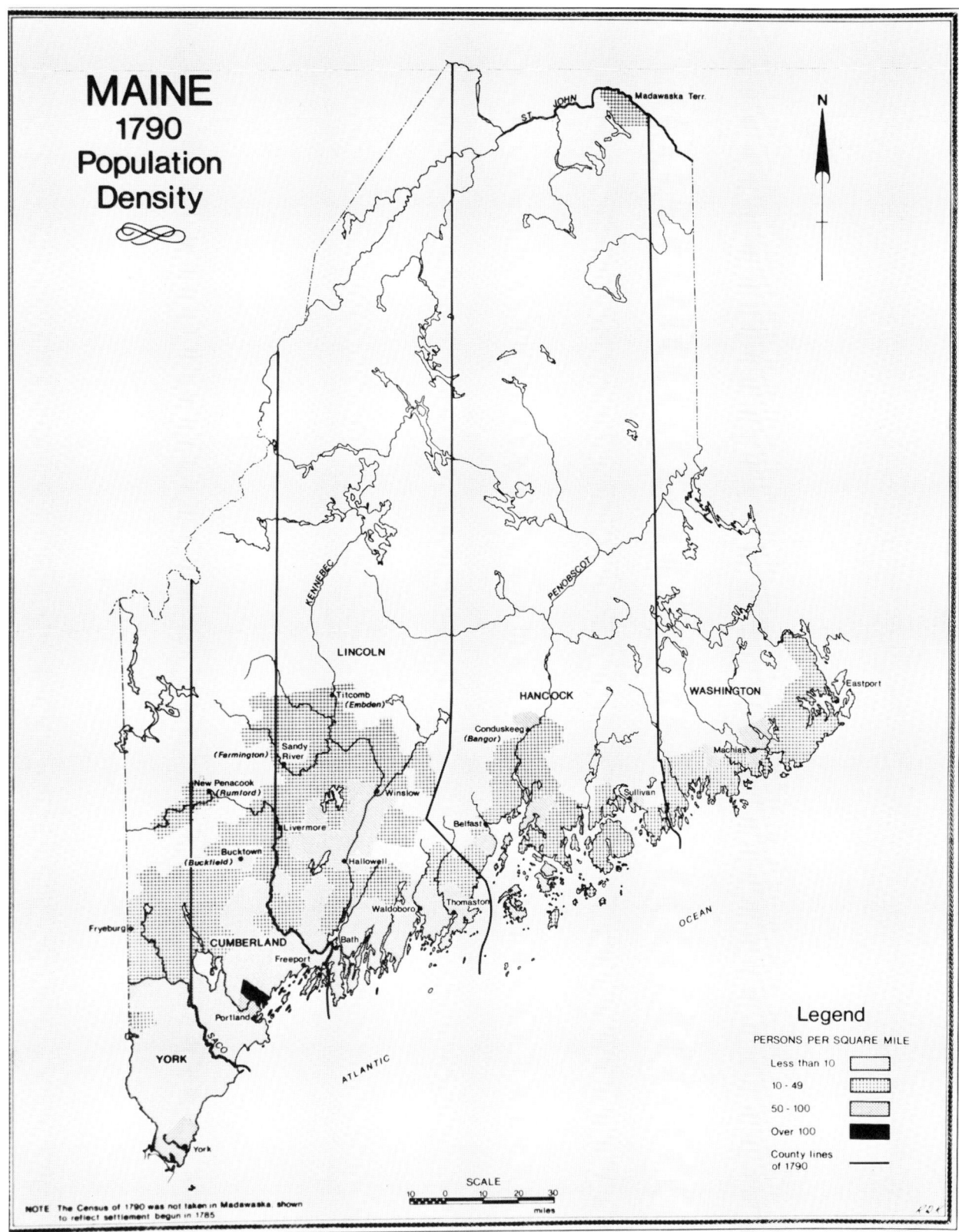

3. *a.* Maine 1790, Population Density.
(Reprinted from *The Maine Bicentennial Atlas: An Historical Survey,* [Portland: 1979])

the Massachusetts government restricted the Indians of Maine to clearly defined reservations. Unlike some of the western tribes, the Maine Indians kept their peace. Almost two hundred years later, however, they won a judicial award of 27 million dollars and 300,000 acres of land as compensation for losses in those treaties with Massachusetts, which had been illegal under the federal Non-Intercourse Act of 1790.

Squatters and settlers in the interior of Maine reacted far more violently than their Indian neighbors in defense of their "natural right" to land won from the British by common effort. In the forty years following the Revolution, organized groups of frontiersmen harassed, terrorized, and murdered agents of the great proprietors. They were drawing on an old tradition of violent protest, a tradition sanctified by successful revolution. This tradition died slowly, especially in sections of the country where inhabitants still felt as isolated from the new American government as they had from the British, as Shays' Rebellion in western Massachusetts and the Whiskey and Fries Rebellions in Pennsylvania amply demonstrated. The violence in Maine did not attract national attention, but leaders in Massachusetts and the eastern counties and their counterparts throughout the country were deeply disturbed by what appeared to be a prevailing tendency toward anarchy in the new republic.

The precarious balance among loyalties and between liberty and authority was a major preoccupation for the delegates who gathered at Philadelphia in the spring of 1787. Shays' Rebellion, put down only three months before, weighed heavily on their minds as they drew a plan for a national republic capable of neutralizing factions by its very size or, if necessary, by force. In Maine, the partly justified fear that the spirit of Shays' Rebellion had infected this outpost society cut short early efforts for statehood and offered a strong argument for ratifying the new Federal Constitution. Maine's dissident elements continued to agitate and resort to sporadic violence until the evolution of the Democratic-Republican party provided a legitimate outlet for the aspirations of the opposition.

Maine prospered under the new constitution and Federalist programs. Rising land prices reflected the continued increase in population, as did the leap in the number of incorporated towns from 71 in 1790 to 126 a decade later.[3] Maine's merchants, who dominated the life of the seaboard, not only regained some of their old markets but also found new ones, while shipping registered in the District rose from 50,000 tons in 1794 to 148,000 tons in 1807.[4] Like other American merchants at this time, Maine shippers shared in the profitable role of neutral carriers for war-torn Europe. Shipbuilding flourished under these conditions throughout the District but nowhere more than in the town of Bath. Where commerce and shipbuilding were already well-established, as in Brunswick and Topsham, textile manufacturing began to take hold. For dramatic recovery from the devastation of war,

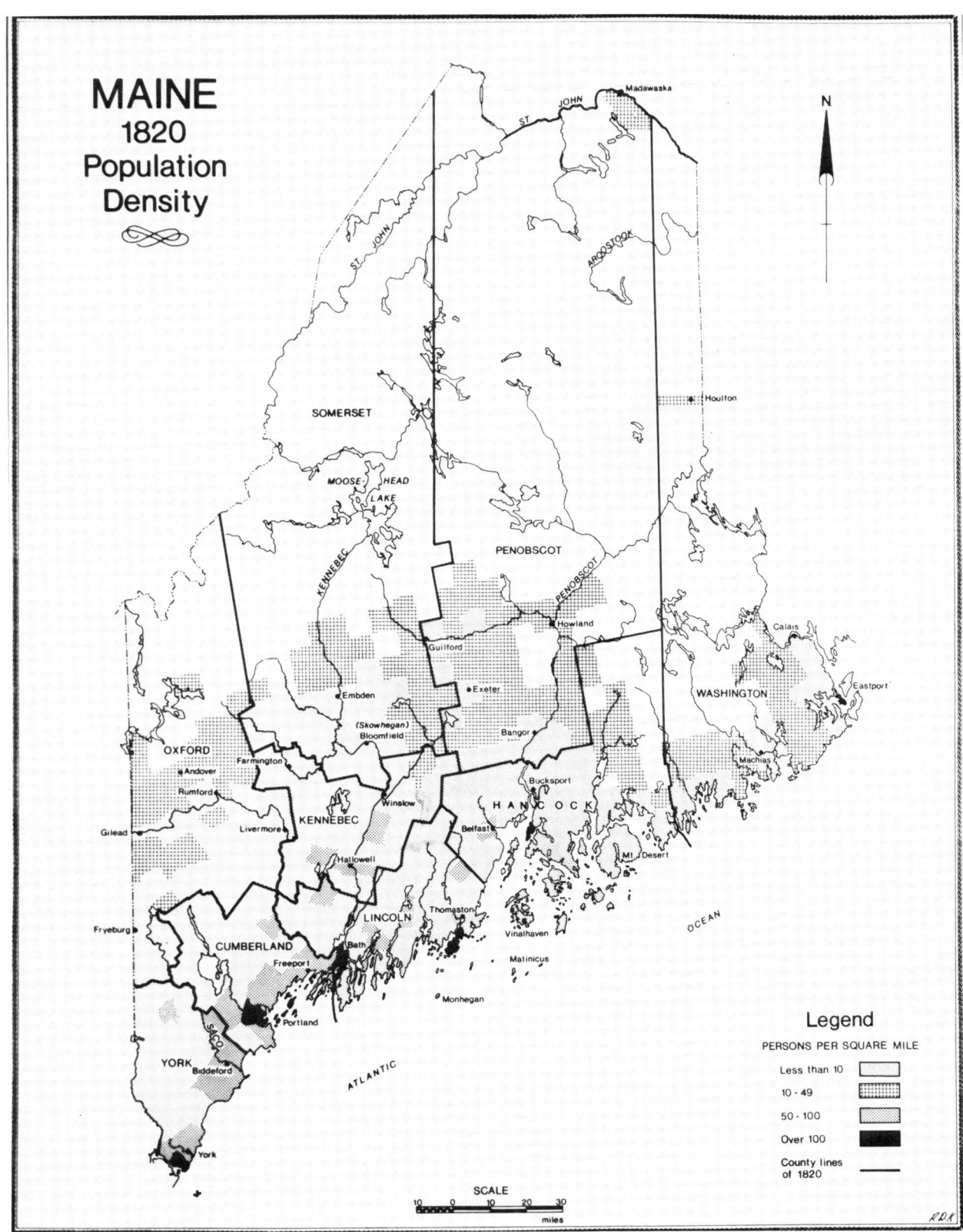

3. *b.* Maine 1820, Population Density.
(Reprinted from *The Maine Bicentennial Atlas: An Historical Survey* [Portland: 1979])

however, no town in the District came close to rivaling Falmouth. Burned by the British in 1775 and almost deserted by its residents, Falmouth reemerged in the half-dozen years after the war to resume its place as Maine's leading seaport—rebuilt, repopulated, revitalized, and renamed Portland.

National growth and prosperity, of which Maine enjoyed more than its share in these brief years, did not, however, bring tranquility. Thomas Jefferson's election in 1800 ushered in a long period of Democratic-Republican ascendency under a series of Virginian presidents. Federalists in New England, suspicious of Jeffersonian motives, remained unreconciled to the political change. Jefferson's brilliant coup in the Louisiana Purchase, extending the nation's borders from the Mississippi to the Rockies, appeared to the Federalists to be a sinister plot to undermine the political power of the northeast.

The War of 1812 and the events leading to it especially incensed the Federalists of New England. With much justification, New Englanders protested that Jefferson's embargo of 1807, and the more selective Non-intercourse Acts that followed, sacrificed their regional economy to a national cause with which New England had little sympathy. New England therefore refused to cooperate, and by 1812, when the United States declared war against Britain, Federalists in the northeast had come to regard the government in Washington as a greater enemy than the one in London. New England states not only refused to contribute their militias and money to the war effort, but continued to trade when possible with the "enemy." In retaliation, the American government withdrew federal troops from New England, claiming that they were needed elsewhere. Massachusetts, unable or unwilling to defend its eastern counties in the District of Maine, watched passively as the nearly unopposed British occupied Eastport, fortified Castine, burned Belfast, and established control over all of Maine east of the Penobscot. Federalist delegates from several New England states, demonstrating the alienation of their section from national policies, met in convention at Hartford, where amidst rumors of actual disunion, they expressed long-standing grievances against Republican administrations and recommended a series of constitutional amendments to protect their region's interests. Unfortunately for the delegates' program and the lasting reputation of their cause, the Hartford Convention occurred just as the war ended in a wave of national euphoria over Andrew Jackson's victory at New Orleans. Federalism, already in decline, never overcame the taint of defeatism and disloyalty.

The decline of the Federalists was as obvious in the District of Maine, where the Democratic-Republicans had been making significant gains over the past decade, as anywhere. As the party of opposition to the Federalist "establishment" in Massachusetts proper and along the Maine seaboard, the Jeffersonians attracted the ambitious, the discontented, and the dispossessed. Contacts between Democratic-

Republicans in Maine and the party's national leaders came through Henry Dearborn of Pittston, Jefferson's secretary of war, who was the personal patron of John Chandler of Monmouth, a party stalwart at the local level. Another important, if informal, connection developed through Richard Cutts of Saco and his sister-in-law, none other than "Dolly" Madison, the wife of the President himself. Ambitious young merchant-lawyer-politicians formed the leadership core of this growing opposition party in the District. In addition to Chandler and Cutts, they included William Pitt Preble of Saco, John Holmes of Alfred, and especially William King of Bath, the acknowledged leader of the party in Maine, who was soon to become the new state's first governor. Around this nucleus of the solidly respectable gathered a diverse group of restless land squatters and religious nonconformists who, while enjoying toleration, still faced discriminatory taxation policies under Massachusetts ecclesiastical law. So powerful became the Democratic-Republicans of Maine that in 1807, 1808, 1810, and 1811 their majorities in the District were sufficient to elect governors of their party for the entire Commonwealth.[5]

The leaders of the new political majority in the District now revived the idea of statehood for Maine, and even Massachusetts Federalists conceded that the notion was a viable one. Their concession, of course, was an act of political self-defense. If Maine were separated, the principal threat to their continued control of Massachusetts would be removed.

Separation certainly made sense to the rising powers within Maine itself because statehood for the District would satisfy the needs of the politically ambitious for their own power base, while at the same time providing a government responsive to the needs of squatters and religious dissidents. Statehood also appealed to a growing number of residents with motives no more tangible than a sense of the impropriety of Maine's continued colonial status, a sense enhanced by resentment at the failure of the Commonwealth to protect the District during the recent war. The physical outpost that was Maine had been abandoned by its metropolis, which therefore, by this reasoning, had no further claim on the District as a political outpost. The debate in this period centered for the most part on economic and political self-interest. The first movement for separation in the 1780s had drawn heavily on the natural-rights philosophy of 1776, as thought by some to apply to Maine's relationship with Massachusetts. This time, that rhetoric was largely missing; the concepts it expressed were simply taken for granted. Nobody needed convincing on those points.

On the national level, statehood for Maine would strengthen the political power of the Democratic-Republican party in congressional and presidential electoral politics, a desirable goal for political leaders in Maine but not for those in Massachusetts. The prospective political cost to Massachusetts and what remained of Federalist New England, however, was more than balanced by the emerging importance of sectional representation in Congress: There would be two more northern Senators.

In fact, by July 1819 when Mainers finally voted overwhelmingly for statehood, sectional divisions in Congress had almost entirely replaced the rivalries of party. The expansion of settlement into the Louisiana Purchase, the old northwest, and Maine aggravated the developing bitterness of the great debate over slavery. As new territories and other entities applied for statehood, the South sought desperately to maintain the balance of slave states and free states in the Senate. The timing of Maine's bid for statehood was such that it could not avoid getting tangled in the web of sectional politics. The price of Maine's identity was a compromise with slavery, a compromise that preserved the balance in the Senate by the simultaneous admission of Missouri and acquiesced in the continued expansion of slavery in the territories. Statehood for Maine, achieved on March 15, 1820, was a moral as well as a political compromise.

Excitement and enthusiasm over a long-sought new political identity in the twenty-third state, however, outweighed by far whatever lingering moral reservations may have clouded the celebration of statehood. Those reservations were sufficiently strong to prevent five of the seven Maine Congressmen in the Massachusetts delegation, committed though they had been to statehood for Maine, from supporting the Missouri Compromise. But self-identity is a powerful force, especially when it has been building and seeking institutional legitimacy over many years. The winning of statehood meant, among other things, the nation's granting of distinct status to a people that had long been developing its own particular ethos.

This does not mean that there was anything unique about the artistic, architectural, or literary forms that had been produced in Maine between Revolution and statehood. On the contrary, expressions of culture were derivative and provincial. Maine borrowed fashion and taste from Boston, New York, and Philadelphia, just as those American capitals were still borrowing from London and Paris. During that forty-year period, however, Maine artists, craftsmen, and writers became increasingly proficient and self-confident in adapting contemporary styles and techniques to older traditions in order to serve a growing population and an expanding economy.

At the same time, the products even of high fashion and academic art made their way into the consciousness of people on Maine's seacoast and in the more-developed towns of the interior by means of publications and visiting artists and skilled craftsmen. When Maine achieved statehood, none but the leading American architect of the day, Boston's great Charles Bulfinch, would do to express the authority of the new state in its capitol building. (See Plate XV.) Augusta's pastoral setting did not detract from the grandeur and dignity achieved by the monu-

INDEPENDENCE!!
July 26th, 1819.

CITIZENS OF MAINE,

Shall Maine be a free, sovereign and independent State, or shall you and your children remain forever the servants of a foreign power? This is the true question that is to be settled by your votes on *Monday next.* The friends of liberty cannot hesitate in the choice between freedom and servitude.

What shall we lose by separation? the privilege of being governed by Massachusetts. What shall we gain? the right of governing ourselves.

☞ The last year we paid Massachusetts EIGHTY EIGHT THOUSAND DOLLARS for governing us. This is proved by the OFFICIAL CERTIFICATE signed by the SECRETARY OF STATE. It will cost us less, probably not more than ONE HALF this sum to govern ourselves. Almost the whole of this is now carried to Boston and expended there. Choose *freedom and independence* and *one half of this sum will be saved* to the people, and the *other half will be spent* at home.

☞ *Six Millions of acres* of Lands in Maine are now owned by *non-resident land holders;* full *one third* of which is *owned in England.* These lands now pay but a *nominal tax.* Two THIRDS of the tax is taken off; and who pays it? ☞ It is paid by the FARMER AND MECHANIC *in addition* to his own proper share of taxes. ☞ It is these non-resident land holders who are afraid of taxes. ☞ Their land is taxed at *two per cent,* yours at *six per cent.*

☞ They now pay a *Boston lawyer* ONE OR TWO THOUSAND DOLLARS A YEAR to manage this business with the legislature. *What is taken from their tax is added to yours.* Their taxes may be increased but yours will be diminished.

These land holders are now traversing Maine in every direction. They have their *agents in pay* in every quarter, and they are all *opposed to your independence.*

If you do not wish that you and your children should forever *pay the taxes of these nabobs of Massachusetts* and ENGLAND, turn out on the next Monday and give your voices for separation.

FELLOW CITIZENS,

The eyes of all America are upon you. Your enemies are active and vigilant, and already boast of their fancied success. We exhort you to turn out in your whole strength. Let not a vote be lost. Leave your private business for a day or half a day or an hour, and convince the world by an overwhelming majority that you deserve FREEDOM AND INDEPENDENCE.

July 21.

4. *INDEPENDENCE!!,* July 26, 1819.
(Broadside. The Pejepscot Historical Society, Brunswick)

mental scale of the building and the academic correctness of its neoclassical details. In its echoes of the Capitol in Washington and of the Massachusetts state house in Boston, which Bulfinch had also designed, the capitol symbolized Maine's participation as an equal partner in the federal union. At the same time, the design of the capitol acknowledged, as did the form and general substance of Maine's new state constitution, the particular political roots from which Maine had sprung. But like the state constitution, the capitol also differed from the Massachusetts state house in significant details.

As Maine moved toward statehood, her citizens participated in the remarkably cosmopolitan cultural life which diffused throughout New England in the years after the Revolution. Alexander Parris of Pembroke, Massachusetts, designed several elegant homes and commercial buildings in Portland, while throughout the District carpenter-builders drew on handbooks which brought the neoclassical style to every village. Gilbert Stuart painted several of the District's most prominent residents; in a plainer style Connecticut-trained John Brewster, Jr., captured the mercantile and commercial families of York County. To the settlement of Farmington, Supply Belcher brought a passion for music characteristic of post-Revolutionary New England. Farmer, town agent, and teacher as well as musician, Belcher in 1794 published the *Harmony of Maine,* a collection of plain and fuguing songs and anthems, which he prefaced with a defense of all cultural pursuits: "As the encouragement of the Arts and Sciences is beneficial to all countries, and especially where the settlement is new . . . the propagation of Sacred Musick will answer a vauluable purpose—that it will not only be a means of forming the people into Societies, but will be ornamental to Civilization."[6]

The cultural expressions of Maine during this forty-year period, while not yet distinctive in form or style, nevertheless reflected and contributed to a growing sense of place. The developing cultural sophistication and artistic competence of the people of Maine occasionally resulted in the portrayal of the particularities of Maine: the beauties of its landscape in Jonathan Fisher's painting, *A Morning View of Blue Hill Village,* the glories of its past and future in James Sullivan's *History of the District of Maine,* and its economic potential in Moses Greenleaf's *Statistical Survey.* More often, Maine's artists, builders, writers, musicians, and craftsmen fused the traditional and the folk with the learned and the new. These artisans simply reflected in less explicit ways the vibrancy, the dynamism, and the self-confidence of a people with an emerging new identity for whom the status of outpost had been outgrown and had become outmoded.

The images—both written and pictorial—in this book focus on several different but related aspects of Maine's quest for identity in the forty or so years following the American Revolution. Here the reader and viewer may contemplate the withering in a number of ways of a relationship once accurately described as that between an outpost and a metropolis.

One aspect of the change was economic and physical growth, which was essential to the region's sense of progress toward statehood. Thus we begin with descriptions of the clearing of the forests, the building and transformation of towns, and the construction and furnishing of one of the District's great mansions.

We then shift to descriptions of conflicting loyalties and the various responses to authority. These loyalties and authorities are political, economic, sectional, professional, stylistic, and religious. At times, individual or sectarian morals and values traditionally associated with the "frontier" are posed against those sanctified by law or social usage and traditionally associated with mature or established societies. In these cases it is the "new" individualism, perhaps relying both for inspiration and legitimacy upon the example of the successful American Revolution, that challenges the "old" ideas of social order. In some cases, however, the challenge is not so much of the old by the new as of the new by the newer still, as when Jacob Cochran in effect contests for souls with the evangelical sects by which he has been influenced. At other times, it is a new academicism or formalism, more metropolitan than provincial and brought in from the outside, that challenges, for example, traditional medical practices or styles of building or decorating. Often, however, such challenges produce not an outright conflict but a subtle blending of authorities, as when Martha Ballard, a midwife, manages a peaceful coexistence with the new obstetrical science and its male practitioners. The blend of academic and vernacular seems especially fruitful in Maine's contribution to the artistic and literary life of the early Republic. The presentation and illustration of these topics suggest a fusion of tradition and innovation in the development of a vigorous expression of regional identity, with an occasional clarion call for statehood.

We are conditioned to think of any thinly settled, subsistence-farming interior (that is, the "frontier") as the source of innovation and democratic change in American society in contrast to the more conservative, commercial coastal settlements—and then to assume an antipathy between them. Above all else, these writings demonstrate the inaccuracy of that polarization. No place or section had a monopoly on tradition or on dynamic change. The transition from established patterns, values, and institutions to newer ones evolved everywhere—sometimes consciously and sometimes not, at times with subtlety and compromise, at other times with violence.

Although the topics in this volume are related primarily to the evolution of Maine's particular identity during this eventful period, their significance is larger than regional. The experiences of Maine, particu-

Introduction 11

12 *Introduction*

lar though they were, can also be regarded as a microcosm of the larger quest for national identity in the years after the Revolution. This collection of writings and visual images stands, we hope, as an example of what an interdisciplinary effort can accomplish in advancing our understanding of a people, a place, and a culture. The scholars who contributed to this volume have used the social laboratory that was Maine from Revolution to statehood to study some of the significant national themes of that period. They offer their findings as a collective effort to their fellow students of the Early Republic.

In a somewhat different but equally fervent spirit, they also offer these findings to those who want to read about Maine simply because it is Maine. Scholars are people, too. Most of these people have written about a place whose attraction to them is more than academic.

NOTES

1. Ronald F. Banks, *Maine Becomes a State: The Movement to Separate Maine from Massachusetts, 1785–1820* (Middletown, Conn.: Wesleyan University Press, 1970; reprinted Somersworth, N.H.: New Hampshire Publishing Company and Maine Historical Society, 1973), p. 5.

2. Evarts B. Greene and Virginia D. Harrington, compilers, *American Population Before the Federal Census of 1790* (New York: Columbia University Press, 1932; Gloucester, Mass.: Peter Smith, 1966), pp. 18, 40–46; *Statistical History of the United States from Colonial Times to the Present* (Stamford, Conn.: Fairfield, undated), p. 13.

3. Banks, *Maine Becomes a State*, p. 41.

4. Ibid.

5. Ibid., p. 42.

6. Supply Belcher, *The Harmony of Maine,* intro. by H. Wiley Hitchcock (New York: DaCapo Press, 1972), author's preface.

David C. Smith

CHAPTER I

MAINE'S CHANGING LANDSCAPE TO 1820

Between the end of the Revolution and the year of Maine's statehood, more than 240,000 people settled in the District. Whatever else they combined with their primary occupations, most of them were farmers. To illustrate some of the realities of their pioneering experience, David Smith, an environmental historian, draws extensively upon the diary of Isaac Hasey, a farmer-preacher in the newly settled town of Lebanon. With incredible energy and persistence, Hasey and his fellow farmers transformed their environment. They cut and burned two million cords of wood between 1784 and 1820—and that was for fuel alone. In addition, they built houses, barns, fences, and rapidly commercialized their activities. Lumber, naval timber, firewood, barrel staves, and shingles—and the labor to produce them—provided farmers with their most ready source of cash and credit in a world where no settlement was entirely self-sufficient. "Land clearing, land modification, and farm making," observes Smith, "was the very core of Maine's history in the decades prior to statehood."

In the past, historians studied the effects of the environment upon human activity; today's historians are equally concerned about the effects of human activity upon the land. In his recent book, *Changes in the Land: Indians, Colonists, and the Ecology of New England* (1983), William Cronon observes that "deforestation was one of the most sweeping transformations wrought by European settlement in New England." David Smith's findings not only confirm Cronon's generalization but demonstrate its application to Maine in particular.

This is a report on work in progress: a study of agriculture and land use in northern New England, the region Harold Wilson once called "the hill country." Wilson's study, completed in 1936, provides a basis for understanding the intricate relationships among the region's resources—its soil, climate, forests, and topography—and its people. In this region human beings have been involved in a constant struggle to survive since the ice receded about 13,000 years ago, although that struggle has taken different forms over the centuries. A comprehensive study of the reciprocal impact of environment and human activity, building upon Wilson's earlier descriptive treatment of the region, should provide a better understanding of the history of land

David C. Smith is professor of history at the University of Maine at Orono.

use in northern New England and a new appreciation for the extent to which this activity has modified—and continues to modify—the landscape of Maine.

To understand agricultural history within this framework, we need to define clearly the areas involved. Topographic features are generally more useful than political boundaries for this purpose; as a result, we focus on the area south of the White Mountains and east of Lake Winnipesaukee. Its northern extent is roughly the frontier of settlement in 1810; it includes Fryeburg, Lovell, Norway, Paris, Bethel, Wilton, Farmington, Skowhegan, Corinth, Bangor, Old Town, and Bucksport, and the coastal towns east to the St. Croix River.[1] Logically, the region should also include the towns in the St. John River valley, but data on land use in that area is sparse.

Agricultural development in this frontier area was dictated by several environmental factors. For instance, towns were located at the falls of rivers in order to utilize water power for gristmills and sawmills. Some form of agriculture may be practiced in the entire area described, although farming becomes increasing marginal above 600 feet in elevation. This area tends to be where white pine was the dominant evergreen, and its early use as a valuable cash crop encouraged settlement and rapid conversion of the land to agriculture. The soil is fairly productive, consisting primarily of sandy loamy till deposited by the glaciers. The valleys in particular had a large amount of land in natural meadows, called *intervales*, much of which had been under some sort of cultivation before European settlement. Since then, these meadows have been used for hay crops and to fatten cattle for overland transport. During periodic warming cycles, the intervales provided land for wheat, which allowed residents of the area to produce their own flour and bread. Since the 1790s or so, their land has chiefly produced Indian corn.[2]

Settlement patterns reflected cultural as well as natural considerations. Before 1785, land was normally allocated in the old New England manner. Prospective settlers from relatively overpopulated Massachusetts towns were organized into a group. A number of the men went to a new area, located potential settlement sites, often built rudimentary cabins and hayed natural fodder grasses, and returned for their families. Occasionally, several trips over a period of years were required to move the citizens to the new towns, and another twenty or more years might go by before the towns would be organized, accepted by the commonwealth, and represented in the General Court. Typical of this method of settlement were several towns on the edge of the agricultural frontier: Lebanon, first settled in 1747 and incorporated as a town twenty years later; Norway and Paris, both explored in the 1770s and settled in the 1790s; and Bethel, settled in 1767 and incorporated in 1796. Machias was the object of haying expeditions as early as 1761; land was allocated in 1784 and settled to considerable degree by 1805. Topsfield was visited around 1818; some cabins were built in the mid-1820s, but settlers did not arrive until the winter of 1828.³

Settlement of the region proceeded slowly until after the Revolutionary War. Beginning about 1784, Massachusetts, wishing to sell land to help meet its bills and other financial obligations, began to encourage settlement in its downeast district. Lotteries were planned to entice settlers and speculators; veterans were given land warrants. With the removal of restrictions on timber cutting, especially of large mast trees, loggers moved into the area. Rising seaboard urbanization and a growing number of draft animals in the larger cities created a booming demand for hay and oats. The District's greatest population growth took place between 1784 and 1810, according to figures compiled by Moses Greenleaf.⁴

1772	29,100	1800	151,719
1777	42,300	1810	228,705
1784	56,321	1820	298,335
1790	96,540		

This growth occurred primarily within the present boundaries of York, Cumberland, and Oxford Counties. Table 1 indicates the population change in the various counties based upon actual census enumerations, either by the Commonwealth of Massachusetts or the federal government.⁵

A population change of this magnitude—tripling in the thirty years from 1790 to 1820 and quintupling between 1784 and 1820—had a profound impact on Maine land and its use. Although we cannot quantify exactly the degree of this change, we can speculate about it by extrapolating the limited amount of data available to the larger areas being considered.

The impact of increasing population and market pressures upon the

TABLE 1
Population Growth, 1784–1820

County	Year				
	1784	1790	1800	1810	1820
York	19,909	27,560	34,284	41,877	46,283
Cumberland	15,621	23,481	31,898	42,831	49,445
Lincoln	20,791	18,668	27,998	38,570	46,843
Waldo		2,432	6,695	13,941	22,253
Hancock		5,763	8,947	13,499	17,856
Washington		2,526	4,536	7,870	12,744
Kennebec		9,105	17,995	31,565	40,150
Oxford		3,333	9,896	18,630	27,104
Somerset		2,146	5,509	12,286	21,775
Penobscot		1,154	3,003	7,841	12,870
TOTAL	56,321	96,168	150,761	228,910	297,325

"hill country" landscape was indeed profound. The most dramatic change was the rapid destruction of the original forest, resulting from intensive clearing between 1784 and 1810. Often the land was burned over after the larger, commercially valuable timber was cut. In other instances, settlers cut the forest systematically to meet their own needs for building materials and fuel. Frontier houses typically used large amounts of fuel wood. Most often cut in four-foot lengths and burned in huge fireplaces, logs were used extravagantly in a society that could envision no end to the trees. In southern Maine on predominantly sandy soils, fences were made of wood: first of smaller trees and later of slabs from the ubiquitous small sawmills. Settlement brought other changes in the coastal landscape; salt marshes were drained and diked from Boston to Machias in an effort to control the quality of the hay produced. These dikes were primarily small and built by single owners; however, in the more populated areas near Newburyport, Massachusetts, along the New Hampshire shore near Rye and Hampton, in the area of Scarborough and farther east in Machias and East Machias, land was diked by mutual companies or by single large capitalists who had consolidated land holdings. By 1840 the extensively diked area had changed much of the coast substantially from its natural state. Coastal land was also transformed by extensive cutting of oak as far north as Merrymeeting Bay. This species, prized for its water-resistant and close-grained wood, was the basis, along with the mast pines, for a prosperous shipbuilding industry along the southern Maine coast.[6]

In many areas of poorer soil, droving had already become an important form of land use by the early 1800s. Land to be used for pasture required less exacting clearing than did land intended for cultivation, but the extent of the clearing was probably greater where droving prevailed, as in Fryeburg, Paris, and Farmington.[7]

Fire also played a major part in altering the northern New England landscape. For instance, in 1761 following a period of drought great fires ravaged large areas of New Hampshire, crossed over into Maine, raced through Lebanon, and spread into Gorham, Casco, and Scarborough, where they were finally extinguished by a heavy rainstorm on August 19 and 20 after burning for six weeks. The next year, large areas in Scarborough and North Yarmouth were devastated by similar fires. As William Williamson said in reporting these conflagrations, "A prodigious quantity of the most valuable forest-timber was destroyed; and so much were crops cut short, that greater supplies from abroad than usual, were necessarily imported for the people's support."[8] During the colonial period—and until as late as 1820—it was not at all unusual for diarists when commenting on the weather, especially in the fall and spring, to mention the hazy air, "smoaky" atmosphere, or the presence of fires and cinder fall in their area. Some fires, of course, were the result of natural causes, but many were set by settlers to clear land for crops and were allowed to burn into the "wasteland" where only rain or an encounter with a lake, river, or swamp would extinguish them.[9]

From the perspective of the original settler, the process of altering the land to meet human needs was an agonizingly slow, labor-intensive effort. The settlers normally established themselves along rivers and streams and in the natural meadow intervales. Here they would plant food crops and after building their houses, use the surrounding areas for lumber, firewood, and finally orchards and fields. This process took about twenty years of hard, continuous labor; an average family could clear and plant three to seven acres of land per year. Usually after about twenty years the first house was replaced with a grander edifice, again with locally manufactured lumber. Occasionally, the original house provided a central focus for the new structure. Many of the houses in Maine bearing dates of 1820 to 1830 shelter a one room cabin, and the facade we see today actually may date from the 1840s. As stoves were introduced, first into the fireplace and later as freestanding elements in the kitchen, such rebuilding became common. These larger houses often consumed close to twenty cords of firewood a year, thus accelerating clearing of the forests. Cutting wood for fuel probably contributed most to the immense change in landscape and land use during this period. The wood lot as a specific harvested section probably emerged in the second generation, if not the third, when distance to undesignated woodlands for fuel wood created a recognizable hardship.[10]

As trees were cut and land opened for cultivation, stream flow in the area was affected almost immediately, and as a result, about twenty years after settlement, farm diarists often complained of freshets and flooding in both fall and spring. The results of clearing on fertility is less well known, but the continuous clearing of adjacent land for the first thirty years or so, while land was relatively inexpensive, suggests an adverse effect. In any case, we know from the available evidence of diarists that fires, floods, constant land clearing, and fence building were normal aspects of the seasonal routine. Such efforts took a surprising amount of time over the course of the entire work year.[11]

Farm diaries are among our most important sources of information about these matters. Entries in the diaries left by Isaac Hasey of Lebanon suggest some further tentative conclusions about the interrelation between human and natural forces in this Maine farming frontier. As a settlement, Lebanon dates from the late 1740s; it was incorporated in 1767. Hasey moved there as one of the earliest settlers and became the town's first resident minister. Since town taxes supported the church, Hasey was the recipient of much work done by others to meet their tax obligations to the town, but he was also a hard worker himself. His diary shows a consistent pattern of work to modify the land from its original forested state. The work performed on Hasey's farm is exemplary of that done on thousands of other small Maine landholdings during this period. Such labor was a legal as well as a moral obligation, so Hasey kept a strict account of the days worked and those who performed the labor.

Wood was constantly being cut and hauled for use as fuel. January, February, and occasionally March were the months of greatest effort, although it was not unusual for additional wood to be cut and hauled in December. Hasey did not often mention the actual cutting; he was more interested in the hauling and the specific amounts of the loads. Land clearing also went on in this period on what were called the "moor" lots, or new land opened up as the town population grew above the estimated 200 in 1770. Clearing was the work of March and April, until plowing and raising crops began to take precedence. On rainy days, wood was split for the fireplace, although not much needed to be done since most fuel wood was used in large pieces in great fireplaces in parts of the main house. Fence making and repair occupied much of the spare time of both Hasey and his hired men. Usually, this work was not part of the legal obligation of his parishioners. After the merchantable wood (fuel wood and fencing stuff) was cut and hauled away, the land was nearly always burned of its undergrowth, preparatory to plowing and seeding. By 1768, Hasey had transformed his land so significantly that he could introduce orchard trees, primarily apple but also pear and currant. These trees were available in Dover from William Hanson, who apparently operated a nursery for the settlers.[12]

In addition, new land was constantly being surveyed; there were few years in which the lines in Hasey's vicinity were not run by a surveyor. Hasey and his neighbors occasionally walked the boundaries to further establish their actual location. After September when the first harvests were in, there was further opportunity to clear new land and to burn the piles of brush that had been collected. The danger of fire apparently was sufficient to create an occasional cooperative effort in the burning. Still, fires got away and destroyed forest and fencing. Hasey found himself and his crew mending burnt fences in 1774, 1775, and 1776, for example. His diary expresses no real feeling about the damage, as it apparently was a common hazard in those early days. As slabs became available from the mill, he frequently used them for fencing in place of the alder and other small stocks. This area is covered with stone walls today, but from the accounts of brush, wood, and slab fencing used, it appears that here, at least, the stone walls came later as the competition for cash crops and the need to control wandering cattle increased.

Farm work, incidentally, was done almost entirely with the aid of oxen. The few horses available were used for pulling carriages or for riding. Hasey kept milch cattle, hogs, and sheep. The sheep normally ran loose year round, except in the coldest weather, when he provided some hay at the barn for them. Since sheep are very close foragers, their grazing must have added to land change. In his orchards, Hasey (along with nearly all the other diarists of the period) planted wheat, indicating more intensive use of relatively small amounts of land. His other crops were peas, oats, turnips, and garden "sass." The farmers grew some corn, but rather less than might be expected. As time went on, they would grow more corn and less wheat, demonstrating the ready availability of crops from other trading areas. Potatoes were widely sown as a crop on the newly cleared and plowed land.

An indication of Hasey's status as an established farmer was his shingled barn, built in 1773. Apparently, he continued to use the earlier unshingled and smaller barn alongside the new structure. By November 23, 1772, Hasey's diary reveals he had begun a modest timber-selling business, demonstrating both his growing economic prestige and his connection with another prominent land use in the frontier region. On December 14, 1772, "a large crowd gathered at the tavern for a vendue of timber lands." Five large lots changed hands in this sale for £84 6s.

The mid-1770s brought increased attention to fencing, suggesting growing population pressures. Logging became a major spring business even when "the ground was barely covered with snow" (February 16, 1775). The year 1775 was an eventful year: Fire was followed by a July windstorm, which tore down fences and moved Hasey's barn from its foundation (July 17). Much time was spent over the next month, as men were available, shoring up the building, leveling the floor, and otherwise mending the barn. The next year even greater fires threatened the area, as new settlers were either less careful or temperature and moisture conditions created hazards (May 20, 21, 29, 1776). That fall Hasey himself burned new areas of land for clearing (September 17, 24, October 14, 19, 1776). In 1777 Hasey and his parishioners began work on a sawmill, which would occupy a good deal of Hasey's time for the remainder of his life. Lumber and land sales had become even more important in the area, which was now ready to leave the pioneer period. In 1778 for instance, Hasey noted the sale of lumber from two lots for a substantial sum, and allowed the purchaser seven years to haul the down timber away (November 20, 1778). As more and more people came to live in Lebanon, wood cutting and hauling became group efforts, entailing many yoke of oxen and many helpers. This development, too, showed a growing sophistication in the local frontier economy.

In 1781, Hasey began to repair, partially reshingle, and build an addition to his house. In the same year, the town voted to supply him with twenty cords of wood each year for as long as he remained as minister (December 7, 1781). At about the same time the town also built a new meeting house, which still stands. With its formal clapboard facing and strong foundation, the building became a focus for the settlement. Although the pioneer stage was nearly over in Lebanon, Hasey noted on December 6, 1782 that wolves—reminders of the still-untamed woods—had killed five of his sheep; the frontier was indeed still very close at hand.

On October 22, 1785, a great freshet carried off the mill. Although many of the old timbers were salvaged downstream, rebuilding took a great deal of Hasey's time. By December 21 the mill was back in working order. During the next year, Hasey was not only still making and mending fence, but also building more permanent stone walls near his house and along the road. We can safely say that with this development the boundaries of the cleared land were relatively fixed, and the process of clearing the forest was over. This process, taking about twenty years in all, would be repeated over much of Maine in the period up to 1820 and less frequently thereafter, as much of the normally usable land was filled up. The upland edge of this frontier, except for Aroostook County, was climatically and agriculturally marginal, and as the American West was opened to settlement, much of Maine's marginal land would begin to revert to forest after the first twenty years or so of pioneer effort. Examples of this cycle include the towns of Madrid, Weld, Cambridge, Salem, Lexington, Concord, Exeter, Topsfield, Waite, and Kossuth, all of them retaining some residential population, but also numerous empty cellar holes, stone walls, and old-field timber—the fading symbols of dashed agricultural dreams.

Table 2 shows the number of days that Hasey or his workers spent on forest-clearing and other pioneer activities in the years 1767–1787. We could construct similar tables for nearly all the towns in the District before the Revolution and during the years between the Revolution and statehood. The table shows, among other things, that as time went on, more and more days were spent hauling fuel wood. This suggests increasingly greater distances to good wood sources and growing fuel needs as houses were enlarged. Hasey's needs for fuel wood increased until 1783–1784, after which the town provided a standard amount, suggesting that Hasey's house had achieved its final form. The Hasey family burned about 20 cords of fuel wood each year, although in the beginning with a smaller house, the amounts were probably smaller—perhaps no more than 15 cords. Clearly, some years would require more. The 1770s and mid-1780s had particularly cold winters, as did the years from about 1805 to 1810 and especially the years 1815–1817.[13]

The amount of time spent clearing land was substantially greater in the earlier years, although some time each year was spent on this task in later periods, as perhaps additional land was acquired or wider food needs developed. Entries regarding fencing—both repairs and new construction—remained prominent in Hasey's diary throughout the period. With labor and materials readily available and the boundaries of cleared land still in flux, there was no pressure to put up permanent fencing until the very end of the period. Hasey spent a fair amount of

TABLE 2
Forest-Related Activities on Isaac Hasey's Farm in Lebanon, Maine, 1768–1787
All Figures in Man-Days, Except Fuel-Wood Amounts*

Year	Hauling	Amounts	Clearing	Fencing	Burning	Plowing	Planting
1768	$10\frac{1}{2}$	9 loads	17	6	3	2	5
1769	$9\frac{1}{2}$	8	6	2	3	2	5
1770	Diary not available except for scattered dates			2			
1771	Diary not available						
1772	$8\frac{1}{4}$	5	1	4	3	1	1
1773	8	10	3	5	3		
1774	12	10		10			
1775	$17\frac{1}{2}$	46		$17\frac{1}{2}$			
1776	7	27	1	14	4		
1777	16	30		5	1		4
1778	37	43		6			
1779	20	$17\frac{1}{2}$		8			
1780	31	3 & 22 cords		2			
1781		$7\frac{1}{2}$ cords		1			1
1782	2	$28\frac{1}{2}$ cords		5		1	
1783		$17\frac{1}{4}$ cords	$\frac{1}{2}$	$3\frac{1}{2}$			
1784		20 cords, 4 loads slabs		$11\frac{1}{2}$			
1785		20 cords, 8 loads slabs		7			3
1786		20 cords		8			
1787	6	20 cords	2	28	3		
TOTAL	185	$220\frac{1}{2}$ loads $155\frac{3}{4}$ cords	$30\frac{1}{2}$	$133\frac{1}{2}$	22	6	19

*Plowing and planting days are for new orchards only and do not include crop days in orchards. Each day recorded is a man-day and may include several men working for part of a day and summed by author. Wood-hauled amounts include estimates based on diarists use of "jag" or "twitch" to indicate partial loads. It does not include logs hauled directly to the sawmill to be made into lumber.

time in burning associated with land clearing and devoted additional time to plowing and planting new orchards. Other source material not analyzed here would indicate more precisely the amounts of time he and his work force spent plowing, planting, harvesting, haying, and tending his animals. Taken together, evidence of this sort reinforces our concept of frontier homemaking as a difficult, time-consuming, and arduous task, but also an effort that dramatically reshaped the Maine landscape.

Of course, the largest single change in Maine's landscape was caused by logging. Wood was the basic commodity of an agricultural-forest economy that had not yet been transformed by steel and steam. Its major, although by no means exclusive uses were in the manufacture of a wide variety of implements, casks and barrels, and fencing, as fuel, and in shipbuilding. Markets existed for many species of northern New England wood, and settlers learned quickly to adapt their economy and land use to the unique composition of the northern New England mixed forest. In turn, this activity, along with changing lumber markets, played an important part in shaping the composition of the forest.

The large pines were cut with great care, frequently felled into beds of smaller pines and spruce in order to preserve their strength for shipmasts and spars. Oak was cut mainly for shipbuilding. Hackmatack, previously called "juniper" and now known as larch, was grubbed for its roots, to be used as ship knees because they are extraordinarily strong. Hornbeam was sought as a source of trunnels for ships and other large structures. All the deciduous species, but mostly maple, beech, birch, and oak, were used for fuel wood, of which pioneer homes used great amounts. Even spruce and hemlock were used for flooring where the prying eyes of the visitor might not notice. In many palatial homes, spruce was used for the second-floor sleeping quarters and hemlock in the attics and servants quarters.

Pine, of course, was the premier wood. It makes marvelous wainscoting and excellent flooring. Used as an exterior lumber, it has the remarkable capacity of hardening when in contact with the open air, so it actually grows stronger with time. The best pines for building—"sapling" or "pumpkin" pines—seem almost to swallow builder's nails and then form a carapace around them as the wood responds to the weather. Even elm was in demand for wheel hubs, thills (wagon shafts), and mangers. The new settlers found wood that was of value to them everywhere they went. Even the act of burning produced potash and pearl ash as a cash crop in a period when chemical compounds, yeasts, and leavening agents were not widely available.

Consumption of wood for fuel may well have been the major factor in changing the forest landscape in frontier Maine. Some cordwood from Maine was sold as far away as the Boston and Cambridge markets by the end of the Revolutionary War, but not as much as from inland Massachusetts and to a lesser extent from New Hampshire. In late December 1775, Hasey recorded in his diary that he and a crew of twenty-four men drew five large loads of fuel wood to Cambridge. The purpose of this trade is unclear. Perhaps it was strictly a commercial transaction. Possibly it was aimed at supplying the Continental Army with fuel during its siege of Boston throughout that winter. In any case, a record of such hauling does not appear in Hasey's diary again before 1785.

If we figure that the average Maine household was made up of six people, we can reduce the census figures to an estimate of about 9,000 households in 1784; 16,000 in 1790; 25,000 in 1800; 38,000 in 1810; and nearly 50,000 in 1820.[14] If we carry our calculations further and estimate that each household burned an average of 15 cords of wood per year, we can arrive at a crude estimate of the amount of fuel wood cut and burned each year. Thus we can estimate that the following amounts of fuel wood were consumed in Maine in the census years from 1784–1820.

1784	135,000	cords
1790	240,000	
1800	375,000	
1810	570,000	
1820	750,000	
Total	2,070,000	cords, or 1,035,000,000 board feet

These figures, of course, do not include the fuel wood used for industrial purposes, which would add substantially to the annual consumption totals. Burning lime rock to produce lime (called *lime burning*) along the central coast, for instance, required prodigious amounts of wood and was largely responsible for the deforestation of Maine's islands and coastal areas. All in all, extraordinary demands for fuel wood accompanied the extension of the Maine frontier between 1784 and 1820.

Gathering this essential fuel supply was itself a demanding part of frontier life. Enormous amounts of energy were consumed by this work, which is one of the reasons why frontier people ate such hearty meals. Their caloric intake had to be immense, and foods used to produce these calories were very heavy by today's standards. This need for energy accounts for the large amounts of barley, rye, buckwheat, turnips, and cabbages, as well as high protein meats, both domestic and wild, that were consumed. We can only wish that Hasey's wife had kept a diary, indicating how much of her time was spent in preparing food and cooking these large meals. However, we can say that these appetites do provide an explanation for the rich recipes contained in reproductions of colonial cookbooks.[15]

Work on the farm, whether initial clearing or later cash-crop production, was a year-round occupation that included a variety of frontier pursuits, which we do not often associate with traditional agricultural practices.[16] Changing the face of the land was a remarkably comprehensive task, and when we drive through this area today (even though it is returning to its original forested form in many places), we can still see many indications of pioneer labor. By the time it attained statehood, Maine was a much different place than it had been in 1784. This extraordinary job of land clearing, land modification, and farm making by thousands of people is the very core of Maine's history in the decades prior to statehood.

ACKNOWLEDGMENT

I wish to express my gratitude to Richard Judd for his valuable editoral assistance.

NOTES

1. Excellent descriptions of the areas being discussed may be found in William D. Williamson, *The History of the State of Maine from Its First Discovery, A. D. 1602, to the Separation, A.D. 1820*, 2 vols. (Hallowell, Me.: Glazier, Masters & Co., 1832), especially vol. 1, pp. 10–182; Jeremy Belknap, *The History of New Hampshire*, 3 vols. (Boston: Bradford and Read, 1813), vol. 3. My concept of the Maine frontier of settlement is based on Paul Coffin, "Memoir and Journals of Rev. Paul Coffin, D.D.," *Collections of the Maine Historical Society*, 1st ser., 4 (1856), 301–357.

2. Mostly based on work in progress, although Clarence Day, *A History of Maine Agriculture* (Orono, Me.: University of Maine Press, 1954) is in general agreement, as is Harold Wilson, *The Hill Country of Northern New England* (New York: Columbia University Press, 1936). For another useful early account of the area, see Thomas Starr King, *The White Hills* (Boston: Crosby and Nichols, 1862); for an early fictional account, see Isaac W. Scribner, *Laconia: or Legends of the White Mountains and Merry Meeting Bay* (Boston: Kelley, 1856); the second edition (1857) is entitled, *Roselle of Laconia*.

3. John Hayward, *The New England Gazeteer* (Concord, Mass.: I. S. Boyd & W. White; Boston: The Author, 1839); William B. Lapham, compiler, *History of Bethel, Maine* (Augusta, Me.: Press of the Maine Farmer, 1891) and others of Lapham's works on these Oxford County towns; Records of Proprietors of Machias; Town Meeting Records, Machias; personal knowledge.

4. Moses Greenleaf, *A Survey of the State of Maine* (Portland, Me.: Shirley and Hyde, 1829), p. 134. Greenleaf does not explain the discrepancies between his figures and those of the censuses.

5. Ibid., pp. 132–151; a discussion of population and population statistics appear in James Sullivan, *History of the District of Maine* (Boston: I. Thomas and E. T. Andrews, 1795), Chapter VIII, pp. 390–92; Lapham, compiler, *History of Bethel*, Chapter XV, which is especially good on Oxford County settlements.

6. Work in progress with W. R. Baron on the use of salt marshes for hay along the Atlantic coast. The techniques for diking and controlling the saline content of the water was established clearly in 1797 by Samuel Deane, *The New England Farmer, or Georgical Dictionary* (Worcester, Mass.: Isaiah Thomas, 1797). Anne Bridges and I have discussed some aspects of this history in "Salt Marsh Dykes [Dikes] as a Factor in Eastern Maine Agriculture," *Maine Historical Society Quarterly*, 21 (Spring 1982), 219–226 (hereafter, *MeHSQ*); related geological and sea-level data can be found in a number of publications of the Maine Geological Society written by me and my associates, and especially in Walter A. Anderson et al., "Crustal Warping in Coastal Maine," *Geology*, 12 (November 1984), 677–680. The early shipbuilding industry, focusing on Kennebunk, has been written about by John G. B. Hutchins, *The American Maritime Industries and Public Policy, 1789–1914* (Cambridge, Mass.: Harvard University Press, 1941). An account of later shipbuilding activities on Maine rivers appears in David C. Smith, "Coastal Shipping on the Eve of the Railroad: Gardiner, Maine, in the Early 1830's," *MeHSQ*, 13 (Winter 1974), 148–177, especially pp. 157–158.

7. Droving is discussed briefly in Belknap, *The History of New-Hampshire*, vol. 3, as a factor in the area under discussion. A detailed analysis, with emphasis on Maine contributions, is presented in David C. Smith and Anne E. Bridges, "The Brighton Market: Feeding Nineteenth Century Boston," *Agricultural History*, 56 (January 1982), 3–21.

8. Williamson, *History of Maine*, vol. 2, pp. 364–365; see p. 259 for a description of earlier fires. See also Catherine Fox, "The Great Fire in the Woods" (M.A. thesis, University of Maine at Orono, 1985).

9. The standard histories of fire, such as Stewart Holbrook, *Burning an Empire* (New York: Macmillan, 1943), do not discuss this sort of burning very much, if at all. They are concerned with larger fires, although Holbrook does devote a chapter to the Miramichi fire, which caused extensive damage in Maine in 1826. Stephen Pyne, *Fire in America* (Princeton, N.J.: Princeton University Press, 1982), recognizes in a disorganized way the relationship of fire to clearing but devotes little attention to the eastern United States. Many paleoecologists have treated fire as an ecological factor of the past several thousand years, but historians have done little as yet to incorporate this knowledge into their work. For examples see Albert M. Swain, "A History of Fire and Vegetation in Northeastern Minnesota as Recorded in Lake Sediments," in "The Ecological Role of Fire in Natural Conifer Forests of Western and Northern America," H. E. Wright, Jr., and M. L. Heinselman (eds.), *Quaternary Research*, 3 (October 1973), 383–396; J. S. Rowe and G. W. Scotter, "Fire in the Boreal Forest," ibid., pp. 444–464; see also R. Scott Anderson, "A Holocene Record of Vegetation and Fire at Upper South Branch Pond in Northern Maine" (M.A. thesis, University of Maine at Orono, 1979). The diary accounts referred to are representative of nearly a thousand such accounts from this period that I or my students have read over the past decade.

10. Land clearing and timber usage is based on Williamson, *History of Maine*, vol. 1, pp. 106–112; Belknap, *The History of New Hampshire*, vol. 3, Chapters VI and VIII. Chapter VI contains a good account of road building in this area, which of course also modified land use substantially.

11. Comments based on diaries of Isaac Hasey, Lebanon, Maine, 1767–1809, MeHS; Caleb Scribner, Paris, Maine, 1809–1821, Bangor Public Library and private collections; Town and Proprietors Records, Machias, 1784–1860; Lapham, *History of Bethel*, and the various historical articles about early Bethel written by Nathaniel T. True between 1850 and 1870. *The Oxford Democrat* of this period is a rich source of such pieces.

12. I do not wish to burden the reader with extensive citations from these diaries. In fact, much of the material is summarized in Table 2, Forest-Related Activities on Isaac Hasey's Farm. For the burning, however, see entries of April 15, 16, 18, 22, 1768. For the nursery purchases, see entry of May 5, 1768: 50 apple trees, 4:13/9d [pounds, shillings, and pence] old tenor.

13. My colleagues and I have dealt with the impact of climate change in a number of writings, but the most accessible for Maine readership is "Climate Fluctuation and Agricultural Change in Southern and Central Maine 1765–1880," *MeHSQ*, 21 (Spring 1982), 179–200.

14. Jim Potter, "Demographic Development and Family Structure," in Jack P. Greene and J. R. Pole (eds.), *Colonial British America: Essays in the New History of the Early Modern Era* (Baltimore, Md.: Johns Hopkins University Press, 1984), p. 146.

15. Two examples are Clarissa M. Silitch (ed.), *The Old Farmers Almanac Colonial Cookbook* (Dublin, N.H.: Yankee, Inc., 1976); Lynne J. Belluschio, *Selected Recipes from the Genessee Farmer, 1831–1856* (LeRoy, N.Y.: The Author, 1981).

16. See David C. Smith, "The Harvest Cycle in Nineteenth Century Maine," in Duncan Howlett (ed.), *The Small Woodland Owner in Maine*, Technical Note No. 85 (Orono, Me.: College of Forest Resources, 1982), pp. 9–11. Other papers in this publication also bear reading.

Richard M. Candee

CHAPTER 2

MAINE TOWNS, MAINE PEOPLE
Architecture and the Community,
1783 – 1820

Part of the changing landscape of Maine was its villages and towns. These included a sizable number of trading and manufacturing towns, but even the primarily agricultural communities were far from static. Over time, the varied demands of commerce, industry, government administration, and farming shaped the function and thereby the physical appearance of communities. By using illustrations from the Maine at Statehood traveling exhibit, entitled "Maine Towns, Maine People: 1783–1820," architectural historian Richard Candee points out that the architecture and layout of Maine's community centers were physical responses to the changes in social organization. They were also cultural responses, and Candee emphasizes that the growing number and importance of village centers throughout Maine stimulated the proliferation of structures both public and private whose facades made a cultural statement in the latest Federal style.

The end of the Revolution ushered in a new era of town building throughout New England. In Maine the rebuilding of coastal communities and the building of new interior settlements took on a special character. "Great numbers of our most enterprising eastern inhabitants, by dint of industry and toil," wrote William D. Williamson, "changed tracts of wood or wild lands into farms, accommodated with dwelling houses, outbuildings and the conveniences of life."[1] Within a few years they also built new sawmills, barns, churches, factories, courthouses, banks, and a wide range of commercial structures, as shown in Illus. 5. Through such intensive building activity the men and women of this era transformed the Maine landscape into patterns that can still be recognized. These patterns of community-building are the result of both cultural and economic factors; Maine's architecture and village centers of that era are physical mani-

Richard M. Candee is well known in northern New England as a museum and historic sites consultant and is Director of Preservation Studies in the American and New England Studies Program at Boston University. He was curator of the "Maine Towns" section of the exhibition, *From Revolution to Statehood*.

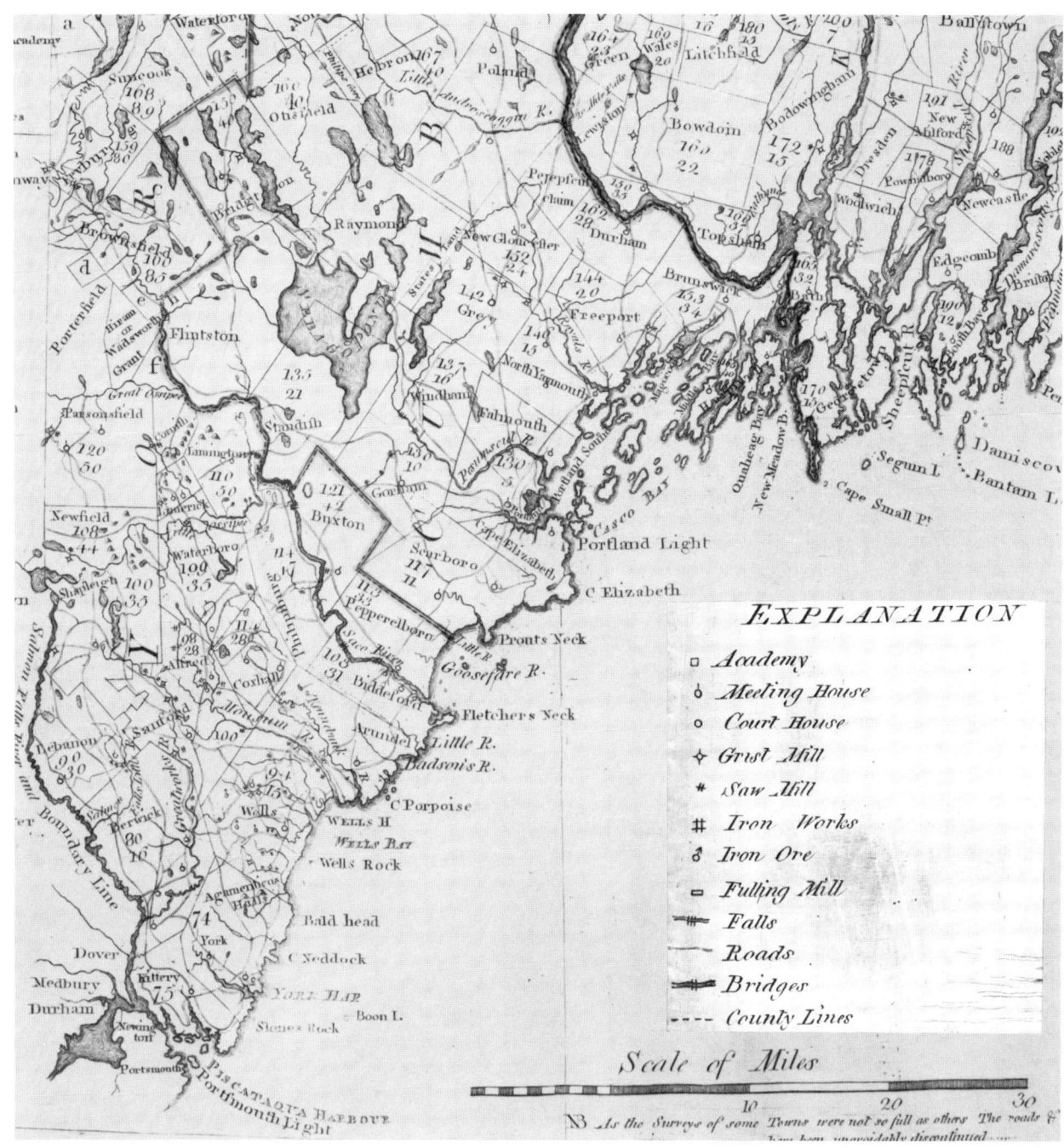

5. *A Map of the District of Maine,* 1798 (detail). Osgood Carleton (1742–1816), cartographer; John Norman (1748–1817), engraver.
(Courtesy of the John Carter Brown Library at Brown University)

6. Raising a meeting house, detail of an overmantel (Plate II) from the Lazarus Hathaway House, Paris Hill, ca. 1803.
(Oil on board. The Hamlin Memorial Library and The Paris Hill Historical Society)

festations of a widespread change in the region's system of social organization. The brief sketches of the physical growth and economic organization of selected communities, with portraits of a few of their better-known citizens, represent the far larger number of examples still awaiting more detailed research.

Village centers, like the one shown in the overmantel painting from the Lazarus Hathaway house of Paris Hill (see Plate II), emerged to serve a variety of social and economic needs. Painted in about 1803, this image of the Paris Hill town common shows men clearing the land of pines. In addition, nearly hidden in the background among the newly built homes, is a rare view of a rural church-raising in progress (Illus. 6). Unlike most rural meeting houses in colonial New England towns, this one is surrounded by a village of homes and businesses. Such post-Revolutionary villages were, in the words of the historical geographer Joseph S. Wood, "new places of commerce, not the simple agricultural-community centers thought to have dotted the colonial landscape. The new village was a central place, what geographers commonly call active market places that dominate and are central to a market area."[2]

There is a traditional image of the New England town as centering on a village of meeting house, dwellings, and stores surrounding an attractive town common. Earlier historians mistakenly equated such places with the "nucleated" settlements of the seventeenth century English colonists, viewing them as "relict artifacts" of an earlier era. More recent study found that the term "village" in colonial records seldom meant the tightly settled cluster of buildings that may have been transplanted here in the first years of settlement. Often it encompassed the farming community of a much more scattered settlement form without a built center. "The village encountered in New England today, white-painted, black-shuttered, classical-revival dwellings, churches, and stores abutting a tree-shaded green, reflects not continuity with New England's colonial past but a most dramatic change."[3] In fact, the emergence of rural village centers was the product of a widespread building boom during the Federal era.

Before the Revolution, most New England towns shared a landscape of isolated individual farms linked by a network of town roads to a public meeting house located in a position that roughly marked the town's center. Rural New Englanders lived on scattered farms, conducted most local economic transactions in these dispersed places, and traveled on the sabbath to nearly isolated geographic centers for their public and religious activities. Even older settled market towns along the coast were less densely built than they would become in the first half century of independence. When the population grew larger in one section of a rural town, religious and political battles either forced a change in the location of the meeting house or caused a new town to be created from that part of the old one.[4]

"The distinguishing feature of the colonial settlement landscape," in this view of New England's historical geography, was "the relative absence of compact settlement" around the public meeting house. "The tavernkeeper-trader was the only townsman to do enough business to require a central location" there.[5] It was not until the last half of the eighteenth century that the rural economy began to be transformed from subsistence to advanced commercial farming. This was marked in southern New England by a corresponding increase in domestic and commercial building at the village core. The economic development of rural New England after the Revolutionary War, encouraged by internal improvements of public highways and private toll roads, forged a network of small market centers in the hinterlands. These, in turn, formed a chain of larger and smaller communities linked by trade to established coastal commercial centers. This increased extralocal exchange began to attract entrepreneurs such as blacksmiths, doctors, and lawyers, who did not necessarily participate themselves in the trading of agricultural and hand-crafted goods between markets. They did, however, depend upon and take advantage of the new wealth that this trade generated. The evidence often survives in homes, public buildings, shops or offices erected during this era on village lots around the meeting house and town common.

While many outlying farmers continued to erect simple one-story ("Cape Cod") houses or one of several larger colonial house forms drawn from the region's vernacular architecture, the new villagers did not. Those who constructed new buildings in nascent commercial centers generally adopted a style thought to be more symbolic of the new republic. Marked by a refinement of proportion and scale in comparison to the heavier detailing of Georgian colonial building, the graceful Federal style was favored by the affluent coastal merchant leadership for its imagery of earlier republics in history. This neoclassical architecture, borrowed from English ideas and influenced by the then recent archaeological investigations of the buildings in Roman antiquity, quickly became the dominant visual statement of the new country. The Revolutionary War had interrupted all forms of new building and delayed the importation of the latest English fashions. By the 1790s, however, London builders' guides of the 1760s and 1770s advocating this new style were republished in Boston. The first architectural handbooks by American architect-builders soon followed. Printed as sources for the country or village carpenter, books such as Asher Benjamin's *Country Builder's Assistant* (1797)—from which Illus. 7 is an example—and *The American Builder's Companion* (1806) provided rules for creating the classical orders, design motifs of interior and exterior finish, and plans that helped to popularize the use of the circle and ellipse as new shapes for rooms and staircases, as well as windows and doorways. Such publications and the simultaneous migration of carpenters from southern New England quickly spread the Federal style to even the most remote Maine towns.

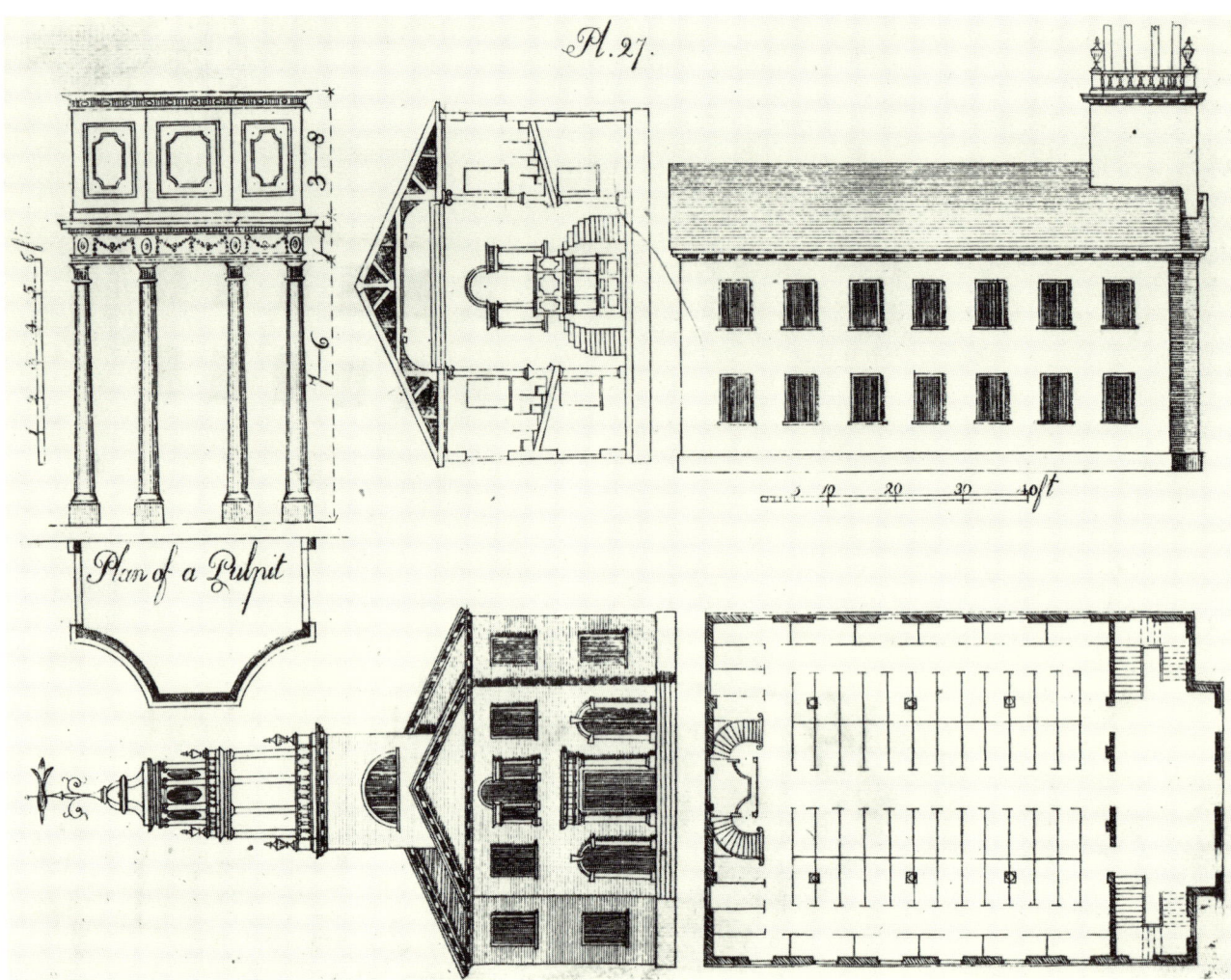

7. "Design for a Meeting House," from *The Country Builder's Assistant* (1805) by Asher Benjamin (1771–1845).
(Courtesy of The Society for the Preservation of New England Antiquities)

The growth of central villages in southern New England, usually around preexisting meeting house locations, was an elaboration of the existing colonial settlement pattern. New roads that were built through such towns as Thompson, Connecticut, or Sturbridge, Massachusetts, between 1790 and 1820, both reinforced and extended the settlement pattern. As shown in Illus. 8, the new roads along the town common or meeting house lot became lined with two- and three-story federal houses. Some were copies of the urban forms popularized by Charles Bulfinch's work for the merchants of Boston. Others were the products of local builders who used their printed guides as sources for architectural details. The new and lighter, classical features might be applied to older house forms, such as the colonial central chimney plan or the Georgian "double-pile" with two rooms on each floor separated by a central hall. But local carpenters could also adapt new plans to meet the sometimes narrow house lots. In Sturbridge, for example, several homes were sited with their gable end toward the street and a front door at one corner of this new facade. Many of these gable-entry

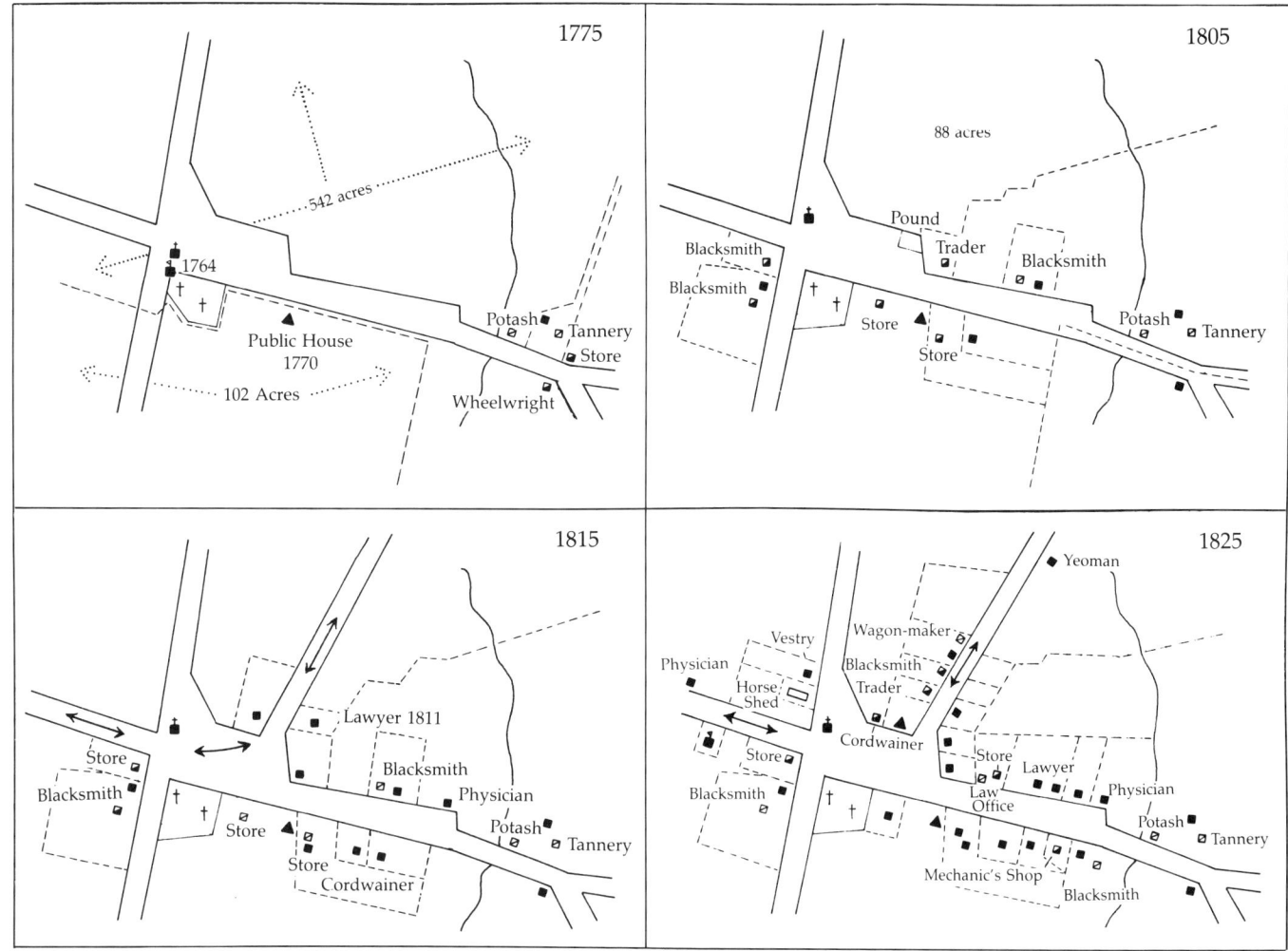

8. Maps of Sturbridge, Massachusetts, 1775, 1805, 1815, and 1825.
(Based on the research of Herbert LeVine and reprinted from "The New England Village as American Vernacular Form," by Joseph Wood in *Perspectives in Vernacular Architecture II,* ed. Camille Wells. Reprinted by permission of the University of Missouri Press. Copyright 1986 by the Curators of the University of Missouri)

houses also had one-story wings on one or both sides of the main block. Built in the second decade of the nineteenth century, this new house type shared Federal style fan lights, lunettes in the attic gable, and other details of this era of town growth. They predate by more than a decade the similar Greek Revival "temple and wing" houses, which would later dot not only Maine's landscape but also villages and farms throughout the West into which New Englanders migrated.

This regional pattern of Anglo-American farm and village development could be seen in the District of Maine. Its growth during the decades before statehood not only paralleled the southern New England evolution from dispersed farm to nucleated rural centers, but reflected that evolution in each of its stages, as towns developed beyond their origins as frontier settlements. As late as 1785, one foreign visitor to York described its land as "dotted with poor cabins where dwell the cultivators who came only a few years ago.... The homes of the inhabitants are quite distant from one another."[6] Although Yankee immigrants into Maine brought older ideas of an agricultural community based on separate farmsteads, they responded as did others of their generation to a variety of economic opportunities, which fostered new village building. Because such activities required commercial farming or other forms of export trade, newly settled farming towns were slow to achieve salable surpluses and remained without much of a village center. Where circumstances permitted, however, trade created a hierarchy of new central places between the inland frontier and the coast. Several types of Maine communities that were settled, incorporated, or simply rebuilt between the Revolutionary War and statehood can thus be differentiated on the basis of their primary economic and service activities. These include newly cleared farming towns, lumbering and manufacturing villages, seats of county government and law, and larger centers of trade and commerce.

AGRICULTURAL SETTLEMENTS: NEW TOWNS, NEW PEOPLE

At one end of the spectrum of Maine's early settlement are the large numbers of newly settled agricultural communities. Some, like Cushing, a town of some 75 dwellings in 1819, had "within it neither settled minister, lawyer, physician, tanner, tailor or shoemaker; each being his own mechanic."[7] Other examples, such as inland Bethel or coastal Blue Hill, remained thinly settled farming and fishing towns in the years before statehood. Individual farms dotted the rural landscape, as in the southern New England agricultural towns of the preceding century. Single-story "Cape Cod" dwellings or larger two-story central-chimney farmhouses might replace the temporary log houses of the first settlers, but village centers in these Maine towns would appear only later in the nineteenth century.

Bethel, known as Sudbury Canada when land grants were first made in 1768, was not settled until after 1774 and not incorporated until twenty years later. None of the original grantees settled his land, which included rich farm tracts laid out in narrow lots along the Androscoggin River and larger wooded lots in the surrounding hills (Illus. 9). In 1781 there were only fourteen families in Bethel. Some of the original patentees sold their rights to the first settlers; others forfeited them for unpaid taxes, and their lands were acquired by local residents. By the 1820 census over 1,000 acres were in pasture, 1,500 acres in mowing and meadow land, and 564 acres of tillage in the rich intervales where most people settled. The population doubled to 1,200 between 1800 and 1820, but the "center" at Bethel Hill was a hamlet of only a dozen families. By tradition the 1813 home of Dr. Moses Mason was the first in this nascent village to be painted and the first to be built on a stone foundation. Mason (Illus. 10) is an outstanding example of the entrepreneurial professional whose presence was often the first stage in the creation of a village center.

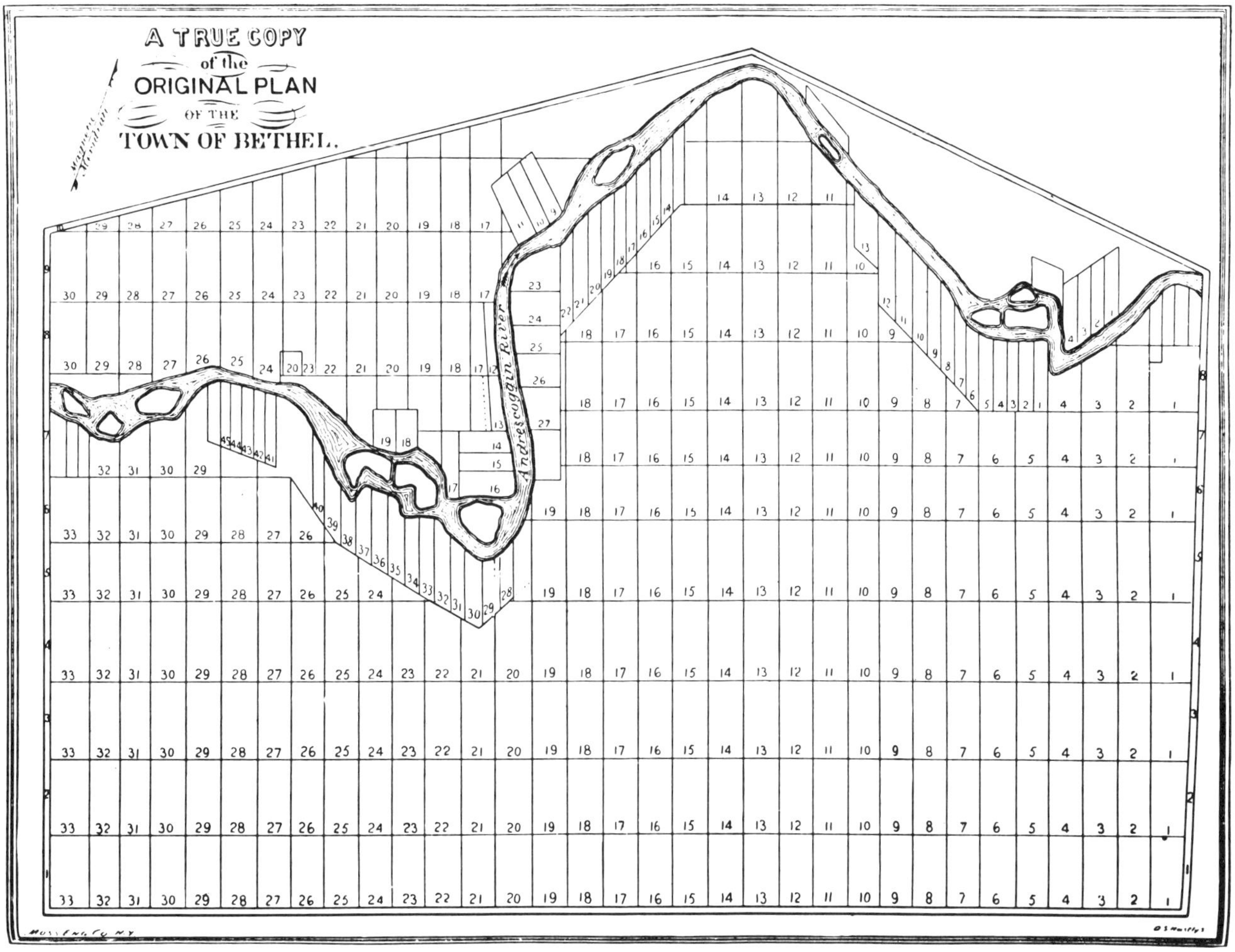

9. Proprietors' map of Bethel. (Reprinted from *History of Bethel, Maine,* by William B. Lapham, [Augusta: 1891])

Born in Dublin, New Hampshire, Moses Mason (1789–1866) came to Bethel with his father, who was a Revolutionary War veteran, a Baptist, a farmer, and a local politician. At the age of twenty-one he began to study medicine under his brother-in-law, Dr. James Ayer of Newfield, supporting himself by teaching school during the winter months. Certified by the Massachusetts Medical Association in 1813, he entered practice, married, and built the new house at Bethel Hill, which was later decorated by the itinerant wall muralists Rufus Porter and Jonathan Poor.

Mason's appointment in 1814 as postmaster, a position he retained until the end of his medical career in 1832, reflected his Jeffersonian politics, his desire to open Oxford County to a wider world, and his own role in the growing community. An active Baptist and agrarian Democrat with his own working farm, Mason later advocated building the Oxford and Cumberland canal to link inland towns to larger markets through water transportation and trade. He also became a land speculator, surveyor, and developer. His own aspirations and achieve-

10. *Moses Mason* (1789–1866), by Chester Harding (1792–1866), ca. 1835. (Oil on canvas. The Bethel Historical Society)

ments sprang from a vision for his town's prosperity and led him in later life to the Governor's Council and the United States Congress.[8]

Another dispersed settlement pattern similar to Bethel's was the coastal farming and fishing community of Blue Hill, which was depicted by Jonathan Fisher in his 1824 painting, *A Morning View of Blue Hill Village*. (See Plate XIII.) There is virtually no identifiable village "center" around Parson Fisher's large Congregational meeting house in the middle distance or the 1817 Baptist church in the right foreground. Rather, as Fisher's maps and land surveys of the community demonstrate, Blue Hill began and stayed a dispersed farming town with its network of rural roads connecting individual farms throughout the town. In time shipbuilding and trade would support a small cluster of buildings along the water and help create a nearby village center, but throughout Fisher's lifetime and into early statehood, Blue Hill continued to have a dispersed economy.

THREE EXCEPTIONS:
INDIANS, ACADIANS, AND SHAKERS

Three exceptions to this common pattern are noteworthy because they reflect the less-well-known diversity of Maine's rural population. For the Indian tribes of the state, the French-speaking settlers of Madawaska Territory, and the utopian communities of the Shakers, the physical arrangement of their settlements and use of their lands varied markedly from those of their contemporaries.

Indian Settlements

The rapid growth and expansion of Maine's population came at the expense of a native-American population that had been literally decimated since the seventeenth century. Reduced to less than 10 percent of their former strength and their fur trade ruined, the Penobscot and Passamaquoddy Indian tribes faced an uncertain future with new settlers eager to claim the Indians' traditional hunting and fishing regions. Some whites, including General Henry Knox, hoped that Maine's native population would eventually disappear through interracial marriage and cultural assimilation. In the meantime, others sought to regularize relations with these allies in the recent Revolution by relegating them to specific land areas.[9]

Treaties in 1786 and 1818 between Massachusetts and the Penobscots provided the tribe with a token annuity, several wilderness townships, Indian Island, and small holdings along the Penobscot River. This tribe contained "250 or 300 souls in 1816, more than two thirds of whom were women and children," while the Passamaquoddy "were about equally numerous. Both had become the objects of public charity and protection" by that date. Relegated to limited land areas, provided with a church at Old Town, and offered education in white farming methods, Maine's Indian population resisted assimilation into the dominant culture. An 1829 visitor to Old Town described the Penobscots as occupying "miserable huts. They have their fire on the ground in the middle of their huts, and sleep on deerskins spread on the ground, or on platforms about six inches high."[10]

Yet, within the native community were those whose images depict various kinds of interaction between the races. A portrait of Denny Soccabeson, a Passamaquoddy, was done at Eastport during the British occupation in 1817. (See Plate III.) That of Sarah Mollasses (ca. 1812–1880) of the Penobscots, painted by Bangor artist Jeremiah P. Hardy after 1827, shows her in commercially manufactured clothing and felt hat as well as silver trade ornaments and crucifix. (See Plate IV.) Such documents are rare testaments to the tribes' continued efforts to maintain a separate cultural identity in the face of overwhelming odds.[11]

French-Speaking Settler Communities

A second exception to typical New England patterns of community land use and development was that of the French-speaking people of the Madawaska Territory who settled along both sides of the St. John River. Arriving here some thirty years after the British uprooted them from their homes in Acadia (Nova Scotia) in 1757, they were a tightly knit group united by their Catholicism, their language, and the experience of exile and migration. Their agricultural economy was distinct from that of the English-speaking Yankees in western Maine; distance made commercial marketing of their produce unprofitable. They adapted to the climate and soil by growing buckwheat, oats, and potatoes; they worked the land with simple locally made tools. They arranged their farmsteads Quebec style, in long strips fronting on the river, as shown in Illus. 11. These were, in the words of an 1825 American observer, "situated from 80 to 100 rods apart on both sides of the river."[12]

This land along the St. John River was claimed by both New Brunswick and Massachusetts, although since the river was a main travel route and emptied into the Atlantic within British territory, the area was simply more accessible to the British for many decades. The uncertain border between the United States and Canada meant little to the Acadian population of Madawaska. They resisted the interference of outsiders in their affairs, even by the priests sent to them by the Bishop of Quebec. Statehood for Maine meant little to those living in the St. John River valley. After being granted statehood, however, Maine was eager to confirm its title to the Madawaska Territory. The resulting conflicts were resolved only by the 1842 Webster-Ashburton Treaty, which fixed the border along the river, splitting Acadian families into American nationals on one side and British subjects on the other.

11. Madawaska farmlots along the St. John River. (Detail of a photograph by Cary Wolinsky © 1980 National Geographic Society)

12. Log houses along the St. John River, New Brunswick, ca. 1850. (The New Brunswick Provincial Archives [*a*. P4–1–42; *b*. P5–94])

Land surveyor Park Holland, writing of Madawaska in 1794, noted that "Their Houses are Chiefly built of Logs but are warm & Convenient." He also saw in Madawaska Village a "temporary thing, built of logs and covered with bark, which served the purpose of a dwelling house and mill."[13] These Madawaska homes and farm buildings were unique in Maine and continued an older Acadian tradition of log construction called *en columbage*. The walls were hewn logs fitted horizontally into a frame of hewn corner posts by means of grooves in the posts (Illus. 12a and b). This type of construction differed from Maine's late seventeenth century sawn log "garrison houses" and the hewn log construction used throughout much of eighteenth century America, both types called "log houses." Hand hewn timbers, roughly squared with an ax, notched at the corners and chinked with daubing, formed walls of the later "log houses." Settlers from southern New England used notched-log buildings only until they could build framed houses. Acadians, however, continued to construct their high-quality log buildings in the St. John valley from the 1780s through much of the nineteenth century. The squared logs of the wall, often up to six inches thick, were chinked with flax and lime to provide a tight, warm home.[14]

Shaker Communities

The third exception to typical patterns of village building in Maine was the utopian Shaker community. Unlike the many other dissenting sects that flourished in Maine and overpowered the publicly supported Congregational ministry, the United Society of Believers, or Shakers, built communities that reflected their communal separatism and religious hierarchy. While their architecture was often a simplified version of the New England Federal style, it embodied the Shaker theology explicitly. The 1794 meeting house at Sabbathday Lake—a separate village created by the Shakers near the northwest corner of New Gloucester—is typical of Shaker religious structures and is shown in Illus. 13. It was designed by masterbuilder Moses Johnson of the Shaker community at Enfield, New Hampshire, but was strongly influenced by the architectural dictates of the Shaker leadership in New (now Mount) Lebanon, New York. The outside walls of the plain-style meeting room on the ground floor were lined with blue-painted pews, and large spanning beams overhead created an uninterrupted open space for the religious dancing of the Believers. The ministry of elder and eldress occupied separate quarters above the meeting room, and the building itself was surrounded by separate communal dwellings for men and women, as well as barns and workshops. Unlike the "worldly" villages in the region, these special communities were built according to a completely planned design growing out of the sect's religious beliefs.

Shaker communities were organized into "Families," each of which had its own cluster of buildings within a Shaker village. One family

13. Shaker Meeting House, Sabbathday Lake, built in 1794.
(Measured drawing. The Historic American Building Survey)

or "Gathering Order" would contain the children, often orphans, and adult novice Shakers; the Church Family included only full members of the faith and was always located around the meeting house. Each Shaker village had an office building, usually situated along a public road, which was the only site where their leaders could meet or do business with "the world." This building was often located across the road from the Church Family dwellings and meeting house. For some years the exterior colors of their buildings were dictated by Millenial Laws which, for example, reserved white paint to be used only on the meeting house as a symbol of purity. Surrounding the clustered buildings of these "families," the communal farm lands were laid out in orchards, fields and pastures. Barns and workshops for various activities of the brothers and sisters were located near their dwellings. Where topography permitted, mill ponds supported waterpowered industries. Besides the Shaker Village of some 75 to 80 individuals at Sabbathday Lake, there was a society in Alfred gathered from New Lebanon in 1784 (see Plate V) and another at Gorham. By 1820, Maine had five communities that shared the cloistered design and gender-segregated domestic architecture of the communal Shaker life.[15]

NEW TOWNS OF ENTERPRISE AND TECHNOLOGY

All along the Maine coast small seaports took advantage of opportunities to trade in lumber, to build ships, and where waterpower permitted, to process raw materials or transform them into manufactured goods. Wharves, warehouses, and ways were built along coastal waterfronts. Small factories began to dot the landscape inland at the falls along many rivers. Thus a new village center might not even be located near the original town meeting house as had been common in southern New England. Rather, the site of the town meeting house might shift with the population to be near new economic activities.

This process of rural industrialization was described clearly by one early visitor to northern New England:

> The place, therefore, at which a village begins is either a sea-harbour or other *landing*, where country-produce is exchanged for foreign merchandise, or it is a cataract on a river, or some situation capable of affording a *mill-seat*. In such a situation, the first fabric that is raised is a solitary saw-mill.... The owner of the saw-mill becomes a rich man; builds a large wooden house, opens a ... store, erects a still, and exchanges rum, mollasses, flower [flour] and port for logs. As the country by this time has begun to be cleared, a flower-mill is erected near the saw-mill. Sheep being brought upon the farms, a carding machine and fulling-mill follow.
>
> For some years, as we may imagine, the *store* answers all the purposes of a public house. The neighbors meet there, and spend half the day in drinking and debating. But the *mills* becoming everyday more and more a point of attraction, a blacksmith, a shoemaker, a taylor, and

various other artisans and artificers, successively assemble. The village, however, has scarcely advanced this far, before half its inhabitants are in debt to the *store*.... What, therefore, is next wanted is a *collecting attorney*.... The attorney is also employed by the neighbors; and as the fees on collecting small debts are high, any tollerable increase of the settlement procures him at least a decent living.

But as the advantage of living near the mills is great ... so a settlement, not only of artisans, but of farmers, is progressively formed in the vicinity; this settlement constitutes itself a society or parish; and, a church being erected, the village, larger or smaller is complete.[16]

The village that developed around the falls of the Saco River at Pepperrellborough (Saco, after 1805) is one of several Maine communities whose history fits this scenario. (See Plate VI.) The land was subdivided after the Revolutionary War from the confiscated property of Sir William Pepperrell, a Tory, and from the sale of a portion granted by the state to his widow. Several merchants located there in the 1790s to join Colonel Thomas Cutts, who since the mid-eighteenth century, had occupied an island in the river connected to shore by his private toll bridge. By 1800 the town had seventeen sawmills, which produced up to 50,000 board feet of lumber a day. There were gristmills on each side of the river, as well as a fulling mill that had been built in 1788.[17] By 1820 there was also a Saco Iron Works corporation, capitalized at $50,000. It consisted of five nail-making machines and two rollers, run by waterpower, to turn imported iron into hoops, plates, rods, and nails.[18]

The 1801 sale of Pepperrell lands created new houselots and business locations. The state also gave a ten-acre lot to the town for a meeting house, a training field, and a burial ground. The new meeting house was erected by the town between 1803 and 1805. It was designed by masterbuilder Bradbury Johnson, who had already built a number of important public and private buildings in the new Federal style throughout southern New Hampshire. Johnson's Pepperrellborough meeting house (Illus. 14) was described by Yale's Timothy Dwight in 1807 as "a new and beautiful church: a structure superior to any other I have seen in this district and inferior to very few in New England."[19]

Two years later another visitor described "the modern village at Saco Falls" as having "the most flourishing appearance; and its new church is built and painted in the gayest style." He noted, however, that the industry and prosperity of the village stood in contrast to the surrounding farms. "On the road, in the intervals between the village, are several dwellings that betray extreme poverty in the inhabitants; and not a few of them have boards hung out, on which are uncouth inscriptions offering *spiritous liquors for sale*."[20]

This same process of village growth around industrial sites was repeated along the Maine coast with many local variations. Bath, Camden, Belfast, Searsport, and Bucksport grew in much the same way as Saco. Among the most interesting Federal-period mill towns are the twin centers of Brunswick and Topsham at the tidal head below the

14. The Pepperrellborough Meeting House, Saco, built between 1803 and 1805. Bradbury Johnson (1766–1819), architect.
(Detail of a lithograph by Charles Henry Granger, 1860. The York Institute Museum, Saco)

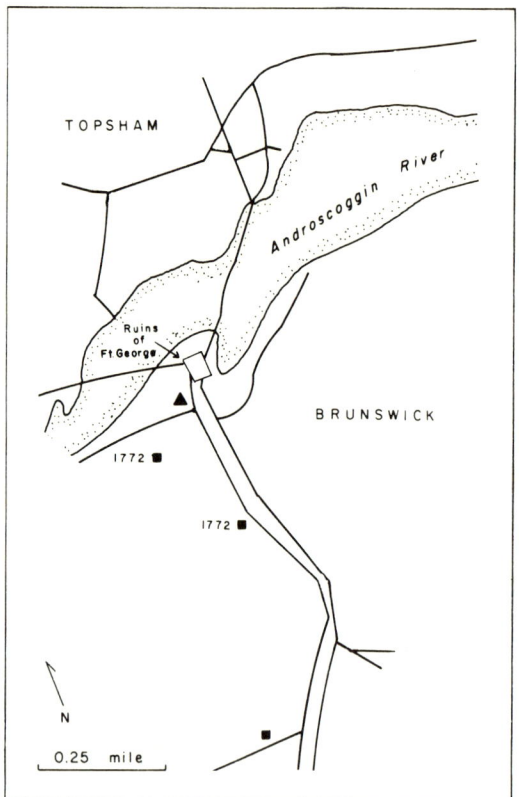 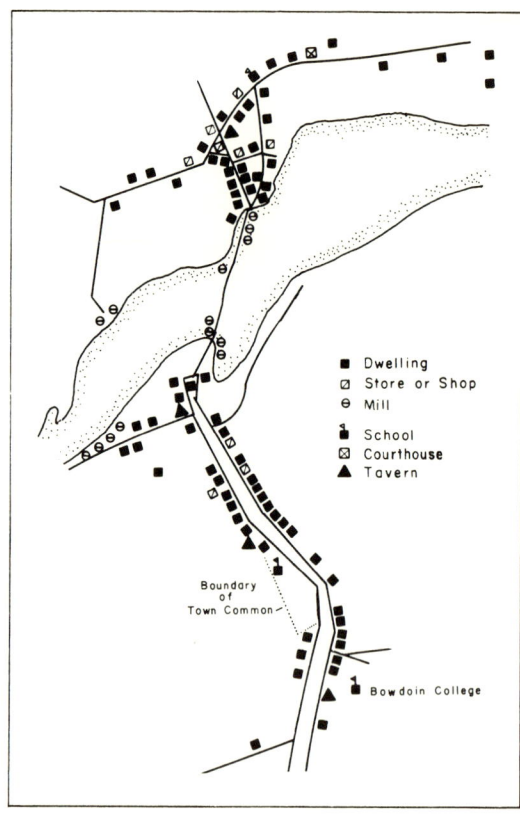

1780   1802

15. Maps of Brunswick and Topsham, 1780 and 1802.
(Based on maps from "The Origins of the New England Village" by Joseph Wood [Ph.D. dissertation, Pennsylvania State University, 1978])

Androscoggin River. Arriving in 1783, a visitor would have seen little evidence of any village. Except for Sabbath services or public meetings at the centrally isolated town meeting house, those living on the area's coastal farms had virtually no reason to gather. By 1802 both towns had formed business centers on opposite sides of the falls; the commercial core was soon surrounded by dozens of new homes (Illus. 15). A decade later Timothy Dwight estimated that the "considerable village" of Brunswick contained some fifty homes and three churches.[21] In 1807 a new First Parish Meeting House designed by Samuel Melcher III, with his brother and father the leading local builders of the new style, had been erected in Brunswick village.

Brunswick's development can be credited only partly to the creation of Bowdoin College, which was chartered by the General Assembly in 1794. (See Plate VII.) Massachusetts Hall, built from designs by Samuel and Aaron Melcher between 1798 and 1803, contained all its initial requirements—"accommodations for a president and family, rooms for students, for a chapel and hall, for lectures and apparatus"—within this single structure.[22] However, the town had already grown rapidly by 1802, the year Bowdoin took its first class.

Rather, the concentration of people and buildings around the falls reflects the economic importance of water power. The first sawmills there were built in Topsham about 1772. Writing in 1795, James Sullivan noted that "a number of very valuable saw mills" had been added. "And although the waters are not navigable within two miles of the mills, yet great quantities of lumber are shipped from the river."[23] By 1802, Topsham and Brunswick were joined by a toll bridge across the river near the falls; eight sawmills, four gristmills, and a fulling mill were being operated. By 1820, someone had also established a clapboard mill using a new waterpowered circular saw. One person recorded "twenty five saw mills, part of which are on the Topsham side" employing some 300 men. He calculated "that there is not less than five hundred thousand feet of boards cut by each saw on an average." From this he estimated that, at seven dollars per thousand, the value approached $175,000, of which $100,000 worth of lumber was shipped from Bath or from wharves south of Brunswick. The remaining $75,000 worth was "directed coastwise," often in ships built along the river below the falls.[24]

The 1807 embargo on foreign goods had a marked impact on towns like Brunswick by spurring local investment in American manufacturing. As the industrial revolution in England had started with the waterpowered manufacture of textiles, so New Englanders took advantage of their waterpower for machine processing of cotton and wool into yarns and threads. These products were initially "put out" to home weavers, but by 1820 New England manufacturers had also mastered machine weaving of cloth on waterpowered looms in their factories.

Thus by 1810, several Maine towns—including Brunswick, Gardiner, Waldoboro, Winthrop, and York—could claim a new cotton mill that was either chartered or already being built.[25] However, most of these mills must have resembled the small cotton factory in Lisbon, described in 1820 as employing three men and three girls and consisting of "one wooden building three stories high about 44 feet by 33 feet." Not only were they small, they were also inefficient; before the embargo, nearly all of Maine's cotton and woolen factories operated at less than capacity because they could not compete with the influx of imported fabrics after the Revolutionary War.[26]

Brunswick was an exception. By 1820 its "extensive manufactory of wool and cotton" contained more cotton spinning machinery than all the other mills in the state and had 24 waterpowered looms for cotton weaving, nine hand looms for wool, as well as carding machines and a fulling mill.[27] This "little world of ingenuity, industry, and discipline" employed about 100 people, including several "poor children."[28] Unlike the rest of Maine's fledgling textile factories—and even in the depressed postwar economy—Brunswick's scale of operation was comparable to that of many factories in southern New England. Together with lumbering, shipbuilding and the maritime trades, factory life contributed to the growth of Brunswick and Topsham. Although much of their prestatehood streetscape has been replaced by later domestic and commercial building, many houses still survive. Some line

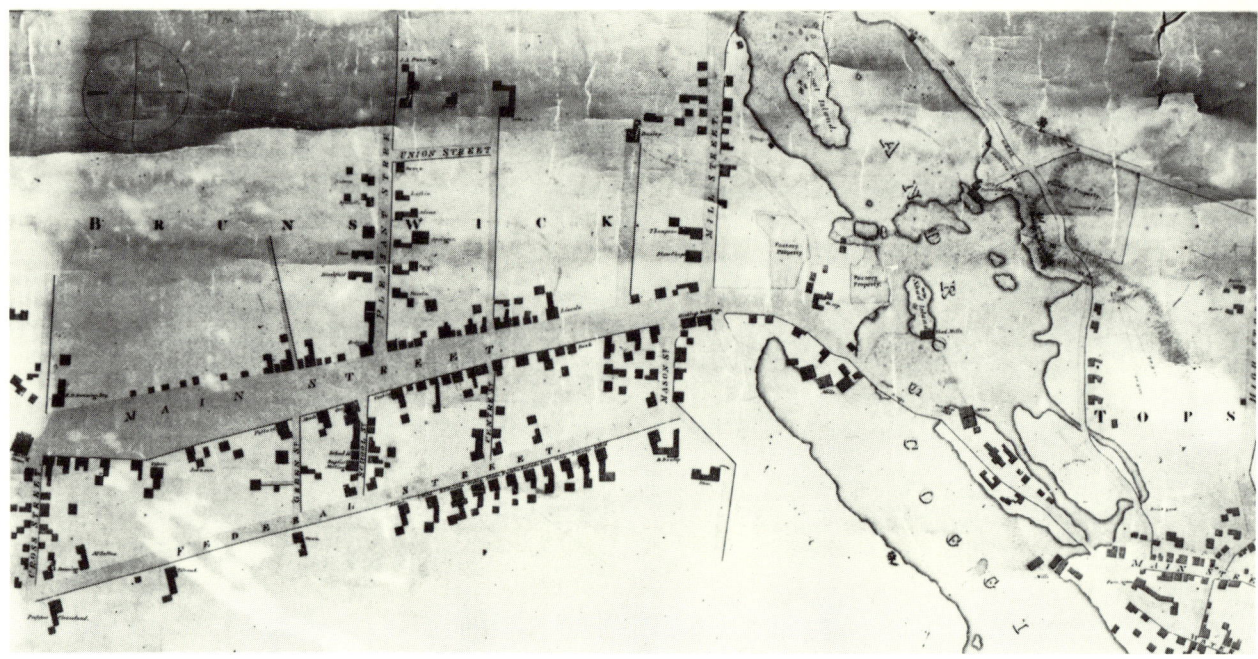

16. *A Plan of the Villages of Brunswick and Topsham,* 1828 (detail).
(The Maine Historical Society)

one side of Brunswick's Maine Street, opposite the town common, but most occupy the streets laid out in a grid pattern during the early nineteenth century. Others, many of which were built by local builders such as Samuel Melcher, still form the core of Topsham's historic district.

Manufacture of woolen cloth in Maine was minimal; small woolen factories were located only in Kennebunk, Parsonsfield, Thomaston, and Brunswick. But there were dozens of small carding mills and fulling mills throughout rural Maine. These smaller mills, such as the Hapgood carding mill in South Waterford (Illus. 17), were usually located on rural waterpower sites owned by an entrepreneurial farmer and employed only one or two workers. They machine-cleaned and prepared wool for local farm families, eliminating the arduous home processing previously required for hand weaving. By being located on small streams or rivers within a local market, the larger number of these dispersed mills probably had even greater impact in many small towns than the introduction of a cotton factory in a few growing villages.[29]

Attempts at textile processing and manufacture were typical of the era's industrial growth, but many Maine towns engaged in other forms of industry. Nearly every coastal community, for example, built ships. The Portsmouth Naval Shipyard was established in Kittery in 1800 and began building government warships during the War of 1812. The flagship of the Mediterranean squadron, the *Washington*, was launched in 1814. (See Plate VIII.) Most Maine shipyards, however, must have been smaller, like the one shown in Fisher's painting of Blue Hill in 1824 (Illus. 18).

Maine Towns, 43
Maine People

17. Interior of the Hapgood Carding Mill, South Waterford, ca. 1835. (Old Sturbridge Village photo by Henry E. Peach)

18. Shipbuilding, detail from *A Morning View of Blue Hill Village* (Plate XIII), by Jonathan Fisher (1768–1847), 1824.
(Oil on canvas. The William A. Farnsworth Art Museum and Library, Rockland)

Lumber was not Maine's only extractive industry. Investors from Newfields, York, Kittery and Portsmouth formed a company in 1792 to mine "ores and Metalick Substances" in Washington Plantation, later named Newfield. "Here is found a mine of *fuller's earth*, which has been wrought by the 'Washington Mining Company' " at the "pit in Davises Field." Despite incorporation in 1806, the company's operation was sporadic and disappointing.[30] Thomaston began burning lime rock as early as 1734, and a lime industry based on this raw material was producing 50,000 casks a year by 1820. It, in turn, created business

19. Interior of the Nash Cooperage, Waldoboro, ca. 1840.
(Old Sturbridge Village photo by Henry E. Peach)

for a large number of coopers (Illus. 19), as well as a great deal of shipping and shipbuilding to get the plaster to urban markets. Also related to Thomaston's lime industry was its marble business, begun in 1809 by a Mr. Dwight. By 1825, the town had two mills, or factories, with 200 saws, employing 12 or 15 men and producing marble slabs for chimney pieces, hearths, and gravestones.[31]

SHIRE TOWNS: GOVERNMENT AND GROWTH

As the District's population grew, so did the need for legal services. Deeds for land, contracts for shipbuilding and commerce, and provisions for inheritance all required lawyers and county courts. Between 1789 and 1820, the Massachusetts legislature created six new Maine counties in addition to the earlier counties of York, Cumberland, and Lincoln. Part of the reason for establishing new public services in rural Maine was the desire of the Massachusetts legislature to undercut local sentiment for separation and to demonstrate that the District's special needs were recognized in Boston.

The administrative center for the county, its "shire town," was by law the site of the sheriff's office. It also contained the offices of various county officials and the courts, and quickly became the home of lawyers, judges, and other political figures. There were also "half-shire" towns, where courts and other county functions served citizens who were too far away from the older county seat. New Gloucester was a half-shire with Portland for Cumberland County from 1794 until Oxford County was created in 1805; Topsham also had a courthouse by 1802. Warren had a courthouse for the courts that were established there in 1799, continuing throughout this period and beyond as half-shire for the western part of Lincoln County (later Knox County). Waterboro was designated half-shire for York County in 1790 and held courts until 1806. In 1799 the county was divided along the Great Ossipee and a new northern district—with its own registry of deeds and a yearly probate court—was established at Fryeburg. In 1802 Alfred became a half-shire town and many services formerly located in York and Waterboro were transferred there. The jail, built in 1720 on town-parish land in York and later enlarged to serve as a debtor's prison, was granted to the county in 1812 for a century if needed. The county treasurer's office moved to Alfred in 1813, the registry of deeds in 1816, the probate court and clerk of courts in 1820, and the full courts in 1832 when Alfred replaced York as the county seat.[32]

Before 1820, Maine's courts were part of the Massachusetts legal system. On the local level, justices of the peace settled minor disputes. Meeting together in the shire town, all the justices in a county formed a County Court, or Court of Sessions, to administer jails, roads, and other business of county government. A Probate Court and a Court of Common Pleas also met there to adjudicate inheritances and civil and criminal complaints. The men who served in these offices were often prominent and wealthy citizens, usually without legal training, appointed by the Governor of Massachusetts. The Supreme Judicial Court met in Boston and on a circuit of all the county seats to resolve appeals from the lower courts throughout the Commonwealth.

Becoming a shire town ensured rapid community growth and prosperity and a developing town center. Court sessions brought law offices, public officials, and tavern trade to these communities, usually elevating them above neighboring towns. Being a shire town also stimulated the building of new homes for judges and lawyers, whose elaborate dwellings were often built in the town center. The impressive new courthouses and jails frequently faced an ornamental town common, such as those that can still be seen in Wiscasset, Castine, and Paris Hill. Even Augusta, established as the shire of Kennebec County in 1799, indulged in such embellishments before the statehouse was built there. (See Illus. 53 on p. 169.)

Towns competed fiercely to be named a county seat, and political leaders in the older shire towns, such as York, worked hard to retain their courts and jails. William Frost, the "Register" of deeds and treasurer for York County, kept many papers showing the town's commitment to retaining its position. He led the subscription for an intended addition to the York courthouse in 1799, the same year that a debtor's cell was added to its old county jail. In 1811, having beaten off earlier bids from Kennebunk and Biddeford to serve as seats of the courts, the town and parish of York voted to donate a site for a new court building. The new two-story courthouse was built a few feet from the

20. *a.* The Lincoln County Courthouse, built between 1824 and 1825.
(The Maine Historic Preservation Commission)

b. The Cumberland County Courthouse, built in 1816.
(The Maine Historic Preservation Commission)

"ancient town and county house," as the meeting house was described, nearly opposite the old jail.[33]

Pownalborough was designated county seat of Lincoln County in 1760 and its three-story colonial courthouse, built the next year under the direction of Boston housewright Gershom Flagg, survives in Dresden. In 1794 Alna and Dresden were split off from the old town, and the courts were moved to Wiscasset Point on the Sheepscot River, which had become the economic center of local trade and foreign shipping. In 1802 the town name was changed from Pownalborough to Wiscasset, and the village's growth was marked not only by new homes "of ample dimensions and the most imposing forms" for shipmasters and lawyers, but new public buildings as well. A brick building for the Lincoln and Kennebec Bank was raised in 1805, as was an academy building in 1807; between 1809 and 1811 a massive granite jail was erected some distance away from the center, and in 1813 a circular brick powderhouse with conical roof was built to store gunpowder during the War of 1812. The village also was the home of a marine insurance company. By 1820, the town supported eight housewrights, two painters and glaziers, three part-time brickmakers and a brickmason, three cabinetmakers with two apprentices, and a joiner.[34]

At the head of the town common a new, brick Lincoln County Courthouse (Illus. 20a) was erected in 1824–1825. It was built under the direction of Nathaniel Coffin, who served as county agent for its construction. Coffin first traveled to Portland to see the 1816 Cumberland County Courthouse (Illus. 20b) and later returned there to examine its plans with master carpenter Tileston Cushing of Bath. The influence of the Portland courthouse (which burned in 1858) can be seen in the use of recessed brick arches around the facade's first floor windows and central doorway, as well as in the chain fence between granite posts in front.[35]

Little remains from Machias's early years as shire town for Washington County after 1789. However, Penobscot, the original county seat of Hancock County formed the same year, has a long history as the site of both French and English coastal forts. Renamed Castine when the peninsula was set off as a separate town in 1796, the village occupied the bluffs above its port. The 1790 county courthouse faced a new meeting house across the town common; a stone jail and the stocks stood beside the courthouse opposite an 1802 school. Community growth was interrupted when the British occupied Castine during the War of 1812 (Illus. 21). After the British evacuated the town in 1815 it revived, gaining a new bank and weekly newspaper, but after the county seat was moved to Ellsworth in 1838, its economy leveled off for many years.[36]

Paris Hill, first settled in the 1780s, became the shire town for inland Oxford County in 1805. Before 1815, when a new brick courthouse was built beside the Paris Hill town common, the court sat in the Baptist meeting house and was called together by a drummer standing at the corner of the church.[37] This 1803 Baptist church may be the structure being erected in the Hathaway overmantel painting done about the same date. (See Illus. 6.) In the years immediately following statehood, the granite Oxford County jail and a jailer's house (1822) were constructed nearby, as was a brick house for offices of the registry of deeds and probate court (1826). The home of Cyrus Hamlin, clerk of courts, was built overlooking the valley in 1806 and was the birthplace three years later of Hannibal Hamlin, Vice President of the United States from 1861 to 1865.

Across the Common a row of handsome Federal-style homes was built between 1802 and 1819, as was the small wooden law office of

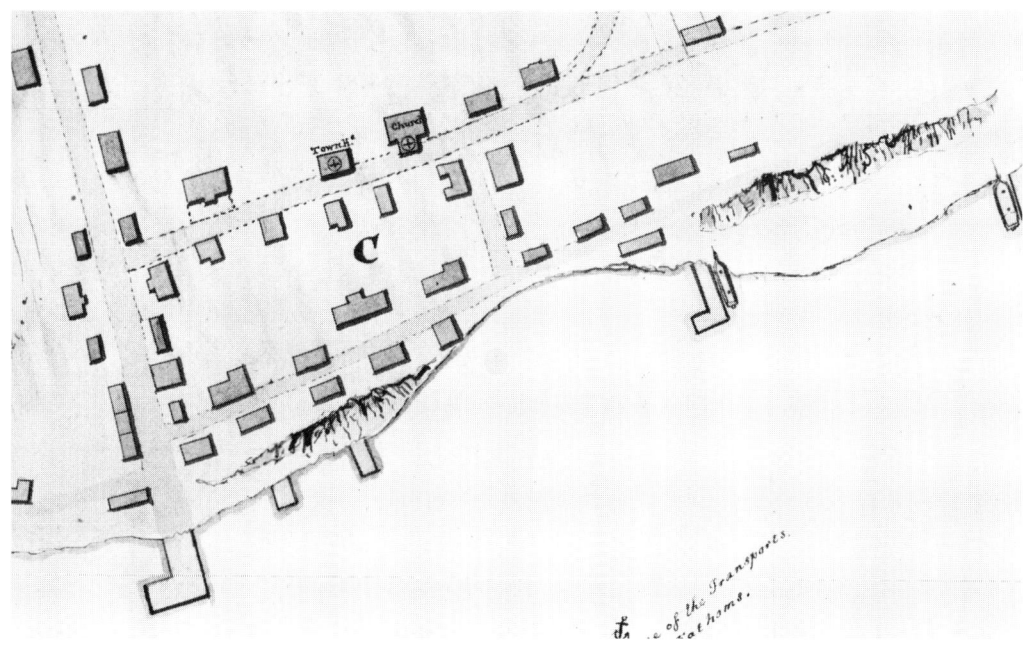

21. *Sketch of the Peninsula of Castine in the Bay of Penobscot and District of Maine in New England,* (detail), by R. H. Bonnycastle, 1814.
(Pen and ink and watercolor. The Public Records Office, London [MPH 499(1)])

Albion K. Parris in 1809. Parris was elected to Congress and was one of the principal leaders in the movement to separate Maine from Massachusetts. In 1819 the law office was taken over by Enoch Lincoln, who later served in Congress and as governor; many later practitioners who occupied this building went on to serve in equally prominent positions.

The original county seat for Somerset County, formed in 1809, was Norridgewock. Its Indian name was thought to mean a village seated on still water because the town is located just below a succession of cataracts on the Kennebec River where a point of land slowed the current. A bridge spanned the river's 650-foot width and led to the town common, which held both a town meeting house and the new County courthouse shown in Illus. 22. The old style meeting house was begun in 1794, six years after the town's incorporation. Its interior remained unfinished, however, until 1807 when it was completed by the sale of square box pews that had been built like those in the old meeting house in Concord, where some of the new citizens had once worshipped. Three religious denominations shared the house, according to the number of pews owned by each. Among these denominations, the Congregationalists were called "Hopkinsians" for the particular theological emphasis they professed. The town was "regarded as the metropolis of Methodism, in this quarter of the country," although it was only part of a traveling circuit for preachers. Near the church, an early visitor noted, "a white-painted house, of large dimensions and the most respectable appearance is the inn; and at the same time the country shop or *store*, at which all the commerce of the neighborhood is carried on."[38]

The town's representative to the General Court in Boston, John Ware, is credited with making Norridgewock the shire town. He gave an acre of land for a jail, contributed eight hundred dollars for its erection, and donated a house for the courts for as long as the county chose to occupy the building. Such community spirit was usually repaid by increased land values in a new shire town, but during the War of 1812 there was "an actual diminution of the value of property in the town. The price of land fell, and there were no purchasers, while the prices of all kinds of merchandise were exorbitant."[39]

Penobscot, established in 1816, was the last county created before statehood. Its shire town, Bangor, was just emerging from its frontier settlement as a lumbering and commercial center in eastern Maine owing to its prominent position at the headwaters of the Penobscot River at its confluence with the Kenduskeag. Although the town was first settled in 1769, title to the land was not granted until 1801. In that year Massachusetts investors commissioned Boston architect Charles Bulfinch to draw up a "Plan of Condeskeag Point on the Penobscot River," which envisioned an urban grid of house and commercial lots.[40] Architectural historian Deborah Thompson finds, however, that as late as 1819, log houses—usually discarded or reused for rear ells as

22. Norridgewock Common, Somerset County Courthouse, and Meeting House.
(Reprinted from *The History of Norridgewock* by Henry Allen [Norridgewock: 1849])

soon as more permanent houses could be built—still outnumbered frame and brick houses in the town.[41]

The community grew rapidly. The post office was established in 1800 and a bridge was built across the Kenduskeag in 1807. A printing office was established in 1815, a fireproof building for county records in 1817, and a bank in 1818.[42] The town meeting house, built in 1812, became the county courthouse in 1816; the Congregationalists built a new church in 1821. An 1825 description of the rapid increase of population and business in Bangor noted 107 dwellings containing 190 families with an average of 14 people each, all located within a mile and a half radius of the center. "There are also 8 lawyers offices, 40 trading houses, 2 bookstores, 7 taverns, two printing offices, 1 bake house, 2 tanneries, 2 victualling cellars,..." and a wide range of smaller shops and businesses.[43] Like several coastal shire towns, Bangor's favorable location combined the administrative services of the county courts, which attracted a class of professional men, with an active lumber trade. The wealth created by lumbering and shipping acted as an economic engine for the continued growth of the town.

PORTLAND:
THE ASCENDANCY OF CAPITAL

"No American town is more entirely commercial" than Portland, "and of course none is more sprightly," wrote Timothy Dwight in 1797. Upon his return ten years later, just before the Embargo closed the port, he wrote:

23. *Falmouth, Now Portland, in Casco Bay*, 1786. An 1849 copy by Charles Harris, after John Seymour, Jr. (1764–1791). (Pencil. The Harvard College Library)

No place on our route hitherto could for its improvement be compared with Portland. We found the buildings extended to the cove, doubled in their number, and still more increased in their appearance. Few towns in New England are equally beautiful and brilliant.[44]

Known as Falmouth until 1786, the town recovered rapidly from its burning by the British during the Revolutionary War to become the District's largest city (Illus. 23; see also Illus. 47 on p. 86). The federal government built a lighthouse to guide ships to the newly expanded wharves and a new customs house to tax imported merchandise. From 1790 to 1820, the population quadrupled to 8,500. Shipping tonnage grew from 5,000 tons in 1789 to eight times that amount in 1806, though trade came to a stop in every American seaport with Jefferson's Embargo Act and the War of 1812. Portland grew faster in the Federal era than Portsmouth, New Hampshire, or either Newburyport or Salem, Massachusetts. Fed by an almost unlimited timber supply, it began to challenge Boston as New England's busiest port.

Success in shipping and finance also made Portland the hub of a new communications system. Maine's first newspaper, *The Falmouth Gazette and Weekly Advertiser*, was established in 1785 by Thomas B. Wait and Benjamin Titcomb, Jr., for the purpose of promoting separation from Massachusetts. (See Illus. 48 on p. 89.) Titcomb (1761–1848), born into a well-to-do Falmouth family, learned the printing trade in Newburyport after graduating from Dummer Academy in Byfield (Illus. 24). Returning to Portland, he continued as a pressman and newspaper owner until 1796, when he became the leader of Portland's first Baptist Society and its first minister in 1800; he later assumed the Baptist pulpit of Brunswick (in 1804). When the Portland Convention for Independence met in 1819, he returned at the request of William King to open it with a prayer, demonstrating the fusion between religious dissent and the separatist movement.[45]

His counterpart in the pulpit of the Congregational First Church of Falmouth was the Reverend Samuel Deane (1733–1814), one of the city's early supporters of separation. The son of a Dedham, Massachusetts, tavern keeper, Deane was educated at Harvard in the years preceding the Revolution and served his Portland parish by dispensing both spiritual and secular wisdom to the District's citizens from 1764 to 1814. (See Illus. 49 on p. 121.) A representative of the established church, Deane instructed his parishioners in every aspect of their daily lives. His *New England Farmer*, published in 1790, testifies that he was as interested in teaching others how to plant and harvest as he was in guiding worship, voting, and obedience to the laws of God and man.[46]

It was Deane who recorded the burning of Falmouth by the British in 1775, "whereby more than three-quarters of the buildings, with much wealth in them, were reduced to ashes, and the remaining ones greatly torn and damaged."[47] In his diary he followed the community's revival, recording the replacement of buildings and their growing numbers over his long pastorate. By 1809 when the embargo brought construction to a halt, more than 500 houses, 150 barns and stables, and 200 shops and stores had been added to the town.[48] While many of these buildings have since been lost to the Great Fire of July 4, 1866, and rebuilding over the years, enough remain—either in fact or as drawings, daguerreotype photographs, and other illustrations—to enable us to recognize that Portland was a small city nearly unique in its fully modern architecture and in being largely unencumbered by its old plan and earlier buildings.

Among the homes erected during the first decade of resurgence, Daniel How's brick house along the waterfront attests to the use of republished English carpenters' guides to permit the local builders to affect the latest fashion. Soon the city would have numerous carpenters-turned-architect—such as John Kimball, Sr. and Jr.—who could combine the new classical motifs in elegant ways. The father, an established local joiner, designed two fine Federal-style townhouses built in 1800 for brothers Hugh and Stephen McLellan, wealthy merchants; the son is best remembered as the designer of the 1816 Cumberland County Courthouse.[49]

24. *The Reverend Benjamin Titcomb, Jr.* (1761–1848) (detail), by Constantine Brumidi, after Thomas Badger (1805–1880). (Oil on canvas. The Portland Public Library)

An innovative architecture served as a symbol of Portland's mercantile energies and reflected both individual and community success. None was more brilliant than the work of the young Alexander Parris (1780–1852), an architect-builder brought up and trained in rural Massachusetts. Parris worked in Portland from 1801 to 1811, building some of the city's major landmarks of that decade, before moving to Boston. After Charles Bulfinch left Boston in 1817 to take over the building of the United States Capitol, Parris soon became the city's leading architect. He emerged as a leader of the Greek Revival style through such projects as St. Paul's Cathedral (1819) and Mayor Quincy's markets (1825).[50]

Among the Portland buildings attributed to Parris is the home of silversmith and land speculator Joseph Holt Ingraham. The owner laid out and developed State Street, then the westernmost street in the city, and built his own home there in 1801. The building's style could have been based on a number of sources, including published ones. Many of the same exterior features appear in the work of Bulfinch and in the unfinished Salem mansion that Samuel McIntire designed in the 1780s for Elias Hasket Derby, the richest man in the country.[51] In addition to designing homes for some of Portland's mercantile elite,

25. Commercial Portland.

a. Central pavilion of the Maine Marine Fire and Insurance Company, built 1803–1804. Alexander Parris (1780–1852), architect. (1848 Daguerreotype. The Maine Historical Society)

b. The Fox Store, Middle Street. (Daguerreotype. The Maine Historical Society)

Parris is thought to have planned a row of commercial buildings, built in 1803–1804 and unified by pilasters and a pediment over the central bays above the ground floor facing Exchange Street. Located in the heart of the commercial city, this elegant home for the Maine Fire and Marine Insurance Company (Illus. 25a) is but one symbol of Portland's role as a financial center.

In an era when most housewrights could produce only simple floor plans and sketches, Parris produced brilliant architectural drawings. Some show that he adapted design elements, like the skylighted interior staircases for the Portland Bank (built in 1806–1807), from the most recent English architectural publications (Illus. 26). Parris also designed a flat roof, weatherproofed with pine tar and gravel, behind the balustrade; however, the Maine climate forced the bank to replace it with a steep roof a few years later. Burned in the 1866 fire, the Portland Bank survives in Parris's drawings as evidence of his innate talent as an architect, artist, engineer, and shaper of Portland during the city's first building boom.

In addition to the mercantile blocks and handsome dwellings that reflected its wealth, the city contained large numbers of utilitarian structures, such as the one shown in Illus. 25b. Wharves, warehouses, small wooden shops, ropewalks, and the several distilleries which transformed molasses into rum all bespoke the commercial nature of the city. Among them the Portland Observatory is perhaps the best known. Captain Lemuel Moody promoted its construction on the highest point of Munjoy Hill in 1807. When the embargo was decreed and many of the city's merchant leaders failed, Moody repurchased all the stock and became its sole owner.[52] Timothy Dwight recorded that the tower was "a frustrum of an octagonal pyramid . . . ascended by

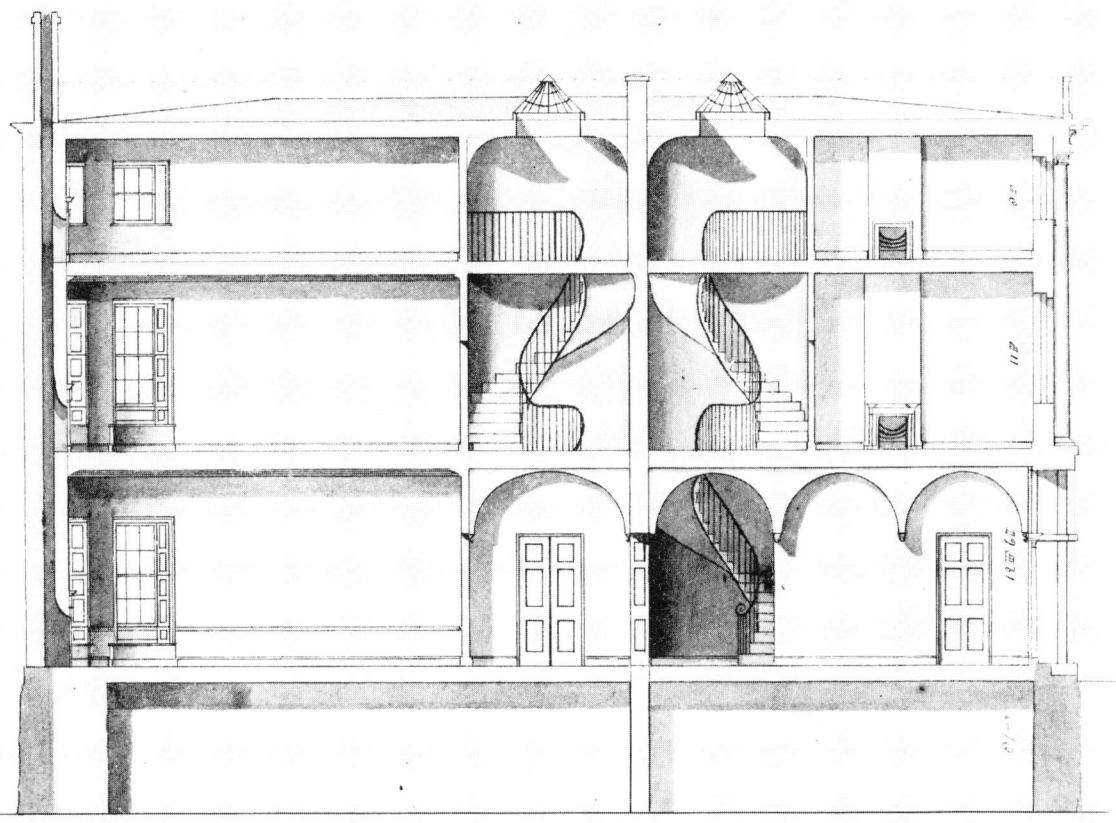

26. Elevation, door, and section of the Portland Bank, built between 1806 and 1807. Alexander Parris, architect.
(The American Antiquarian Society)

27. *Billy Hans* (ca. 1755–1831) (detail), by Charles Codman (1800–1842), ca. 1825. (Oil on panel. Private collection)

successive flights of stairs, the last of them spiral. The design in erecting this structure is to descry vessels off at sea." Flags of the city's merchants flown from its height were matched with those on incoming ships to alert the city of their approach. (See Plate IX.) "It is the only work of the kind, as far as my knowledge, in the United States," he noted.[53]

Portland's economic progress during the Federal era did not affect all its citizens alike. The fourteen-month-long embargo destroyed much of Portland's mercantile base. Import duties, which had totaled more than $342,000 in 1806, were down to $41,369 in 1808. The Portland Bank failed, and many of the city's leading citizens went bankrupt. Charles Codman's later portrait of rum-soaked "Billy" Hans (1755–1831) serves as a reminder that the lower classes suffered, too (Illus. 27). A Falmouth native, Hans served three years with the Massachusetts Line in the Revolution. Returning to Portland he married, built a house and made his living at odd jobs. By 1807, he had succumbed to the products of the city's several distilleries, had sold his house, and had become a town character. Living as a war pensioner in a smaller dwelling, he remained one of the city's least successful residents during this time of change.[54]

Life was also hard on the young men who went to sea from Portland and other seaports. In Beverly, Massachusetts, the mean age at death of mariners in the late eighteenth century was fifty-one years, or younger than artisans (55) and farmers, tradesmen, and gentlemen in less adventurous occupations (66, on average). Young mariners were especially vulnerable to early death at sea.[55] The dangers of the sea were multiplied by the harassment of American ships by warring European powers and the impressment of American sailors into the British navy. When the United States went to war with Great Britain in 1812, these dangers increased. Only one naval engagement was fought in Maine waters: a bloody fight off Monhegan in 1813 that resulted in the capture of the Royal Navy brig *Boxer* by the U.S. Navy brig *Enterprise*. But many Maine sailors manned privateers—private merchant vessels commissioned by the government to capture enemy ships—and in some cases ended up among the six thousand Americans in England's Dartmoor prison.[56]

Despite Portland's preeminent position as the center of shipping and trade, other commercial centers also emerged during the thirty years of prestatehood development. Shire towns like Castine, Wiscasset, and Machias were all active ports. By the year of statehood, Bath, located twelve miles from the sea up the Kennebec River, boasted four churches, two banks, two newspapers, and some 250 houses, as well as a growing number of locally built ships to support its "considerable commerce." Even more interesting to consider is another ocean port and center of commercial activity located on the same river. Hallowell, just below Augusta, which was separated from it in 1797, was the most inland community that could be reached by ship; it was forty-six miles up the Kennebec River at the head of tidewater. Hallowell's river harbor made it "a seat of commerce for all the upper and surrounding country," and it became second only to Portland as a market town.[57]

A recollection of Hallowell in 1792 by a visitor in September of that year gave little indication of the commercial character that it would soon attain and might have been written about many rural towns in Maine.

> There were about a dozen houses in the village of Hallowell and three or four stores. Isaac Clark was an inn holder and lived in a two story house. There was a large house called the Dutton house, the inside unfinished, in which a family lived. I lodged there ten years afterwards [1802] when the lower rooms were finished, but the chambers were partitioned off with rough boards and not nailed down.... There was no painted house in the village in 1792, no meeting house or other public building. Moses Sewall kept a few goods to sell in a room at the end of his house next to the street, and Rowland Smith kept a small assortment of goods in the little building opposite Clark's Tavern, used as a hatters shop.[58]

An academy was established in Hallowell in 1791, the first bank in 1804. By then the first of 100 warehouses, shops, and stores along the river's edge were being built, with over 60,000 feet of wharf and nearly 4,000 tons of locally owned ships by statehood.[59] *View of Hallowell* (Illus. 28), sketched about 1817, shows the river port and the hillside village spawned by the rich trade with agricultural towns to the west and coastal towns to the east.

Old South Meeting House in the center of the town was erected in 1796, but is shown with the handsome cupola added in 1806 from designs by Charles Bulfinch. As built, the cupola is related to several Bulfinch church designs, which may have been requested by his brother-in-law, Charles Vaughan, who was in Hallowell as early as 1791. "Contiguous to the upper street is the elegant residence of Dr. Benjamin Vaughan," his elder brother, "an English gentleman and late a member of the House of Commons," who arrived in 1797 from Europe with an independent fortune and the largest private library in New England. Next to Benjamin's country seat with its landscaped grounds was the farm of Charles Vaughan, an active promoter of improved livestock and agricultural reform. Together these brothers also established one of Maine's first commercial nurseries and orchards on the ridge to the west.[60]

The ascendency of capital in Maine's many commercial centers during the years between the Revolution and statehood transformed the Maine landscape. The handsome Federal-style architecture of Portland and Hallowell are reflections of the vitality of that young society. Likewise, the early settlement of farm towns can be traced today in the neat wooden or brick farm homes, which were later connected to barns by a series of additions made during the nineteenth century. Even the

28. *View of Hallowell,* by Jacques Gerard Milbert (1766–1840), ca. 1820. (Pen and brown wash. Courtesy, Museum of Fine Arts, Boston)

connected farmhouses of later date, which in many parts of Maine predominate over the earlier separate house and barn, reflect some of the outward character of Federal-period merchants' houses of more prosperous coastal towns with their connected carriage houses and stables.[61] Such design interaction drew upon the wealth of prestatehood building forms that flowered in the District in this largely forgotten period.

While the greatest concentration of Federal-style architecture is found in the least altered shire towns established during these years—places like Paris Hill, Alfred, Castine, and Wiscasset—smaller clusters of equally fine buildings can be found in every corner of the state. The mercantile mansions and many smaller houses of Kennebunk and Kennebunkport are well-known, but Federal-style houses of equal presence are also found in such towns as Fryeburg, Parsonsfield, and Waterford. The oldest extant Roman Catholic church in New England is St. Patrick's Church (1807) in Newcastle. The carved Irish harps above its interior doors reflect the origins of both designer, Nicholas Codd, and major patrons, James Kavanaugh of Damariscotta Mills and Matthew Cottrill of Damariscotta. Codd not only built the brick church and wooden homes for Irish lumber baron and shipowner

Kavanaugh and Irish-born merchant Cottrill, but set his hand to a series of grand houses throughout the state, including several of the finest in Wiscasset. Another group of excellently detailed Federal-style houses is found unexpectedly in Washington County's Columbia Falls. The most impressive is the one built in 1820 by Aaron Sherman of Duxbury Falls, Massachusetts, for the wealthy lumber merchant and store owner, Captain Thomas Ruggles. Unlike Portland, where much has been lost to fire as well as to later economic growth, these small towns seem defined by what is often their earliest architectural expression.

Although most stylistic pretentions of the new architecture in the District were expressed in neoclassical details, two buildings of this era provide clear examples of Gothic style. In Gardiner the granite Christ Episcopal Church facing the town common was built in 1819–1820 from plans of the Reverend Samuel Forman Jarvis of Bloomingdale, New York. Jarvis advocated the use of the "Gothick" style, drawn from similar eighteenth century English forms transmitted by architectural writers like Batty Langley. He sought to provide a new identity to the Episcopal church after the Revolution by drawing on a unique style with allusions to medieval ecclesiastic design. Yet this early example of Gothic Revival in Maine is not the first. A decade earlier a stone farmhouse outside the center of Bath was built with gothic arched windows and other applied detail of this romantic style (Illus. 29). The house is believed to date from between 1809 and 1812, making it one of the first examples of Gothic Revival design not only in Maine but in all

29. Gothic Cottage, home of Governor William King, built ca. 1810.
(The Maine Historic Preservation Commission)

New England. Why the future first governor of Maine, William King, chose to build this gothic cottage for his working farm is unknown. King himself occupied a large house in the village and owned a number of ships on which he exported from Bath the produce of this farm. Despite the mystery of why "The King of Bath" selected a style that might be the forerunner of the later nineteenth century development of stylistic revivals in Maine, it is an individual statement about the unsuspected range of choice that came with his own prosperity during Maine's transformation.

ACKNOWLEDGMENTS

The interpretations and images that form the core of this chapter were first presented in the form of the exhibition *From Revolution to Statehood: Maine Towns, Maine People, 1783–1820*. *Maine Towns* was prepared by the American History Workshop of Boston: Richard Rabinowitz, project director; William Braverman, researcher; Allen Moore, Jr., designer; Christine Gebhard, graphic designer; Gary Kincaid and Chandler's Lane, builders. *Maine People* was developed by William Barry, curator; Peter Simmons, preparator; and Kevin Murphy, coordinator.

NOTES

1. William D. Williamson, *History of the State of Maine from Its First Discovery, A.D. 1602, to the Separation, A.D. 1820*, 2 vols. (Hallowell: Glazier, Masters & Co., 1832; reprinted Freeport, Me.: Cumberland Press, 1966), vol. 2, p. 606.

2. Joseph S. Wood, "Elaboration of a settlement system: The New England village in the Federal period," *Journal of Historical Geography*, 10 (October 1984), 331.

3. Joseph S. Wood, "Village and community in early colonial New England," *Journal of Historical Geography*, 8 (October 1982), 333–346.

4. Ibid., pp. 334–341; also see Joseph S. Wood, "The Origins of the New England Village" (Ph.D. dissertation, Pennsylvania State University, 1978) and a brief published summary in Joseph S. Wood, "The New England Village as an American Vernacular Form" in Camille Wells (ed.) *Perspectives in Vernacular Architecture II* (Columbia, Mo.: University of Missouri Press for the Vernacular Architecture Forum, 1986), pp. 54–63. For a description of the internal migration of individuals to farming and commercial towns, see Douglas Lamar Jones, *Village and Seaport, Migration and Society in Eighteenth Century Massachusetts* (Hanover, N.H.: University Press of New England, 1981).

5. Wood "Elaboration of a Settlement System," p. 336.

6. Count Luigi Castiglioni, *Viaggio negli Stati Uniti dell' America Settentrionale*, vol. I, C.II, S.4, p. 46, cited in Charles Edward Banks, *History of York, Maine*, 2 vols. (Boston: Calkins Press, 1931–1935; reprinted Baltimore: Regional Publishing, 1967), vol. 2, p. 340.

7. Williamson, *History of Maine*, vol. 2, p. 541n. Williamson's footnotes are a goldmine of contemporary descriptions of Maine communities such as this, based upon an 1819 letter from Cushing. Many of his correspondents are identified and a good number describe their towns in 1820.

8. William B. Lapham, *History of Bethel, Maine* (Augusta, Me.: Press of the Maine Farmer, 1891), pp. 141, 243–245; Stanley Russell Howe, *Dr. Moses Mason and His House* (Bethel, Me.: Bethel Historical Society, 1981).

9. North Callahan, *Henry Knox, General Washington's General* (New York: A. S. Barnes & Co., 1958), pp. 322–323; Knox advocated a national program to encourage intermarriage and transform tribes into husbandmen.

10. Williamson, *History of Maine*, vol. 2, pp. 669–670; "Charlemagne Tower—His Journey Through Maine in the Summer of 1829," *Down East*, 16 (June 1970), 76, 80.

11. Nin Fletcher Little, *Six Decades of Collecting American Decorative Arts* (New York: Dutton, 1984), pp. 260, 262; James Vickery, *Jeremiah Pearson Hardy* (Waterville, Me.: Colby College Art Museum, 1966), unpaged.

12. George W. Coffin, Land Agent for Massachusetts, Journal of a Trip to Madawaska Territory, October 5, 1825, MS, Maine State Archives (hereafter MeSA).

13. Diary of Park Holland, November 10, 1794, MS, MeSA; *Park Holland Life and Diaries* transcription by Mary H. Curran, Bangor Public Library, p. 56.

14. Richard W. Hale, Jr., "The French Side of the Log Cabin Myth," *Proceedings of the Massachusetts Historical Society*, 72 (October 1957-December 1960), 118–125; Donald Cyr, "Acadian Architecture Evident in Restored Family Home," *St. John Valley Times*, July 22, 1981. Charles E. Clark, *The Eastern Frontier: The Settlement of Northern New England, 1610–1763* (New York: Alfred A. Knopf, 1970), pp. 194–197, attempts to differentiate the two New England log house types partly on the basis of arguments posed by Samuel Eliot Morison, who brought to publication the research of Harold R. Shurtleff in *The Log Cabin Myth* (Cambridge, Mass.: Harvard University, 1939; reprinted Gloucester, Mass.: Peter Smith, 1967). In disproving that Anglo-American building practices of the seventeenth century included the "log cabin," as many romantic nineteenth century writers had supposed, Morison and Shurtleff argue that the "blockhouse" type of log building in seventeenth century northern New England was hand hewn like English timber framing but nondomestic by virtue of its military function and therefore not really a log house. Both assumptions are false; see Richard M. Candee, "Wooden Building in Early Maine and New Hampshire: A Technological and Cultural History, 1600–1720." (Ph.D. dissertation, University of Pennsylvania, 1976), Chapter V.

Both documentary evidence and photographic evidence (as well as a few remnants in Vermont) show that eighteenth and early nineteenth century "log houses" in northern New England were more closely akin to the mixed origins of the "log houses" (later called cabins) of the Pennsylvania culture that was spread primarily south and west by the Germans and Scotch-Irish (who quickly adopted Pennsylvania German building techniques). See Fred Kniffen and Henry Glassie, "Building in Wood in the Eastern United States," *Geographical Review*, 56 (January 1966), 40–66. The log "cabin" myth was just that when applied to seventeenth century English settlement, but temporary houses of rough-hewn logs built later in eighteenth and early nineteenth century New England may have shared a common origin with those of the western frontier. A 1792 memoir by William Allen about Hallowell, Maine, "Now and Then," *Collections of the Maine Historical Society*, 1st ser., 7 (1876), 276 (hereafter *Coll. MeHS*) describes both log and frame houses:

> All lived in log houses at first, five to ten years until they were able to commence building a framed house, and could procure boards, and they usually moved in as soon as the outside and single room inside was finished, and lived in that condition sometimes for years, not so comfortably as in a log house, the seams of which could be stopped on the outside with clay, and caulked on the inside with moss; then with a large fire the house could be kept warm all day and night.

15. Robert P. Emlen, "The early drawings of Elder Joshua Bussell," *Antiques*, 113 (March 1978), 632–637; Delores Hayden, *Seven American Utopias: The Architecture of Communitarian Socialism 1790–1975* (Cambridge, Mass.: MIT Press, 1976), pp. 81–99; Williamson, *History of Maine*, vol. 2, pp. 406n, 565n, 699.

16. Edward A. Kendall, *Travels Through the Northern Parts of the United States in the Years 1807–1808*, 3 vols. (New York: I. Riley, 1809), vol. 3, pp. 33–34.

17. George Folsom, *History of Saco and Biddeford* (Saco: Alex C. Putnam, 1830), pp. 305–308.

18. U.S. Bureau of the Census, *Records of the 1820 Census of Manufacturers*, MS returns, National Archives Mirofilm #279, Roll 1, New Hampshire and Maine (York County, Saco Iron Works), p. 2.

19. Folsom, *Saco and Biddeford*, p. 305; James L. Garvin, "Academic Architecture and the Building Trades in the Piscataqua Region of New Hampshire and Maine, 1715–1815." (Ph.D. dissertation, Boston University, 1983), pp. 403–409; Dwight, *Travels in New England and New York*, 4 vols. (New Haven: Timothy Dwight, 1821–1822), vol. 2, p. 227.

20. Kendall, *Travels*, vol. 3, p. 45.

21. See maps from Wood, "Origins of the New England Village," redrawn from George A. and Henry W. Wheeler, *History of Brunswick, Topsham, and Harpswell, Maine* (Boston: Alfred Mudge and Son, 1878), pp. 11, 261; Dwight, *Travels*, vol. 2, pp. 211–214.

22. Quoted in William B. Miller, *The Early Architecture of Bowdoin College and Brunswick* (Brunswick, Me.: Pejepscot Historical Society, 1973), p. 18.

23. James Sullivan, *The History of the District of Maine* (Boston: I. Thomas & E. T. Andrews, 1795), p. 29.

24. [Henry Putnam], *A Description of Brunswick (Maine) in Letters. By a Gentleman From South Carolina to a Friend in that State* (Brunswick: Joseph Griffin, 1820), pp. 6–7, 12, 17.

25. Tench Coxe, *A Statement of the Arts and Manufactures of the United States of America for the Year 1810* (Philadelphia: A. Cornman, Jr., Printer, 1814).

26. *1820 Census of Manufacturers*.

27. Ibid.

28. [Putnam], *A Description of Brunswick*, p. 16.

29. *1820 Census of Manufacturers*; 1820 letter from Rufus McIntire in Williamson, *History of Maine*, vol. 2, pp. 519n, 461; Coxe, *Arts and Manufactures*, Part II, pp. 2–28 lists 75 carding mills and 59 fulling mills in the District of Maine.

30. William Frost MSS at Old York Historical Society and the Maine Historical Society contain records of the "Washington Mining Company" of which he was clerk from 1793 to 1810; Williamson, *History of Maine*, vol. 2, p. 567n. Also see the MSS records of the Washington Mining Company 1792–1810, Baker Library, Harvard School of Business, Boston, which show that the company was active 1793–1796, reorganized and incorporated in 1806, and operated through 1809. Fuller's earth is a highly absorbent claylike material used, among other things, to remove grease from woolen cloth in the fulling process.

31. Williamson, *History of Maine*, vol. 2, p. 461n.

32. Ibid., pp. 407n, 535n, 556n, 582–583; also see Topsham 1802 map; Banks, *History of York, Maine*, vol. 2, p. 238; Stanley B. Attwood, *The Length and Breadth of Maine* (Augusta, Me.: Kennebec Journal Print Shop, 1946), p. 38.

33. List of subscribers for an addition to the court house July 25, 1799; draft for town meeting vote, September 3, 1799; "The County of York in Accot. Current with Wm. Frost their Treasurer for the year 1806;" vote of First Parish in York, November 25, 1811 in William Frost MS, Old York Historical Society; Town Meeting record, Kittery, March 14, 1803, vote number 188 and Town Meeting record, York, March 15, 1803, vote number 167 in contemporary copies, William Frost MS, Maine Historical Society.

34. Frank A. Beard and Bette A. Smith, *Maine's Historic Places* (Camden, Me.: Down East Books, 1982), pp. 253–257; Kendall, *Travels*, vol. 3, pp. 129–130; *1820 Census of Manufacturers*, return of John Langdon for Wiscasset, Maine.

35. Tony P. Wrenn "Documenting an 1824 Court House: Lincoln County, Wiscasset, Maine," *Pioneer America*, 3 (January 1971); 3–18.

36. Williamson, *History of Maine*, vol. 2, p. 573n.

37. Charles E. Hamlin, *The Life and Times of Hannibal Hamlin* (Cambridge, Mass.: Riverside Press, 1899), p. 14.

38. Kendall, *Travels*, vol. 3, pp. 52, 104–106; William Allen, *The History of Norridgewock* (Norridgewock, Me.: Edward J. Peet, 1849), pp. 98–99.

39. Allen, *History of Norridgewock*, pp. 99, 102–103.

40. James H. Mundy and Earle Shettleworth, Jr., *The Flight of the Grand Eagle* (Augusta: Maine Historic Preservation Commission, 1977), pp. 2–3, 55–56; Penobscot County Plan Book, vol. 2, p. 44, Registry of Deeds, Bangor, Me.

41. Deborah Thompson, "Bangor in the Federal Period: Catching Up and Competing." Paper presented to the Maine at Statehood symposium delineates these buildings. The subject will be covered more fully in Deborah Thompson, *Bangor, Maine, 1769–1914: An Architectural History* (Orono, Me.: University of Maine Press, forthcoming). Williamson, *History of Maine*, vol. 2, p. 509, cites 11 log houses built in Machias's 1763 settlement around the sawmill. Paul Coffin, "Memoir and Journals of the Rev. Paul Coffin, D.D.," *Coll. MeHS*, 1st ser., 4 (1856), 330–331 states that the first house in Pownalborough, built by Wyman Bradbury, "of hewed timber" was still standing in 1796.

42. Williamson, *History of Maine*, vol. 2, p. 553n.

43. *Eastern Argus*, November 22, 1825, cited in Mundy and Shettleworth, *The Flight of the Grand Eagle*, p. 3.

44. Dwight, *Travels*, vol. 2, p. 208.

45. William Willis, *History of Portland from 1632 to 1864*, 2 vols. (Portland: Bailey & Noyes, 1865), vol. 2, pp. 596–597n, 687, 843–844.

46. William Willis (ed.), *Journals of the Rev. Thomas Smith and the Rev. Samuel Deane* (Portland: Joseph S. Bailey, 1849), pp. 290–299.

47. Ibid., p. 341n.

48. Ibid., pp. 408–417.

49. Denys Peter Myers, "The Historic Architecture of Maine" in the Maine Catalog of the Historic American Building Survey (Washington, D.C.: U.S. Government Printing Office, 1974), pp. 38–40, 66.

50. Edward Francis Zimmer, "The Architectural Career of Alexander Parris (1780–1852)" (Ph.D. dissertation, Boston University, 1984).

51. *Ibid.*, pp. 32–43.

52. Beard and Smith, *Maine's Historic Places*, p. 310.

53. Dwight, *Travels*, vol. 2, p. 209.

54. Research on Hans by William David Barry, Curator, Maine at Statehood exhibit. Charles Codman (1800–1842) worked as a sign and decorative painter in Portland as early as 1823. After his discovery as a landscape painter in 1828, his works were displayed in the Boston Athenaeum and the National Academy. His painting of Billy Hans is one of his rare portraits. See Maine Library *Bulletin*, 13 (July–October 1927), and "American Painters: Charles Codman," *Portland Magazine*, 1 (1834), 121–123.

55. Jones, *Village and Seaport*, pp. 38–39.

56. Martha Gandy Fles, "Saga of a Shipmaster's Portrait," *Down East*, 27 (April 1981), 16.

57. Dwight, *Travels*, vol. 2, p. 215; Williamson, *History of Maine*, vol. 2, p. 489n; Kendall, *Travels*, vol. 3, p. 47; *Historic Hallowell*, Katherine H. Snell and Vincent P. Ledrew, compilers (Hallowell, Me.: Kennebec Journal Print Shop, 1962), p. 19.

58. Allen, "Now and Then," p. 276.

59. Williamson, *History of Maine*, vol. 2, p. 390n.

60. *Historic Hallowell*, pp. 18–19, 32–33; Harold Kirker, *The Architecture of Charles Bulfinch* (Cambridge: Harvard University Press, 1969), p. 373; the church burned in 1878; Kendall, *Travels*, vol. 3, pp. 121–122.

61. Thomas Hubka, *Big House, Little House, Back House, Barn: Connected Farm Buildings of New England* (Hanover, N.H.: University Press of New England, 1984), pp. 14–18.

Carolyn S. Parsons

CHAPTER 3

"BORDERING ON MAGNIFICENCE"
Urban Domestic Planning in the Maine Woods

General Henry Knox was one of the more prestigious emigres to Maine who helped transform the region physically and culturally. Though he might properly be called a "pioneer" in the strictest sense, he did not even remotely fit the stereotype of the pioneer wilderness settler. By marriage and purchase, he acquired extensive property in Maine and from the nation's bustling capital of Philadelphia, where he had served as Washington's Secretary of War, Knox moved to the remote settlement of Thomaston in the District of Maine. There he supervised the exploitation of his land, lumber, and limestone resources. There he also built a grand Federal-style mansion, "Montpelier," in which he lived a life befitting the new revolutionary elite. By examining in detail the manner in which Knox built and furnished his splendid residence, Carolyn Parsons, a historian of the decorative arts, recaptures the special ambiance of Montpelier and describes some of the innovations that Knox brought there from Boston, Philadelphia, and even France. Economically, socially, and culturally, Thomaston was not as remote from the main centers of civilization in America as its location might suggest.

General Henry Knox was a self-made man. He began his career at the age of nine, working in a Boston bookstore to support his mother and brother. By 1771, he had opened his own shop. Appointed by George Washington as commander of Continental Artillery, Knox served with distinction throughout the Revolutionary War and subsequently became the first Secretary of War (Illus. 30). He also had the good fortune to marry Lucy Flucker, daughter of the Honorable Thomas Flucker, Royal Secretary of the Province of Massachusetts Bay, and Hannah Waldo, whose father was Brigadier General Samuel Waldo. Through Lucy's inheritance, the Knoxes came into possession of the Waldo Patent, a large piece of Maine land, which they supplemented with additional purchases. In 1794, Knox resigned his cabinet post and prepared to move from Philadelphia, the new

Carolyn S. Parsons is registrar at Strawbery Banke, the outdoor museum in Portsmouth, New Hampshire.

30. *General Henry Knox* (1750–1806), by Gilbert Stuart (1755–1828), ca. 1805.
(Oil on panel. Courtesy, Museum of Fine Arts, Boston)

31. Montpelier and farmhouse, ca. 1871.
(The Maine Historical Society)

nation's capital, to Thomaston, in order to oversee the development of his land. He looked forward to success in business ventures like lumbering, lime production, and shipping and sought, as well, the role of gentleman farmer in the best Enlightenment tradition.

Unfortunately, little physical evidence of Knox's plan for Montpelier, his Thomaston estate, survives. The present building, a replica owned by the State of Maine, was constructed in 1930 and does not stand on the original site. Knox's estate was closer to the St. George River in the vicinity of present day Knox Street and was far more extensive, including the mansion, outbuildings, gardens, orchard, wooded areas, and wharves. Knox conceived of Montpelier as the "nerve center" of an ambitious complex of outlying farms for raising livestock according to the latest scientific methods, growing market crops, developing extractive industries such as logging and the manufacture of lime, and the marketing of all these products, which involved shipbuilding and coopering. By 1853 the remainder of the Knox estate had been divided into house lots and split into four equal parts for the heirs of Lucy Flucker Knox Thatcher, the last child of Henry Knox and Lucy Flucker. The mansion house survived in a state of disrepair until 1872, when the railroad purchased the property and tore down what remained except the farmhouse, which served as the railroad station[1] (see Illus. 31).

Although the integrity of the site has been destroyed and the original mansion demolished, we can reconstruct the visual appearance of the house and its furnishings through surviving correspondence, bills and receipts, probate inventories, visitors' accounts, architectural fragments, pieces of original wallpaper, and furnishings owned by the Knox family. In this chapter we examine the Knox household between 1793 and 1806 when, upon the premature death of Henry Knox, the family's finances took a decided turn for the worse and Montpelier, as conceived by Knox, ceased to exist.

The design of the dwelling house and the selection of the furnishings were deliberate and emphasized the Knoxes' social position. Montpelier reflected the best in current neoclassical architecture and country living, but the estate was situated in near-wilderness and lacked the support systems necessary to maintain an opulent, urban household. Cyrus Eaton, writing almost seventy years later, described the Thomaston of 1796 as:

> Still a woody region, interspersed with straggling clearings, dotted here and there with small low, unpainted houses, many of them of logs and some few of hewn timber, distant from each other, along half made or newly laid out highways scarcely fit for wheel vehicles of any kind.[2]

Eaton's words describe the town at the time the Knoxes were moving into their house, three years after the initial plans were drafted. Henry Knox had no idea of how long it would take to build Montpelier into a thriving farm and to equip Thomaston with the support systems that his ventures required. But Knox was spurred by speculation. Harrison Gray Otis aptly described the General's eagerness:

> When this great and good man left the Federal cabinet, he became a victim to anticipation ... he expected to accelerate, and to realize in few years, not merely the growth and prosperity which Maine has now attained, but the high destination to which she may probably arrive in another half century.... He regarded his lime-kilns as mines of gold, and his standing timber as if cut and dried in the markets of Boston.[3]

Henry Thatcher Fowler, a great-grandson of the General, felt that the house and grounds drew inspiration from the Philadelphia area and farther south.[4] Noah Brooks, an early biographer, saw the outbuildings, cookhouses, and stables as arranged "after the ample and generous style of the best Virginia homesteads...."[5]

It is not, however, the plantations of the South but the country estates surrounding Boston that served as the main inspiration for Montpelier. With the creation of these estates came the development of a comprehensive plan for land management, emphasizing correct taste in architecture, landscape design, and agricultural reform in equal measure; business principles held the same importance as esthetic conceits. The essence of this kind of estate, or *ferme ornee*, was to "dignify and render ultimately pleasurable the sequence of agricultural processes throughout the year." The men involved in these design projects were not "content to live within the confines of a rectilinear mansion or the restrictions of an adjacent foreyard, nor to conduct their farms as luxurious (but profitless) ventures...."[6] Instead, Boston's elite utilized site and structure to fashion new environments mirroring new social and economic needs. In Thomaston, Knox intended to construct a *ferme ornee* on a grand scale. There he expected not only to make his estate a center of fine architecture, landscape design, and agriculture, but also to engage in extractive industries and mercantile ventures. He expected that the raw port would quickly grow into a bustling community, visually commanded by his home. That Knox was doing his part in developing the area was recorded in 1796 by Alexander Baring, who accompanied William Bingham on a trip to the latter's Maine property in August of 1796:

> He farms about 200 acres of land in high order as an example and carries on besides a lime-kiln, brick-making, shipbuilding, lumber trade, saw and grist mills, and a store for all imported articles. He breeds a vast number of horses and is excessively active in all sorts of projects such as cutting canals etc. . . . The soil of his tract at a distance from the sea is fine and near his house he has discovered and works a vein of limestone which is very soluable and the more singular as it is not otherwise met with on any part of the Atlantic coast. . . . Upon the whole the property is really well managed and thriving, at the same time that Knox from being near us is of great benefit to our property.[7]

Baring also indicated that such progress was not without great personal sacrifice to Knox. "For his own interest he does too much, as I believe he is a loser by most of his undertakings, but they are of vast advantage to his surrounding lands and to the country in general."[8]

The earliest example of a *ferme ornee* in the Boston area was Pleasant Hill, the merchant Joseph Barrell's estate in Charlestown, well situated at the most commanding position along the Charles River and within sight of Boston. Dr. William Bentley of Salem noted the novelty of Pleasant Hill in his diary when he recorded a visit on May 31, 1793:

> The plan of the Building is to me new, & not entirely executed. The Saloon is oval fronting the Town. the Cellars are in the best order. The flights of stairs in a vast entry opening towards the country & meet upon the first floor. There is an oval opening above which preserves the communication above, with a neat balustrade & the stairs are back. Everything discovered expence, but taste, & elegance. The prospect is the best I ever beheld.[9]

Pleasant Hill had an immediate and long-lasting influence on other country estates. During the next three decades at least a dozen other oval-on-axis residences with similar surroundings were erected in the Boston area.[10]

Henry Knox followed the lead of Joseph Barrell by taking advantage of the natural topography of Thomaston. He focused on the preferred entry into Thomaston—the water route—and built a mansion quite similar to Barrell's above the banks of the St. George, overlooking the harbor. In so doing, Knox emphasized his association with Boston's "new nobility," the people who were utilizing site and structure to create environments to reflect post-Revolutionary social and economic status.

32. Pleasant Hill, Charlestown, Massachusetts, built ca. 1796. Charles Bulfinch (1763–1844), architect. (Watercolor by an unknown artist, ca. 1830. Source unknown. Photograph courtesy of The Society for the Preservation of New England Antiquities)

Harold Kirker confidently assigned the design of Montpelier to Charles Bulfinch, primarily on the basis of stylistic analogies and published descriptions.[11] Montpelier compared quite favorably with Joseph Barrell's house, shown in Illus. 32. Pleasant Hill was designed by Bulfinch in 1791, or perhaps earlier, since the architect was first employed by Barrell as a merchant apprentice upon graduation from Harvard in 1782. Through the Barrell house, erected in 1792–1793, Bulfinch introduced to New England a style of domestic architecture featuring an elliptical salon flanked by two corresponding rooms and fronting on a garden.[12] A vestibule and stair hall were the other principal features of this new oval-on-axis plan. A sketch of Montpelier's floor plan penciled on the back of a scrap of wallpaper (Illus. 33) was very similar to the floor plan of the Barrell house.

Montpelier also shared design features with two other country houses designed by Bulfinch for Boston gentlemen. James Swan built a house in Dorchester in about 1796, which featured a circular drawing room with walk-through windows opening onto the piazza. Likewise, a monitor roof crowned the Perez Morton house in Roxbury, erected in 1796.[13] Thus, while Montpelier was not necessarily in a class by itself, it was certainly in the forefront of New England architecture during the last decade of the eighteenth century.

Knox may have discussed his intentions to create a country estate with Charles Bulfinch when the architect was in Philadelphia to examine the Chestnut Street Theatre. At about the same time, Bulfinch submitted estimates for constructing a theater in Boston, which was

33. Sketch of Montpelier floor plan, ca. 1850.
(Source unknown. Photograph courtesy of The Society for the Preservation of New England Antiquities)

erected in 1793. Henry Jackson, a proprietor of the Boston theatre wrote to Knox, possibly as a warning:

> Mr. Charles Bulfinch . . . calculated the cost of our Theatre to a Brick, a foot of Boards, and every other material and to complete the workmanship, and to his calculations added 10 percent: the whole expense did not amount to twenty thousand dollars—although every article has been purchased with the cash, at the cheapest rates, and the work performed on the most reasonable terms, the theatre will cost forty thousand . . . double the sum contemplated.[14]

Bulfinch's method was to supply only the plan for a grand scheme and to leave it to the master craftsmen, in consultation with the owner, to work out the details with the aid of published architectural design books. The extensive list of "Instructions to the House Builder," in Knox's hand and sent from Philadelphia, March 10, 1794, recapitulated an equally specific document addressed to the contracted builder, Ebenezer Dunton, the previous fall.[15] The involvement of the owner with the minutiae of construction was consistent with building practices of the period. Knox specified that all was to be completed, "according to the rules of work laid down in Ye Town and Country Builders Assistant engraved and printed in Boston."[16] Most of the workmen employed by Knox in the building of Montpelier were from the Boston area and they completed much of the finish work, such as window sash, doors and frames, balusters, and newel posts (Illus. 34) during 1793 in their shops. In the spring of 1794, these craftsmen were brought to the District of Maine to build a Boston-area house.

The result of their labors was documented by several travelers and guests at the Knox mansion, the novel design having aroused much interest. According to Alexander Baring:

> The house he has built is a very fine one and the whole of his stile rather bordering on magnificence. I think he is right in his calculations on this subject, although to himself it is an unnecessary expence. It attracts very much the attention of every part of the country. His house is talked of everywhere and is certainly equalled by nothing out of the large towns. He has besides being known for a man of refined manners and as a lover of society shewn the country to be a comfortable and agreeable one to inhabit and I am persuaded more strangers have visited it from curiosity the short time he has been there than in any ten years before.[17]

Among the curious visitors was the Reverend Paul Coffin, who stopped at Montpelier on his way home to Buxton after a missionary trip during the summer of 1796. Coffin left an intimate record of Montpelier:

> Dined at General Knox'. His house is admirably situated, looking south, almost directly down George's river, which makes a kind of a bay, and salt water here.... The General has a garden fenced ovally. Indeed circles and semi-circles in his fences &c. seem to be all the mode here. His house draws air beyond all the ventilators which I had before seen. I was almost frozen for three hours before we took dinner and plenty of wine.... The General's house with double piazzas round the whole of it, &c., exceeded all I had seen. The General being absent, gone East, in a Portland Packet with Mr. Bingham, I dined with Mrs. Knox and her daughters, and Mrs. Bingham and her sister and daughter. We had a merry dinner, the little Misses talking French in a gay mood. Mrs. Bingham was sensible, had been in France, could talk of European politicks, and give the history of the family of the late King of France &c.[18]

Both Baring and Coffin's comments were colored with practicality and a certain dissatisfaction with Knox's house in spite of its magnificence. The latter's physical discomfort underscored the impracticality of Montpelier's design for the Maine climate—perhaps the best reason for the failure of the design concept in its entirety in the District. Coffin, however, was the willing recipient of the kind of light-hearted, informal entertaining for which Montpelier was best suited and which fashionable Americans had absorbed as part of their affection for anything French.

The placement of Montpelier was calculated by Knox to impress all who saw it; the design of the house was avant-garde and magnificent. While Alexander Baring commented on the unnecessary expense in constructing such a building in Thomaston, perhaps the biggest extravagance lay in the Knoxes' plan to use Montpelier only as a part-time residence; they planned to spend the winter months in rented quarters in Boston. In a letter to George Washington, Knox elaborated upon their intentions:

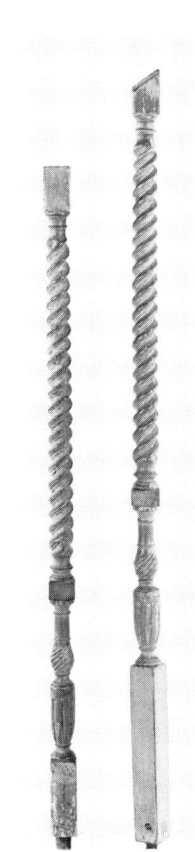

34. Two balusters from the center hall stairway, Montpelier, ca. 1795. (Montpelier, Bureau of Parks and Recreation, Maine Department of Conservation)

We have lately come from St. George's to pass the winter in this town. Indeed, this is our general plan: we may, however, as we grow older find it inconvenient. We are distant about two hundred miles by land, which we may easily ride in six days when the snow is on the ground; or with wheels, with a very little improvement of a small part of the road. I am beginning to experience the good effects of my residence upon my lands. I may truly say that it is more than doubled in its value since I determined to make it my home. The only inconvenience we experience is the want of society: this will probably lessen daily. Our communication by water to this town is constant and cheap. We can obtain transportation here cheaper than the same article can be carted from my store to the vessel. This egotism would require an apology to any other than you.[19]

Montpelier's use as a summer residence affected the appearance of the interior of the house. In particular, the furnishings, while fashionable, did not fulfill the promise of the public facade. Henry Knox was not fond of ostentatious ornament, especially where cost was concerned. In instructions to his builder, Ebenezer Dunton, Knox wrote, "You must understand clearly that altho I am desirous of having a well built house, yet I am also desirous of having it plain without carving or other expensive ornaments."[20]

Surviving bills and receipts indicate the General's wishes were carried out; there is no reference to payment for a carver's work. The walls, however, provided ample space for interior ornamentation of another kind. Undoubtedly Knox acquired a taste for wallpapers during his career as a bookseller in Boston, for such shops usually offered fine imported and domestic papers for sale. Excellent documentation for the use of wallpaper at Montpelier survives in the Knox papers, memoirs of visitors to the house, and actual fragments of the papers. In the stair hall on "a paper of yellow ground work" were "pictures some distance apart of men, nearly life size standing on pedastels in various stages of mutilation."[21] In all likelihood, these figures were similar to the "Cornices and pillars, with statues for halls and entries," offered for sale by William Mooney in New York in 1796 and the "Ancient Statues" advertised by a Boston wallpaper seller in 1800.[22] Knox purchased eleven figures in February 1794 from George Bertault in Philadelphia[23] (Illus. 35). These were the same figures included in Henry Simpson's bill of June 30, 1795, for work at Montpelier, which read in part:

"puting on 215 rolles of paper 3/ per roll" 33..5..0
"puting up and cuting out 12 figers" 0..18..0[24]

The discrepancy in the number of figures purchased from Bertault and those hung by Simpson may be explained by the entry for "4 seasons paper" purchased at the same time from Bertault. If so, then figures depicting the four seasons were intermingled with classical "pictures" to account for the dozen figures hung, twelve being a more symmetrical number. The installation of the classical statues is an early

35. Receipt for "4 Seasons paper" and "11 figures," purchased by Knox from George Bertault, 1794. (The Maine Historical Society)

reference to the use of such figures in America and especially in Maine; they remained in vogue, or at least for sale, throughout the first half of the nineteenth century.

The paper "of yellow ground work" was a color that was not yet popular at the time of Montpelier's construction. Papers of "plain sky blue" and "plain pea green" were the colors Thomas Jefferson desired when ordering wallpapers from Paris in 1790.[25] George Washington was partial to plain blue and green papers, as were the majority of American consumers around the turn of the nineteenth century.[26]

Knox's choice of wallpaper motifs varied widely. From Moses Grant, a Boston merchant and wallpaper manufacturer whom Knox patronized, the General purchased (Illus. 36) in 1795 the "festoon" border, a fragment of which exists at Montpelier over "a paper of yellow ground work."[27] (See Plate Xa and b.) A French paper that featured an eagle motif—a favorite of Knox's—combined with the symbols of Cupid (a quiver, arrows, and a torch) was hung in the drawing room. The paper was enhanced with mica particles scattered over areas prepared with varnish. The ground mica accentuated the pattern, incorporated the various colors present in the surrounding area within the visual surface of the paper, and added, as well, an element of light to the room. (See Plate Xc.) Another French paper depicting fruit on a pale blue or gray ground with a typical rose-type narrow border paper was used in the dining room. (See Plate Xd.) On the walls of a chamber, Knox hung a chinoiserie paper, similar to one depicted in the 1794 billhead of a Boston paper stainer, Appleton Prentiss, and known as "China fig" in a Prentiss' factory inventory.[28] (See Plate Xe and Illus. 37.)

36. Knox account for wallpapers and borders purchased from Moses Grant, 1794–1795.
(The Maine Historical Society)

Several fragments of another border used at Montpelier survive (but none containing a full repeat). This French paper featured landscape scenes within lozenge and octagonal shapes interspersed with seated figures in round medallions. It was designed to be hung vertically and horizontally to create visual interest in interiors where architectural details were light and subdued. Banding and stringing with contrasting woods, the hallmark of early neoclassical furniture, served the same purpose. We cannot determine whether Knox used this border vertically as well as horizontally because no records or fragments exist.[29] The modern reproduction of the border (See Plate Xf) shows, like the original, Greek-inspired orange pottery shapes on black ground. The same colors and shapes were featured by Josiah Wedgwood in his "Etruscan vases."

Against the bright backgrounds of wallpaper were placed a variety of furnishings typical of the late eighteenth century. The General's probate inventory of 1806—recorded in room-by-room fashion—is the most useful in determining the function of certain rooms during Knox's lifetime and the location of goods that were purchased for Montpelier prior to his death.[30]

With the exception of a few major pieces of furniture—a bookcase, the area's first pianoforte, and a billiard table—the furnishings were neither ostentatious nor avant garde in the context of Boston wealth similar to the Knoxes' and were purchased from Massachusetts merchants or moved from Philadelphia. The two formal rooms—the dining room and the oval room—were furnished simply yet fashionably. "Kane bottom[d]" chairs and settees, or painted fancy chairs with cane seats, served as the seating furniture in many formal rooms in fashionable New England households during the early years of the Federal period. With the exception of the few mahogany pieces, the Knoxes seemed to have relied heavily upon less expensive painted and pine furniture when furnishing Montpelier. No sideboard, a form that was introduced in the Federal period, is mentioned in the 1806 probate inventory. Nor do card tables appear in the mansion before Knox's death in spite of the fact that Lucy was devoted to games. Both sideboards and card tables are included in later inventories. The one

"Bordering on Magnificence"

37. Appleton Prentiss billhead, Boston, 1794.
(Courtesy of The Society for the Preservation of New England Antiquities)

38. Armchair (William Cox, Philadelphia), ca. 1795. (Montpelier, Bureau of Parks and Recreation, Maine Department of Conservation)

39. Square looking glass, ca. 1790. (Montpelier, Bureau of Parks and Recreation, Maine Department of Conservation)

real excess seems to be in the number of looking glasses and toilet glasses—twenty in all and several to a room—which served as prominent decorative features that reflected available light.

When Henry Knox's estate was appraised, the drawing room contained fourteen cane-bottomed chairs and a settee, a sofa upholstered with horsehair, a pembroke table, a pair of large looking glasses, a set of marble ornaments, fire tools, and a carpet. Set against the yellow walls of the oval room were a pair of painted settees and two smaller ones that he had purchased along with 96 chairs from William Cox of Philadelphia, on May 19, 1795.[31] Earlier, Cox had billed Knox for "12 Oval back'd white colord Arm chairs with Mahogany Arms 18/9" and for "12 Oval back white colord chairs without Arms 11/3."[32]

Several bowback Windsor armchairs painted white with mahogany arms (Illus. 38) survive at the reconstructed Montpelier. These chairs are branded "W. Cox" and stamped "HI" or "IH" on the seat bottom along with an illegible stenciled name. Undoubtedly the chairs are the ones that were purchased from Cox, who used the term "oval backed" to describe Windsor chairs with rounded or bowed backs.[33] Also in the oval room were a set of dining tables with oval ends, a pair of oval looking glasses, and a square one (Illus. 39). Another square looking-glass hung in the entry. An eight-day clock that had been purchased from Simon Willard on July 6, 1795, may have been the one the inventory located in the entry.[34]

Owing to the presence of the oval room, the dining room was used less formally than it would have been otherwise. A writing desk, easy chair, an "old sopha," one pembroke and one square dining table, one large looking glass, fire tools, and a carpet or floorcloth made up the contents of the dining room, along with the area's first piano forte.

The two remaining rooms on the parlor floor were used as bedrooms. One contained a mahogany bedstead and bedding, bureau, writing desk, twelve painted "flag-bottom[d]" chairs, a dressing glass, a large glass, a pair of mahogany framed glasses, three pine tables, and a pine washstand. The other room contained two painted bedsteads, a pine table, and pembroke table, a desk and bookcase, a bureau, and an old carpet, in addition to a large amount of bedding.

The china room was large enough to contain a "variety of glass, crockery, and china" worth sixty dollars; two liquor cases, a mahogany plate tray, six sets of knives and forks, and a pine washstand. This room was fairly substantial in size, undoubtedly larger than the pass-through allotted for storage in the reconstructed mansion, and would have made a sideboard superfluous. It contained, according to Lucy's 1824 inventory, three tables, "1 Set Italian China on 3 Shelves including dining set &c" and "China ware marked H.L.K.," along with other table wares.[35] The Italian china may have been expensive porcelain or pearlware decorated with scenes of landscapes or ruins. The H.L.K. set, worth five dollars in the inventory, was the Knoxes' Cincinnati service decorated with the order's eagle insignia and is the only set in which the husband's and wife's initials are combined (Illus. 40). The service was ordered in China by Samuel Shaw in 1790.[36] Knox had been instrumental in organizing the Society of the Cincinnati after the Revolution.

"Bordering on Magnificence"

40. Chocolate pot and cups, Chinese export porcelain, 1790.
(Montpelier, Bureau of Parks and Recreation, Maine Department of Conservation)

41. Bedstead (Benjamin Frothingham, Charlestown), 1796.
(Mahogany with painted cornice. Montpelier, Bureau of Parks and Recreation, Maine Department of Conservation)

42. Detail of post and cleat, Frothingham bedstead.
(Montpelier, Bureau of Parks and Recreation, Maine Department of Conservation)

In the west chamber stood the most expensive mahogany bedstead in the house (Illus. 41). Valued at $12.00 in the inventory, it was made by Benjamin Frothingham of Charlestown. Including the painted cornice, it cost £14.12.0 when purchased. Sideboards, now lost, were originally included with the bed and the posts were fitted with cleats to receive them, as shown in Illus. 42. Knox also purchased several of his bureaus and pembroke, or small drop-leaf, tables from Frothingham as well as a large mahogany wardrobe.[37]

The other two chambers contained painted bedsteads, bedding, wash stands, and other typical furnishings. One housed a mahogany wardrobe, the other a chest of drawers. The final listing of objects "in different parts of the house" is composed primarily of furniture and bedding, most items being rather unremarkable in their values. There was, however, a notation for 32 framed back chairs and 20 armed chairs—the Windsor chairs sold by William Cox. The appraisers found them in use throughout the house.

Three fine examples of early American portraiture are not included in Knox's inventory but were known to have been at Montpelier: Hannah Waldo Flucker by Joseph Blackburn; Thomas Flucker by John Singleton Copley; and Brigadier General Samuel Waldo (Illus. 43), attributed to Robert Feke. While there is no mention in the Knox papers of the Flucker portraits hanging in Philadelphia, correspondence concerning the Samuel Waldo portrait survives. Writing to Samuel Hodgdon, his aide in Philadelphia, from "Mount Pelier," July 4, 1796, Knox asks that he:

"Bordering on Magnificence"

77

43. *Brigadier General Samuel Waldo* (1695–1759), ca. 1748, attributed to Robert Feke (fl. 1741–1750). (Oil on canvas. The Bowdoin College Museum of Art, Brunswick)

44. Demi-lune table (Isaac Ashton, Philadelphia), ca. 1796.
(Mahogany primary wood. Montpelier, Bureau of Parks and Recreation, Maine Department of Conservation)

[N]ot forget to [pack] the old Brigadier as you mentioned that is carefully fold up the canvas and have the frame pack.ᵈ up—I wish you would have the frame regilt[,] The Brigadier['s] wig mended & perhaps the Dres[s] bugled by Peal or some other artist [who] also will be moderate in his Expenses....[38]

Four days later Knox wrote, "If you cannot have the Brigadier wig and frame Repared and Reguilt ship them packed up as you proposed."[39] The portrait left Philadelphia, August 13, 1796, on board the schooner *Friendship* with, among other things, "5 cases containing a Ward Robe and a sett of dining Tables."[40] The wardrobe and set of dining tables were made by the Philadelphia cabinetmaker Isaac Ashton. The tables may be the "Dining table with oval ends" listed in Lucy Knox's 1824 inventory as being in the yellow, or oval, parlor.[41] The oval ends survive (Illus. 44). "One set of dining tables" was in the oval room at the time of Knox's death.

There is some confusion about which furnishings the Knoxes used at Montpelier and which they used in the several houses they leased in Boston between 1796 and 1806. Some furniture known to have been at Montpelier is now lost.[42] For example, the office contained a billiard table, fire tools, a pine table, surveyor's instruments, 1221 English and 364 French books, maps and charts, and the bookcase brought from Philadelphia (Illus. 45). A note attached to a turned wooden handle—now in the collections of the Maine Historical Society—documents the demise of the billiard table:

This Handle was made from a part of the rail of a Billiard Table which was given by Genˡ George Washington to Genˡ Knox. It was broken up about 1856 by its owner Chaˢ Q. Clapp Esq & a piece given to my father. I turned this handle from a part of that piece. Portland, May 8ᵗʰ 91[,] Edwin S. Drake.[43]

The billiard table actually was not a gift from Washington to Knox; it cost Knox £34.16, including "casing and carting" and "liquer furnished the workmen."[44] Made by Benjamin Frothingham, the table featured molded rails (held together by screws with gilded heads) and green baize upholstery.

The study of Montpelier helps to illuminate important aspects of life in Maine between the Revolution and statehood in 1820. New styles were necessary emblems of aims and ambition in an expanding economy and influenced taste in more modest households. Henry Knox and Montpelier introduced neoclassical architecture and interior decoration, and the concepts of the *ferme ornee* and scientific farming to coastal Maine. At the same time Knox initiated the development of extractive industries and mercantile activities, which provided a base for the local economy and stimulated population growth.

This discussion is the result of preliminary work with the Knox papers. There is a need to study the papers further and to combine that effort with work now in progress on land and economic developments that were begun by Knox but were not a part of Montpelier per

45. Bookcase with looking glass, ca. 1795.
(Montpelier, Bureau of Parks and Recreation, Maine Department of Conservation)

se. The Thomaston of about 1790 must be analyzed and compared with the town as Knox left it in 1806 in order to document his role as a catalyst in the area's development.

ACKNOWLEDGMENTS

The author wishes to thank the following people for their insights, contributions, and assistance in the preparation of this chapter: Richard M. Candee, Tacy A. French, Thomas L. Gaffney, Sheila McDonald, Richard C. Nylander, Laura Fecych Sprague, and Philip Zea.

NOTES

1. A brick farmhouse, one of the outbuildings arranged in a semicircle behind the mansion, remains in its original location and serves as the home of the Thomaston Historical Society.

2. Cyrus Eaton, *History of Thomaston, Rockland, and South Thomaston, Maine*, 2 vols. (Hallowell, Me.: Masters, Smith & Co., Printers, 1865), vol. 1, p. 231. John Gleason, Knox's overseer at Montpelier for several years left a different impression. A ledger entry for September 6, 1789, Henry Knox debtor, reads in part: "To . . . 5 Roles Paper hang^g" and "To 5 yds of bordering. . . ." (Accounts kept by John Gleason with Henry Knox, 1789–1794, Thomaston, Maine, Knox Pps., Maine Historical Society (hereafter MeHS). Wallpaper was rather expensive and its presence in Thomaston indicates that not all houses were as crude as Eaton implied. Covering Gleason's account book is a piece of wallpaper in the "Peacocks" pattern, a woodblock printed paper in black, white, blue, and red on a cream-colored ground and may be an unused piece of the paper that Gleason hung for Knox by virtue of the fact that the entry occurs early in the account book. It is attributable to Boston paper stainers. (Author's conversation with Richard C. Nylander, February 1, 1984).

3. Noah Brooks, *Henry Knox a Soldier of the Revolution* (New York: G. P. Putman's Sons, 1900), pp. 265–266.

4. Henry Thatcher Fowler, *General Knox and His Home in Maine* (Rockland, Me.: Courier-Gazette Press, 1931), p. 29.

5. Brooks, *Henry Knox*, p. 233.

6. Charles Arthur Hammond, "'Where the Arts and the Virtues Unite': Country Life Near Boston 1637–1864" (Ph.D. dissertation, Boston University, 1982), pp. 144, 153. This dissertation is a comprehensive study of several Boston-area country estates, with particular emphasis on those established in the last decade of the eighteenth century and the first quarter of the nineteenth and which followed the precepts of a well-conceived *ferme ornee*.

7. Frederick Allis, Jr., *William Bingham's Maine Lands 1790–1820*, 2 vols. (Boston: Colonial Society of Massachusetts, 1954), vol. 2, p. 770.

8. Ibid.

9. William Bentley, *The Diary of William Bentley, D.D.*, 4 vols. (Gloucester, Mass.: Peter Smith, 1962), vol. 2, p. 28.

10. The closest inspiration for Barrell's estate was "The Woodlands," built by William Hamilton near Philadelphia in 1782, which combined picturesque exoticism with classical correctness. Its construction marked the creation of a country seat complete with mansion house, barns, stables, carriage house, greenhouses, and kitchen gardens—all constructed according to the fundamental principles of neoclassicism. Landscaped green lawns sloped toward the Schuylkill River; lanes and drives were planted with over-arching shade trees and fences, walls, and hedges enclosed meadows and pastures (see Hammond, p. 91). Knox undoubtedly was familiar with "The Woodlands" from his life in Philadelphia.

11. Harold Kirker, *The Architecture of Charles Bulfinch* (Cambridge, Mass.: Harvard University Press, 1969), pp. 93–100 for discussion.

12. Ibid., pp. 45–47.   13. Ibid., pp. 128–140.

14. General Henry Jackson to General Henry Knox, Boston, April 13, 1794, cited in ibid., p. 69.

15. Henry Knox to House Builder, Philadelphia, March 10, 1794, Knox Pps., Massachusetts Historical Society (hereafter MaHS).

16. Tacy A. French, *Montpelier* (Southborough, Mass.: Yankee Color Corporation, 1979), pp. 8, 11.

17. Allis, *Bingham's Maine Lands*, vol. 2, p. 770.

18. Paul Coffin, "Memoir and Journals of Rev. Paul Coffin, D.D.," *Collections of the Maine Historical Society*, 1st ser., 4 (1856), 326–327.

19. Francis S. Drake, *Life and Correspondence of Henry Knox* (Boston: Samuel G. Drake, 1873), pp. 113–114.

20. Henry Knox to Ebenezer Dunton, March 10, 1794, Knox Pps., MaHS.

21. French, *Montpelier*, p. 24.

22. Catherine Lynn, *Wallpaper in America from the Seventeenth Century to World War I* (New York: W. W. Norton, 1980), p. 121.

23. Henry Knox bought from George Bertault, Philadelphia, February 14, 1794, Knox Pps., MeHS.

24. Henry Simpson to Henry Knox, June 30, 1795, Knox Pps., MeHS.

25. Lynn, *Wallpaper*, p. 125.

26. Ibid., p. 148.

27. General Henry Knox bought from Moses Grant, Boston, receipt dated October 13, 1794, Knox Pps., MeHS.

28. Lynn, *Wallpaper*, 112–113. See also Ellen Paul Denker, *After the Chinese Taste: China's Influence in America, 1730–1930* (Salem, Mass.: Peabody Museum of Salem, 1985), catalog no. 23, p. 37.

29. The author wishes to thank Richard C. Nylander for bringing to her attention a photograph of this border installed with the medallions and lozenges running horizontally below the cornice and above the dado, as well as vertically between doors, so that wall sections are treated as several discrete units. Although the subject of the photograph is not mentioned, the following is printed on the back: "Isabella Barclay, Inc./ 136 East 57th Street/ New York/ #3819 Serie de papier peint, Sphinx avec/ corbeilles de fleurs, Louis XVI, attributed / to Pergolesi." (From the files of the Society for the Preservation of New England Antiquities, Boston) For further information on Knox's "festoon" and lozenge and medallion borders see Richard C. Nylander, Elizabeth Redmond, and Penny J. Sander, *Wallpaper in New England* (Boston: Society for the Preservation of New England Antiquities, 1986), pp. 72–74.

30. Probate inventory of Henry Knox, November 1, 1806, Lincoln County Probate Records, 12:202–208, Lincoln County Court House, Wiscasset, Me.

31. Henry Knox bought from William Cox, Philadelphia, May 19, 1795, Knox Pps., MeHS. The list of purchases is as follows:

```
36 Ovel Back'd white Colord Chairs ...   @ 12/6 ea   22..10.-
36 Arm'd do with Mahogany arms           @ 20/ea     36.-
 4 Arm'd do Settees wth do               @ 90/ea     18..-
 2 Arm'd do do          do               @ 40/ea      4..10-
24 Fann'd back'd Brown Colord Chairs     @  8/4 ea   10..- -
```

32. General Knox bought from William Cox, Philadelphia, March 29, 1794, Knox Pps., MeHS.

33. A year and a half later, Joseph Anthony and Company, also of Philadelphia, billed Elias Hasket Derby for "24 Oval Back Chairs ... 34/£40:16:0," Charles F. Montgomery, *American Furniture The Federal Period* (New York: Bonanza Books, 1978), p. 78. Several examples of sophisticated oval-backed chairs with painted and gilt decoration and Derby family provenance survive in the collections of the Museum of Fine Arts, Boston, and the Winterthur Museum. These chairs are believed to be the ones ordered from Anthony. Although the same terminology was used in describing the chairs, Knox's were significantly less expensive, and therefore the purchase of the Cox chairs that survive at Montpelier, as well as one at the Maine Historical Society, can be firmly documented by these two bills.

34. Mr. Joseph Pope bought from Simon Willard, Roxbury, July 6, 1795, Knox Pps., MeHS.

35. Lucy Flucker Knox Probate Inventory, September 11, 1824, Lincoln County Probate Records, 26:122.

36. *The Society of the Cincinnati 1783–1983* (Salem, Mass.: Peabody Museum of Salem, 1983), pp. 5–9, 18. See also John Quentin Feller, "China Trade Porcelain Decorated with the Emblem of the Society of the Cincinnati," *Antiques*, 118 (October 1980), p. 763, Figs. 5 and 5a.

37. General Henry Knox from Benjamin Frothingham, Charlestown, November 10, 1796, Knox Pps., MeHS. Knox tended to patronize tradesmen who had served with him in the Revolutionary War or were active in militia companies before the war, such as Samuel Gore, Moses Grant, and Stephen Badlam. Benjamin Frothingham and Thomas Vose served with Knox in the artillery. Vose became Knox's clerk and later his partner in a store in Thomaston.

38. Henry Knox to Samuel Hodgdon, Mount Pelier, July 4, 1796, Knox Pps., MeHS.

39. Henry Knox to Samuel Hodgdon, Thomaston, July 8, 1796, ibid. The Waldo portrait and those of the Fluckers were included in the inventories of Knox's wife and daughters. All three portraits are now in the collection of Bowdoin College, the gift of Mrs. Lucy Flucker Knox Thatcher in 1854. See Marvin S. Sadik, *Colonial and Federal Portraits at Bowdoin College* (Brunswick, Me.: Bowdoin College Museum of Art, 1966), pp. 57–62, 73–76, 79–85.

40. Invoice for shipping, August 13, 1796, Knox Pps., MeHS.

41. Lucy Flucker Knox Probate Inventory, p. 124, LCC.

42. No inventory exists for Henry Knox in Probate Court records, Suffolk County Court House, Boston, Massachusetts. The author wishes to thank Kevin Murphy for supplying this information.

43. The author wishes to thank Laura Sprague for bringing this information to her attention.

44. French, *Montpelier*, p. 18.

James S. Leamon

CHAPTER 4

REVOLUTION AND SEPARATION
Maine's First Efforts at Statehood

Rapid physical growth accompanied by social and economic diversity often led to clashing ambitions, challenges to authority, and conflicting loyalties within Maine and between groups in Maine and Massachusetts proper. Religion, economics, and politics were persistent sources of contention, but no issue was more divisive than the question of separation from Massachusetts. James Leamon finds the origins of the statehood issue in the period of the Revolutionary War. Down-east neutralists wanted to escape war taxation and British devastation; frontier farmers hoped that a Maine legislature would protect them from proprietary claims, and a group of professional men in Falmouth (Portland) viewed statehood as a means to gain political leadership for themselves. All employed the philosophy of the Revolution and the experience of war in seeking their objectives. Yet these proponents of an independent Maine were too few in number and too lacking in unity to overcome the bonds that still linked Maine to Massachusetts. They nonetheless initiated the cause of statehood, which persisted through seven distinct referenda, until in 1819 the idea of separation coincided with the perceived self-interest of the District at large.

On March 15, 1820, Maine joined the union as the twenty-third state, bringing to a climax a movement for statehood that had persisted for almost forty years, and concluding a political union with Massachusetts that had lasted since 1691. That was the year in which the king of England granted to Massachusetts a new charter which reorganized its government and expanded its jurisdiction to include the struggling frontier communities in Maine, over which Massachusetts had already begun to exercise authority.[1] By the time the Revolutionary War broke out, Maine's 40,000 inhabitants had come to accept the union as normal and beneficial. They retained close family ties with the communities in Massachusetts from which many had come; their own incorporated towns, when they could bear the expense, sent representatives to the legislature in Boston; and they were constantly aware of their dependence on Massachusetts for economic and military support. In 1778 the Continental Congress divided Mas-

James S. Leamon is professor of history at Bates College.

sachusetts into three maritime districts of which Maine was one, and the region then became known as the District of Maine.² The new designation did not suggest any weakening of the political union with Massachusetts; indeed, townsmen of the new District almost immediately participated in creating a new state constitution for Massachusetts, which retained the former political connection. The advantages of union for Maine so far outweighed the disadvantages that separation simply was not an issue.

The Revolution changed that. The war, independence, and the political philosophy justifying revolution not only gave rise to Maine's first efforts to separate from Massachusetts, but they also stimulated public debate over the nature of government, political allegiance, and the right and the means of opposing popular government. The debate soon fused with that over ratification of the Federal Constitution so that Mainers had to consider simultaneously the merits of union and disunion on the local as well as on the national level. Separationists and Anti-Federalists together went down in defeat, but the debate about representative government, allegiance, and resistance reveals a high degree of political sophistication over questions that have never lost their significance throughout American history.

The initial movement for separation occurred as a plea for neutrality in eastern Maine during the Revolution when Massachusetts seemed unable to protect a frontier so extended and vulnerable as that in Maine. The local militia was generally ineffectual in protecting the towns, and only the friendly eastern Indians provided any sort of deterrent against British incursions. By sea, Maine was defenseless (Illus. 47); Massachusetts had no vessels to spare for patrolling the coast, and most of the towns hoped that their own insignificance would ensure their safety.³

However, inconspicuousness provided poor protection. In June 1779, a British expedition from Nova Scotia occupied what is now the town of Castine on the east side of Penobscot Bay (Illus. 46). Although Massachusetts responded vigorously with an armada of some forty vessels and a thousand Maine militiamen to drive the enemy out, their commanders disagreed over tactics. While they argued, a British naval squadron arrived and sent the Americans fleeing up the Penobscot River.⁴ From 1779 until the end of the war, Maine had to contend with an enemy base in its midst. From this base the British (aided by local loyalists) ravaged the land, destroying vessels, burning houses and barns, slaughtering livestock, and kidnapping local leaders.⁵ No settlement was too small or too impoverished to escape the enemy's attention. In addition, Maine had to face endless demands from Massachusetts for taxes, troops, and provisions.

Maine towns barraged the General Court with appeals for relief and increasingly criticized the ineffectiveness of the government. From Machias a resident accused the government of thinking that the best policy for the eastern district was "to neglect it utterly."⁶ A critic from

46. *A Southeast View of Fort George with the Peninsula and Harbor of Majabigwaduce* (detail), by Lieutenant Jones, 1780.
(Source unknown. Library of Congress photoreproduction)

Boothbay chided the General Court by stating that although the region had little political importance, "its inhabitants suppose themselves entitled to the protection of Government in common with other parts of the State."[7] After 1779, petitions seldom addressed the government in former terms of filial loyalty as "Fathers of the People" or "our avowed, beloved, & beneficient *Guardians*" or "An Indulgent & Affectionate Parent."[8] Instead, they demanded relief almost without formality and occasionally with heavy sarcasm compared the taxing policies of the General Court with those of the British Parliament.[9] An alarming willingness to cooperate with the British at Castine revealed a growing disillusionment with Massachusetts and the war. The General Court tried to counter the trend by placing Lincoln County, the eastern-most half of Maine, under martial law. The commanding officer imprisoned those whose loyalty was suspect and even executed one known collaborator.[10]

Such repressive measures in the name of freedom only reinforced the prevailing pessimism and led to a movement in Lincoln County to abandon the war entirely. The initiative came from Francis Shaw, Jr., of Gouldsborough, a merchant, colonel of militia, and chairman of the local Committee of Correspondence, Safety, and Inspection. According to Shaw, even Governor John Hancock agreed that since the state could not protect the eastern communities, the inhabitants had an "undoubted Right" to make the best terms they could to protect their lives, families, and property.[11] A committee from the eastern towns conse-

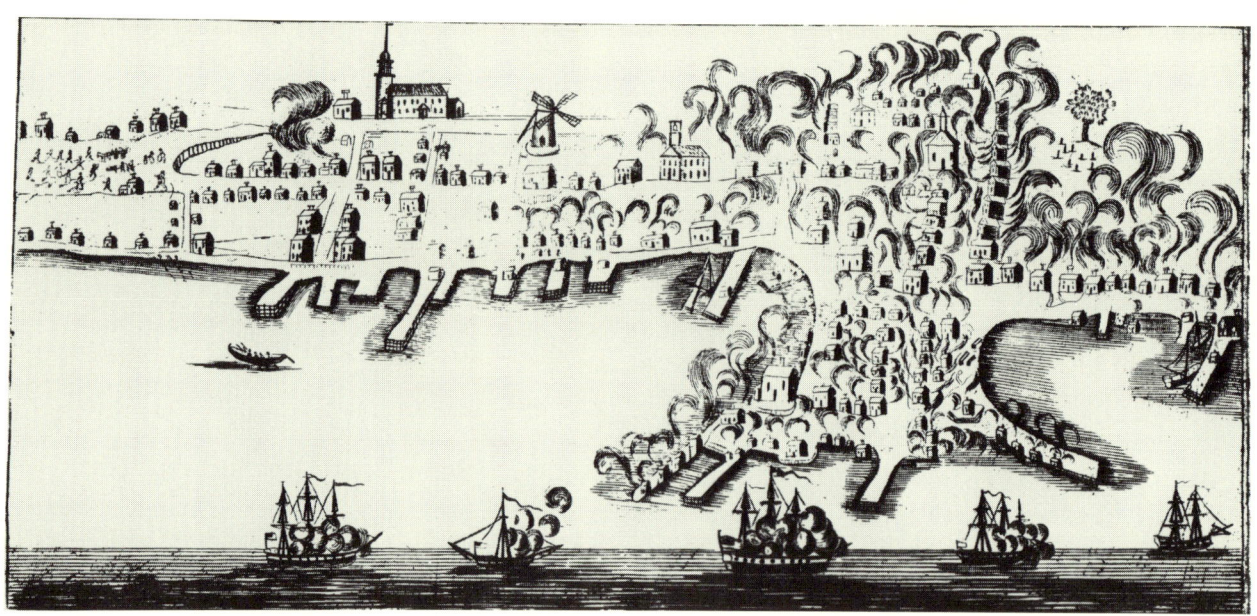

47. "THE TOWN of FALMOUTH, Burnt by Captain MOET . . . 1775" (detail), from *An Impartial History of the War in America* by James Murray (Boston: 1782).
(The American Antiquarian Society)

quently drafted a petition in March 1781 requesting the state of Massachusetts to recognize a condition of neutrality from Penobscot Bay eastward to the Saint Croix River.

The neutralist argument rested on the unstated but widely held conviction that governments exist to protect the lives, liberty, and property of their citizens. It followed then that "Allegience & Protection are Reciprocal." Maine's eastern towns had done more than their fair share in the war against Great Britain, but the Massachusetts government had left them defenseless and subject to plundering, devastation, and the additional grievance of martial law. Therefore, "the Government of Massachusetts (from what cause is totally Immaterial,) have Refused or Neglected to give Protection to us the said Inhabitants in Return for our Allegiance, so that in Justice to our selves, our Families, & Posterity founded on the Universal Concurrance of Nations we are constrained to Ask of your Excellency & Honours, an Act of Neutrallity."[12]

Not only had the Massachusetts government broken the contractual relationship with its eastern-most subjects, but the petition clearly hints that it was more than accidental. It suggests darker motives, even a plot behind such actions. Belief in conspiracy pervaded the revolutionary mentality, with King George III as the arch-conspirator of all.[13] Francis Shaw, Jr., and his fellow petitioners never explained their suspicions, nor did they go so far as to equate the Massachusetts governor, John Hancock, with King George III. On the contrary, they cleverly used Hancock, one of the leading patriots, to support their cause by quoting his alleged expressions of sympathy for the plight of the people down east and by using his prestige to sanction the cause of neutrality. The petition clearly applied the political thought of the Revolution to the particular advantage of the eastern-Maine communities. Given the circumstances in Lincoln County, the argument may have seemed persuasive, but even within the county itself the petition raised a storm of protest, and the movement collapsed with the vilification of its proponents.

The town of Machias was particularly hostile to the scheme. In a spirit of outraged patriotism, Machias expressed its "utmost abhorrence" of neutrality and accused Francis Shaw of seeking his private interest rather than the good of his country.[14] The town's Committee of Correspondence, Safety, and Inspection drafted its own resolves denouncing Shaw and his fellow neutralists for trying to restore the region east of Penobscot Bay to British control merely to continue their illegal trade with the enemy without fear of interruption.[15]

Machias's vehement opposition to neutrality arose from the fact that the war had affected that community differently from those around it. Gouldsborough, Jonesborough, Narraguagus, and Frenchman's Bay had all suffered from British depredations. Machias, by contrast, enjoyed a more protected location and increased importance as the war continued. It was the eastern-most fortified town in Maine, a haven for Nova Scotian refugees, a staging area for invasions of British-held territory, and the center for rallying the eastern Indians. So important was Machias that both Massachusetts and the Continental Congress contributed to its defense. Screened by friendly Indians, supported by state and nation, and located well up the Machias River beyond the easy reach of unfriendly vessels, Machias could afford to assume the uncompromising attitude which effectively killed Shaw's neutralist scheme.

Actually, Massachusetts had not neglected the plight of its eastern communities, defenseless though they may have been. The General Court did try to provide supplies of food and even funds with which needy towns could purchase provisions. The government interceded with other states and with the Continental Congress to relax embargoes so food might be sent down east, and it promised credit to towns that were unable to pay.[16] After 1779, when British cruisers out of Castine put a stop to shipments of food, the General Court provided relief by suspending or reducing its demands for men, money, and goods. So great was the need that it is doubtful whether government aid had much physical benefit, but it had a political benefit in helping to reduce a sense of resentment and isolation from Massachusetts, which could have flared into yet more serious sectional hostility. As it was, the wartime neutralist movement down east briefly raised the spectre of separation and demonstrated a novel application of revolutionary political theory concerning natural rights and conditional allegiance—and then collapsed. However, these arguments soon reappeared after the war was over.

The postwar movement for separation had little in common with eastern Maine neutralism, except that they both evolved from the local elites and drew heavily on the political ideology of the American Revolution for self-justification. Inspiration and leadership for postwar separation came from a group of leading citizens in the Portland-Gorham area. Included were several prominent merchants, such as Enoch Ilsley and Peleg Wadsworth, the latter a former brigadier general; two Congregational ministers, Thomas Smith and Samuel Deane; Thomas Wait, a newspaper editor; a gentleman farmer named Stephen Longfellow; and the leading resident in the town of Gorham, Judge of Probate William Gorham, one of the few separationists to hold a civil or judicial commission. Later, two leading spokesmen for the interior represented the rural, populist wing: William Widgery, a lawyer from New Gloucester, and Topsham's Samuel Thompson, former mob leader, now risen through the ranks to brigadier general of militia, state representative, and finally state senator.[17]

In their own way, these proponents of separation were as much speculators in Maine's future as those who were investing in Maine land. Forty thousand new settlers surged into Maine in the six years following the end of the war, swelling the population from 56,000 to 96,000.[18] The promoters of separation were acutely aware that the region had the potential to become a state in its own right, and those who led the movement might find a suitable reward for their political ambitions in the many new offices that would be created.

From 1785 through 1789, these men provided the stimulus and direction for a series of conventions that met at Portland to promote the cause of statehood for Maine. The conventions produced a list of grievances, an Address to the People, a referendum, and eventually a petition to the General Court requesting separation. Once more a lively debate ensued over the nature of representative government and whether one group of people could legitimately withdraw from a political union they voluntarily had helped to create. Advocates and opponents argued over the theoretical and practical aspects of separation in a series of essays printed under pseudonyms in Maine's first newspaper, the *Falmouth Gazette*, which was established in 1785 to further the cause of statehood for Maine[19] (Illus. 48).

Proponents no longer accused the state government of any particular failings or of a conspiracy against the District; instead they invoked the "principle of self-preservation" to rectify the practical disadvantages caused by the existing political connection. They argued that Maine's geographical distance from the seat of government, the expense of sending delegates, and its poverty and lack of population all placed it at a comparative disadvantage relative to the other regions of the Commonwealth. Therefore, whenever a part of any body of people "bear an unequal share of the public burthen," they have a right, which they "derive from nature, and the principles of self-preservation," to demand a separation.[20]

To justify separation, advocates had to do more than emphasize the inequities of the existing union with Massachusetts. They had to demonstrate that *any* political connection with the Commonwealth was

48. First issue of *The Falmouth Gazette and Weekly Advertiser,* 1785, Benjamin Titcomb, Jr., and Thomas B. Wait, publishers.
(The Maine Historical Society)

unacceptable and that Maine had a legitimate, autonomous existence of its own prior to and independent of union with Massachusetts. Separationists therefore ransacked the past to discover historical precedents for a territorial state of Maine with powers of self-government. King Charles I's early seventeenth century charter to Sir Ferdinando Gorges for the Province of Maine provided just what they were looking for. The *Falmouth Gazette* published the entire charter in three successive installments. Commentators emphasized the salient points that Gorges, his heirs, and assigns had power to make laws, ordinances, and constitutions, and although later monarchs had abrogated the charter, their actions were arbitrary and without legal basis. Therefore Maine had every right to resume its powers of self-government, which it had never actually surrendered.[21]

Necessity, natural right, and history all justified an autonomous Maine, but did the region possess the ability and the means to govern itself? Critics of separation denied that it did. Some even stigmatized separationists as Tory sympathizers who, if successful, would welcome the return of Tory refugees and admit them to a share in the new government. At the very least, the returning loyalists "will be continually endeavouring to instill their pernicious principles into the minds of their neighbours, And what friend to American liberty would not tremble at the consequence?"[22] One proponent of separation responded to the charge by admitting that he, at least, would welcome to Maine anyone whose character, skills, and wealth might strengthen the government.[23] In general, separationists ignored the slander and tried to convince the public that Maine did indeed possess sufficient resources, human and material, for self-government. "Government is a very simple, easy thing," declared the convention's Address to the People, adding that "Mysteries in politicks are mere absurdities—invented entirely to gratify the ambitions of princes and designing men—to aggrandize those who govern, at the expense of those who are governed."[24] Although opponents doubted, proponents were confident that Maine had the human skills needed for self-government.

Proponents were also convinced that Maine could afford its own government if it were kept small, simple, and inexpensive like those in Connecticut, Rhode Island, and New Hampshire. Separationists went to great lengths to prove that even if the costs per capita increased somewhat, the increase would be absorbed quickly by the flood of immigrants that statehood was bound to attract.[25] Numerous schemes of economical government appeared in the newspapers, some stressing the desirability of low salaries to ensure attracting public servants who would serve for the honor alone. Several writers proposed reducing the size of various components of government. One writer even suggested abandoning town representation in favor of districts and a unicameral legislature, not because they were more democratic, but simply because they were cheaper.[26]

Without exception, proposals for separation assumed that Massachusetts would consent to its own dismemberment if a majority of Maine's population favored it. The problem then became how to organize popular support for the cause. Advocates finally hit upon a technique used effectively during the Revolution: the convention. In the period of agitation just before the outbreak of war, Massachusetts patriots had employed popularly elected conventions to nullify royal government and to exercise political power in the name of the people.[27] This time, however, the conventions were not aimed at an arbitrary royal government, but at a state republic that the separationists themselves had helped to create. Was it logical, was it legitimate to employ such revolutionary techniques against the legal, republican government of Massachusetts? The issue turned on the nature of the state's constitution. Supporters of conventions and of separation pointed out that provisions in the state constitution guaranteeing the right to address and petition implied a right to hold conventions in which to formulate popular sentiment. Even if this were not the case, advocates of separation recalled that during the Revolution, American colonists had defied Parliament's opposition to conventions and had met anyway. Maine had every right to do the same, for "we can be considered in no light very different from a Colony to Massachusetts."[28]

Opponents of separation developed a narrow view of the state constitution in countering the separationists' broad interpretation. Nervous over a recent outbreak of rebellion in western Massachusetts, they insisted that the constitution allowed for legal change only through the legislative process and through addresses and petitions submitted in an orderly fashion. The Revolution was over, and Massachusetts now possessed a republican form of government. The constitution of Massachusetts, stated one writer, provides no legitimate way of addressing the people apart from their legislators.[29] Another writer went so far as to denounce conventions as "usurpers of the rights of our legislators, strangers and enemies to the Constitution."[30] The conclusion was clear: Now that the Revolution was over, conventions were dangerous incitements to violence and, by implication, unconstitutional.

Despite their energy and ingenuity, the advocates of separation suffered the same fate as the neutralists before them, and for basically the same reason: a lack of popular support. From the beginning, leadership rested in the hands of a few ambitious, elite leaders in the Portland area. The only popular support the movement aroused came from the restless towns in the interior where squatters and settlers, engaged in a bitter struggle with land companies and great proprietors, such as General Henry Knox, hoped that a separate state of Maine would be more receptive to their needs. One observer accurately summed up the composition of the separationists in the comment that "the whole matter is set on foot & carried by people who either expect places in the New Government or persons called squatters (of which there are many

Revolution and Separation

in these parts of considerable influence)."[31] Such an alliance was politically unstable. The urban leaders feared the potential radicalism of their rural followers who, in turn, became disillusioned with the conservatism of the leaders. One eastern separationist described his more radical colleagues as "infested" with the sentiments of "genuine insurgents," who speak of the senate and the attorney general as grievances and seek relief through paper money and legal-tender acts.[32] Attendance at the separationist conventions gradually dwindled until at the last one in March 1789, only three members were present—all from Portland.[33]

Separation received virtually no support from the District's population centers along the coast, which were fearful of disrupting valuable commercial and financial connections with the rest of the state. York, Scarborough, and North Yarmouth showed no interest; Portland officially repudiated its own separationists.[34] The leading town down east, Machias, rejected separation as vigorously as it had neutrality, in eager anticipation that under Massachusetts it might become the shire town for a new county jurisdiction.[35] Only about one-third of Maine towns responded to the referendum on separation in 1786, and although the popular vote favored separation, only a fraction of the electorate bothered to participate.[36] In addition, the District's leading men generally opposed separation because it would jeopardize the fees, prestige, and political influence they enjoyed by holding Massachusetts commissions as justices of the peace, court officials, judges, customs agents, and militia officers.[37] The cause of separation had little appeal against such obvious and powerful advantages of union.

The lack of popular support probably would have been sufficient to destroy the separation movement, but Shays' Rebellion and the ratification of the Federal Constitution provided additional obstacles. In the winter of 1786–1787, farmers in western Massachusetts rose in rebellion to force the state government to redress their grievances. Claiming discrimination, the westerners demanded that state government be reformed and relocated from Boston to Worcester and that it provide cheaper, more efficient justice, debtor relief, and paper money. Although the state militia quickly restored order, the rebellion shocked leaders in Massachusetts, as well as those who were soon to gather at Philadelphia to consider ways of reconstituting the national government. In Maine, opponents of separation were quick to link separation with Shaysism, a synonym for social revolution and violence. One critic of separation pointed out that separationists were worse than Shaysites in that the latter wanted only to alter a part of the state constitution, while separationists wanted to destroy the entire thing.[38] "This spirit of novelty and revolution," declared another commentator, had to be subdued even though "the expense of blood and treasure be ever so great."[39] A rumor circulated that unredeemed Shaysites in western Massachusetts favored statehood for Maine in hopes that once Maine separated, the capital of the Commonwealth could be shifted to

Worcester.⁴⁰ Earlier, there had been just enough discussion of that possibility in the *Falmouth Gazette* to lend credence to what was merely political slander.

Shays' Rebellion had a telling impact on the separation movement, dividing the membership between those who wanted to push for separation by taking advantage of that unrest and of rumblings of separation in Nantucket, and the more conservative separationists who wanted to proceed more slowly. Thomas Wait, editor of the separationist *Falmouth Gazette*, asked rhetorically whether it would not be cruel, in the present circumstances "to perplex government with a request of this kind."⁴¹ Radical separationists retorted that now was the time; the government "will not dare to refuse our request; and if they do, we can drive them into a compliance, by threatening to join in the insurrection."⁴² The conservatives had their way, however, and even radical-minded Samuel Thompson, chairman of the convention's petition committee, publicly declared that "considering the peculiar embarrassments of government and the alarming and distressed situation of the western counties," the committee would delay submitting its petition for separation to the General Court.⁴³ The document that Thompson's committee did eventually present was devoid of radicalism and politely requested an orderly separation of the three Maine counties on purely pragmatic grounds.⁴⁴

The debate over ratification of the Federal Constitution diverted attention from separation but continued to polarize its advocates. The *Cumberland Gazette*, formerly the *Falmouth Gazette*, reflected the shift in concern. From October 1787 and for about a year, editor Wait devoted the paper almost exclusively to articles supporting the new framework of government. He had not abandoned separation totally, but he was convinced that ratification was of primary importance. Once that was achieved, he explained, statehood would follow naturally, since northern states would welcome additional support to offset southern influence in the new government.⁴⁵ Other separationists disagreed. In September 1787, a rare article devoted to statehood rather than ratification warned Mainers, "If ever you intend to be a state, now is the time, before an alteration in the Confederation renders it impossible, unless on very disadvantageous terms."⁴⁶

The rift among separationists widened as they themselves split between Federalists and Anti-Federalists. In Maine, support for the Federal Constitution tended to be concentrated in the commercial centers along the coast where traders, merchants, and shipbuilders—even lawyers and preachers—eagerly anticipated the benefits from a more highly centralized, effective national government.⁴⁷ The interior towns of Maine, however, looked with suspicion at the new framework of government. To squatters and farmers already contending against great land owners and their political influence, the proposed government was too distant, too big, and too powerful to be trusted. Such a government was sure to be expensive and oppressive, a threat to the very liberties the Revolution was supposed to preserve. Since Maine's interior supplied the only popular support for separation, Anti-Federalism and separation tended to coalesce. Separationist spokesmen from the interior, such as Samuel Thompson and William Widgery, personified the link with Anti-Federalism by their energetic opposition to the Constitution as members of the state ratifying convention at Boston.

Samuel Thompson's notorious belligerency virtually confirmed the connection. Following ratification of the Constitution in Massachusetts, which he had strenuously opposed, Thompson refused to join other Anti-Federalists in expressions of unity for the new government. Instead, he was quoted as threatening to visit the western counties, the source of Shays' Rebellion, where he promised to "throw the State into Confusion."[48] On the way he declared he might look in at New Hampshire's ratifying convention to "stir up what strife he could."[49] Thompson, if he made good on his threats, would thereby reverse the path of Samuel Ely who, having led anticourt riots in western Massachusetts, would soon arrive in Maine to employ his talents for turbulence on behalf of the District's embattled farmers and squatters.[50] Ely and Thompson illustrate the close affinity between the rebellious people of western Massachusetts and the restless people in Maine, which tainted the cause of separation and even Anti-Federalism in Maine.

Separation suffered one final setback when Massachusetts responded to the threat of disunion by agreeing to remedy many of the District's grievances. The government's initial reaction was far from sympathetic. Governor James Bowdoin condemned separation, and the legislature ominously warned that "The social compact solemnly entered into by the people of this Commonwealth, ought, we conceive, to be attended to, and guarded with utmost care; and it shall ever be the aim of this Legislature, to prevent any infraction upon it, and preserve it entire."[51] Yet instead of punitive action, the government continued its wartime policy of trying to redress Maine's grievances. In 1789 the General Court agreed to divide Lincoln County into three separate counties, thereby expanding the judicial system. Not incidentally, the additional courts would require a large number of new officials, who would tend to regard Massachusetts—rather than an independent Maine—as a source of patronage. Machias finally had the satisfaction of becoming the shire town for the new county of Washington. New counties also required the wholesale incorporation of settlements so they could raise taxes and elect juries to support the legal system. Incorporation also meant additional representation for Maine in the state legislature. The General Court also suspended or abated taxes for over 30 percent of the towns in the District and revised the fees for land transfers. It exempted wild lands from taxation for ten years, quieted squatters occupying public lands, and pressured private land companies to compromise differences with their tenants. In addition, at public expense, the state laid out roads running from the Kennebec River to the Penobscot, and from there to Passamaquoddy Bay—and even approved in principle the establishment of a college for the District.[52]

By the time the long-delayed petition for separation finally reached the General Court in March 1788, separation was a dead issue. Lacking a wide popular base to begin with, the movement was discredited by its apparent association with Shaysism, divided by the debate over the Federal Constitution, and then undercut by the government's reforms. The last few separation conventions met only to adjourn. For almost a year the petition lay before the legislature, its fate a foregone conclusion. Nonetheless, the die-hard separationists among the representatives, such as William Widgery and Samuel Thompson, did not give up. When the legislature finally acted on the petition, they once more emphasized the advantages of statehood, not merely for Maine, but for Massachusetts as well, because the Commonwealth could enjoy a more compact, efficient government without its eastern counties. They argued that the nation would also benefit from the addition of another northern state to counterbalance southern influence in Congress. It was a hopeless cause, but the separationists did enjoy a victory of sorts. As a conciliatory gesture, the General Court refrained from rejecting the petition outright. Instead, on January 22, 1789, it accepted the report of its committee that the petition be tabled, or "lay on the files."[53] Technically, the matter was still alive; practically speaking, the first phase of Maine's movement for separation and statehood had come to an end.

If the separation movement is presented as an example of radicalism, then it is hard to disagree with Professor Ronald Banks' observation that what passed for radicalism in Maine was of a "shallow and tepid variety."[54] Neutralists and separationists alike confined their radicalism to political theory and conventions to justify their proposals. They did not resort to armed violence, attacks on courts, and calls for paper money and laws deferring the payment of debts, all of which characterized Shays' Rebellion. By contrast, that first separation movement in Maine seems very limited and conservative.

Differences between the counties in Maine and those in western Massachusetts help to explain the contrast in movements. Berkshire, Hampshire, and Worcester Counties, the heart of Shays' Rebellion, were safely isolated from the physical impact of the Revolution. They did not have to contend with British privateers, invasion, guerilla war, and the costs of self-defense. Instead, they experienced unusual prosperity because of the demand for agricultural goods by French and American forces and because of inflated prices. With the shift of the war to the south, currency deflation, and then the disbanding of the armies at the end of the war, the west experienced a sudden economic reversal, accompanied by bitter social and political unrest and culminating in the violence of Shays' Rebellion.[55]

Conditions in Maine during the postwar period were hard, but they were nothing new. In fact, despite the heavy taxes, debts, and economic dislocations, conditions were slowly improving because Maine no longer had to face enemy raids and the costs of defense. Private journals and newspapers complained about the dullness of trade and the scarcity of cash, but the town of Falmouth reemerged from wartime destruction, severed its connections with its agricultural hinterland, and assumed a new commercial identity and a new name, Portland.[56] Throughout the District, population was increasing rapidly, creating higher land values. The atmosphere seemed to be one of cautious optimism despite present difficulties and frustrations. The movement for separation evolved from leaders who were optimistic about the District's future. Aspiring to leadership in a new state, the leaders of separation feared radical action and Shaysism as much as their counterparts in the rest of the Commonwealth. Their own political futures would depend on an orderly and legitimate separation.

In effect, the separation movement was radical only in seeking to dismember a preexisting state. There is no indication that Francis Shaw, Jr., and his fellow neutralists in eastern Maine, or the spokesmen for separation, such as Stephen Longfellow, Thomas B. Wait, Enoch Ilsley, and the Reverend Samuel Deane, had any desire to alter the traditional social or economic order in which they were leaders. When separationists complained about the judiciary, they did not demand reform, but simply an extension of the present system. If successful, they would have presided over a very orthodox state of Maine.

Maine did not lack manifestations of radicalism; the District's frontiersmen and squatters interpreted the Revolution as a promise of social and economic reform, and they joined in a popular, violence-prone movement aimed especially at the great land monopolizers. Frontier radicalism, however, was a phenomenon in itself, independent of separation. These radicals supported separation in the hope of gaining a state they could influence in their own behalf. When this first stage of separation disintegrated in 1788–1789, frontier radicalism continued to grow in organization and articulation.[57] While the movement for separation existed, its frontier following gave it a reputation for radicalism that it neither wanted nor deserved. In most cases, spokesmen for separation were orderly, polite, and respectable. They had to convince a skeptical citizenry who had no grievances against Massachusetts, and even the Massachusetts legislature itself, that separation was safe, just, and reasonable. Professor Banks correctly implied that separation was shallow and tepid radicalism; he might just as well have questioned whether separation was radical at all.

Despite its apparent defeat, the cause of separation did not die; it persisted with only limited appeal into the nineteenth century. Conditions favorable to the movement evolved, especially in the years following the War of 1812. The writings of James Sullivan and Moses Greenleaf reflect a growing sense of regional identity, which Maine had lacked at the end of the Revolution. In addition, the cause of statehood now fused with a series of broad-based grievances with Massachusetts, which involved not only ambitious politicians and turbulent frontiersmen as before, but also newly self-confident merchants and religious dissidents who complained of restraints under the Massachusetts constitution. These elements now merged in the new Democratic-Republican political party that came to champion separation from a Federalist-dominated Massachusetts. These political differences between Massachusetts and the District help to explain why Massachusetts again left her eastern counties undefended against the British in the War of 1812. Separationists could have found evidence of a plot to explain this lack of protection, but appeals to separation no longer had to resort to conspiracies or to the natural-rights philosophy from the time of the Revolution; self-interest was reason enough. One old argument, however, did recur, which in retrospect, seems prophetic and even ironic. Several of the original separationists, such as Thomas B. Wait and Samuel Thompson, had urged statehood for Maine on grounds that an additional northern state would help to offset southern influence in the national government.[58] In 1820, Maine's successful bid for statehood was part of the Missouri Compromise, which helped to preserve the balance between northern and southern states in the U.S. Senate; Wait and Thompson were prophets indeed. Few of Maine's separationists, however, could have foreseen that their own emancipation from Massachusetts would involve a compromise with the institution of slavery for others.

NOTES

1. Charles E. Clark, *The Eastern Frontier: The Settlement of Northern New England, 1610–1763* (New York: Alfred A. Knopf, 1970), Chapter III.

2. William Williamson, *History of the State of Maine from Its First Discovery, A.D. 1602, to the Separation, A.D. 1820*, 2 vols. (Hallowell, Me.: Glazer, Masters, Co., 1832; reprinted Freeport, Me.: Cumberland Press, undated), vol. 2, p. 467.

3. John H. Ahlin, *Maine Rubicon: Downeast Settlers During the American Revolution* (Calais, Me.: Calais Advertiser Press, 1966), pp. 98–111, 140–144; Rev. Samuel Deane to Jedediah Preble, Falmouth, March 21, 1776, Willis Pps., Autograph Letters, Maine Historical Society (hereafter MeHS); John Allan to Jeremiah Powell, October 12, 1777, in James P. Baxter (ed.), *Documentary History of the State of Maine*, 24 vols. (Portland, Me.: Maine Historical Society, 1869–1916), vol. 15, p. 241 (hereafter *Doc. Hist. Me.*); Committee of Inspection, Correspondence, and Safety of Boothbay to the General Court, June 24, 1778, ibid., vol. 16, p. 33–35.

4. For a popular account, see Russell Bourne, "The Penobscot Fiasco," *American Heritage*, 25 (October 1974), 28–33, 100–101. For a scholarly account, see Peter Elliot, "The Penobscot Expedition of 1779: A Study in Naval Frustration" (M.A. thesis, University of Maine at Orono, 1974).

5. Timothy Dwight, *Travels in New England and New York*, Barbara M. Solomon (ed.), 4 vols. (Cambridge, Mass.: Harvard University Press, 1968), vol. 2, pp. 117–135.

6. Rev. John Lyon to the General Court, September 1776, *Doc. Hist. Me.*, vol. 14, p. 379.

7. Rev. James Murray to Jeremiah Powell, June 18, 1779, ibid., vol. 16, p. 289.

8. Committee of Safety of Machias to the General Court, October 14, 1775, ibid., vol. 14, p. 312; Petition of ... A Committee chosen by the Sufferers in Falmouth, January 4, 1779, ibid., vol. 16, p. 151; Narroguages to the General Court, undated, ibid., p. 180; Petition of the Inhabitants of Lincoln County, October 1, 1779, ibid., vol. 17, p. 338.

9. For example, see the petition of the towns in Lincoln County, November 16, 1779, ibid., vol. 17, p. 449.

10. Proclamation of martial law, Thomaston, April 18, 1780, ibid., vol. 18, pp. 222–224; John Allan's Proclamation of martial law, Machias, June 26, 1780, ibid., pp. 333–335; Peleg Wadsworth to the Council, April 28, May 26, September 14, 1780, ibid., pp. 241, 280, 414–415;

Peleg Wadsworth to William D. Williamson, January 1, 1828, *Collections and Proceedings of the Maine Historical Society*, 2nd ser., 2 (1891), 160.

11. Francis Shaw, Jr., to Stephen Jones, March 17, 1781, *Doc. Hist. Me.*, vol. 19, pp. 235–236.

12. Petition to his Excelly the Governor, The Honble His Council, The Honble the Senate & the Honble the House of Representatives, Gouldsborough, March 17, 1781, ibid., pp. 243–246.

13. Gordon Wood, "Conspiracy and the Paranoid Style: Causality and Deceit in the Eighteenth Century," *William and Mary Quarterly*, 39 (July 1982), 401–441 (hereafter *WMQ*).

14. Resolves of Machias, March 29-April 10, 1781, *Doc. Hist. Me.*, vol. 19, pp. 236–237.

15. Machias Committee of Correspondence, Safety, and Inspection to Governor John Hancock, April 10, 1781, ibid., pp. 238–241.

16. Report on the Petition of Thomas Donnel & others, July 8, 1775, ibid., vol. 14, p. 290; Resolve of the Provincial Congress, June 23, 1775, ibid., pp. 284–285; Receipt of the Inhabitants of Deer Isle, June 23, 1775, ibid., p. 285; Resolve of the General Court, January 12, 1778, ibid., vol. 15, pp. 323–324. Compare with the following: Resolve of the General Court re Thomaston, November 7, 1780, ibid., vol. 19, pp. 37–38; Resolve of the General Court on behalf of Washington, November 24, 1780, and Cape Elizabeth, February 17, 1780, and Brunswick and Harpswell, June 12, 1781, ibid., pp. 47–48, 87, 280–281; Petition of Berwick and the response of the General Court, June 21, June 23, 1781, ibid., vol. 19, pp. 289–290.

17. William Willis, *History of Portland*, 2 vols. (Portland, Me.: Bailey & Noyes, 1865), vol. 2, pp. 252–254; Williamson, *History of Maine*, vol. 2, pp. 521–522; Ronald F. Banks, *Maine Becomes a State: The Movement to Separate Maine from Massachusetts, 1785–1820* (Middletown, Conn.: Wesleyan University Press, 1970; reprinted Somersworth, N.H.: New Hampshire Publishing Company and Maine Historical Society, 1973), pp. 4, 10–12.

18. Banks, *Maine Becomes a State*, p. 5.

19. Ibid., p. 13.

20. *Falmouth Gazette*, November 5, 12, 1785 (hereafter *Fal. Gaz.*). Name changes to *Cumberland Gazette* after April 7, 1786 (hereafter *Cumb. Gaz.*).

21. *Fal. Gaz.*, May 21, July 2, 16, 23, 30, August 6, 13, 1785.

22. *Fal. Gaz.*, October 15, 22, 1785.

23. Ibid., October 22, 1785.

24. Daniel Davis, "The Proceedings of the Two Conventions, Held at Portland, to Consider the Expediency of a Separate Government in the District of Maine," *Massachusetts Historical Society Collections*, 4 (1795), 39.

25. *Fal. Gaz.*, June 4, 11, 1785.

26. Ibid., June 4, 11, 1785; March 9, 23, 1786; *Cumb. Gaz.*, May 4, September 21, 1786.

27. Richard D. Brown, *Revolutionary Politics in Massachusetts: The Boston Committee of Correspondence and the Towns, 1772–1774* (Cambridge, Mass.: Harvard University Press, 1970), pp. 29–31; L. Kinvin Wroth (ed.), *Province in Rebellion: A Documentary History of the Founding of the Commonwealth of Massachusetts, 1774–1775* (Cambridge, Mass.: Harvard University Press, 1975), pp. 62–67.

28. *Fal. Gaz.*, March 16, 1786; see also *Cumb. Gaz.*, December 8, 1786; March 2, 16, 23, 1787.

29. *Fal. Gaz.*, March 30, 1786.

30. *Cumb. Gaz.*, November 31, 1786; see also ibid., September 21, 28, November 24, 1786; February 23, 1787.

31. Jonas Clark, Jr., to Jonas Clark, Sr., October 17, 1785, Jonas Clark Pps., Mss. Div., Library of Congress, Washington, D.C.

32. Davis, "Proceedings of the Two Conventions," p. 33.

33. Ibid., p. 35; Willis, *Portland*, vol. 2, p. 256n; Banks, *Maine Becomes a State*, p. 24.

34. *Fal. Gaz.*, December 10, 1785, March 9, 16, 1786; *Cumb. Gaz.*, August 31, September 7, November 13, 1786; petition from Hallowell to the General Court, read March 15, 1788, *Doc. Hist. Me.*, vol. 21, pp. 457–458; Davis, "Proceedings of the Two Conventions," p. 29.

35. Petition from Machias to the General Court, December 18, 1782, *Doc. Hist. Me.*, vol. 20, pp. 302–303; Machias Committee of Correspondence to the General Court, May 12, 1784, ibid., pp. 337–341; Petition from Machias to the General Court, undated, ibid., vol. 21, pp. 128–131; Stephen Jones and others for Machias to Caleb Davis, May 22, 1786, Caleb Davis Pps., Massachusetts Historical Society; same to same, December 23, 1786, ibid.

36. Davis, "Proceedings of the Two Conventions," p. 32; Banks, *Maine Becomes a State*, p. 23.

37. *Cumb. Gaz.*, July 20, 1786; Davis, "Proceedings of the Two Conventions," p. 25.

38. *Cumb. Gaz.*, November 24, 1786.

39. *Fal. Gaz.*, November 19, 1785.

40. Ibid., August 17, 1785; *Cumb. Gaz.*, April 18, 1788; David Sewall to George Thatcher, February 11, 1788, in William Goodwin (ed.), "Thatcher Papers," *Historical Magazine*, 2nd ser., 6 (1869), 271.

41. *Cumb. Gaz.*, February 9, 1787.

42. Davis, "Proceedings of the Two Conventions," p. 33.

43. Ibid., pp. 32–34; *Cumb. Gaz.*, March 23, 1787.

44. Davis, "Proceedings of the Two Conventions," p. 40.

45. Thomas Wait to George Thatcher, February 29, 1788, "Thatcher Papers," pp. 342–343.

46. *Cumb. Gaz.*, September 15, 1787; see also ibid., September 6, 1787.

47. For sectional divisions in Maine over ratification of the Federal Constitution, see Orin G. Libby, *The Geographical Distribution of the Vote . . . on the Federal Constitution* (Madison, Wisc.: University of Wisconsin Press, 1894), pp. 14, 49, 54–57, 77–78; Van Beck Hall, *Politics Without Parties: Massachusetts, 1780–1791* (Pittsburgh: University of Pittsburgh Press, 1972), pp. 7, 26, 178.

48. Quoted by Thomas Wait to George Thatcher, February 29, 1788, "Thatcher Papers," pp. 342–343.

49. Quoted by Jeremiah Hill to George Thatcher, February 28, 1788, ibid., p. 342.

50. Robert Moody, "Samuel Ely: Forerunner of Shays," *New England Quarterly*, 5 (January 1932), 117–134; Alan Taylor, "The Disciples of Samuel Ely: Settler Resistence Against Henry Knox on the Waldo Patent, 1785–1801," *Maine Historical Society Quarterly*, 26 (Fall 1986), 66–100.

51. Gov. James Bowdoin's speech to the General Court, October 20, 1785, *Doc. Hist. Me.*, vol. 21, pp. 49–50; Legislative response in *Fal. Gaz.*, December 17, 1785; Williamson, *Maine*, vol. 2, p. 523.

52. Williamson, *History of Maine*, vol. 2, pp. 532–548; Hall, *Politics Without Parties*, p. 169n; Banks, *Maine Becomes a State*, pp. 24–25; *Acts and Laws of Massachusetts, 1780–1805*, 13 vols. (Boston: Wright & Potter, 1890–1898), vol. 1788–1789, pp. 237, 350, 426–429, 626–628; Report of a Committee of the General Court, February 17–19, 1790, *Doc. Hist. Me.*, vol. 22, p. 107.

53. *Cumb. Gaz.*, March 27, 1788; January 29, 1789.

54. Banks, *Maine Becomes a State*, p. 24.

55. Robert J. Taylor, *Western Massachusetts in the Revolution* (Providence, R.I.: Brown University Press, 1954), pp. 103–127.

56. William Willis (ed.), *Journals of the Reverend Thomas Smith and the Reverend Samuel Deane* (Portland, Me.: Joseph S. Bailey, 1849), pp. 252–254, 260; Willis, *Portland*, vol. 2, pp. 179–180; *Fal. Gaz.*, February 5, October 15, 1785.

57. Alan Taylor, "'Stopping the Progres of Rogues and Deceivers': A White Indian Recruiting Notice of 1808," *WMQ*, 42 (January 1985), 90–103.

58. *Cumb. Gaz.*, January 2, 1789; Daniel George to George Thatcher, June 5, 1789, Thacher [sic] Pps., Essex Institute, Salem, Mass.; Thomas B. Wait to George Thatcher, Feb. 29, 1788, "Thatcher Papers," pp. 342–343.

Alan S. Taylor

CHAPTER 5

NATHAN BARLOW'S JOURNEY
Mysticism and Popular Protest on the Northeastern Frontier

Only in the long run could statehood provide Maine's backcountry farmers with relief from grasping proprietors, merchant creditors, lawyers, and sheriffs. In the short run, frontiersmen had to rely on their own efforts against a hostile world through organized violence. In mobs thinly disguised as Indians, frontiersmen terrorized, beat, and occasionally murdered those—or their agents—who threatened their existence. Alan Taylor's analysis of "Indian" leader Nathan Barlow reveals a popular culture suffused with poverty, primitive democracy, and millenarianism. This explosive mix provided a legitimacy for resisting the power of evil even when that power was the government itself. Taylor points out that Barlow's mystical experience in particular gave him the credentials necessary for leadership among the frontier folk. When he was arrested, convicted, and imprisoned, however, the high expectations that he had aroused quickly crumbled and resistance to authority dwindled.

When the nineteenth century began, Maine's backcountry settlers felt that they were becoming free. Most were poor men and women seeking a modest prosperity by investing their labor to transform wilderness land slowly and arduously into comfortable farms. They meant to be independent producers, owners of their own land and labor, and free from the dictates of a superior. This constituted true "liberty," as they understood it. Constructing that liberty in a dense wilderness, from thin soil, and within a cold environment was no easy task. They began with little more than their own labor. As the first claimants to occupy and improve their particular lots of land, they hoped to get title by squatter's right. To develop that land and sustain their labor, they acquired needed capital from local traders and merchants on credit in the form of tools, livestock, and provisions.[1]

To succeed, these settlers needed time: time to pay off their debts and time to parry the financial demands of absentee proprietors, who

Alan S. Taylor is assistant professor of history at Boston University.

claimed the settlers' land by virtue of vague and conflicting seventeenth century crown grants and Indian deeds. In late 1807, the settlers in central Maine's Kennebec Valley ran out of time with the conjunction of two events: a commercial depression induced by President Jefferson's embargo on foreign trade and the decision by the region's dominant proprietary company, the Kennebeck Proprietors (or Plymouth Company), to open a legal offensive against the settlers. To forestall bankruptcy, traders and merchants demanded immediate payment in full from their debtors. Those who could not pay faced a date in court. To obtain legal possession of their claims and oust their settler competitors from the land, the proprietors commenced dozens of ejectment suits. Consequently, for both the hard-pressed creditors and the aggressive Kennebeck Proprietors, the courts issued a flood of writs impounding settler livestock and homesteads. These writs obliged their recipients to stand trial for debt or ejectment. In late 1807 and early 1808, constables and deputy sheriffs fanned out across the countryside to serve writs upon particular settlers.[2] (See Plate 1.)

Even in the best of times few settlers could afford to pay their debts suddenly in full, buy their homesteads, or employ a lawyer to defend their interests in court. They certainly could not do so when a commercial depression undercut the value of their livestock, grain, and lumber. As a result, the sudden upsurge in suits for debt or ejectment threatened to pry the settlers from their hard-earned homesteads. To preserve their shaky hold on independence, the settlers needed to buy more time: time to fend off creditors until the depression abated, time to obstruct proprietary claims until the passage of thirty years invested an occupant with squatter's title. As they had done intermittently since the 1760s when confronted with similar threats, Maine's backcountry settlers once again donned Indian disguises and formed secret armed bands to patrol the outskirts of their settlements and intimidate approaching deputy sheriffs and proprietary surveyors.[3]

These tactics pitted settlers against the prestige of the law and the power of the state government. The entire legal and political framework of authority from the local justices of the peace to the governor and the General Court in Boston upheld the interests of creditors and the claims of nonresident proprietors. Such sources of authority insist that they alone can legitimately wield power; that they define and uphold the law that men must obey. Consequently, to resist that power successfully, men must begin by convincing themselves that existing authority does not represent justice and therefore that it may and must be resisted.[4]

In the past the settlers had tried to sidestep this problem with the argument that the government latently supported their resistance against the rich and powerful. This notion accepted the equation of existing authority with abstract justice; settlers concluded that since their cause was just, government must inexorably, even though slowly, embrace it. Indeed, it followed that settlers were doing their duty as citizens by obstructing the unjust schemes of grasping proprietors and creditors. This wishful illusion was akin to that associated with the primitive rebellions of the early modern European peasantry; those peasant rebels believed that their king or tsar would eventually placate their grievances as a reward for calling to his attention the exploitations practiced by the aristocracy.[5]

In the short run, this shortcut to legitimacy enabled the settlers to organize and expand their resistance quickly. Many believed the report that the chief justice of the state's Supreme Judicial Court had let it slip that the Kennebeck Proprietors' title was worthless and would not stand up in court. In 1796 the settler leader and preacher Samuel Ely quickly accumulated a wide following by assuring his listeners that the governor and General Court quietly favored the settlers' resistance and would wink at their burning down the buildings belonging to General Henry Knox, a leading proprietor, and his land agents. Similarly, a Patricktown (now Somerville), Maine settler told two emissaries from General Knox that the General Court "had determined that proprietors & settlers should 'fight it out' & passed an act or resolve to that affect," thoughtfully stipulating the use of "guns & swords" in this conflict.[6]

This approach contained a fundamental flaw: It reiterated and reinforced the legitimacy of the government. As a result, resistance flagged whenever the governor, General Court, or Supreme Judicial Court went on record condemning the settlers' violence. For example, the Ely-led opposition in western Hancock County (now Waldo County) to Henry Knox suddenly collapsed in the spring of 1796 when Governor Samuel Adams issued a proclamation denouncing the unrest and calling for the parson's arrest. By 1808, sustained evidence that the existing structure of authority consistently supported creditors and proprietors provoked an intellectual crisis among the backcountry settlers. It became apparent that they could not resist their foes without attacking the legitimacy of the government. Consequently, settlers needed to convince themselves that they obeyed a higher law, that they were in contact with the original source of true justice. They needed, in short, an appeal directly to God. This alone can account for the influence exercised among the settlers by a religious mystic named Nathan Barlow.[7]

On January 8, 1801 Nathan Barlow of Fairfax (now Albion), Maine, and his neighbors in that recently settled community gathered in a private house. They sought one another's company, to escape from monotony and the cold, and to hear an itinerant evangelical preacher who warmed his winter-chilled audience with a vivid landscape of hell and its horrors. Barlow later recalled how he left the company "much agitated about it ... for reflecting on the life I had lived, I considered myself in the most imminent danger and begged of God to convince me of it if it was so."[8]

Shortly after Barlow returned to his crude log cabin, the early winter twilight crept across Fairfax. Barlow remembered that at that moment he was "taken all at once with a strange kind of feeling and laid me down: I began to grow stiff and to lose the power of moving by degrees, til I was totally unable to stir. I am very clear that I did not fall asleep." Suddenly Christ appeared "with a glorious countenance" and took Barlow by the hand. Barlow recalled that Christ then "carried me away as quick as a flash of lightning (my spirit I mean, for I was sensible at the time that I had left my body behind, and had no feeling of weight, but light as air)."[9]

They traveled first to hell "and a blue smoke rose from it and I heard the roaring of fierce fire. There was an innumerable multitude of people in it, who all seemed to be in great agony." Barlow found this no pleasant experience:

> Oh, the groans that filled my astonished soul, the wringing and twisting of the tormented, their shocking countenances; and when I considered that they were once on the earth as we are now, busied as we are, engaged in the same pursuits, had the same hopes, intended likely to repent and find mercy by and by, as many of us do now; and as I have done my self, I was filled with inexpressible horror. I floated out over this dreadful pit like a feather carried by a small breeze of wind, Christ being with me, and holding me by the hand.[10]

To counterpoint the experience, Christ suddenly carried Barlow to the gates of heaven where he saw God and the saved. The latter "looked very smiling, and appeared perfectly happy, their faces were all toward God; and they were singing praises to him in a most melodious manner." Alas, few of the approaching procession of the newly dead "entered into glory without difficulty" while the great majority "with sad countenances ... sank down to the place of torment as if something attracted them."[11]

Christ then returned Barlow's spirit to his body and charged him with a mission: to narrate his experience to local religious gatherings. But as soon as Barlow began to regain his senses, he began to doubt the whole experience. At that point Christ wrenched Barlow back into the trance for a second whirlwind tour of hell and heaven. Restored once again to his body, Barlow forsook his doubts and accepted the necessity of his special mission on earth.[12]

Seven years later a very different but equally dramatic incident occurred in Fairfax. On April 18, 1808, town constable Moses Robinson mounted his horse to serve writs of attachment and execution on local debtors. No doubt he eagerly anticipated the fees he would earn for each successful service; the fees were a welcome cash supplement to the small income of a frontier settler. Nonetheless, Robinson must have been a resolute man to proceed on this day's work because one of his writs called for the arrest of Daniel Brackett, a leader of the local band of Indian-disguised settlers determined to forbid the service of all writs in the vicinity.[13]

Robinson arrested Brackett only to find himself suddenly surrounded by a handful of determined men armed with loaded muskets and disguised as Indians. Quite sensibly, Robinson released his man. Less sensibly, he proceeded to the local magistrate to obtain a new warrant for the arrest of Brackett and his rescuers for resisting an arrest. Reinforced by a deputy sheriff, Robinson again found Brackett and once more placed him under arrest. En route back to the magistrate with his prisoner, Robinson ran into an eight-man patrol of armed "White Indians" who had come from the adjoining settlement of Beaver Hill (now Freedom) to assist their Fairfax brethren. One man fired "a brace of balls through" Robinson's horse which reared, throwing the constable to the ground.[14]

The patrol then exercised the rough retribution customarily visited on fellow settlers so reckless of their personal safety as to assist outside creditors and landholders in serving their writs. Seizing Robinson's pocketbook, the party removed his writs and tore them into "attoms." They then carried the struggling constable into a nearby house, tore off his clothing "at the points of six bayonets," shredded those clothes into rags, and proceeded to beat him "in a merciless manner, with sticks prepared for that purpose." Robinson was then "turned, naked as he was born, into the woods, in which situation he was obliged to travel three miles to his family, in an inclement season of the year."[15]

This incident is particularly noteworthy because Nathan Barlow led that White Indian patrol. Nor was this the first time he violently disciplined a traitor to the settlers' resistance. Nearly two years before, on June 1, 1806, Nathan Barlow and three of his lieutenants seized John Harvey of Fairfax, "placed him naked astride a rail, and in that position forcibly carried [him] along the highway for ... three miles, and then & there threw [him] on the ground & bismeared his naked body with dirt & filth & in that condition exposed [him] to the contempt & derision" of his neighbors.[16]

What, then, is the link between Nathan Barlow, religious mystic, and Nathan Barlow, "White Indian?" The apparent answer is that his neighbors regarded the rough justice meted out to John Harvey and Moses Robinson as entirely compatible with, indeed as an extension of, Nathan Barlow's divinely charged mission. His local paramilitary authority seems to have rested on his reputation as a man who had encountered the divine.

The evidence of a direct link is no more than inferential. Although Barlow recounted his mystical experience at a time of growing tensions between the squatters and the great proprietors, he made no direct reference to that conflict. In narrating his experience to settler gatherings and in dictating it to someone more literate for publication, Barlow sought to impart a sincerely held and purely religious experience. But it would be a mistake to disentangle Barlow's mysticism from his social rebellion. Indeed, throughout late eighteenth and early nineteenth century America, agrarian rebels understood their world in religious terms and turned to direct experience with divinity for legitimacy. A very similar set of land riots against nonresident proprietors occurred in New Jersey in the 1740s. A local preacher drafted the settlers' public defense, penning a pamphlet condemning the land barons for corrupting America with their covetous example. Early America's most famous and most peripatetic backcountry rebel, Herman Husbands, figured prominently in both North Carolina's Regulation of 1768–1772 and in Pennsylvania's Whiskey Rebellion of 1794. He wrote numerous tracts on astrology, politics, and mysticism. He prophesied the emergence of "a New Jerusalem" in the backcountry and predicted that this "New Government of Liberty" by small farmers and artisans ultimately would conquer the corrupt and exploitative towns along the Atlantic seaboard.[17]

Emotional, often mystical, religion was closely associated with settler resistance to authority in Maine. Another settler leader in Maine, William Jones of Bristol, also recorded and published a mystical experience that may help account for his influence. The agrarian unrest in Maine produced five protest pamphlets. All utilized a religious language of persuasion, and two of the three authors, Samuel Ely and James Davis, were frontier preachers. Similarly, a "White Indian" recruiting notice, posted in Fairfax in January 1808 and authored by Daniel Brackett, lumped wealthy proprietors, lawyers, merchant creditors, and magistrates into a common enemy determined "to impoverish the people and to bring them under lordships and slaveourey." Recruits were assured that "our indian king" meant "to cut down all popery and kill the devil and give the world of mankind some piece [sic] by stopping the progres of rogues and deceivers and helping every man to his right and privilidges and liberty, the same as our indian nation injoys." This passage recalls the transcriber's postscript to Barlow's pamphlet, which insisted that such visions were credible in an age when true Christians expected "wonderful things to be effected by the power of almighty God in the world; such as the total downfall of popery and Mahometanism." In smiting proprietors and creditors, the settlers, it seems, saw themselves as assisting God in the introduction of His millennium.[18]

The pamphlets and the recruiting notice all conceived of the settler rebellion as part of the great cosmic struggle between good and evil. They cast the settlers as the true heirs of both Christ and the American Revolution; they characterized men of wealth and power in general, and proprietors in particular, as just different embodiments of the same demons who at other times appeared in the guise of Tories and Popes. Because backcountry men and women perceived their problems in terms of an ongoing supernatural struggle over the fate of humanity, a man like Barlow, who could claim direct experience with divinity and a special mission to advance its cause on earth, was just the sort of man these settlers looked to for leadership.[19]

A second reason for linking Nathan Barlow's mysticism with his rebellion is the difficulty in accounting for his leadership in any other way. In rural New England local influence and authority accrued to those who demonstrated their ability to acquire and manage landed property. Men who enclosed extensive, well-kept fields with well-repaired fences and who could boast of commodious, sturdily built farmhouses were the sort who routinely served as selectmen, moderators, town clerks, and town treasurers. It was felt that men who successfully managed their own property, or the sons of such men, could be counted on to manage town concerns prudently.[20]

Usually, the same men who ran town affairs also led their communities' defense against outside proprietors. Unity's two foremost men, Deacon Stephen Chase and Squire Ezekiel Pattee, led that town's White Indians. In Palermo, the six identifiable leaders of the local resistance ranked first, second, fifth, eighth, tenth, and thirteenth in taxable property out of 108 taxpayers on an 1806 highway tax list. By the standards of the wealthier outside world, these men were hardly well-to-do, but by internal, backcountry standards, they were men of superior accomplishment in the slow acquisition of property. Men of recognized spiritual authority were the only exceptions to the usual source of leadership. For instance, in the 1790s, Northport's itinerant preacher, Samuel Ely, led the resistance in the Waldo Patent despite his lack of important town office and his low ranking—seventy-fourth out of his settlement's eight-three taxpayers—on a 1798 tax list. Leaders like Ely seemed to have emerged when the town fathers broke with their poorer neighbors to support the proprietors, as was the case in the Waldo Patent.[21]

Not a town father, Nathan Barlow more closely fits the Ely mold. In 1813 when Beaver Hill incorporated as the town of Freedom and chose its first set of town officers, the most prestigious offices—moderator, clerk, selectmen, and treasurer—went to others. Nathan Barlow was not excluded from office; he was chosen one of the town's seven highway surveyors and one of its two field drivers. These were middle-level posts that were below the prestigious positions but above the humble hog reeves and those entrusted with no town offices. In the eyes of his neighbors, Nathan Barlow was neither a town father nor a pariah. Some factor, other than civic leadership, must have accounted for the respect accorded him as a White Indian.[22]

Neither Nathan Barlow's parentage nor his own economic accomplishments recommended him for leadership. He was born in about 1775 on Cape Cod in Sandwich, Massachusetts, the son of Obed Barlow, one of that town's poorest men. In 1784, Obed Barlow owned no house and no real estate except a small shop. A single cow comprised his only other taxable property. Seven years did not significantly improve his lot; of the 427 taxpayers on a 1791 tax list, only 128 were as poor or poorer than Obed Barlow, and most of those were far younger men just starting out as independent householders. In 1792, at age

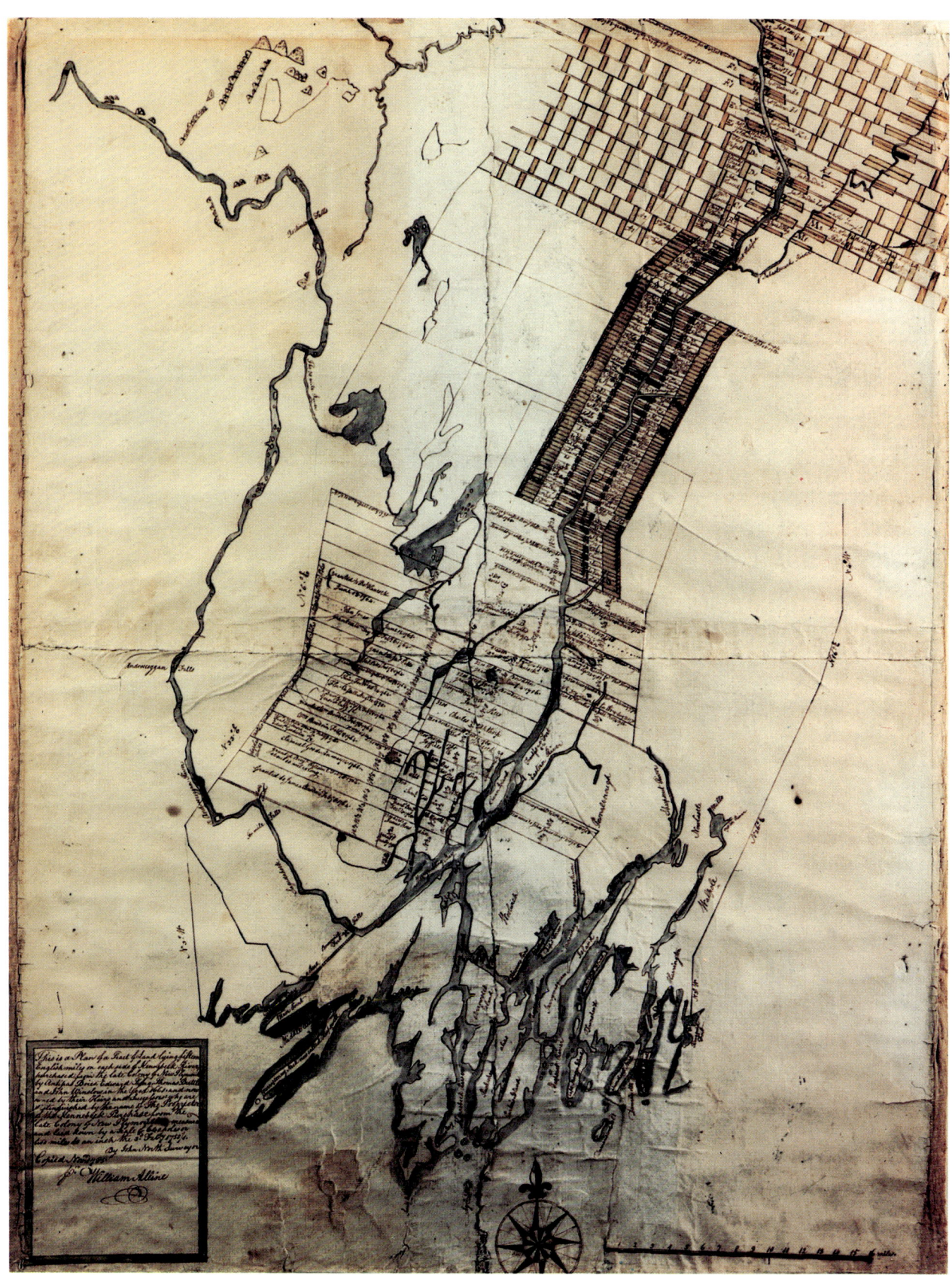

1. *Map of the Proprietors of the Kennebeck Purchase,* by William Alline, 1785.
(Pen and ink and watercolor. The Bowdoin College Library)

11. *A View of Paris Hill,* overmantel from the Lazarus Hathaway House, Paris Hill, ca. 1803. Artist unknown.
(Oil on board. The Hamlin Memorial Library and the Paris Hill Historical Society)

111. *Denny Soccabeson,* September 18, 1817. Artist unknown.
(Watercolor. The Collection of Bertram K. and Nina Fletcher Little)

iv. *Sarah Mollasses* (ca. 1812–1880), by Jeremiah Pearson Hardy (1800–1887), after 1827. (Oil on canvas. The Tarratine Club, Bangor)

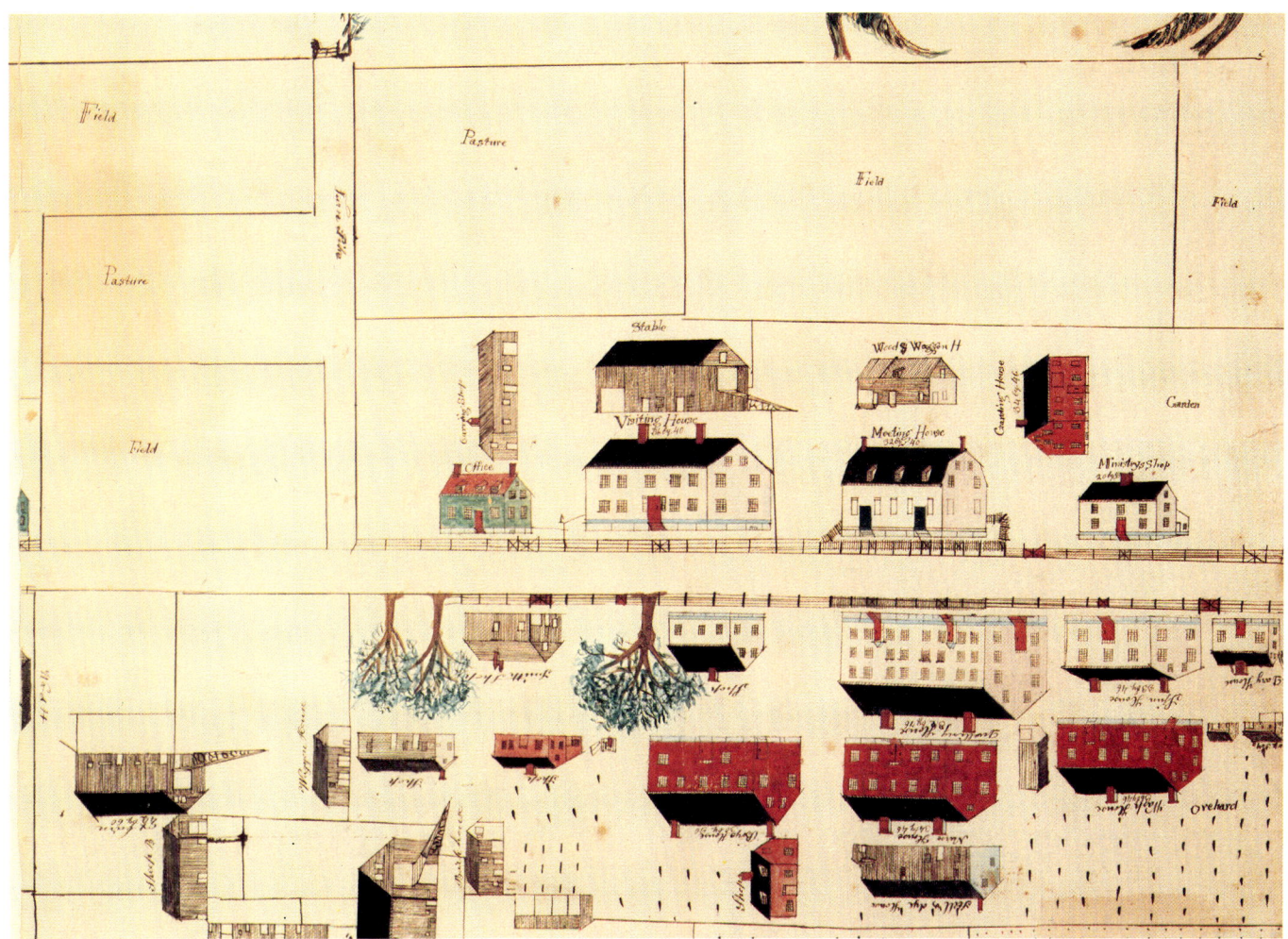

v. *A Plan of Alfred Maine* (detail), by Elder Joshua Bussell (1816–1900), 1845.
(Pen and ink and watercolor. The Library of Congress)

VI. *View of Saco Falls,* by William Stoodley Gookin (1799–after 1872), 1829.
(Oil on canvas. The York Institute Museum, Saco)

vii. *The Bowdoin College Campus,* by John G. Brown (fl. 1821–1858), 1822.
(Oil on canvas. The Bowdoin College Museum of Art, Brunswick)

VIII. *The Launching of the U.S.S. Washington,* Kittery, by John S. Blunt (1798–1835), 1814.
(Oil on canvas. The Collection of Bertram K. and Nina Fletcher Little)

forty, Obed disappeared from the Sandwich tax rolls—only to reappear later that year in a new settlement located just east of Winslow, Maine. This settlement was later incorporated as Fairfax and is now known as Albion, but the pioneer settlers, determined to pay no outside proprietors for their lands, called it "Freetown." Obed laid squatter's claim to a lot of 100 acres of wilderness land and gradually cut a clearing and erected a cabin.[23]

Mounting debts, however, were the almost inescapable burden of a poor man trying to capitalize a new farm. Debt proved an almost constant companion to the Barlows. In June 1798, Obed Barlow lost the first of three suits brought against him by creditors. Acting on behalf of a creditor, a deputy sheriff tried to seize some of Barlow's property on June 7, 1803. Obed violently defended his livestock and did "beat, wound & evilly entreat" the offending officer. This cost Barlow a conviction for assault, a sentence of two months in the local jail, a twenty dollar fine, and an order to pay the state's costs to prosecute him. Meanwhile, in August, Obed lost a suit for debt to Benjamin Whitwell, an Augusta esquire, and in December he lost another suit to Nathan Breed, a Vassalborough trader. The last suit seems to have obliged Obed to sell his homestead within a month to the same Nathan Breed for $800. Much of that sum must have been used to pay off his debts to Breed. Obed then moved eastward into the adjoining Beaver Hill settlement. Again he became a squatter, for there is no record of his having bought the land. Sometime between the 1810 and 1820 censuses—apparently frustrated in his hopes of finding frontier prosperity—Obed Barlow left the region to return to Sandwich, where he died in 1839.[24]

Nathan accompanied his father to the northeastern frontier in 1792 and proved to be no more successful. He first appeared as an independent householder in March 1799, when the Federal direct tax assessors found him dwelling in the northernmost part of Harlem (now China), just to the south of Freetown. His property was meager: a 100-acre squatter's lot assessed at $186 and a rough log cabin worth a mere $30. Overall, he ranked thirty-ninth among Harlem's forty-nine taxpayers. Nor was he able or willing to pay the modest tax; in March 1801, the federal government advertised the property for sale to meet the unpaid tax. Nathan moved northward into Freetown where he purchased 290 undeveloped acres from another squatter and took up another 100 unclaimed acres. But repeating his father's experience, Nathan fell so deeply into debt that he had to sell his land to meet the demands of local merchants. On the same day in June 1804, he sold 50 acres to Nathan Breed and another 50 acres to another Vassalborough trader, Stephen Bragg. In December 1805, he sold his remaining 290 acres to a third Vassalborough merchant, Benjamin Colby.[25]

Nathan followed his father eastward into the Beaver Hill settlement where he too squatted on a new lot of land. Barlow was in his forties when he prematurely died in the winter or spring of 1817. According to his probate inventory, he owned no legal title to any real estate and held a mere $100 in personal property. One cow, a single mare, a yoke of yearling steers, eight sheep, a pig, and a set of blacksmith's tools comprised the bulk of his modest estate. In contrast, three years earlier, the same appraisers assessed the Beaver Hill property of Bradstreet Wiggins at $1000 real and $420 personal, for a combined total in excess of fourteen times what Nathan Barlow owned. It is noteworthy that Bradstreet Wiggins had opposed Barlow and most of his neighbors by assisting the proprietors as a land surveyor.[26]

Obed and Nathan Barlow's experience with debt attest that in opening and improving wilderness lands, the poorest newcomers worked less for themselves than for their merchant creditors, who advanced the provisions, rum, tools, and livestock that sustained a settler and his family through their first hardship-filled years on the land. In return, the creditors entered high prices on their books and set annual interest rates at more than 25 percent. In 1807, the English traveler, Edward Augustus Kendall, toured the Kennebec valley and reported:

> The farmer is commonly in debt to the merchant to an amount exceeding the value of his whole property. The merchant considers the farm, the crops, the oxen and the utensils of his debtor as his own; but reckons upon the industry of the farmer, and on the security of the property; and, so long as he is satisfied with these, he reckons on his outstanding debts as on money put out to use, and from which he is to derive yearly interest.[27]

When a settler failed to meet the annual interest payment or when the merchant suddenly needed the return of his principal, he could bring a debt suit that could compel the settler to sell his homestead and move on. As a result of this process, local merchants obtained partially improved homesteads that they could lucratively resell. In sum, as a return on their initial investment, these merchant creditors ultimately reaped the fruits of some settlers' labor. It is small wonder, then, that Nathan Barlow participated in the settlers' resistance to debt collection, as well as to proprietary demands.

The third reason for drawing a connection between Nathan Barlow's mysticism and his role as a leading White Indian lies in the striking similarity between his mystical experience and another described in a pamphlet penned and published the year before by another settler leader, James Shurtleff of Litchfield. Entitled, *The Substance of a Late Remarkable Dream in Which was Presented the Celestial Worlds and the Infernal Regions with the Arch Enemy of Mankind with his Legions Paraded, Together with his Instructions to Them in Which was Discovered his Deep-Laid Plot Against the United States of America*, and written in verse, this pamphlet explicitly linked the cause of Christianity and the American Revolution with the poor squatters' struggle to preserve their property from wealthy proprietors.[28]

According to the pamphlet, Shurtleff fell asleep and into a deep dream. A celestial ball descended to him and its conductor with a "visage most sweet" invited him aboard. They then ascended "thro clouds and thro ether" to the moon, which proved to be "a world . . . with groves, seas and fields, which fruits in abundance to industry yields." After a brief pause "for refreshment" they continued upward toward "a bright star" passing several other worlds and suns on the way. These worlds were paradises where "ambrosial cakes" and "bowls over-flowing with nectar" were freely given by the loving inhabitants. From the perspective of these socialist paradises the Earth appeared to be:

> The fag-end of nature, of various classes,
> Scenes tragic presenting, mixed with farces,
> The good over power'd, while each daring fool
> Affects to be greatest, and strives for to rule,
> . . .
> Adieu to that bedlam, entail'd to the curse,
> Among millions of worlds I can't find a worse.[29]

At last they came amidst "the gracious behests of heaven's great King" and were greeted by the heavenly host "all sparkling in radiant sheen." Their contrast with corrupt man was marked:

> None deform'd or wrinkled with age here are found,
> All young, gay and sprightly, and healthy and sound.

When they spoke, it was "with music," and they spent their time picking flowers and "sporting on the skirts of a cloud." All was brotherhood and bliss because possession was collective:

> They in friendship and love were firmly combin'd:
> Here none sue for justice, none wrong'd or oppress'd,
> For each happy being of all was possess'd;
> No grieving known there at the good of another,
> For each view'd himself in viewing a brother.[30]

En route back to earth a cosmic storm seized Shurtleff's celestial ball and blew it past earth to "the verges of hell." He found Satan addressing his massed horde of demons who were preparing to depart for earth to subvert the morals and liberty of mankind. Satan insisted that their task would be simplest in Europe because "it is well known the chief of that old world has long been our own." The demons were then to proceed to America to stifle the virtue and freedom inspired there by the recent Revolution. Satan advised his minions to proceed by posing as political leaders:

> Of patriotism your robes must be woven,
> To places of honor then straight you'll be chosen,
> But mind that you cover the foot that is cloven
> . . .
> You'll command attention with noddles capacious,
> And tongues smooth and flippant, sublimely falacious,

> Thro' sophistical mazes, then play round and round,
> Common sense, plain reason, and justice confound.

Or the demons were to pass themselves off as preachers in order to discredit religion and so bring down freedom:

> For religion and freedom, of old 'twas decided,
> Springs both from one root, and can't be divided.

Their mission assumed special importance, for Satan's longstanding control over the earth lay in jeopardy:

> Yet now 'tis disputed, for what do I hear?
> Strange rumor of late, which alarms and affrights,
> Strange rumor of freedom and human rights;
> Tho men are but squatters, vile squatters, you see,
> Who settle on earth, holding not under me;
> But, alas! human rights, as urg'd by the squatter,
> Makes my kingdom and hell's foundation to totter.[31]

Then Shurtleff was suddenly cast from the ball back to earth, where with newly widened eyes he beheld the injustices perpetrated by the wealthy and powerful upon the poor and powerless. America stood imperiled by the rule of men "prefer'd not for wisdom but the wealth they inherit." Justice and equity had been turned upon their heads:

> The swift too I saw, who ne'er gained the prize,
> And bread oft they lacked, who were truly wise,
> . . .
>
> Nor was always the battle obtain'd by the strong,
> Nor did copious heads wealth accumulate,
> But th' fool gaining richer was call'd wise and great.

In Maine he found:

> Courts sitting and rising, and justice delay'd,
> And peasants dejected, on the doubtful soil,
> While claimers stood ready to seize of their toil.[32]

In sum, Shurtleff insisted that the squatters were struggling to preserve the American Revolution from a corrupt elite, betrayers of that revolution whatever their lip service to it. This struggle occurred in the context of God's contest with Satan for the fate of the earth. The settlers upheld God's purpose while the corrupt elite were demons at work for Satan. Presenting the settlers' cause in these Manichaean terms was the ultimate rejection of the existing fabric of authority. It denied the validity of anyone, any institution, or any argument that spoke out against the settlers' resistance. Anyone who opposed the settlers merely proved that he was one of Satan's minions. According to Shurtleff, any source of authority—lawyer, magistrate, sheriff, merchant, preacher, legislator, or governor—that a foe could invoke only demonstrated that Satan did indeed install his demons in positions of worldly power. This insistence nicely fit the needs of a humble people confronted by the combined strength of proprietors, creditors, and their political leaders.[33]

As in Barlow's vision, Shurtleff fell into a "dream" and traveled to heaven and hell before returning with a call for mankind to repent. Yet there were also important differences between the two visions—beyond Shurtleff's reverse itinerary and greater flair for color and detail. Shurtleff's pamphlet drew explicit political conclusions from his "dream." Indeed, the dream seems to have been a literary method of presenting his social critique. Barlow and his transcriber went to great pains to describe his physical state during the trance, to reveal personal details about others that he could only have learned by meeting and conversing with the dead, and to stress the emotional transformation wrought on Barlow and those who later heard his account of this journey. Powerful mystical experiences seem to have characterized the "new births" of evangelicals on the Maine frontier. Shurtleff, in contrast, was not concerned with proving the spiritual validity of his journey. Rather, in choosing the format of a dream experienced and revealed, Shurtleff consciously sought to maximize the impact of his social message; for as the traveler Edward Augustus Kendall noted after his 1807 tour of the Kennebec valley, the settlers there put great stock in the supernatural inspiration and predictive power of dreams. Apparently, the retelling of vivid dreams played an important part in the oral culture of these rural folk. Indeed during the Revolution, New England authors often communicated subversive ideas to the common people through apocryphal visions.[34]

Despite the differences, the similar plots suggest that Barlow may have been familiar with Shurtleff's pamphlet. It would be surprising, indeed, if such a pamphlet intended for cheap circulation among the settlers of the valley had not reached Fairfax and Beaver Hill. It seems that Shurtleff's pamphlet had an impact on Barlow sufficiently powerful to seep into his unconscious. What Barlow knew and what concerned him at twilight on January 8, 1801, colored his experience within his trance. For maximum impact, Shurtleff used the mode of a prophetic dream; this was so successful that it helped shape an actual revelation. By pointing out the divine source to which settlers must look for guidance, Shurtleff's poem played some small role in forming Barlow's mysticism. This divine contact then invested Barlow with particular prestige among fellow settlers who were seeking a higher justification for their resistance to worldly authority.[35]

In the end, because his encounter with the divine was merely fictional, Shurtleff could not be sure that Massachusetts' rulers were literal demons. He could never quite bring himself to justify organized violence against the state. Instead, he hoped that electing different leaders would rescue the settlers from proprietary demands. When the election of new Jeffersonian officials resulted in only mild reform, and when it became obvious that no election could replace the staunchly pro-proprietor state Supreme Judicial Court justices, Shurtleff could fight no longer. In January 1808, he explained to William King,

Maine's leading Jeffersonian politician, that "the torrent of influence" employed in the legislature and in the courts against the settlers' search for radical reform "caus'd me to despair of its accomplishment." Chagrined by mounting legal costs, he "concluded it would be safer & best to purchase, provided we could be secur'd in the premises."[36]

Shurtleff's quandary was that of many modestly successful settlers who had initially supported the resistance to protect their growing property, but who worried that if they held out too long and resistance collapsed, they would lose the opportunity to buy title to their land at a relatively modest rate. An 1810 valuation return for Litchfield shows that Shurtleff was a middling farmer who held a 78-acre homestead that included nine improved acres. He also owned a frame house and frame barn, a horse, three cows, five steers, and three swine. Although far from rich, he was much better off than Nathan Barlow. Shurtleff's circumstances were a substantial improvement from what he had known in his original home town of Plymouth, Massachusetts, where in 1771 he owned no livestock and no land except a small tannery. Among Plymouth's 255 real property owners, only nine possessed as little as Shurtleff. So, with the passing years and his improving circumstances, Shurtleff's passion gradually cooled; he grew ever less confident that the settlers could prevail against their powerful foes; by 1808, he concluded that they should buy before it was too late. Most of his poorer neighbors disagreed. "The utmost discontent still possesses the minds of the settlers," he sadly noted.[37]

In contrast to Shurtleff, Barlow and his followers were more thoroughly fortified against despair and compromise by the apparent authenticity of his spiritual authority. In their minds, opposition from the courts, the legislature, the governor, and the county sheriff carried little moral weight when matched against that of a man who had traveled with Christ. Accordingly, in late 1807 and early 1808, the White Indian bands in Barlow's vicinity attained considerable notoriety among the "friends of order" as the most radical of the settlers. God's blessing on their efforts seemed apparent in the dramatic expansion of active participants in their bands. According to Lemuel Paine of Winslow, the resistance in Barlow's district was "gaining strength by the accession of disaffected, unprincipled persons, by inflated hopes & confirmed habits of audacity." He estimated that as many as 700 men had joined the White Indian bands in Beaver Hill, Fairfax, and Unity. They "frequently assembled in large parties at their places of rendezvous, where they organize their system of opposition, and enact their savage laws." They exulted, he concluded, "in the anticipated revolution they intend to effect." But beyond some loose talk about marching on Augusta, the county seat, to burn the public buildings and the homes of proprietors and their supporters, the White Indians did not proceed beyond defensive measures and hopes that God would do the rest to secure His millennium.[38]

Nonetheless, the proprietors and the officers of the law rejoiced in May 1808 when they succeeded in arresting and imprisoning Barlow in the Kennebec County jail in Augusta. In early June the Supreme Judicial Court convicted him of felonious assault in the Moses Robinson incident. The justices sentenced Barlow to thirty days' solitary imprisonment and two years of hard labor at the state prison in Charlestown, Massachusetts. To the authorities' surprise and relief, they were able to get the convicted man out of the county and to Charlestown on June 3, before the White Indians could descend in force to rescue him.[39]

Thereafter resistance steadily declined. Occasional assaults on deputy sheriffs and periodic obstructions of proprietary surveys continued but at a diminishing rate through the balance of 1808 and into 1809–1811. The armed resistance in central Maine peaked during the two years 1807–1808, when at least thirty-six violent incidents occurred. They fell off markedly to nineteen during the next two-year period, 1808–1810, and virtually ceased thereafter, with but two incidents in 1811–1812. In one settlement after another the settlers stopped obstructing the writs issued for merchant creditors and began negotiating with proprietors to pay for their lands. Those settlers who could not afford to buy moved on. In late 1810, the Fairfax settlers at last permitted a comprehensive survey of their parcels by the Kennebeck Proprietors and began to make land payments. True to the example of Nathan Barlow, who returned home in mid-1810 after the expiration of his sentence, Freedom remained the last pocket of settler resistance. Not until the autumn of 1818, a year after Barlow's death, did the inhabitants permit the first survey by the assigns of the Kennebeck Proprietors. During the early 1820s, Freedom's settlers gradually purchased their lots. Anson, James, and William Barlow, sons or brothers of Nathan Barlow, were among the purchasers, paying about three dollars an acre to prevent eviction by their triumphant foes.[40]

Why did the White Indians' millenarian hopes collapse so quickly and completely? In the end, the resistance could not survive the loss of people like James Shurtleff—settlers who now had more property and less daring, men who by early 1808 had begun to despair that radical reform was possible. Without their support, the Nathan Barlows, the poorer men with less to lose and more to gain from millenarian hopes, lost the united front essential to resisting their wealthier and more powerful foes. Once the Shurtleffs began to waver, they came to fear the Barlows in their midst. Barlow went too far in visiting a savage beating on Moses Robinson, a man who was respected by many of the settlers. In reporting the incident to Governor James Sullivan, Kennebec County sheriff John Chandler expressed confidence that it would shock the more cautious settlers, disrupting the united front that comprised the insurgents' chief bulwark against prosecution. Chandler claimed that many settlers who "once countenanced the opposition . . .

now see that they are not safe among themselves, and [I] have no doubt they will aid in securing the offenders." Barlow's arrest, successful prosecution with the aid of several witnesses from Fairfax, and safe removal to state prison proved Chandler a prophet about the crippling division in the settler's ranks.[41]

In the end, mystical experience proved too volatile a source of social authority. Its resort to divinity overrode the legitimacy of all worldly sources of authority, nullifying the influence of human laws and government and encouraging a willingness to confront any foe. But, in the long run, it aroused false expectations that, because settlers did God's bidding, sweeping success would come swiftly and without fail. Such vague millenarianism encourages the hope that because God intends for His people to succeed, He will show the way and supply the instruments—provided they continue to believe and spread the faith. With such millenarian movements, any setback that stymies the movement's dramatic growth punctures the utopian expectations necessary for its existence. Hopes collapse suddenly. Consequently, the vivid demonstration of the state's power to seize and hold the most divinely powerful of the settler leaders had a profoundly discouraging effect on the settlers' resistance. Too much had hinged on Barlow's charisma as Christ's traveling companion.[42]

ACKNOWLEDGMENTS

I would like to thank Samuel K. Cohn, Robert A. Gross, David A. Kaplan, Laurel Thatcher Ulrich, and, especially, Marvin Meyers for their encouragement and criticism of this chapter. Danny D. Smith and James B. Vickery III provided fruitful research suggestions. Thomas Gaffney of the Maine Historical Society and Martha Clark of the Massachusetts State Archives made my task much easier. Research and travel support from the Irving and Rose Crown fund at Brandeis University made this work possible. My thanks also to Ruth Friedman of Brandeis University for running down a Barlow lead in the course of her research in Sandwich. Finally, I am very grateful to Karen Bowden and Julia Walkling for their skill in organizing and seeing through the Maine at Statehood program, which provided the original forum for my presentation.

NOTES

1. For the best introduction to frontier conditions and settler aspirations in Maine, see William Allen, "Now and Then," *Collections of the Maine Historical Society*, 1st ser., 7 (1876), 267–290 (hereafter *Coll. MeHS*); William Allen, *History of Industry, Maine From the First Settlement in 1791*, 2nd ed. (Skowhegan, Me.: Smith and Emery, 1869); William Allen, "The Journal of William Allen, Esq.," in William Collins Hatch, *A History of the Town of Industry, Franklin County, Maine* (Farmington, Me.: Knowlton, McLeary and Co., 1893), pp. 72–89.

2. On the origins of the unrest over land, see Robert Hallowell Gardiner, "History of the Kennebeck Purchase," *Coll. MeHS*, 1st ser., 2 (1847), 269–294; Gordon E. Kershaw, *The*

Kennebeck Proprietors, 1749–1775 (Portland, Me.: Maine Historical Society, 1975). For the troubles in 1807–1808, see Thomas Jeffrey, "The Malta War" (M.A. thesis, University of Maine at Orono, 1976); Alan Taylor, " 'Stopping the Progres of Rogues and Deceivers': a White Indian Recruiting Notice of 1808," *William and Mary Quarterly* 42 (January 1985), 90–103 (hereafter *WMQ*).

3. Arthur Lithgow's memorial to the Governor and Council, February 1808, Box 16 (August 1807-May 1808) Council Files, Massachusetts State Archives (hereafter MaSA); James W. North, *The History of Augusta From the Earliest Settlement to the Present Time* (Augusta, Me.: Clapp & North, 1870), p. 357.

4. On this issue, see especially Christopher Hill, *The World Turned Upside Down; Radical Ideas During the English Revolution* (New York: Viking Press, 1972); Alfred F. Young, "English Plebeian Culture and Eighteenth-Century American Radicalism," in Margaret and James Jacob (eds.), *The Origins of Anglo-American Radicalism* (London: Allen & Unwin, 1983), pp. 185–212.

5. Eric J. Hobsbawm, *Primitive Rebels; Studies in Archaic Forms of Social Movement in the Nineteenth- and Twentieth-Centuries* (Manchester, U.K.: University of Manchester Press, 1959), pp. 108–124; George Rude, *Paris and London in the Eighteenth-Century; Studies in Popular Protest* (New York: Viking Press, 1975), pp. 17–34.

6. On the chief justice rumor, see Charles Vaughan to Thomas L. Winthrop, October 10, 1803, Box 5, Kennebeck Proprietors Papers, Maine Historical Society (hereafter MeHS). On Ely, see James Nesmith to Isaac Parker, March 7, 1796, Henry Knox Pps. 38, 160, Massachusetts Historical Society (hereafter MaHS). On Patricktown, see Thurston Whiting and Benjamin Brackett, "Journal," August 26, 1801 entry, Henry Knox Pps., 44, 54, MaHS.

7. Robert E. Moody, "Samuel Ely: Forerunner of Daniel Shays," *New England Quarterly* 5 (January 1932), 105–134.

8. Nathan Barlow, *A Vision Seen by Nathan Barlow, of Freetown (Called so by the Inhabitants) Adjacent to the North-End of Harlem, in the County of Kennebec, District of Maine, January 8, 1801* (Boston: 1802, Shaw-Shoemaker #1838), p. 3.

9. Ibid.
10. Ibid., p. 4.
11. Ibid.
12. Ibid.

13. Moses Robinson's petition to the General Court, February 14, 1809, General Court Related Papers for Resolve CCXCIII (February 25, 1809), MaSA; John Chandler to Governor James Sullivan, April 25, 1808, House File of Unpassed Legislation #6381, MaSA.

14. Ibid.
15. Ibid.

16. "Harvey v. Fowler *et al*," December 1807, Kennebec County Court of Common Pleas (hereafter CCP) Record Book 7, p. 13, Maine State Archives (hereafter MeSA); writ, "Harvey v. Fowler *et al*," March 27, 1807, Box 9, Files of the Kennebec County CCP, MeSA. See also North, *Augusta*, 357.

17. Barlow, *Vision*, pp. 1–11; Gary S. Horowitz, "New Jersey Land Riots, 1745–1755" (Ph.D. dissertation, Ohio State University, 1966), p. 169; A. Roger Ekirch, "A New Government of Liberty: Hermon Husband's Vision of Backcountry North Carolina, 1755," *WMQ*, 34 (October 1977), 632–646; James P. Whittenburg, " 'The Common Farmer (Number 2)': Hermon Husband's Plan for Peace Between the United States and the Indians, 1792," *WMQ*, 34 (October 1977), 647–660; Richard Maxwell Brown, "Back-Country Rebellions and the Homestead Ethic in America, 1740–1799," in Brown and Don E. Fehrenbacher (eds.), *Tradition, Conflict, and Modernization; Perspectives on the American Revolution* (New York: Academic Press, 1977), pp. 73–99.

18. William Jones, *The Inconsistency and Deception of the Methodist Ministers Together with the Abuses Exercised Towards Their Church Members, Exposed* (no location: The Author, undated), pp. 14–16. The five pamphlets are: Samuel Ely, *The Deformity of a Hideous Monster Discovered in the Province of Maine, by a Man in the Woods, Looking After Liberty* (Boston: 1797, Evans #32081); Samuel Ely, *The Unmasked Nabob of Hancock County or the Scales Dropt from the Eyes of the People* (Portsmouth, N.H.: 1796, Evans #31477); [Samuel Ely and James Davis], *The Appeal of the Two Counties of Lincoln and Hancock from the Forlorn Hope, or Mount of Distress; to the General Court, or to All the World* (Portsmouth, N.H.: 1796, Evans #31477, paired with *Unmasked Nabob*); James Shurtleff, *A Concise Review of the Spirit Which Seemed to Govern in the time of the American War, Compared with the Spirit which Now Prevails: With the Speech of the Goddess of Freedom, Who is Represented as Making her Appearance on the Alarming Occasion* (Augusta, Me.: 1798, Evans #34548); James Shurtleff, *The Substance of a Late Remarkable Dream in Which was Presented the Celestial Worlds and the Infernal Regions with the Arch Enemy of Mankind with His Legions Paraded, Together with His Instructions to Them In Which was Discovered His Deep-Laid Plot Against the United States of America* (Hallowell, Me.: 1800, Evans #38584). For Brackett's notice, see Taylor, "Stopping the Progress." William Taylor of Freetown transcribed Barlow's account. See Barlow, *Vision*, p. 7.

19. Ibid.

20. On the local political prowess of propertied men in eighteenth century New England, see James T. Lemon, "Comment on James A. Henretta's 'Families and Farms: Mentalite in Pre-Industrial America'," *WMQ*, 37 (October 1980), 688–696; Robert Zemsky, *Merchants, Farmers, and River Gods; An Essay in Eighteenth-Century American Politics* (Boston: Gambit, 1971), pp. 28–38; Edwin M. Cook, Jr., *The Fathers of the Towns: Leadership and Community Structure in Eighteenth-Century New England* (Baltimore: Johns Hopkins University Press, 1976), pp. 23–118.

21. On Chase and Pattee, see Abraham Welch to George Ulmer, July 11, 1801, Henry Knox Pps., 44, 24, MaHS. The six identifiable Palermo leaders were Benjamin and David Turner, Jacob Greely, Captain Daniel Clay, Jonathan Bartlett, and Stephen Marden. See Thurston Whiting and Benjamin Brackett, "Journal," August-September 1801, Knox Pps., 44, 54, MaHS. The Palermo tax list is reprinted in Millard Howard, *An Introduction to the Early History of Palermo, Maine* (no location: no publisher, 1976), pp. 28–31. For Ely, see Moody, "Samuel Ely," pp. 105–134. For his standing, see the Northport return, Hancock County, Massachusetts-Maine returns, 1798 Federal Direct Tax, New England Historic Genealogical Society Library (hereafter NEHGSL).

22. Freedom Town Meeting, August 11, 1813, first book of Freedom Town Records, microfilm copy at the MeSA.

23. Sandwich Valuation Return for 1784, Box 382 (microfilm), Massachusetts Town Valuations, Massachusetts State Library (hereafter MaSL); Sandwich Valuation Return for 1791, Box 384, Massachusetts Town Valuations, MaSL; Sandwich Valuation Return for 1792, Box 387, Massachusetts Town Valuations, MaSL. For Obed Barlow's arrival in the Kennebec valley, see "Submissions of Settlers, Kennebeck Purchase," I, 27, MaSA. See also Laura Campbell Hawkins and Emma Campbell Devries, "Barlow and Allied Families," manuscript on deposit at the NEHGSL, pp. 57–60.

24. Hawkins and Devries, "Barlow," pp. 57–60; "Philbrook v. Barlow," June 1799, Lincoln County CCP Record Book 11, p. 44, Lincoln County Courthouse, Wiscasset, Maine; "Whitwell v. Barlow," August 1803, Kennebec County CCP Record Book 3, p. 172; "Breed v. Barlow," December 1803, Kennebec County CCP Record Book 3, p. 245; "Barlow to Breed," January 11, 1804, Kennebec County Deeds 6, p. 90; "Commonwealth v. Barlow," September 1803, Kennebec County Supreme Judical Court (hereafter SJC), 2, case #91; "Commonwealth v. Barlow," September 1803, Box 70 (criminal cases), Files of the Kennebec County SJC.

25. Harlem Return, Lincoln County, Massachusetts-Maine Returns, 1798 Federal Direct Tax, NEHGSL. On the same tax list William Taylor, who transcribed Barlow's experience into pamphlet form possessed $250 of property. On Barlow's default, see *Castine Journal* (Castine, Me.), March 27, 1801. For the land transactions, see "Barlow to Breed," "Barlow to Bragg," and "Barlow to Colby," Kennebec County Deeds 6, pp. 162, 336; 9, p. 142, Kennebec County Registry of Deeds, Augusta, Me.

26. Inventory of Nathan Barlow's estate, April 9, 1817 and Inventory of Bradstreet Wiggins's estate, July 8, 1814, both Kennebec County Probate Court, Augusta, Maine. For Wiggins's assistance to proprietors see Arodi Thayer to James Bridge and Reuel Williams, August 1, 1808, Letterbook 1: 250 Kennebeck Proprietors Pps., MeHS. No pre-1817 tax lists survive for Beaver Hill/Freedom.

27. Edward Augustus Kendall, *Travels Through the Northern Parts of the United States in the Years 1807 and 1808* (New York: I. Riley, 1809), vol. 3, p. 89. Later in life Nathan Barlow incurred yet more debts to Vassalborough trader Philip Colby. See "Colby v. Barlow," and "Cutler v. Barlow" both December 1814, Kennebec County CCP Record Book, 16: 295, 296, MeSA.

28. Shurtleff, *Substance*, pp. 3–4. Shurtleff was born in Plymouth, Massachusetts, on July 21, 1745. He married Priscilla Torrey in Plymouth on August 22, 1773. He moved to the future town of Litchfield before the 1784 Plymouth valuation. Relatively well-educated, although penurious in his early years, he became a respected schoolteacher, surveyor, and farmer. He even served a term in the General Court. He died in Litchfield, January 16, 1832. See *Centennial History of Litchfield, Maine*, p. 305; Benjamin Shurtleff (ed.), *Descendants of William Shurtleff of Plymouth and Marshfield, Massachusetts*, 2 vols. (Revere, Mass.: Shurtleff, 1912), Vol. 1, pp. 70–71.

29. Shurtleff, *Substance*, pp. 3–4.

30. Ibid., pp. 4–5. 31. Ibid., pp. 8, 14. 32. Ibid., p. 16.

33. See also Shurtleff, *Concise Review*.

34. Barlow, *Vision*, pp. 3, 6–9; Kendall, *Travels*, Vol. 3, pp. 84–85. On the vision genre, see Robert Girouard, "A Survey of Apocryphal Visions in Late Eighteenth-Century America," *Sibley's Heir: A Volume in Memory of Clifford Kenyon Shipton. Collections of the Colonial Society of Massachusetts*, 59 (1982), 191–194. For other examples of religious mysticism, see Paul Coffin, "Memoir and Journals of Rev. Paul Coffin, D.D.," *Coll. MeHS*, 1st ser., 4 (1856), 315–316, Jotham Sewell, "Autobiography," MS, undated, in MeHS.

35. My interpretation follows Christopher Hill, *The Religion of Gerrard Winstanley; Past and Present Supplement #5* (London: 1978).

36. James Shurtleff to William King, January 11, 1808, Box 7, William King Pps., MeHS. On Shurtleff's distaste for extralegal violence see *Concise Review*, p. 38.

37. For his property holdings, see Litchfield Valuation Return for 1810, Box 399, Maine Valuations Returns for 1810, MaSL. For his 1771 property holdings, see Bettye Hobbs Pruitt, *The Massachusetts Tax Valuation List of 1771* (Boston: G. K. Hall, 1978), p. 656.

38. Lemuel Paine to Governor James Sullivan, February 13, 1808. Similar accounts appear in A. Mann to Sullivan, February 15, 1808, and E.J. Warren to Sullivan, February 16, 1808. All three letters can be found in Box 16 (August 1807-May 1808) Council Files, MaSA.

39. Moses Robinson's petition to the General Court, February 14, 1809 in General Court Related Papers for Resolve CCXCIII (February 25, 1809), MaSA; "Commonwealth v. Barlow," May 1808 (criminal cases), Box 73, Kennebec County SJC files; *Eastern Argus* (Portland, Me.), June 16, 1808; North, *Augusta*, pp. 357 claims, "After serving his sentence he returned a finished rogue, and engaged in burglarious operations up and down the river." Court documents provide no evidence to confirm or to refute this assertion.

40. I define an *incident* as any illegal act committed against proprietors, their agents, or their supporters. I confined my search for incidents to the then three mid-Maine counties—Hancock, Lincoln, and Kennebec—and to the years 1790–1815, when and where documentation was most complete. I culled the incidents from (1) the Kennebeck Proprietors' Pps., MeHS; (2) the Henry Knox Pps., MaHS and MeHS; (3) the Supreme Judical Court records for the three counties, LCC, MeSA; (4) the papers filed by General Court resolves compensating victims of insurgent attacks, MaSA; and (5) any stray reference I could find. Because reporting was often inconsistent and incomplete; the 132 confrontations so discovered certainly do not represent the total number of such incidents that must have occurred. For a more complete examination, see Alan S. Taylor, "Liberty-Men and White Indians; Popular Protest and the Frontier Pursuit of Property in the Wake of the American Revolution" (Ph.D. dissertation, Brandeis University, 1985). For the settlers' gradual submission, see Gardiner, "History of the Kennebec Purchase," pp. 290–294; Reuel Williams' account with the Kennebeck Proprietors, March 1, 1811, Box 7, Kennebeck Proprietors' Pps., MeHS; Matthew Randall to William D. Williamson, March 3, N.Y. [ca. 1820], filed under "Freedom," town file, William D. Williamson Pps., MeHS. For Barlow purchases, see Kennebec County Deeds 37, p. 198, 200; 43, p. 231; 46, p. 412. The earliest of the four Barlow mortgages dates to March 23, 1821, the last to September 10, 1824.

41. John Chandler to Governor James Sullivan, April 25, 1808, House File of Unpassed Legislation; #6381, MaSA.

42. On the weaknesses of millennial movements, see Hobsbawm, *Primitive Rebels*, pp. 57–107. For a more mechanistic reading of millennial movements, see Norman Cohn, *The Pursuit of the Millennium: Revolutionary Millenarians and Mystical Anarchists of the Middle Ages* (New York: Oxford University Press, 1970).

Stephen A. Marini

CHAPTER 6

RELIGIOUS REVOLUTION IN THE DISTRICT OF MAINE
1780 – 1820

Religious individualism—the search for a direct, personal experience of the divine outside the institutional church—ran unchecked through Maine's backcountry in the years following the Revolution. The Congregational churches failed to keep pace with Maine's expanding population and were able to retain their domination over religious life only in the older coastal communities. Into the spiritual vacuum of the interior settlements flowed a wide variety of sectarian opinions and practices, which provided spiritual alternatives to the Congregational establishment. Stephen Marini, a historian of American religion, shows that Maine's religious dissenters shared a common bond with separationists, anti-Federalists, and opponents of proprietors. Only in part was this bond one of sectional self-interest; more significant, Marini argues, was a common set of values and world outlook that unified Maine's backcountry radicals and attracted them to the Democratic-Republican party, which embodied a similar world view.

A religious revolution in the District of Maine paralleled in time, space, and cultural tendency the movement for statehood. The transformation began in 1774 with a revival that for ten years swept across the rural interior. The revival, called the New Light Stir, fostered the rise of radical evangelical sects, including Separate Baptists, Freewill Baptists, Universalists, Methodists, Shakers, and Christ-ians. With dramatic speed these sects broke the religious hegemony of traditional Congregationalism, and by 1820 they had emerged as the dominant religious movement among the new inland majority of the District. It was among this same rural constituency that Jeffersonian Democratic-Republicans forged the political movement that finally achieved separation from Massachusetts.

By contrast, the older coastal settlements continued to sustain both Congregationalist religion and Federalist politics, but found themselves increasingly unable to check burgeoning religious dissent and popular democracy in the District. The evidence indicates that Maine's

Stephen A. Marini is associate professor of religion at Wellesley College and lecturer in church history at the Weston School of Theology.

religion and politics developed simultaneously geographically and sociologically between 1780 and 1820. Closely inspecting the little-studied religious dimension of Maine's transit to autonomy therefore seems warranted, as does asking whether its correlation with political patterns is substantive or merely coincidental.

Cultural transformation is highly complex, and debate over its definition and structure has been central to recent interpretations of the American Revolution. These interpretations are divided into those stressing the importance of socioeconomic forces and those emphasizing ideologies in the formation of the American republic. Both schools of thought have acknowledged the significance of religion in cultural change, but neither has encompassed fully the complex nature of American religion in the late eighteenth century. The most eminent contemporary works are those by Rhys Isaac, who has brilliantly described the ethnographic impact of dissenting religion on social and political behavior, and by Alan Heimert, Bernard Bailyn, and Gordon Wood, who have tied religious thought to revolutionary thought in different ways.[1]

In each of their works these authors have identified religion, and especially religious conflict, as an important contributory source of revolutionary change, but in each case the interpretation lacks what would seem to be essential to such a claim: an overview of denominational and theological patterns. Without solid empirical data on which religious groups were growing and which were failing, where change was taking place, and what issues characterized change, the place of religion in American Revolutionary culture cannot fully be assessed. It is far beyond the capacity of a single chapter to resolve the theoretical and interpretive issues raised. Thus my purpose is to describe the process of religious change in one Revolutionary society—the District of Maine—and to suggest its larger significance in the emergent culture of Maine at statehood.

THE DOMINANCE OF CONGREGATIONALISM

During the eighteenth century, Maine developed slowly into a colony's colony, reproducing in its small coastal towns and cities a provincial society modeled after that of Boston and Massachusetts Bay. Population increased steadily from 10,000 in 1750 to 29,100 in 1772. By 1776, settlement had proceeded down east past the Penobscot River, and the valleys and the backcountry had begun to fill with immigrants, many of them from eastern Massachusetts. Maine enjoyed substantial representation in the Great and General Court of Massachusetts Bay and its leading families were not without influence in Boston and Salem.[2]

The legally established religion was Congregationalism. The thirty-eight Congregationalist parishes that had been organized by 1780 far outnumbered the divided and far-flung churches of dissenters more than two to one. (See Table 3 on p. 120.) The Society of Friends (Quak-

TABLE 3
Religious Bodies in the District of Maine, 1780–1820

Denomination	Number of Churches				1820		
	1780	1790	1800	1810	Churches	Ministers	Members
Congregational	38	47	66	81	97	69	9,000*
Friends	6	8	19	25	36	—	2,150*
Episcopal	3	4	5	5	5	5	500*
Presbyterian	2	8	6	4	0	0	100*
Catholic	2	2	4	4	4	4	1,000*
Separate Baptist	3	15	38	148	154	122	9,373
Freewill Baptist	0	16	37	59	87	77	7,500*
Methodist	0	0	9	45	73	102	6,192
Shaker	0	0	10	14	10	32	700*
Universalist	0	0	1	10	25	20	2,000*
Christian	0	0	0	10	23	18	2,000*
TOTAL	54	108	205	389	560	485	39,865*

*Approximate number of members.

ers), the largest dissenting body, had organized only six meetings, most of them in isolated settlements along the east shore of the Piscataqua. Other denominations were present in even smaller numbers. Anglicans had been able to assemble small parishes only among British military and imperial personnel in garrison and commercial towns. Quebecois Catholics and Scotch-Irish Presbyterians each supported a few churches, as did Separate-Baptist migrants from southeastern New England.[3]

None of the others even began to approach Maine Congregationalists in size, resources, or influence at the outbreak of the American Revolution. With a meeting house, a parsonage, a university-trained minister, and public revenue in virtually every town, Congregationalism in Maine was arguably the most successful of New England's religious establishments in 1776. Rooted in Puritan Calvinism, the English Civil War, and a century and a half of successful New England colonization, Congregationalism transmitted a vision of a deferential, hierarchic, and godly society. The church defined the world view and maintained the moral order of Maine towns, and where coercion was necessary for the task, it could call upon the agencies of the state.

Congregationalism produced a complex and extensive religious culture: From artifacts such as the meeting house and parsonage to the life of the mind, from child-rearing to politics, the established church wielded its influence throughout colonial New England life. At the center of Congregationalist culture stood the minister. During the Revolution, Maine ministers still occupied what Donald Scott has termed the "office" of ministry, a social station and religious vocation placed above—and for the most part beyond—the average citizen or saint. Educated at Harvard, or occasionally at Yale, and protected by a

49. *The Reverend Samuel Deane* (1733–1814), by John Brewster, Jr. (1766–1854), ca. 1810.
(Oil on canvas. The Maine Historical Society)

lifetime contract to town and parish, ministers in Maine's deferential society held credentials to arbitrate taste and determine cultural legitimacy in their communities. Heavy obligations were placed on ministers to embody the ideal Christian life of traditional New England: pastor, spouse, and parent, teaching by precept and example the sacred norms of spiritual, moral, economic, and public life.[4]

THE COSMOPOLITAN MINISTERIAL STYLE

The career of Samuel Deane (Illus. 49) of Falmouth's First Parish clearly illustrates the nature of the Congregationalist establishment during the period. Deane (1733–1814) epitomized what social historians have called the "cosmopolitan" or "metropolitan" cultural style of colonial American elites.[5] The eldest son of Deacon Samuel and Rachel Dwight Deane of Norton, Massachusetts, Deane graduated from Harvard in 1760 and three years later was appointed a tutor in the college. His vocational interest, however, was the ministry. The summer after his graduation Deane served as chaplain to Massachusetts troops stationed in Halifax for duty in the French and Indian War. As a tutor, Deane received regular invitations to preach in eastern Massachusetts pulpits. On one such occasion in May, 1764, Deane was in Dunstable, where he met Colonel Eleazar Tyng, who brought him to Falmouth to preach at Thomas Smith's First Parish. Deane's sermon pleased the majority of the congregation and opened the way to a call to join them as junior minister. At Falmouth, Deane entered a world that closely corresponded to the traditional archetypes of town and parish. Falmouth was Maine's most dynamic settlement and Deane enjoyed the benefits of his predecessor's successful pastorate. Smith (1700?-1795; Harvard, 1720) had ministered at Falmouth for almost forty years when Deane arrived. His steady leadership had steered the congregation through the acrimonies of the Great Awakening and the crisis of the French and Indian War without a major schism or separation.[6]

Like most Maine parishes, Falmouth First had been divided in its response to the Great Awakening. Smith himself had initially embraced the strategies of George Whitefield and Jonathan Edwards, leaders of the prorevival New Light or Evangelical party. Smith joined Samuel Moody of York, John Rogers of Kittery, and many other Maine colleagues in supporting Whitefield's controversial preaching tours of New England.[7] Whitefield and the New Lights preached "the necessity of the New Birth," the doctrine that true Christianity began with a conscious experience of spiritual regeneration by the Holy Spirit. Their impassioned sermons strove to arouse in their listeners an awareness of the soul's sinfulness and its need for salvation by God through Christ. Many who heard were deeply affected by this message and professed to have experienced authentic conversion in the revival.[8]

Others rejected both the techniques and the theology of the New Lights, arguing that the human soul, though not perfect, was endowed by God with sufficient ability to discover true religion through reasoned understanding of the Bible rather than emotional excess of conversion. These opponents of the Awakening were called Old Lights; their leaders were Charles Chauncy, minister of Boston's prestigious First Church, and most of the Harvard College faculty. In Maine as elsewhere in New England, many of the elite sided with the Old Lights, viewing the New Light campaign as a dangerous outbreak of "enthusiasm," threatening the traditional social order they dominated.[9]

When Whitefield and Gilbert Tennent openly encouraged New Lights to separate from "unconverted" ministers and congregations, Old Lights—and many socially conservative New Lights, among them, Smith—found their worst fears of anarchy confirmed. In the 1740s all over New England, but especially in eastern Connecticut and southeastern Massachusetts, radical New Lights declared themselves unable to remain in fellowship and communion with unconverted people or ministers. Withdrawing from the town parish, they organized their own independent churches, called Separate or Strict Congregational.

The Separates defied law and custom by refusing to pay ministerial taxes, sponsoring itinerants and lay exhorters, ordaining as ministers those having no university training, demanding the New Birth and separation from all worldliness as qualifications for membership, and obeying what they called "impressions" of the Holy Spirit dwelling in the heart, soul, and mind. A few established ministers joined the Separates, but the vast majority—both Old and New Light—endorsed denunciations of them by the Harvard faculty and the Boston ministerium. The battle lines had been drawn in a theological and constitutional conflict between the Separates and the establishment that continued unabated during the Revolution and beyond.[10]

In Maine, however, traditional norms and institutions were strong enough to bend without breaking under the strain of the Great Awakening. Falmouth was a case in point: Thomas Smith's prestige and leadership had prevented schism, while promoting revival during the turbulent early 1740s. After 1745, however, Smith distanced himself from Whitefield and the Separates, while the Old Lights built a majority in the congregation. The First Parish New Lights remained loyal to Smith's moderate evangelicalism, though they were less certain of their welcome by the Old Light majority. When the growing congregation searched for an assistant to their aging minister, Deane appeared to be a perfect candidate. He was a moderate Old Light and thus established, with Smith, a balanced theological spectrum within which all members could feel comfortable.

Deane's teaching pleased the Old Light majority while his geniality, tolerance, and dedication helped keep New Lights comfortable. For almost fifty-five years—thirty of them alongside Smith—Deane successfully served his congregation without suffering a major separation. Between them the two men served more than a century in the Falmouth pulpit, living exemplars of the traditional ministerial office.[11] As he matured, Deane took up his pastoral obligation to provide public moral instruction. His principal effort in this regard was a series of sermons to young men. Taken together, these sermons represent a classic Congregationalist statement of traditional personal morality on the eve of political rebellion. Deane exhorted young people "to avoid all those sins, irregularities, and excesses, into which our senses are apt to carry us," and of which "it is likely young men are, on the whole, in greater danger than other sorts of persons."[12]

But true sober-mindedness, in Deane's view, required more than the external performance of duty, important as that undoubtedly was. He demanded that the sober "must be chaste and moderate in their tho'ts and meditations . . . must have a frame and temper of mind habitually correspondent to external sobriety." Deane located the center of this moral discipline in the mind, not the heart. "A mind that dwells much on the forbidden pleasures of sense," he warned, "is not a sound mind, but a mind sadly disordered, and full of corruption." The truly sober would obtain proper guidance in moral life by obeying the authority of traditional New England religious culture, and under its aegis they would cultivate "an anxious concern, desire, and endeavor to avoid all sin and temptation, and to walk 'in all the ordinances and commandments of the Lord blameless.'"[13]

During and after the Revolution, Deane espoused an increasingly liberal theology, criticizing the orthodox doctrines of the Trinity, predestination and election, and substitutionary atonement, and advocating the Arminian position in support of free will. Deane was a proto-Unitarian, espousing what Conrad Wright has called the "supernatural rationalism" characteristic of the generation of liberal Congregationalists between the Old Lights of the 1740s and the Unitarians of 1824, a blend of Enlightenment humanism and Arminian theology aligned with traditional New England concepts of religious establishment and public morality.[14]

Deane was also notable for his pursuit of scientific observation and comment. A fellow of the American Academy of Arts and Sciences and a founder of Bowdoin College, he was a keen meteorological observer and student of agriculture. As a man of learning and of God, Deane cut a substantial public profile in Revolutionary Maine. His politics, like his theology and science, followed that of Boston's Federalist elite. Deane was part of the "black regiment" of New England ministers who early advocated revolution and who sustained religious zeal for the cause both in the pulpit and on the field of battle. After the war this group of clerics joined conservative mercantile, landed, and professional interests to form the Federalist party, which controlled New England politics until 1805. The Federalists—Deane among them—stood for maintaining traditional institutions and ideals, including the Congregationalist establishment. In the words of one of his biographers, "Dr. Deane frankly described [Federalism] as a virtue equal to patriotism." He remained firm in his Federalist conviction until his death shortly before the Hartford Convention.[15]

Deane's diaries and publications reflect his close ties to the Federalist elite in Maine. In his popular agricultural manual, *The New England Farmer*, which appeared in 1790 and 1797 editions, Deane urged a "spirited attention" not merely to farming, but also to manufacturing in the expectation that the increasing wealth would cancel the public debt and enable the republic to become an "opulent, respectable, and very powerful nation."[16] Deane's concern with wealth, power, and legitimacy was characteristically Federalist.

Deane's greatest opportunity to defend the system came in 1794 when he was invited to deliver the annual election sermon before the Great and General Court of Massachusetts. He made the most of his chance, aroused, no doubt, by the presence in the Governor's chair of Samuel Adams, the only Democratic-Republican with sufficient stature to defy the Federalist hold on Massachusetts politics. Deane exhorted saint and magistrate alike to uphold the ideals of spiritual union, moral discipline, social deference, and political obedience that had characterized Massachusetts Bay since the days of John Winthrop. Deane not only assumed the correctness of publicly supported religion, but argued for its aggressive use as an agent for promoting political virtue and preventing vice. Inquiring rhetorically about the legitimate powers of the governor and the legislature under the state constitution, Deane called for enforcement of mandatory Sabbath attendance:

> If . . . they may enforce the support of schools for the instruction of youth, why not that of meetings for the instruction of grown up children in religion and morality, so far as they shall judge it needful to promote the welfare of society? Why not oblige a dishonest person to attend these meetings, of the denomination he prefers, if it were only to prevent his invading the property of the Christian neighbours, while they are at the place of public worship? And why not constrain the profane person to do the same, in hope that he may learn to be afraid of perjury, the practice of which vice would be pernicious to a community, as it would render good government impracticable. All that is indisputably beneficial to society, and consistent with the rights of individuals, is within their line.[17]

Yet on the question of statehood Deane joined with his Maine brethren against Boston's power. He was a leader in the early stages of the Maine separation movement. As Ronald Banks has shown, the post-Revolutionary campaign for Maine statehood was spearheaded by the elite families of coastal towns, the sort of people to whom Deane and Smith principally ministered. Theirs was an attempt by conservative District Federalists to wrest political and economic control of their province from the distant authority of Massachusetts. As one of this "cocked hat" faction, Deane had complained as early as 1785 on behalf of one Maine community that "this plantation is taxed without the least shadow of representation and they have indeed no more voice in making laws, than the late British colonies . . . ever had in the parliament of Britain."[18] Though horrified by Shays' Rebellion, Deane supported separation in 1792, and he hosted a separation convention in 1794, the very same year in which he so zealously defended the religious establishment clause of the Massachusetts state convention before the Great and General Court. For the balance of the eighteenth century Deane campaigned for Maine statehood, but like most Federalists he reversed himself after 1800, when a new Jeffersonian majority captured the issue as a symbol of rural independence against both Boston and Falmouth.[19]

A VARIATION OF THE COSMOPOLITAN MINISTERIAL STYLE

Although Deane represents the archetype for the cosmopolitan Maine ministry, it is important to remember that there were many variations. No two parishes were the same. But an overall pattern did characterize the Congregationalist establishment: In general, the farther inland from the coast, the weaker the parish system became, and the stronger the New Light persuasion of the people. The career of Tristram Gilman at North Yarmouth is a good example. His parish, located on Royal's River ten miles from Falmouth, was badly divided by the Awakening, and his own growth into the ministry was protracted and troubled. Gilman was born in Durham, New Hampshire, on November 24, 1735. His parents were the Reverend Nicholas and Mary Thing Gilman. Both parents held elite socioeconomic status, and until the Great Awakening they enjoyed the privileges of sacred status and social prestige. During the revival, however, Nicholas Gilman (Harvard, 1724) suddenly emerged as the most radical of the New Lights, demanding the display of charismatic gifts as a sign of authentic conversion. His adherence to "the Durham Dancers," a charismatic and ecstatic assembly, broke up the Durham parish and caused Gilman's dismissal in 1747. Within a year he died, and in another year Tristram's grandfather Gilman also passed away, leaving the young man independently wealthy.[20]

Tristram attended Harvard (Class of 1757) and for several years after graduation he taught school in Exeter. He then presented himself for ordination, which he received on September 27, 1763. For more than five years Gilman searched for a parish before North Yarmouth called him in August, 1769. The parish was predominantly New Light; the majority made Gilman's call possible by forcing out his Old Light predecessor and Harvard classmate, Edward Brooks. In Gilman the New Lights found a candidate of clear evangelical lineage to reinforce their convictions. One memorial biography described the New Light orthodoxy of Gilman's proclamation: "In his preaching, he dwelt much upon the doctrines of total depravity, particular and eternal election, regeneration by the special influences of the Holy Spirit, justification by the righteousness of Christ, and the perseverance of the saints."[21]

However, the divided votes of both parish and town—29 to 13 and 40 to 29, respectively—revealed a deep division between New and Old Lights, with most elite families on the minority side. Undaunted, Gilman accepted the invitation, and for twenty years he labored to reconcile the Old Lights. Clifford Shipton observes that "the success of [Gilman] in conciliating the faction that had opposed his call is amazing, and particularly so because his vigorous physical frame was matched by his strong will and almost obstinate independence."[22] Then in 1790 Gilman's wife of almost twenty years, Elizabeth Sayer of Wells, died. Ironically, even as he struggled to overcome this devastating blow, events were conspiring to bring fame to Gilman and his congregation. In 1791 and 1792 Gilman presided over the largest Congregationalist revival in Maine since the Great Awakening. Both Gilman's contemporaries and later historians, however, have interpreted Gilman's North Yarmouth revival as a prototype for the Second Awakening in New England. One source described Gilman in 1791–1792 as:

Indefatigable; either reading or preaching four lectures a week besides the Sabbath.... The work was carried on with great calmness and deliberation. Some indeed were so affected as not to be able to attend to their business for some time. There were no instances of crying out or fainting, except once in the time of lecture a woman fell into a fainting hysteric fit. A boy also cryed because of his sins.[23]

The key aspect of this account is its emphasis on orderliness and decorum. If Samuel Deane could maintain unity at Falmouth with Old Light theology, Gilman proved that New Light evangelism could also successfully be employed without disrupting a congregation. Moreover, a well-executed revival could bring new members into the established church better than any other evangelistic technique. From 1770 through 1774, the earliest years of his ministry, Gilman's preaching brought a modest but steady number of converts. From 1775 through 1790, however, North Yarmouth parish was on a steep and constant decline despite Gilman's best efforts to unite Old Lights and New Lights. For those fifteen years, deaths outnumbered admissions 233 to 53. Then in just three revival years, from 1791 to 1793, Gilman attracted 149 new members, almost restoring in one stroke the losses of fifteen years and revitalizing the life of his parish.[24]

Though his tenure was far less stable and his New Light theology quite the opposite of Samuel Deane's, Gilman in other ways resembled his Falmouth colleague. Gilman, like Deane, enjoyed long tenure and parish harmony; he served North Yarmouth for forty years from 1769 to 1809 without serious division. In Gilman's case the task was more difficult, for he faced directly the itinerant evangelists of other sects, specifically Elder James Potter of the Separate Baptists. Potter, "a prosperous farmer and man of influence" from Bowdoin, Maine, preached at North Yarmouth in 1793. Gilman quietly joined the congregation; then, when given leave to speak after Potter's sermon, "warned the people to beware 'strange fire' and 'new lights,' but told them that they would hear nothing from Potter which they would not hear from him."[25] In this critical situation, Gilman was able to call upon his own New Light credentials as well as his traditional prestige to weaken the appeal of Potter and keep his flock intact.

Another similarity between Deane and Gilman was their common allegiance to the Federalist elite. Throughout the Revolution Gilman remained a strong, if sometimes critical, supporter of American independence, and after the war he dutifully entered the Federalist ranks. In this political persuasion he mirrored his people, who made North Yarmouth a Federalist bastion. Gilman wrote letters to both John Adams and Thomas Jefferson endorsing the former's policies in the XYZ Affair, and he remained a strong supporter of the religious establishment. In addition, Gilman joined Deane and other elite ministers, merchants, and landowners in the founding of Bowdoin College, and served as the first president of its Board of Trustees.[26]

As the careers of the two men indicate, theological persuasion made little difference in the conservative cultural milieu of Congregationalism. Deane and Gilman, along with virtually all Maine ministers of every theological stripe, shared the same traditional religious-political vision of a unified, hierarchic, and godly society. Through decades of service, revered religious leaders such as Deane and Gilman were able to preserve and extend the colonial world view and cultural authority of Congregationalism in their cosmopolitan towns into the nineteenth century.

FACTORS INFLUENCING RELIGIOUS CHANGE

The growth of Congregationalism in Maine from 1780 to 1820 appeared to be solid and substantial. As Table 3 indicates, the number of parishes grew at a relatively constant rate throughout that period. In relation to most of their earlier colonial rivals, Congregationalists maintained their numerical advantage. But these indications of continuing Congregational dominance tell only part of the story. By 1820 the parish system was in perceptible decline. Almost one-third of the District's Congregational pulpits were vacant.

This shortage reflected several grim institutional realities. The very longevity and cohesion that made Deane's and Gilman's clerical generation so powerful also made its passing traumatic to the parish system. Gilman died in 1809, Deane in 1814, and along with them virtually the entire Revolutionary generation. Of at least equal importance was a reduced supply of young ministers. The Revolution disrupted the education of several student generations, and after 1783 the colonial custom of preparing students for college and then the ministry—by residential study in a ministerial household—declined. The result was fewer ordinands in the decades before the passing of the Revolutionary generation. Fewer available ministers meant greater cost to the parish for competitive salary. In new towns, establishing a parish also entailed funding and construction of a meeting house and parsonage. These high costs grew even more burdensome to communities because of postwar inflation and economic insecurity.[27]

It was during the economically and politically troubled 1780s and 1790s that the expensive and cumbersome Congregationalist establishment faltered in Maine. The dimensions of the breakdown were far more serious than aggregate growth and vacancy statistics indicate. Two other sets of data place the Congregationalist numbers in proper context: population growth and its geographical distribution. Maine's population grew much faster than the Congregationalist parish system did. As Table 4 shows, between 1772 and 1820 Maine's total population increased by a factor of ten—the most rapid growth in the new nation—while the number of Congregationalist parishes grew by a factor of only two and a half between 1780 and 1820. (See Table 3 on p. 120.)[28] The parish system, then, far from growing steadily, was actually in steep relative decline.

TABLE 4
Maine Population by County, 1772–1820

County	1772	1777	1784	1790	1800	1810	1820
York	13,398	15,908	19,909	27,560	34,284	41,877	46,283
Cumberland	10,139	13,476	15,621	23,481	31,898	42,831	49,445
Oxford						17,630	27,104
Lincoln	5,563	12,916	20,791	29,723	30,100	42,992	53,189
Kennebec					24,402	32,564	42,623
Somerset						12,910	21,787
Hancock				9,549	16,316	30,031	31,290
Penobscot							13,870
Washington				2,759	4,436	7,870	12,744
TOTAL	29,100	42,300	56,321	96,540	151,719	228,705	298,335

The other important developmental pattern was geographical. Although immigrants poured into all parts of the district, the areas of most rapid development were in the Saco, Androscoggin, Kennebec, and Penobscot river valleys and the tiers of hill country towns extending inland from the coast. To the three pre-Revolutionary counties of York, Cumberland, and Lincoln were added Hancock and Washington down east in 1789 and later the interior counties of Kennebec (1799), Oxford (1805), Somerset (1809), and Penobscot (1816).

By 1776, the old colonial counties had reached rough parity in size and for the balance of the period they grew at fairly even rates. The new settlements, by contrast, grew explosively, particularly in the upper Kennebec and Androscoggin river valleys. These differential rates of development combined with frontier economic conditions and the diverse origins of the settlers to produce a new pattern of small decentralized towns, subsistence agriculture, physical isolation, and social tribalization. Social historians have called these characteristics "localist" or "country" culture in contrast to the cosmopolitan, or metropolitan, characteristics of the old coastal colonial towns. It was in these new settlements, and above all in the interior, that Congregationalism failed decisively and a new religious majority was born.

The crucial episode of religious change in the District of Maine was a revival that swept across the new settlements between 1774 and 1784. Beginning with the preaching tour of the Quaker David Sands through the eastern settlements on the eve of the Revolution, the spiritual quickening increased steadily through the war years, urged on by a host of radical and dissenting itinerant preachers. I have described this revival, known as "the New Light Stir," elsewhere at length.[29] Here I simply want to note several aspects of the Stir that were most salient to the process of religious-political transformation.

In one sense the Stir was important merely as a renewal of the emotional and charismatic religious style of the Great Awakening. The New Lights of the 1774–1784 revival were so called because their visionary preaching and powerful personal religious experiences reminded settlers of Jonathan Edwards, George Whitefield, and the other preachers of the Great Awakening. Here the similarity ended, however, because the Stir, unlike the Awakening, was led not by settled ministers and authorized Congregational itinerants, but by dissenters—most notably Separate Baptists—who opposed the religious establishment and its traditional teachings. A related and highly significant dimension of change in the backcountry during the Stir was the appearance of indigenous sects, which created new theologies and polities to challenge the standing order. Freewill Baptists from New Hampshire, Universalists from the Connecticut Valley, and Shakers from the Berkshires and central Massachusetts sent effective missionaries into the burgeoning Maine backcountry. Encountering the fundamental weakness of the Congregationalist parish system in rural settlements, the forces of radical revivalism and religious revision swept to sudden triumph.

THE PROCESS OF RELIGIOUS CHANGE

The process of religious change was carried out locally. It was a matter of itinerant preachers converting settlers gathered in farmhouses, barns, and fields to hear revival preaching. For this reason the New Light Stir is best viewed through a typical example, that of New Gloucester, located on Royal's River ten miles above North Yarmouth and twenty miles above Falmouth. New Gloucester's first settled minister was Samuel Foxcroft (1723–1807), son of the Reverend Thomas Foxcroft of Boston's prestigious First Church, Harvard graduate (1754), theological student of the eminent Aaron Burr, Sr., at Princeton, and already an experienced itinerant minister. With these impeccable New Light credentials, Foxcroft seemed perfectly suited to the call issued in 1765 by the small rural parish and the town's proprietors in Gloucester, Massachusetts.[30]

For a decade things apparently went well for both pastor and people. Then in 1775, the proprietors' subsidy of Foxcroft's salary ended, and a number of leading citizens requested exemption from the new ministerial tax as religious dissenters. These New Light dissenters complained that Foxcroft's preaching was "cold and lifeless" and "did not appear . . . to be soul searching."[31] For another five years Foxcroft's supporters and the dissenters drifted toward a break when in the autumn of 1780 the New Light Stir broke upon them in the form of Separate Baptist Elders Hezekiah Smith (Princeton, 1762) and Nathaniel Lord. Separate Baptists were the descendants of the Separate, or Strict, Congregationalists of the Great Awakening, most of whom eventually joined forces with New Light Particular Baptists, forming the Warren, Rhode Island, Baptist Association in 1767. The preaching of Smith and Lord converted several of the New Gloucester dissenters, who were baptized and formed into a new congregation before the elders moved on to the next stop in their evangelistic campaign.[32]

No sooner had the spring thaw of 1781 begun than New Gloucester greeted Benjamin Randel of New Durham, New Hampshire, founder of the Freewill Baptists. Randel, raised an Old Light in coastal Newcastle, New Hampshire, was literally George Whitefield's last convert. Receiving a visionary call to preach, he proclaimed a combination of the Arminian theology of human free will, the general atonement of Christ, and a "day of grace" granted to all souls for their free choice of salvation or damnation, with consensus as the polity for Christ's church, and the "open communion" of all true Christians—all in the Grand Itinerant's emotional and rhetorical style.

Examined and rejected by the Separate Baptists for his denial of Calvinism, Randel nonetheless obtained a call from New Light settlers in New Durham, a New Hampshire town not far from the Maine border, whom he organized into "the Church of Christ at New Durham," the first Freewill Baptist church in America. New Gloucester was one of Randel's early stops on his first evangelistic tour. His earnest preaching roused the dissenters and converted others. Adolescent females and young men returning from service in the Revolutionary army took the charismatic lead in the revival, while the dissenters debated among themselves which gospel was the true one.[33]

For almost a year Baptist itinerant preachers fanned the New Light Stir in New Gloucester and organized rival Separate and Freewill churches. Then the revival took a still more radical turn with the arrival of Shaker missionaries in the autumn of 1782. Founded by Mother Ann Lee of Manchester, England, and brought by her in 1774 to a frontier farmstead near Albany called Niskeyuna, the Shakers exercised a powerful array of spiritual gifts: prophecy, healing, vision, speaking in tongues, and ecstatic dance. They taught that the Second Coming of Christ was spiritual, not physical, and had already begun to perfect their souls. They made converts confess all their sins to Mother Ann and the Shaker Elders for forgiveness and embarkation on the perfect life, to become celibate in order to overcome the original sin of sexual intercourse, and to share all things in common according to apostolic precedent.[34]

At the height of the New Light Stir, from 1780 to 1784, Mother Ann traveled and preached across Massachusetts and Connecticut, gaining thousands of converts, especially among Separate Baptists. Her travels took her as far east as Harvard, Massachusetts; from there she dispatched trusted converts to evangelize in northern New England locations where the Stir had been particularly intense. She sent Ebenezer Cooley of Pittsfield, Massachusetts, to Alfred and Gorham, Maine. Three of his converts in Gorham—Elisha Pote, Nathan Freeman, and Joseph Stone—in turn carried the Shaker message to relatives in the Poland Hill neighborhood of New Gloucester. They "opened the gospel" there in November, 1782, and soon brought a dozen large families to Shakerism in Poland Hill and New Gloucester town.[35]

Religious Revolution in the District of Maine

Yet even the Shaker advent did not complete the New Light Stir in New Gloucester. In 1783 Joseph Pearce brought Universalism to the town from old Gloucester in Massachusetts, where he had been a member of the first Universalist church in America, organized by John Murray, a British New Light and onetime convert and colleague of Whitefield. Murray taught that a benevolent God would not damn human beings who lacked the natural ability to be sinless. Instead, Murray followed his mentor James Relly—another former colleague of Whitefield at Moorfields Tabernacle in London—claiming that Christ's atoning death on the cross was universal, extending its infinite merit to the salvation of every human soul. Hence all will eventually be saved. Murray argued further that realization of this truth would generate the greatest love to God and humanity. Murray was a controversial but popular preacher in Gloucester, and several of his followers (including Joseph Pearce) joined in settling the town's Maine outpost. Pearce's lay ministry in New Gloucester and his work in the interior drew a steady stream of converts and established Universalism's first permanent presence in the District.[36]

The revival eventually subsided, but its aftermath only heightened the religious-political divisions in the town. The New Gloucester dissenters were by now better organized and continued to press their claim to exemption from ministerial taxes. In November, 1783, thirty-nine dissenters—more than one-quarter of the registered polls, holding more than one-third of the town's wealth—were excused from the annual levee. With this victory, the sectarians swiftly gained political control of town meeting and then used their new majority to dismantle the religious establishment. All Baptists were granted exemption in 1786, Universalists the next year. In 1789 the town voted to share ministerial tax money between Foxcroft and the Separate Baptist congregation. Each of these actions reduced Parson Foxcroft's income and prestige until finally on November 13, 1792, the town unanimously voted that it did not "choose or approve of Mr. Foxcroft's ministerial labors any longer."[37] He resigned three days later, after twenty-seven years in the New Gloucester pulpit.

Yet all was not lost for the Congregationalists. New Gloucester parish shared in Tristram Gilman's North Yarmouth revival of 1791 and 1792 and gained badly needed new members, particularly through the efforts of young Yale-trained itinerant ministers who aided in the work. Almost immediately, however, sectarian preachers returned to exploit successfully the revival's energy for their own purposes. Benjamin Randel revitalized the Freewill Baptist church in 1793 and Elder James Potter did the same for the Separate Baptists in 1794. Also, during that same year, the Shakers "gathered into order" at Sabbathday Lake and the first Methodist itinerant, Jesse Lee, preached in New Gloucester. Universalist Elder John Barnes moved to neighboring Poland in 1798, completing the permanent organization of the new sects.[38]

Meanwhile the Congregationalist parish remained vacant, its religious appeal sharply diminished and its political control rendered ineffective. At last successful in their 1802 call to Elisha Moseley, the New Gloucester parish again rallied under the new pastor's revivalistic influence. This third New Gloucester revival since the Revolution was part of what is known as "the Second Great Awakening," a national crest of evangelical fervor reminiscent in its intensity to the Awakening of 1734–1745. But again, as in 1791–1792, Congregationalist revival invited sectarian exploitation. From 1802 to 1807 the renewal of piety spurred many new conversions, from which Methodists and Universalists especially benefited, while the Baptists and Shakers also grew at Congregationalist expense. This later revival brought Methodist Bishop Francis Asbury—and a company of his fellow circuit-riders—through New Gloucester on their way to the 1802 New England Conference, held at Monmouth, Maine.

New Gloucester's situation reveals in microcosm the ironic transformations of culture through revival. The Stir both increased popular religious interest and weakened traditional religious institutions by division and conflict. It was this explosion of piety and pluralism that engulfed the Congregationalist establishment in New Gloucester and towns like it throughout the District. In less than three years between 1780 and 1783 the New Light Stir divided Samuel Foxcroft's parish and brought four new sectarian religions into the community. The homogeneous parish of colonial days had become a religious minority succumbing to the competition of radical evangelical sectarians.

Fully as important was the political impact of this religious polarization. Despite theological differences, the sectarians were united and highly politicized in categorical opposition to the Congregationalist legal monopoly on religion. The sectarians' attainment of a majority in town meeting and their rapid development into effective managers of the local political system may have been the most crucial transformation of all in the New Light Stir. From 1783 on, the new religious groups, especially the Baptists, used the traditional operations of town government against the establishment rather than for it. At precisely the same time, the town polarized around state and national political issues, with the sectarians sustaining a new Anti-Federalist and separatist majority, voting against the unamended Federal Constitution in the ratification election of 1787, demanding Maine statehood, and supporting an act of indemnity for the Shaysite rebels.[39]

This change was profound because the Puritan vision and New England's colonial experience had always linked town meeting and parish together as civil and sacred guardians of a single societal faith. Yet even as the Revolution reached its successful conclusion, radical evangelical sectarians in Maine and throughout New England converted the religious fervor of the New Light Stir into local political power capable of dismantling the establishment that the Federalist elite regarded as essential for a successful republic. By 1790, Foxcroft and New Gloucester's Federalists had lost control of their town. The Congregationalist revivals in 1791–1792 and 1802–1807 proved futile, succeeding only in offering the sects a fresh opportunity to increase their advantage.

What happened in New Gloucester happened everywhere in rural Maine. Although the specific scenario of change varied from town to town, the larger pattern is clearly shown in Table 5 for the four largest denominations in Maine and in Table 3, which graphically illustrates the chronology of revival and sectarian ascendancy. Clearly the New Light Stir (1774–1784) launched both the Separate and Freewill Baptists, while the revivals of the 1790s helped introduce Methodism and organized Shakerism into the District. The Second Great Awakening of 1802–1807 produced enormous growth for Separate Baptists and Methodists and gave an opening both to Universalists and to yet another indigenous sect, the Christian Connection.

This last communion was founded by Elias Smith in Portsmouth in 1805. Smith, a product of rural New England culture, moved through a series of conversions from New Light Congregationalist to Separate Baptist to Freewill Baptist before proclaiming his own gospel of ecumenism and restoration of the apostolic church. His message marked a new stage in New England religious pluralism. Smith perceived the divisions that had so profited the sects in the eighteenth century as a source of disunion and confusion for the church of Christ. Appealing to the model of the New Testament church, he preached a single communion of all believers, who would be indissolubly bound together in spiritual union and who would take scripture as the only rule for their lives. He called his movement only by the scriptural names "disciples of Christ" or simply "the Christian church." This appeal, together with Smith's own version of theology and revival fervor, quickly established his "connection" of converts as a significant Maine denomination at the time of statehood.[40]

The War of 1812 severely curtailed all revival activity, but after 1815, Freewill Baptists and Methodists continued to expand and Congregationalists pursued an aggressive evangelistic program. But by 1820, the cumulative impact of revivalism and sectarianism had simply overwhelmed the still-legal Congregationalist establishment. At statehood the combined churches of Separate Baptists, Methodists, and indigenous sects outnumbered Congregationalist parishes four to one. Even more revealing is the geographical pattern of the dissenters' triumph. Table 5 shows that Congregationalism was able to maintain itself fairly well in the old colonial counties of York, Cumberland, and Lincoln, but experienced sharply decreasing success moving inland to Oxford, Kennebec, Somerset, and Penobscot or down east to Hancock and Washington counties. The figures for the three largest sects—Separate Baptist, Freewill Baptist, and Methodist—reveal the opposite: modest growth in colonial areas and an explosive increase in the new settlements.

TABLE 5
Geographical and Chronological Growth of Major Denominations by County, 1780–1820

County	Number of Congregationalist Churches Added					Total
	1780	1790	1800	1810	1820	
York	14	1	5	3	0	23
Cumberland	14	3	4	1	2	24
Oxford	1	1	2	3	4	11
Lincoln	7	1	1	7	0	16
Kennebec	0	2	2	1	4	9
Somerset	0	1	0	0	1	2
Hancock	0	1	5	1	2	9
Penobscot	0	1	0	0	1	2
Washington	0	1	0	0	2	3
TOTAL	35	12	19	15	16	97

County	Number of Separate Baptist Churches Added					Total
	1780	1790	1800	1810	1820	
York	2	3	5	9	0	19
Cumberland	1	3	2	6	0	12
Oxford	0	0	7	11	0	18
Lincoln	0	5	5	19	2	31
Kennebec	0	1	2	22	0	25
Somerset	0	0	1	14	0	15
Hancock	0	0	1	16	4	21
Penobscot	0	0	0	9	0	9
Washington	0	0	0	4	0	4
TOTAL	3	12	23	110	6	154

County	Number of Freewill Baptist Churches Added				Total
	1790	1800	1810	1820	
York	2	9	1	2	14
Cumberland	4	2	2	4	12
Oxford	1	1	0	3	5
Lincoln	8	2	7	12	29
Kennebec	0	4	4	4	12
Somerset	1	3	5	2	11
Hancock	0	0	0	0	0
Penobscot	0	0	3	1	4
Washington	0	0	0	0	0
TOTAL	16	21	22	28	87

County	Number of Methodist Churches Added			1820	
	1800	1810	1820	Churches	Members
York	0	0	3	3	460
Cumberland	3	8	6	17	1,185
Oxford	0	5	0	5	644
Lincoln	3	8	3	14	946
Kennebec	3	8	0	11	1,017
Somerset	3	0	3	6	619
Hancock	0	3	3	6	224
Penobscot	0	5	3	8	801
Washington	0	0	3	3	124
TOTAL	12	37	24	73	6,192

Of special significance for all communions was the Kennebec valley and its counties of Lincoln, Kennebec, and Somerset, comprising the old Kennebec Purchase. Table 4 illustrates the magnitude of the Kennebec migration. In 1772 Kennebec valley settlements accounted for less than 20 percent of Maine's population; in 1820 that proportion had grown to nearly 40 percent. The Congregationalist parish system did not match the pace of settlement, placing only one-quarter of its churches in the Kennebec valley. Each of the major sects, on the other hand, concentrated on this region. Table 6 shows the development of denominations by county rather than by denomination, providing a different perspective on the changes in relative strength among the churches. Even in York and Cumberland counties, the sectarians outnumbered Congregationalists; in the Kennebec valley, however, the disintegration of traditional religion was almost complete by 1820: Congregationalists were outnumbered 74–16 in Lincoln, 48–11 in Kennebec, and 32–2 in Somerset. Congregationalism had ended its sudden transition from the center of a flourishing traditional culture to a minority religion, surrounded on all sides by vigorous new sectarian competitors.

RELIGIOUS DISSENT AND THE MOVEMENT FOR STATEHOOD

As Ronald Banks has shown, it was in the Kennebec valley and other new settlements that a Democratic-Republican majority first emerged.[41] After 1800, it was this faction, not the Federalists, that finally mounted the successful drive for statehood. Table 7 summarizes the shifting distribution of proseparation sentiment from the old-county Federalists to the Jeffersonians in the new settlements. As the Federalists began to lose their grip on the District, they appealed to traditional social norms and power relationships—including the religious establishment—as the only way to preserve the District from radicalism and chaos.

And radicalism and chaos abounded in the new settlements, especially in the Kennebec valley. There political questions had assumed more than simply ideological significance, because the majority of the new settlers were squatters on the land and enforcement of tradition meant their dispossession. Much of the Kennebec valley was owned by proprietors, many of them wealthy absentees of the Massachusetts Federalist elite, but the valley was settled by Revolutionary War veterans and eastern New England families displaced by the war and an unstable postwar economy. The settlers typically had little means and virtually no money to pay for their land. What they could and did do was to improve their wilderness tracts by clearing, planting, fencing, and building.

The inevitable conflict between owner and squatter ensued, as pro-

TABLE 6
Religious Composition of Maine Counties, 1780–1820

County/Denomination	Number of Churches		
	1780	1800	1820
York			
Congregationalist	14	20	23
Separate Baptist	2	10	19
Freewill Baptist	0	11	14
Methodist	0	0	3
Cumberland			
Congregationalist	14	21	24
Separate Baptist	1	6	12
Freewill Baptist	4	8	12
Methodist	0	3	17
Oxford			
Congregationalist	1	4	11
Separate Baptist	0	7	18
Freewill Baptist	0	2	5
Methodist	0	0	5
Lincoln			
Congregationalist	7	9	16
Separate Baptist	0	10	31
Freewill Baptist	0	10	29
Methodist	0	3	14
Kennebec			
Congregationalist	0	4	11
Separate Baptist	0	3	25
Freewill Baptist	0	4	12
Methodist	0	3	11
Somerset			
Congregationalist	0	1	2
Separate Baptist	0	1	15
Freewill Baptist	0	9	11
Methodist	0	6	6
Hancock			
Congregationalist	0	6	9
Separate Baptist	0	1	21
Freewill Baptist	0	0	0
Methodist	0	0	6
Penobscot			
Congregationalist	0	1	9
Separate Baptist	0	0	9
Freewill Baptist	0	0	4
Methodist	0	0	8
Washington			
Congregationalist	0	1	3
Separate Baptist	0	0	4
Freewill Baptist	0	0	0
Methodist	0	0	3

TABLE 7
Maine Separation Elections by County

County	May 1792		September 1816		July 1819	
	For	Against	For	Against	For	Against
York	202	991	1,788	1,573	2,086	1,646
Cumberland	618	596	2,369	2,148	3,315	1,394
Oxford			1,563	828	1,893	550
Lincoln	1,090	501	1,758	2,357	2,523	1,534
Kennebec			2,646	1,175	3,950	641
Somerset			847	668	1,440	237
Hancock	163	345	447	1,257	820	761
Penobscot			544	200	584	231
Washington	1	91	55	176	480	138
TOTAL	2,074	2,524	12,007	10,382	17,091	7,132

prietors claimed their lands under Massachusetts titles and sheriffs conducted legal evictions of settlers without compensating them for improvements they had made. The squatters resisted with increasing violence and searched for a political strategy that would grant them relief. These militants, along with independent subsistence farmers, formed the permanent electoral base of the Democratic-Republicans in the new settlements. Led by cosmopolitan coastal politicians like William King, they rolled up increasing majorities from 1800 until the War of 1812 crisis and again after 1815. They organized and achieved separation from Massachusetts, and they elected William King (Illus. 50) the first governor of Maine.[42]

Strong geographical and chronological correlations existed, then, between the movement for Maine statehood and the dissenting sects. One further question remains to be treated here: What was the substantive relationship between them? There has been considerable debate in recent years about the relationship of Revolutionary and early national politics to religion, but most scholars have either denied any direct connection or have accepted an indirect influence at best. Several reasons may be cited for these opinions, including a theory that attributes cultural creativity in the Revolutionary period to the political sphere alone, the absence of any convincing evidence of religious-political correlations, and the unfamiliarity of scholars with the teachings of the emerging American religious sects.

Dissenting religion and radical politics, however, coexisted in subsistence farm families everywhere in the Maine hill country. While simple coincidence and mutual action may be enough to explain their gradual combination into a dominating cultural movement, explanations of this sort largely miss an essential element of rural and sectarian culture, namely, its mentality. Much of Rhys Isaac's description of evangelical dissenters in late eighteenth century Virginia also applies to the district of Maine. As Isaac has shown, sectarians in Virginia

Religious Revolution in the District of Maine

50. *William King* (1768–1852), by Gilbert Stuart (1755–1828), 1806. (Oil on canvas. The Maine State Museum)

separated themselves socially, stylistically, religiously, and politically from the authority of the traditional elite. One of the key aspects of their dissent was its expression in public behavior. They withheld deference to the wealthy and powerful, they defied the law of religious establishment and flouted its enforcement, and they wore costumes having no ornaments or excess. They shunned the public society of taverns, balls, trainings, and court sessions, and they denounced worldly corruption in commerce, government, and the established church. They banded together in "gathered churches" made up exclusively of members who had experienced authentic spiritual rebirth as defined by their doctrine. These tightly knit church communities provided a new and vital primary community for their members in contrast to the "fallen" world.[43] In return, sectarians submitted to strict and comprehensive moral discipline from their congregations. All this occurred in Maine—as the example of New Gloucester shows—as well as in Virginia, although a generation later, just as the Virginia case followed the pattern set by Connecticut's Separates in the Great Awakening. Nor should the similarity between Maine and Virginia be surprising in light of the prominence of Separate Baptists and Methodists in both places.[44]

In everyday life, then, Maine sectarians were arrayed against the social and cultural norms of the Federalist elite, both in the District and in the distant capital at Boston. They were also politicized in their struggle against the religious establishment; the great Separate Baptist leader Isaac Backus led an unsuccessful fight for disestablishment and freedom of conscience in Massachusetts from before the Revolution until his death in 1809. The Democratic-Republicans finally gained passage of the Betterment Act of 1808 and the Toleration Act of 1811, measures that permitted exemption of individual dissenters from ministerial taxes even if their sect had not organized an incorporated congregation in town. As an indication of the growing political power of the sects, the Toleration Act passed the Massachusetts General Court because of a four-to-one majority for it among Maine representatives.[45]

One of the most revealing religious-political events of the long separation struggle was William King's campaign against the educational monopoly of Bowdoin College, the intellectual center of Maine Federalism and Congregationalism, of which he had once been an Overseer. From 1816 to 1819 King campaigned for state aid to the new Maine Literary and Theological Institute at Waterville, a venture of the Separate Baptists. King's petitions for equal aid to both schools were defeated by Federalists in the General Court. The last confrontation occurred in March 1819, on the eve of what proved to be the crucial separation plebescite in the District. King's bill was defeated in the state Senate by only two votes, responsibility for which King fixed on Maine Senators Samuel Fessenden and Lathrop Lewis, both of them Federalists, Congregationalists, and unionists.

After the defeat, King published an account of the confrontation in the *Eastern Argus*, quoting Fessenden's opposition speech on the Senate floor: "One college is all that is necessary in the District of Maine, and I have no idea of conveying or giving away any aid to any College whatever, that is to be in the way, or a rival to Brunswick [Bowdoin] College. If the Baptists want a College ... I have no objections ... providing that they can afford it."[46] Fessenden's remarks outraged Waterville's President Jeremiah Chaplin and brought the Separate Baptists solidly into the separation camp in order to save their school. Not surprisingly, they gratefully delivered their votes to King—a liberal Old Light Congregationalist—in the first gubernatorial election in the new state.

THE CONGRUENCE OF SECTARIANISM AND POLITICS

These episodes document the growing alliance between the Democratic-Republicans and the sectarians through the first decades of the nineteenth century. Their alliance could be accounted for simply on the basis of mutual self-interest, but far more was involved. Cosmopolitan Federalists and Congregationalists held fast to the traditional world view and the institutions that maintained it. But as their experience proved, traditionalism could be a serious liability in a democratic revolution. Sectarians and Democratic-Republicans faced the challenge of appropriating the Revolutionary fervor for change while creating new cultural norms for a partly formed society. They succeeded, and in that success they wove strands of theology and political philosophy into a coherent new world view.

In the first volume of his monumental seven-volume work *The Complete Anti-Federalist*, Herbert F. Storing outlines "what the Anti-Federalists were for," a political outlook that continued to inform Democratic-Republicans until after the War of 1812. Storing's presentation emphasizes three central Anti-Federalist affirmations: (1) a conservative impulse to preserve the liberties for which the Revolution was fought; (2) a governmental theory grounded in the necessity of a small republic—that is, the reservation of primary political powers to the states—to guarantee the obedience of the people to laws and legislatures of their own making; and (3) a political philosophy based strictly on popular sovereignty and natural rights that presumed the private virtue and public morality of the individual citizen.[47] From these convictions flowed the Bill of Rights and the Jeffersonian program of minimal government, maximal personal liberty, and direct political control by the yeoman farmer majority.

The new sectarian faiths articulated much the same understandings of self and society in terms of religious culture. Just as Anti-Federalists in Maine challenged the traditional political ideologies of the Federalist elite, so too the radical evangelical sects assaulted the theology and polity of the Congregationalist establishment. The central element of all the sectarian gospels was the radical transformation of the self through the operation of the Holy Spirit. Separate and Freewill Baptists, Methodists and Shakers, Universalists and Christians—all taught that the authentic spiritual experience of the human soul lay in the New Birth. By their definition the New Birth entailed the personal rejection of an individual's former habits and beliefs and the embrace of new ones. This conversionism contrasted sharply with traditional Congregationalisms' containment of personal religious experience—whether Old Light or New Light—within a continuity of fixed behavioral norms and social relationships. Both traditional and sectarian faiths affirmed the Christian claim that the soul's relation to God was the most important human reality. Where they differed was in the understanding of the nature of that reality. For Congregationalism the dynamic of spiritual growth worked within the constraints of tradition; for the radicals, the transformation of New Birth was itself the essence of religious action, overturning the bonds of tradition and launching the self on a lifelong quest for spiritual purity—even perfection—and restless separation from the world.[48]

Radical doctrines of the New Birth led to a series of cultural imperatives that all the sectarians shared to some degree. Most central was the categorical claim that government had no jurisdiction in matters of religious experience. A person's spiritual destiny, they argued, took precedence over any earthly principalities and powers. Hence a person could not tender obedience to a state religion, for to do so would place the person's eternal salvation at risk. In their view the true church of God was comprised exclusively of those who had experienced the authentic New Birth, and that experience was dictated exclusively by the Holy Spirit. Government, no matter how well intentioned, was a human institution subject to the corruptions of the flesh. From these axioms the sectarians drew an uncompromising political program: religious liberty as a fundamental human right and the absolute separation of church and state.[49]

This program, however, was not the only or even the most important political dimension of sectarian religious culture. As dissenters, they faced the problem of creating their own church institutions. It was here in the local congregations that the sectarians gained their primary political experience. These experiments in polity consisted of a variable mixture of local autonomy, individual conscience, charismatic authority, and denominational consensus.

The Baptists—both Separate and Freewill—led the way, insisting on the authority of the local church of gathered saints and stipulating spiritual union as the sure sign of that authority's proper exercise. The Separate Baptists organized regional associations to govern discipline within and among congregations while the Freewill Baptists constructed a system that closely resembled the Quaker system of consensual monthly, quarterly, and yearly meetings. Universalists and Christians also followed the pattern of localism and consensus but permitted a generous amount of doctrinal and moral discipline to be reserved to individual private judgment. Methodists, observing the episcopal government prescribed by John Wesley and the Shakers, constructed perhaps the most innovative polity, combining absolute and centralized charismatic hierarchy with semiautonomous communal settlements. But in Maine, even these latter polities yielded to the realities of physical isolation and locally gathered converts. In all cases these new polities provided the sectarians with alternative models of self-governance, consciously differing from the hierarchic, homogeneous system of Congregationalist parishes.[50]

The sects also occupied a broad theological spectrum ranging from the Whitefieldian Calvinism of the Separate Baptists to the evangelical Arminianism of the Freewill Baptists, Methodists, and Christians to the utopian perfectionism of Shakers and Universalists. The significant divide on this spectrum both theologically and numerically lay between the Separate Baptists and all the other sects. The Separate Baptists were the largest sect and chief Calvinist competitors of the New Light Congregationalists. The New Lights, a still larger but far more diversified group, challenged the liberal theology of Old Light Congregationalists.

Yet as was the case with polity, the cumulative effect of this theological diversity was to supply substantive alternatives to the Congregationalist tradition. The sects occupied the extremes on both sides of the Congregationalist synthesis. Separate Baptists seized on the Calvinist doctrine of predestination and election to proclaim the eternal security of the saved and the unconditional demand to separate from Congregationalism. On the other end of the spectrum the indigenous sects and the Methodists rejected Calvinist determinism and announced the freedom of the human will to accept or reject God's universal offer of salvation in Christ. For these Arminian sects the cosmos was radically free and abounded with opportunity for any human soul to attain not only salvation but also perfection in this life.[51]

From this summary of sectarian ideology it becomes clear that religion was not simply a passive or coincident factor in Maine's development into an autonomous society dominated by Jeffersonian politics. In fact, the religious revolution paralleled the political transformation of the District in terms of time, place and cultural content and impact. The new sectarian movements provided a religious articulation of the emerging rural localist culture simultaneous and fully congruent with its political expression in Jeffersonianism. The sects taught that ultimate human destiny resided in the individual's personal experience of God, not conformity to the traditional means of grace; that the fundamental reality of the self was spiritual transformation and its corallary of radical behavioral change in search of perfection, not slow incremental growth and observance of deferential social norms; and that the ancient Puritan alliance of church and state was corrupt and could be overcome only by the militant separation of true saints into local communities governed solely by their own spiritual consensus and by the political guarantee of religious liberty as a natural right.

Radical change, localism, liberty, inalienable rights, autonomy—these were the cultural imperatives of religious sectarianism, just as they were of political Jeffersonianism. By 1800, the forces of radical religion and radical politics had become merged in the new settlements of rural Maine. Once they matured and united in the struggle for separation from Massachusetts, their alliance proved irresistable and indispensable in creating the new society that was Maine at statehood.

NOTES

1. Rhys Isaac, *The Transformation of Virginia, 1740–1790* (Chapel Hill, N.C.: University of North Carolina Press, 1983); Gordon S. Wood, *The Creation of the American Republic, 1776–1787* (Chapel Hill, N.C.: University of North Carolina Press, 1969); Bernard Bailyn, *The Ideological Origins of the American Revolution*, (Cambridge, Mass.: Harvard University Press, 1967); Alan Heimert, *Religion and the American Mind from the Great Awakening to the Revolution* (Cambridge, Mass.: Harvard University Press, 1966).

2. Moses Greenleaf, *A Survey of the State of Maine* (Portland, Me.: Shirley and Hyde, 1829), pp. 134, 144–150.

3. Jonathan Greenleaf, *Sketches of the Ecclesiastical History of the State of Maine* (Portsmouth, N.H.: Harrison Gray, 1821).

4. Donald Scott, *From Office to Profession: The New England Ministry* (Philadelphia: University of Pennsylvania Press, 1976); Perry Miller, *The New England Mind: The Seventeenth Century* (New York: Macmillan, 1939), and *The New England Mind: From Colony to Province* (Cambridge, Mass.: Harvard University Press, 1953); David D. Hall, *The Faithful Shepherd: The New England Ministry in the Seventeenth Century* (Chapel Hill, N.C.: University of North Carolina Press, 1980).

5. John L. Sibley, *Biographical Sketches of Graduates of Harvard University*, and Clifford K. Shipton, *Biographical Sketches of those who Attended Harvard College*, 17 vols. (Boston: Massachusetts Historical Society, 1873–1975), vol. 14, pp. 590–597 (hereafter *Sibley's Harvard Graduates*); William Willis (ed.), *Journals of the Rev. Thomas Smith and the Rev. Samuel Deane* (Portland, Me.: J. S. Bailey, 1849).

6. *Sibley's Harvard Graduates*, vol. 6, pp. 400–410; Willis (ed.), *Journals of Smith and Deane*.

7. [Iain Murray (ed.)], *George Whitefield's Journals* (London: Banner of Truth Trust, 1960), pp. 516–523; Joseph Tracy, *The Great Awakening* (Boston: Tappan and Dennet, 1842), pp. 300–301.

8. See Stephen Marini, "The Great Awakening," in Charles Lippy and Peter Williams (eds.), *The Encyclopedia of Religion in America* (New York: Charles Scribner's Sons, 1986), and Perry Miller and Alan Heimert (eds.), *The Great Awakening* (Indianapolis: Bobs Merrill, 1967) for general treatments of the Awakening.

9. See Conrad Wright, *The Beginnings of Unitarianism in America* (Boston: Beacon Press, 1955) for the standard account of Old Lights and their New England successors.

10. See Clarence C. Goen, *Revivalism and Separatism in New England, 1740–1800* (New Haven: Yale University Press, 1962), and Richard L. Bushman, *From Puritan to Yankee: Character and Society in Connecticut, 1700–1760* (Cambridge, Mass.: Harvard University Press, 1967) for standard accounts of early Separates. The cosmopolitan-localist distinction appeared first in Robert K. Merton, *Social Theory and Social Structure* (Glencoe, Ill.: Free Press, 1949), pp. 387–420. See also Jackson Turner Main, *The Social Structure of Revolutionary America* (Princeton, N.J.: Princeton University Press, 1965); Thomas Bender, *Community and Social Change in America* (New Brunswick, N.J.: Rutgers University Press, 1978), pp. 15–44. The most comprehensive application to Revolutionary New England is Thomas Szatmary, *Shays' Rebellion* (Amherst, Mass.: University of Massachusetts Press, 1980), pp. 1–18.

11. *Sibley's Harvard Graduates*, vol. 14, pp. 592–593.

12. Samuel Deane, *Sermons to Young Men* (Salem, Mass.: Samuel and Ebenezer Hall, 1774), pp. 4–7, passim.

13. Ibid, pp. 9–10.

14. Wright, *The Beginnings of Unitarianism in America*, pp. 135–137.

15. Samuel Deane, *The New England Farmer: or Georgical Dictionary* (Worcester, Mass.: Isaiah Thomas, 1791).

16. Ibid., pp. 7–8.

17. *Sibley's Harvard Graduates*, vol. 14, p. 596.

18. Ibid.

19. Ronald F. Banks, *Maine Becomes A State: The Movement to Separate Maine from Massachusetts, 1785–1820* (Middletown, Conn.: Wesleyan University Press, 1970), p. 42.

20. *Sibley's Harvard Graduates*, vol. 7, pp. 338–344.

21. Ibid., vol. 14, p. 171.

22. Ibid., pp. 169–170.

23. Ibid., p. 171.

24. Records of the First Congregational Church of North Yarmouth, MS, Yarmouth Historical Society.

25. *Sibley's Harvard Graduates*, vol. 14, p. 172.

26. Ibid., pp. 169–174, passim.

27. Stephen Marini, *Radical Sects of Revolutionary New England* (Cambridge, Mass.: Harvard University Press, 1982), pp. 35–38.

28. Greenleaf, *A Survey of the State of Maine*, pp. 132–140.

29. Marini, *Radical Sects*, pp. 40–59.

30. Isaac Parsons, "Some Account of New Gloucester," *Maine Historical Society Collections* lst ser., 2 (1847), 152–153; Calvin M. Clark, *History of the Congregational Churches in Maine*, 2 vols. (Portland, Me.: Southworth Press, 1926–1935), vol. 2, pp. 112–113; *Sibley's Harvard Graduates*, vol. 13, pp. 410–411.

31. Records of the First Congregational Church of New Gloucester, Me., 1765–1853, MS, pp. 7–9, New Gloucester Historical Society.

32. Henry S. Burrage, *History of the Baptists in Maine* (Portland, Me.: Marks Printing House, 1904), pp. 98–99. See also Reuben A. Guild, *Chaplain Smith and the Baptists* (Philadelphia: American Baptist Publication Society, 1885), and John Peak, *The Memoir of Elder John Peak* (Boston: J. Howe, printer, 1832) for detailed descriptions of Separate Baptist itinerant networks and the impact of believer's baptism. See also C. C. Goen, *Revivalism and Separatism in New England*; William G. McLoughlin, *New England Dissent* (Cambridge, Mass.: Harvard University Press, 1971).

33. Marini, *Radical Sects*, pp. 64–67. See also John Buzzell, *The Life of Elder Benjamin Randal* (Limerick, Me.: Hobbs, Woodman, & Co., 1827), the first biography of the Freewill Baptist founder, and I. D. Stewart, *History of the Freewill Baptists, for Half a Century* (Dover, N.H.: Freewill Baptists Printing Establishment, 1862), still the definitive history of the denomination.

34. Marini, *Radical Sects*, pp. 75–80, 88–96. Standard accounts of Shakerism are Edward Deming Andrews, *The People Called Shakers*, 2nd ed. (New York: Dover, 1963); Marguerite Melcher, *The Shaker Adventure* (Princeton, N.J.: Princeton University Press, 1941).

35. Otis Sawyer, "The Shakers," in W. W. Clayton, *History of Cumberland County, Maine* (Philadelphia: Everts & Peck, 1880), p. 328.

36. Russell E. Miller, *The Larger Hope: The First Century of the Universalist Church in America, 1770–1870*, (Boston: Beacon Press, 1979), pp. 3–49, 649.

37. New Gloucester Book of Records, 1774–1810, MS, New Gloucester Public Library, vol. 1, pp. 101–102, 106, 177–178.

38. Stephen Allen and W. H. Pilsbury, *History of Methodism in Maine* (Augusta, Me.: C. E. Nash, 1887), pp. 14, 66–67; Levisa Buck, *Memoir of Thomas Barnes* (Portland, Me.: Colesworthy, 1856), pp. 51–53; Russell Miller, *The Larger Hope*, pp. 649–650.

39. New Gloucester Book of Records, vol. I, p. 124.

40. See Elias Smith, *The Life, Conversion, Preaching, Travels, and Sufferings of Elias Smith* (Portsmouth, N.H.: Beck and Foster, 1816).

41. Banks, *Maine Becomes A State*, pp. 41–56.

42. Ibid., pp. 116–149.

43. Isaac, *The Transformation of Virginia*, pp. 143–180.

44. Bushman, *From Puritan to Yankee*; Goen, *Revivalism and Separatism in New England*.

45. William G. McLoughlin, *Isaac Backus and the American Pietist Tradition* (Boston: Little, Brown, 1967), and *Isaac Backus on Church, State, and Calvinism: Pamphlets, 1754–1789* (Cambridge, Mass.: Harvard University Press, 1968); Banks, *Maine Becomes A State*, pp. 139–141.

46. Banks, *Maine Becomes A State*, pp. 141–143.

47. Herbert J. Storing, *What The Anti-Federalists Were For* (Chicago: University of Chicago Press, 1981), pp. 7–37.

48. Marini, *Radical Sects*, pp. 11–24.

49. Bushman, *From Puritan to Yankee*, pp. 221–267; Goen, *Revivalism and Separatism*, pp. 148–158.

50. Marini, *Radical Sects*, pp. 116–135.

51. Ibid., pp. 136–155.

Sources for the data in Tables 3, 5, and 6 are: Calvin M. Clark, *History of the Congregational Churches in Maine*; Henry S. Burrage, *History of the Baptists in Maine*; Stephen Allen and W. H. Pilsbury, *History of Methodism in Maine*; I. D. Stewart, *History of the Freewill Baptists for Half A Century*; Jonathan Greenleaf, *Sketches of the Ecclesiastical History of the State of Maine*. Tables 4 and 7 are adapted from Ronald F. Banks, *Maine Becomes A State*, pp. 5, 32, 97.

Joyce Butler

CHAPTER 7

COCHRANISM DELINEATED
A Twentieth-Century Study

Radical challenge to the established church was not confined to the backcountry. In examining the life of Jacob Cochran, Joyce Butler demonstrates that the forces of modernization that were transforming Maine's older coastal communities produced an environment as receptive to religious and social radicalism as the frontier. Many of the substantial residents of the Saco area renounced their orthodox religious heritage to follow the ecstatic—even erotic—preaching of Jacob Cochran, who appeared in their midst in 1816. Butler traces Cochran's theological dependence on contemporary indigenous American sects, such as Shakers and Free Will Baptists, and then suggests his contributions to later utopian movements such as Mormonism and the Oneida community.

On a spring day in the year 1817 Mrs. Betsy Foss stood in the doorway of the Warren Tavern at Salmon Falls in Buxton and looked across the Saco River to the old Hollis Town House on Brigadier Hill, where a huge crowd of people had gathered to hear Jacob Cochran preach.[1] Indeed, so many had come in from outlying areas to hear the eloquent oratory of the evangelist that the town house was not large enough to hold them all, and the meeting was being moved to Captain Gideon Elden's pasture a third of a mile away. Betsy Foss could see the teams and horses of the meeting-goers hitched to fences and trees as far as the eye could see along the Alfred and Union Falls roads, which converged at the foot of Brigadier Hill. From the large, unpainted, dismal-looking town house the people were streaming down the hill, "the whole caboodle of 'em," as Betsy described them years later, "com[ing] down Brigadier hill, with old Cochrane leading 'em, and they were singing and hollering and the women and girls waiving [sic] handkerchiefs and the Lord only knows what all, for I don't."[2]

Betsy Foss had reason to remember that day, for two years later on May 19, 1819, in what must have been one of the most sensational

---

Joyce Butler is a writer on historical subjects and manuscript curator at the Brick Store Museum in Kennebunk.

COCHRANISM DELINEATED;

OR

A DESCRIPTION OF, AND SPECIFIC FOR,

A

RELIGIOUS HYDROPHOBIA,

WHICH HAS SPREAD, AND IS STILL SPREADING,

IN A NUMBER OF TOWNS IN THE

COUNTIES OF

YORK AND CUMBERLAND,

DISTRICT OF MAINE.

BY A WATCHMAN.

For thus hath the Lord said unto me, Go set a watchman; let him declare what he seeth.—PROPHET ISAIAH.

BOSTON:
PRINTED BY HEWS & GOSS.
1819.

51. Title page, *Cochranism Delineated . . .* by a Watchman [Ephraim Stinchfield] (Boston: 1819). (The York Institute Museum, Saco)

trials of the century in York County, Jacob Cochran would be tried and found guilty of the crimes of adultery and "open gross lewdness and lascivious behavior." For these crimes against society he was sentenced to the state prison at Charlestown for four years and eighteen days.[3]

Jacob Cochran made his first appearance in York County in 1816, and from that date to the present his life history and religious career have excited the curiosity of York County residents and Maine historians.[4] Studies of Cochran and Cochranism, the radical religious sect he founded, have surfaced with perhaps predictable regularity; so unusual, fascinating, and titillating a fragment of Maine history has invited reexamination. Although some of these studies were genuine attempts to analyze and understand the phenomena that brought confusion and discord to at least three generations of certain Maine families, most ranged in purpose from vituperative judgment to playful condemnation.[5]

A reevaluation of Cochranism is justified and seems to be called for by current interest in the District of Maine in the years just prior to statehood. What does Cochranism tell us about the religious and social climate in Maine in the Federal period, and how does it fit into the religious history of New England, and indeed America? Answering these questions, as well as examining Cochranism from our twentieth century perspective, is the purpose of this chapter.

Cochranism was part of a mass movement of religious dissent against orthodox Calvinism called the Second Great Awakening, which swept the country early in the nineteenth century. This creative religious ferment drew inspiration from the First Great Awakening of 1740–1770 and the American revivalism it fostered.[6] America's earliest indigenous religious sects, the Freewill Baptists and Universalists, and England's transplanted Shakers all flourished and became established during the Second Great Awakening.[7] A study of the doctrine and practices preached by Jacob Cochran, as they are known, clearly shows that he borrowed freely from the forms of worship of the Shakers and Baptists and drew upon Universalism to develop his own theological response to what was being viewed increasingly in those years as a repressive Calvinism.

Moreover, Cochranism has significant ties to mid-nineteenth century American religious dissent. In the years following Cochran's downfall and death, the form and theology of two of America's most successful Utopian societies, the Mormons and the Oneidan Perfectionists, would closely parallel Cochran's. Of particular interest is the Mormon and Oneidan practice in varying forms of spiritual wifery, the tenet that proved to be Cochran's Achilles' heel, and for which he has been vilified by sanctimonious and gleeful critics for 167 years.[8] Even in its most extreme forms, Cochranism fits into the mainstream of religious dissent in nineteenth-century America.

A unique aspect of Cochranism might seem to be the success of Cochran's ministry in southern Maine's long-settled coastal towns. Generally, historians associate the sectarian impulse with frontier communities where social and cultural instability led to "an incessant demand for new religious forms."[9] However, rapid economic change in a traditional society, as well as the development of an "exuberant democratic national character," are also recognized as catalysts for sectarianism.[10] All three forces—the frontier experience, rapid economic change, and manifestations of democratic thinking—were at work in the communities where Cochran achieved his greatest success. Following the Revolution a surge in population and rapid economic growth in the District of Maine had created a frontier climate in established coastal towns. The immigrants who flooded into Maine from southern New England came infused with a hunger for new freedoms and new beginnings. Thus even in "old" towns, Jacob Cochran found potential converts.

Most of those who are at all familiar with Cochranism have gotten their information from Gideon T. Ridlon's "The Cochran Delusion" in his 1895 tome, *Saco Valley Settlements*.[11] Ridlon, a native of the Saco valley, which was the center of Jacob Cochran's ministry and witnessed his greatest success, was a minister whose account of Cochranism perpetuated the emotional condemnation of its earlier nineteenth century critics. Ridlon's account, abstracted here and liberally sprinkled with his hyperbole, provides a useful way of presenting that historical view, as well as contrasting it to a more reasoned twentieth century analysis of Cochranism.

Ridlon stated correctly that Jacob Cochran, the son of a prosperous farmer and his wife, was born in Enfield, New Hampshire, on July 9, 1782.[12] Although uncertain of Cochran's early education, Ridlon credits him with being a schoolteacher whose disgust with the "religious societies known as 'the standing order' " led him to begin preaching his own brand of religion. It was a "somewhat chaotic and remarkably elastic" doctrine, in substance the same as Universalism, yet mixed with a "primitive kind of spiritualism and free love, upon which he had engrafted many of the ceremonies practiced by the Shakers," as well as the "forms of the primitive Freewill Baptists." Ridlon presents Cochran as a man of extraordinary "intellectual, mesmeric and physical powers" with, moreover, some kind of "occult power" that influenced his hearers: a calculating man whose musical voice, "eye of penetrating fire," and graceful agility caused conservative, "resolute" men to "surrender unconditionally" to his dictates. As for women, even those who had been reared in the most "puritanical" homes and were "models of virtuous propriety" were so caught up in the "delusive spell woven about them by the mesmeric power of Cochran, [that they] renounced . . . their former principles and habits of rectitude, and with unblushing boldness" followed his teaching.

Cochranism Delineated

Cochran's earliest doctrines were "in harmony" with those of the "orthodox" churches, and therefore unremarkable, but once he had "secured a firm foot-hold in the community" he began to preach a more radical theology. In response, "settled pastors" closed their churches against him, so that Cochran was obliged to preach in "schoolhouses, dwellings, and barns." The most objectionable part of his doctrine was his opposition to "the legal marriage bond." Those who were married were to be prepared to renounce their vows and to take spiritual—that is, divinely designated—consorts. "All revelations to this end were to come through Cochran, of course, and in the allotment of the spoils the leader ... was ... to get the 'lion's share.' Tradition assumes," wrote Ridlon, "that [Cochran] received frequent consignments, ... and that such were invariably the most robust and attractive women in the community."

Ridlon had little information about just when Cochran came into the Saco valley, but he correctly placed his "principal stronghold, and the hot-bed of his delusion" in North Saco and the town of Buxton. Here "the Cochranites fairly reveled in the enthusiasm of their mock worship and disgraceful practices." The Cochranites' meetings and their "disgraceful practices," although not their theology, were of great interest to Ridlon, and his account is filled with numerous colorful anecdotes. Two are worth repeating. It was customary for the Cochranites in their meetings to illustrate scriptural incidents with tableaux. One of the favorite reenactments was the Garden of Eden with "the ideal Adam, in the person of Cochran, and Eve, in the person of some chosen female," appearing as they would have "before fig-leaf aprons were in fashion." Following one such reenactment, Cochran was warned by Saco's authorities that the "most severe penalty of the law would be visited upon him" if such conduct was repeated. Thereafter, the performers appeared in "costumes of ample dimensions."

The other anecdote concerns the Cochranites' proclivity to "swoon away" during meetings, which were marked by the "lively singing" of "rollicking" songs, "attended with clapping of hands and dancing." While "absent from the body" these elect would receive "marvelous revelations" which they would share with the others upon their return from "the realms of the spirit." On one occasion in Saco "a certain sister, named Mercy, who was a maiden of great personal beauty, sank down upon the floor.... and failing to come back ... to relate her experiences..." was put to bed. The next night the Cochranites gathered at the same house and were allowed to view the eighteen-year-old girl where she lay on her bed "dressed in a long, white night-robe. Her classic features were as white and rigid as ... marble, and her profusion of dark hair [spread] over the snow-white pillow. Her eyes were nearly closed and the long, silken lashes lay upon her cheek. There was no movement or change of expression observable as the long line of spectators silently filed through the room to gaze upon her saintly face and graceful form. About the bed her relatives stood weeping." These relatives importuned "Brother Jacob" to return Mercy to them, whereupon he announced solemnly that she was not able to return from the realms of the spirit without assistance. Then "passing his magic hand across her fair brow [he] said: 'Mercy arise.' In a twinkling she sprang from the bed with a scream and swept through the congregation."

The "resurrection ... caused great commotion in the community, and public rage became menacing," resulting in a "moral cyclone." Ridlon paints a dire picture of ensuing events: a vigilante committee, whose meetings were infiltrated by Cochranite spies; secret gatherings of the Cochranites, to which they traveled by circuitous routes in the dark of night in order to escape detection by their enemies; and finally Cochran's arrest "after a desperate struggle." Ridlon was not sure whether Cochran was locked up in the state prison or whether he escaped on the way to prison and fled to New Hampshire. He *was* sure that after Cochran's death his body was brought back to Saco for burial "at night, near one of his [disciples'] dwellings" or "under the cemented floor of a cellar" somewhere in the North Saco-Lower Buxton district.

Ridlon explained that the source of his information about Cochranism was "venerable persons, of unimpaired mental faculties, who had listened to the preaching and witnessed the peculiar practices of Jacob Cochran." Ridlon was careful to point out, however, that he did not quote from "a bundle of yellow documents," which were in the hands of "a magistrate who lived in Buxton at the time these things occurred, [because] some of [the] affidavits [were] too sensational and personal." Ridlon concluded, "I have not torn the veil asunder from the top to the bottom, by any means, and have left out enough of tradition and documentary evidence, relating to this remarkable delusion, to fill a volume." Indeed he did!

Because of the nature of Jacob Cochran's alleged crimes, and the response they elicited from his contemporary critics, it is difficult to discover the truth about his career in southern Maine between 1816 and 1819. Almost without exception, nineteenth century accounts of Cochranism are marred by sanctimonious prejudice and a reliance upon oral history that is more gossip than history and from which the names of actual participants were often withheld in order to protect their descendants from old family scandals.[13] Particular and important details concerning the sect's sexual practices were also suppressed as too sensational for publication. As Cochran's most thorough chronicler wrote, "the most objectionable features" were "eliminated and trimmed."[14]

More seriously, primary documentary evidence is fragmentary. The "bundle of yellow documents" referred to by Ridlon was probably a collection of court depositions taken in February 1819, when Cochran appeared before Justice Daniel Granger who found probable guilt and bound him over to the May term of the Supreme Judicial Court at

York. These depositions, which are missing from the collection of other documents from that preliminary trial now in the State Archives, were described as "obscene, disgusting, scandalous" by Ephraim Stinchfield, a Freewill Baptist minister from New Gloucester. Stinchfield undertook a personal crusade against Cochran, which included publishing *Cochranism Delineated*, a pamphlet describing Cochranism as a "religious hydrophobia" and Jacob Cochran as "one of the most scandalous frauds ever imposed on any people under the name of religion."[15]

Also lost, or at least not yet rediscovered, are a diary kept by Moses McDaniel of Hollis, one of Cochran's missionary disciples, letters of followers, and a few letters written by Cochran himself. These were in the hands of Joel M. Marshall of Buxton, who wrote a carefully researched series of articles about Cochranism that were published in the *Biddeford Daily Journal* and the *Biddeford Weekly Journal* between 1893 and 1896.[16]

An important source of facts about Cochran and Cochranism should be the records of his trial before the Supreme Judicial Court; however, those records do not include a transcript of the actual proceedings.[17] A transcript *was* taken and published by an interested bystander, Gamaliel E. Smith of Newfield, and it is an invaluable source. Regrettably, however, the pamphlet that Smith published is only an abstract of the trial.[18] But perhaps the most serious stumbling block to a full analysis of Cochranism is the absence of any written record or explanation of his theology by Cochran himself.

Despite these handicaps, it is possible to present a fairly complete picture of this fascinating religious teacher and his sect. Accounts of Jacob Cochran invariably describe him as a fine-looking man, something above the ordinary, whose physical appearance attracted much attention. An eyewitness to Cochran's activities, writing in 1839, described him as "preposessing" in his person, "somewhat above the middle stature" with a "florid complexion, light hair, high forehead, a singular dark and penetrating eye, with a wen or protuberance on the fore part of his head, in a line with his right eye."[19] Prison records reveal that in actuality Cochran was five-feet ten-inches tall, with black eyes, brown hair, and a sandy complexion.[20]

The details of Cochran's history before his appearance in York County are unclear. Most observers found him "well-educated for his day," although there is no indication that his formal schooling went beyond a "common-school" education.[21] He was generally recognized as highly intelligent, with a considerable knowledge of history and reading.[22] Ridlon claimed that Cochran was "well read in law."[23] In 1805 at Enfield he married Abigail Colcord Stephenson, and by 1816 they had three children: Rachel, Helen, and John.[24] Cochran was said to have been a schoolteacher and to have served with the Army as a sutler during the War of 1812.[25] Neither of these claims can be documented. Probably the contention of Daniel Remich, a Kennebunk historian, that by 1815 Cochran "had lived several years in Fryeburg, where he kept a small stock of goods, chiefly groceries, and was very fairly patronized" is accurate.[26]

Remich was the only historian who wrote with certainty about Cochran's place of residence and occupation before his appearance in York County as a religious teacher. He was also the only one to profess knowledge of how Cochran began his religious career. Remich describes in some detail an incident that occurred in Cochran's Fryeburg store on a "dull afternoon." In a playful confrontation Cochran inadvertently "put to sleep" (hypnotized) a man who had come into the store with some friends to pass the time of day. The "experiment" was repeated successfully over the next several days, leading Cochran to believe that "he had been endowed with supernatural power ... that could not be otherwise interpreted than as a call to preach."[27] The precise nature of Cochran's "power" remains uncertain. What is certain is that coupling it with his ready wit, shrewd understanding of human nature, fine singing voice, physical grace, and exceptional speaking ability, Jacob Cochran was able to effect the most successful and memorable religious revival ever to sweep southern Maine.[28]

When Cochran made his appearance in York County in the spring of 1816, a revival was underway within Maine's New Light churches.[29] Cochran, in the tested tradition of revivalist preachers,[30] took part in the revival under the aegis of Gorham's newly ordained Clement Phinney and other Freewill Baptist ministers.[31] He was so successful that it appears in retrospect there was general uncertainty as to whether he had been a follower in or the catalyst of the revival.[32] In time this uncertainty would harden into a firm belief that Cochran had deviously presented himself as a Freewill Baptist in order to gain acceptance with the full intention of leading people away into his own "ministry of iniquity."[33]

Historians have looked for an explanation for the revival. Joel M. Marshall described 1816 as "a dismal year." The weather was "cold and backward" with a black frost every month,[34] and in the aftermath of the War of 1812, which ended in 1815, "business was dull, money was scarce, our shipping [was nearly paralyzed and our] prostrated commerce [had resulted in widespread unemployment and] left our credit to the mercy of other nations."[35] It has been noted that "many people [seek] God more earnestly in adversity than in prosperity,"[36] but that is a simplistic explanation for southern Maine's revival of 1816. There were more diverse forces involved.

Dissent against the Calvinist preachings of the orthodox church was raging in New England, particularly in the hill country and on the frontiers.[37] In the District of Maine religious dissent was not confined to frontier communities. Even in long-established coastal communities, such as Saco, whose first year-round settlement occurred in 1614, the old ways were being questioned. An influx of settlers eager to begin a new life had created social and cultural instability much like that of a frontier community. The newcomers, many of whom were veterans of the Revolutionary War, had come not only looking for a fresh economic start but also with a firm belief in themselves as rightful heirs to whatever position and privilege they could garner. Out of the Revolution had come a yearning for new freedoms, and many people were no longer willing to leave religious, political, and economic decisions to the favored few—New England's merchant aristocracy and their Harvard-educated clergymen. This attitude, coupled with the religious credulity of the times, made people receptive to new religious thought and eager for a prophet to lead them.[38] In southern Maine Jacob Cochran was to be their prophet.

And there was a place for him. In most of the communities where Cochran gained large numbers of converts, there was weakness or dissension in the organized churches. In North Saco the Baptists were split; both the Calvinist and Freewill Baptists had built their own small churches.[39] The Baptist ministry was further weakened by the divisive influence of the Christian Society. This offshoot of the Freewill Baptist faith had been successfully founded in Maine by Elias Smith and was being carried on by a new, younger group of ministers, including Mark Fernald and Peter Young.[40]

Vacant pulpits were another problem. In Arundel (Kennebunkport) the decision of the Baptist minister, Andrew Sherburne, to emigrate west left his congregation without a minister. His parishioners, anxious to fill the pulpit of the small church that had been built only after a great struggle against the orthodox clergy, were eager to accept the preaching of whomever would come. Jacob Cochran filled that void with great success.[41]

Even within the orthodox churches there were problems beyond basic doctrinal dissatisfaction that left room for a new voice to be heard. In Kennebunk (then part of Wells) a dispute between the Reverend Jonathan Greenleaf and the Reverend Nathaniel Fletcher may have contributed to Cochran's success in that town. Without doubt the extreme age of Buxton's Paul Coffin was influential in the decision of so many from his church to follow the new prophet.[42]

Pressing in upon this theological disarray were the people who truly were seeking new ways and new answers. The diary of Benjamin Simpson, one of Cochran's Saco converts, illustrates clearly the search that many followed for their faith.[43] From 1781 until the spring of 1817, when Simpson began to attend Cochran's meetings, the pages of the diary reflect a pattern of wide participation in church services. Simpson, who lived in North Saco on what is now called Simpson Road, attended services at the Congregational Church in Saco village and Baptist services in North Saco. He also went to Congregational and Baptist services in Buxton. It was not unusual for him to attend a Congregational service in the morning and a Baptist service in the afternoon. He traveled to church in neighboring Scarborough as well as throughout the nearby countryside to hear any exhorter who came to preach in a schoolhouse or in a private home. Among these was a Methodist circuit rider, a black man from Portland, the Christian Society evangelist Elias Smith, and a woman. On at least one occasion he went to Alfred to a Shaker meeting. It seems that no new church was dedicated and no minister ordained or dismissed without Benjamin Simpson being in attendance. He was a church man; the affairs of the church—any church—were his business.

But in thirty-seven years of diary notations about his church attendance, he does not comment once on the quality of a service. Then on April 20, 1818, after a meeting at which the wife of a neighbor was baptized by Jacob Cochran, Simpson wrote in his diary, "a powerful meeting." Two days later his own wife began a month-long travail of emotional and mental derangement marked by praying and trances. After a week of observing her and a day in which Mrs. Simpson revived enough to sing hymns and "praise the Lord," Simpson wrote, "I trust I felt some of the love of God to my soul, bless the Lord for it." On Saturday May 23, Mrs. Simpson, the Simpsons' son George, and others were baptized by Jacob Cochran. On June 28, another son, Ebenezer Simpson, after "a powerful and happy meeting" was "brought to Praise the Lord." On July 12, Simpson wrote, "Sunday to meeting at McKenneys barn, then to Benja[men] Haines barn to Commemmorate the death & sufferings of the Lord Jesus then went into the watter with five others and Baptized by Jacob Cockran." Simpson was sixty-three years old.

Benjamin Simpson was without doubt one of the "resolute" North Saco men whose conversion to Cochranism puzzled Cochran's critics. He was a native of York and a Revolutionary War veteran who had taken part in the Boston Tea Party and had served at Valley Forge. He was a prosperous farmer and bricklayer and a member of the First Baptist Society of Buxton. Simpson was a respected citizen of Saco who had served his town as surveyor of highways, hog reeve, and tax collector, and the county as a grand juror.[44] He was also a staunch Cochranite, or to use the name Cochran gave his sect, a member of the "Society of Free Brethren and Sisters."[45]

Cochran preached freedom from all organized churches, their ministerial hierarchies, and theological restraints. He called for a return to the apostolic church, advocating rebaptism to cleanse his followers of sectarianism. Cochran's 1839 chronicler provided a list of his basic beliefs along with biblical citations.[46] Reference to these and a careful reading of the New Testament, particularly the Acts and Letters of the Apostles, provide a general knowledge of the doctrine of the Society of Free Brethren and Sisters. Here we can only briefly summarize the results of such a study. In his early ministry Cochran preached one God and one Mediator to whom repentance was due, faith in the Lord Jesus Christ and baptism by immersion in his name, and Christian perfection. His doctrines became more radical as he gained converts. From the epistles of Paul, Cochran culled and preached the possibility of baptism by the Holy Ghost and fire, spiritual healing and the working of miracles, communal living, and spiritual wifery. With his followers he observed both Holy Communion and a Passover feast.[47]

In their worship services the Cochranites practiced "holy marches," lively dancing and singing, and exercises of reaping and winnowing that resembled the worship exercises of the Shakers. Without doubt this reflected Cochran's exposure to Shaker forms of worship in his hometown of Enfield, New Hampshire, site of one of the most successful Shaker communities. Like the Freewill Baptists, the Cochranites practiced the ancient biblical custom of footwashing. When Cochran preached, sometimes standing upon a table in order to be seen by all in the crowded room, his enthusiasm evoked applause and shouts of "Amen" and "Glory to God."[48] Listeners sometimes fell into trances from which they brought back visions of the spirit world. One Cochranite reported, "I saw my Jesus; O, I saw my Jesus; ... I saw heaven, I saw my Jesus there and ... my grandmother ... I saw my father and mother almost into hell.... I saw P.D. enter the kingdom of heaven. I saw I.C. almost to hell. O, what a dreadful place hell is...."[49] Shouting, groaning, weeping, clapping, something called the "holy roll," and whirling and dancing that participants often took to the nearby streets accompanied these revelations.[50]

To those outside the Society, these manifestations of religious hysteria were considered sinful excesses, but actually they were in the best tradition of radical evangelism and revivalism.[51] More to the point, in them lay the appeal of Cochranism. His eloquent oratory, the joyous singing, the dancing, even the physical excesses were a relief after "the solemn psalm tunes and hymns, the pausing and hanging on the parts in slow long metre" and all the other "rigid discipline" connected at that time with accepted religious observance.[52]

Peter Young, who became an itinerant minister of the Christian Society, in describing his own conversion from Congregationalism, wrote of the Baptist elders who inspired him, "But oh! How different was the preaching of those unlearned and despised preachers, from the letter-learned and world-applauded rabbis! These only made sounds of words in the ears and did not reach the heart.... But those despised ones spoke as men having authority from heaven...."[53] The appeal of Jacob Cochran was greater even than that of the Baptist preachers who before his arrival had seemed to speak with supreme authority from heaven. To quote one historian, Cochran's "commanding presence, his pleasing manners, his dark penetrating eyes, his fluent tongue and copious language, his melodious voice, his familiarity with the scripture and his untramelled interpretation of its text, his intense earnestness ... all ... engineered by a superb masculine vigor, made him a dreaded rival."[54]

Cochran weaned men and women of all ages and levels of society away from the organized churches by the hundreds. Estimates of the number of his converts range from 1,000 to 4,000. Cochran claimed to have 2,000 followers. This claim seems possible when we read that his disciple, Moses McDaniel, recorded that at one meeting "about 500 went forward to [the Lord's] supper."[55] It is not surprising that the 1818 minutes of the Cumberland Baptist Association reported, "The state of religion in our churches, is not so lively as it was last year."[56] Many Baptists, like North Saco's Benjamin Simpson, had turned aside to follow Jacob Cochran. Indeed, it was with the leaders of the *dissenting* churches that he competed most strongly for converts.

By late 1817, the Baptists were sufficiently alarmed by the "Cochrane spirit" to form a vigilance mission to crusade against what they considered Cochran's "heresy." Chief among these guardians of the public morals was Ephraim Stinchfield of New Gloucester. Stories of Cochran's denial of legal marriage vows, of the Garden of Eden tableau, of secret late night meetings for the select few at which there was free exchange of sexual partners, and of the pairing of fathers with stepdaughters and neighbor with neighbor as spiritual consorts, provided the ministers with just cause for their crusade. But not until the social leaders of Saco and Biddeford went after Cochran was he brought down.

Whereas the Baptist ministers had confronted Cochran himself and gone among the people warning them of their danger, Saco's Dr. Richard Cutts Shannon and Ichabod Jordan of Biddeford filed legal complaints against Cochran, which led to his arrest and a preliminary trial before Saco's Justice of the Peace Daniel Granger on February 18–19, 1819. Ichabod Jordan and his brother Rishworth, who would assist in the actual arrest of Cochran, were members of one of Saco/Biddeford's most prestigious families. Jordans had been landowners, town officials, magistrates, and Congregationalists in the two towns for generations.[57] Dr. Shannon, Harvard-educated and a deacon of the First Church, was Saco's principal physician.[58]

It may have been Cochran's supposed attack on Freemasonry (which he would have seen as just another form of sectarianism) that stirred them.[59] Years later Cochran would claim that it was "through the influence of Masons" that he was imprisoned.[60] Some said it was the involvement with the Cochranites of a daughter of one of Saco's leading families that moved them to action. This probably was Mary King, daughter of the Honorable Cyrus King, former Congressman of the District of Maine.[61] (There is, in turn, reason to believe Mary King may be the "Sister Mercy" described by Ridlon.)[62]

The appeal of Cochran and his theology for women is another aspect of Cochranism that deserves lengthy examination. Here we can only refer those who are interested in this aspect of his ministry to Whitney Cross's *The Burned-Over District*. Cross states that owing in part to the socially limited and unexciting lives of women, they "comprise the great majority of members in all churches [and] dominated revivals and praying circles, pressing husbands, fathers, and sons toward conversion...."[63] Cochran's appeal to women had long concerned his critics. The prevailing opinion of men of that time was that women were more credulous and sentimental than men and also needed to be protected from their own sexuality.[64] There are many recorded instances of the ready response of women to Cochran's teachings. Benjamin Simpson is but one example of a "resolute" North Saco farmer who was led to Cochran by his wife.[65] Yet at the same time Cochran was noted for the number of men he converted, rivaling the great revivalist George Whitefield.[66]

Cochran was brought to trial at the May term of the Supreme Judicial Court of Massachusetts at York, Maine, on five indictments for adultery and varying forms of "gross and lascivious behavior" with five different women. Mary King and Eunice and Abigail Bond, all young, single women from Saco, were the chief witnesses against him.[67] The courtroom was crowded with men who had left their spring planting to hear the testimony of the women which was "given in most expressive and unmistakable terms."[68] Cochran, who pleaded not guilty, was defended by two of York county's most prestigious lawyers, George Wallingford of Kennebunk and John Holmes of Alfred.[69]

Cochran's trial on the first indictment—"Going to bed with Eliza Hill and Sally Dennet for 1 hour on December 25, 1818"—ended in a hung jury. The following day he was tried for "lying in bed with Abigail Clark, a married woman, and committing adultery, lewdness, etc., with said Abigail Clark on the 6th and 10th day of July [1818]." He was found guilty despite John Holmes's contention that the testimony against him was inconclusive and that Cochran was really being tried for his religious beliefs. Said Holmes, "If the testimony of a people is to be measured by their religious tenets, I know no bounds to the evil."[70] Years later a fair-minded historian would write, "[Cochran] was tried on assumptions."[71] Smith's abstract of the trial does not present conclusive evidence of guilt. Cochran's greatest proven crime seems to have been lying beside Nabby Clark in his "linen."

Cochran did not wait to be sentenced. When he was called to the bar for sentencing he was not to be found. Throughout the spring and summer, sheriffs and constables would search York county for him. In late October he was arrested at the home of John Berry in North Saco and taken to the county jail at Alfred. On November 2, 1819, he was "brought to the bar" at Alfred and sentenced to eighteen days in solitary confinement and four years at hard labor at the state prison in Charlestown.[72]

Joel Marshall, who made such a complete study of Cochranism in the 1890s, questioned the severity of that sentence, calling it "disproportionate" to the crime.[73] From our twentieth century perspective it does seem so. But in the nineteenth century Cochran's espousal of spiritual wifery was a heinous crime against society.[74] As the Reverend Amasa Loring explained in his polemic against Cochranism, marriage was the "divine [institution] given in Eden [to guard] the most precious social enjoyments [and to] defy barbarism, ignorance, heathenism, and lust."[75]

Jacob Cochran served his sentence to the day despite efforts by his friends to secure his early release. Petitions to the Governor of Massachusetts and his Council were filed by York County residents, Cochran's old neighbors in Enfield, New Hampshire, and his wife. Cochran himself petitioned regularly for release from prison, citing the need to support his family, which now included four children.[76]

His life following his release from prison is shadowy and—like the rest of his history—has been the subject of lurid and exaggerated stories. Briefly, the facts are the following. In 1824 he visited James Remich in Kennebunk and tried without success to convince Remich to release the copyright on Gamaliel Smith's report of the trial in order that he might write his autobiography. Subsequently, he is known to have been in Hamburg, New York, attempting to gain converts, and to have gathered followers in South Hadley, Massachusetts, and Stratham, New Hampshire.[77] He died in Stratham on March 5, 1836.[78] His body was brought back to North Saco where it was buried on the John Dennet farm. A few years later it was disinterred and moved to an unknown site in Enfield.[79]

But the story of Cochranism does not end with Jacob Cochran's death. Although most of the supposed 2,000 followers he converted turned to other faiths where they were numbered among the "most valuable members," a dedicated nucleus remembered his teachings.[80] Some of them had turned to Mormonism even before Cochran's death. Mormon missionaries came into Maine in 1832 and 1833 and "brought in a harvest" of converts in the towns where Cochran had been active.[81] As many of Cochran's converts had been Smithites (converts of Elias Smith),[82] so too many of southern Maine's converts to Mormonism had first been Cochranites. As Ridlon expressed it, "Jake Cochran was a John the Baptist for the Mormon's apostles" and "a full-blooded Cochranite made a first-class Mormon."[83]

Much has been made by historians, including Ridlon, of the appeal of the Mormon faith to the Cochranites,[84] but even a cursory study of the history of the Mormon church indicates that Cochran's Free Brethren and Sisters may have made significant contributions to that society. The practice of polygamy, for which the Mormons are known, grew out of an earlier form of spiritual wifery. Louis J. Kern, whose book *An Ordered Love* is a detailed study of sex roles and sexuality in Victorian utopias, wrote that "Mormon social life in the 1830s was characterized by a practice akin to spiritual wifery."[85] Kern further states that "the system of polygamy as it evolved in its early years at Nauvoo ... seems to have been little more than an institutionalized spiritual wifery."[86]

There is evidence that Cochranites may have brought other practices to the Mormons. For example, Kern notes that one early Mormon ceremony of initiation involved "a re-enactment of the Edenic temptation in which those who portray Adam and Eve wear very little clothing."[87]

The teachings and practices of the Cochranites parallel those of another of America's early utopian societies, John Humphrey Noyes's Perfectionists, whose community flourished at Oneida, New York, from 1848 to 1879. The parallels of the Oneidan Perfectionists to Cochran's Society of Free Brethren and Sisters are startling. Noyes rejected organized churches as "in opposition to the everlasting gospel." Like Cochran, he called for a return to the primitive, apostolic church as preached by Paul. The Oneidans were a communal society whose members practiced spiritual healing as well as "complex marriage," a form of spiritual wifery. There are many other minor and detailed similarities between the two societies.

Indeed, there are enough similarities between Cochran and Noyes and their societies that we must ask: Did the two men find their ways independently, or did Cochran influence Noyes, either through his missionary disciples or through direct confrontation?[88] The latter is possible. We know that Cochran was in Hamburg, New York, in 1829 because of the existence of a letter from the Hamburg selectmen to the selectmen of Saco asking for information about his character. "Said Cochran," wrote the Hamburg selectmen, "is now residing in this town and is trying to Establish a Religious Society.... He has produced some considerable excitement in this Vicinity."[89] Noyes's search for his faith took him into upstate New York, as well as to parts of New England, where he might have met or been exposed to the charismatic preaching of Jacob Cochran. However, for the purposes of this chapter it is enough to point out the similarities between the Cochranites and Oneidans. The larger and more intriguing question of influence must await further study.

If we cannot answer many questions about Jacob Cochran's history, his motives as a religious teacher, his theology, the closing years of his life, and his influence on the Mormons and Oneidans, we can state with certainty that he was a significant, not just a colorful, figure. Jacob Cochran and his Society were more than an aberration, more than a bizarre religious manifestation that happened to appear in southern Maine, as their nineteenth century critics have led us to believe. They represent in microcosm all the forces at work in the creative religious ferment of Federal-period New England, and closely parallel later religious developments in America. Moreover, to examine Cochranism from our twentieth century perspective is to gain important insight not only into the religious but also into the social and cultural climate in the District of Maine as it moved toward statehood.

NOTES

1. Primary documents and historical accounts of the career of Jacob Cochran spell his name variously as "Cochran" and "Cochrane." Cochran himself spelled his name without the

"e." See Commonwealth of Massachusetts, Governor's Council, Pardons Rejected, [1819–1822], Petition for Pardon to His Excellency John Brooks, Governor of the Commonwealth of Massachusetts and Honorable Council, October 8, 1821, Archives of the Commonwealth, Boston (hereafter MaSA).

2. Joel M. Marshall, "Cochrane's Craze," *Biddeford Daily Journal*, February 14, 1895.

3. York County Supreme Judicial Court, Proceedings and Judgments, 1819, Commonwealth vs. Cochran, Archives of the State of Maine, Augusta (hereafter MeSA).

4. As with most aspects of Cochran's life, published accounts differ as to when he came into York County. Correlation of all available data indicates that he probably made his first appearance in southern Maine in the spring of 1816 as stated in Joel M. Marshall, "First of a Series: Full and Accurate History of Cochranism," *Biddeford Daily Journal*, December 22, 1893.

5. Honest attempts to explain and understand Cochranism were "Jacob Cochran. Reminisces," written by "An Eye Witness" and published in the Freewill Baptist newspaper *Morning Star*, July 7, 1839; Daniel Remich, "Cochranism," *History of Kennebunk* (Kennebunk, Me.: no publisher, 1911), pp. 268–278; a series of articles written by Joel M. Marshall of Buxton, which were published in the *Biddeford Daily Journal* and *Biddeford Weekly Journal* between 1893 and 1896. The "Cochran Fanaticism in York County," an 1867 paper reprinted in the *Maine Historical Society Quarterly* 19 (Summer 1980), 23–39, which was probably written by the Reverend Amasa Loring and read by his son, Lincoln Loring, to a meeting of the Maine Historical Society in 1892 (see *Biddeford Weekly Journal*, December 16, 1892), is typical of the harsh and abusive commentary on Cochran produced by a number of nineteenth century ministers. Cochran's most recent chronicler, Bill Caldwell, in his *Rivers of Fortune* (Portland, Me.: Guy Gannett Publishing Company, 1983), dismisses Cochranism as a "delightfully scandalous, religious sect" that engaged in "wife swapping."

6. For a more detailed discussion of the Great Awakening and the Second Great Awakening, see Harvey Wish, *Society and Thought in Early America*, 2 vols. (New York: Longmans, Green and Co., 1955), vol. 1; Stephen A. Marini, *Radical Sects of Revolutionary New England* (Cambridge, Mass.: Harvard University Press, 1982).

7. Marini, *Radical Sects*, pp. 1–7.

8. Lawrence Foster, *Religion and Sexuality: Three American Communal Experiments of the Nineteenth Century* (New York: Oxford University Press, 1981), p. 131, explains that in the nineteenth century "spiritual wifery" was a "pejorative generic term [used to refer to] marital experimentation..., a catchall suggesting rationalized infidelity."

9. Marini, *Radical Sects*, p. 2.

10. Ibid.

11. Gideon T. Ridlon, *Saco Valley Settlements* (Portland, Me.: The Author, 1895), pp. 269–280.

12. Ridlon's information concerning Cochran's birth and parentage agrees with that of Joel M. Marshall in his essay "Cochrane's Power," *Biddeford Daily Journal*, December 28, 1893. In 1983 Jeanette Haarala, Town Historian of Enfield, New Hampshire, also stated that Jacob Cochran was born in Enfield July 9, 1782, to Jacob and Rachel (Webster) Cochran. It should be noted that Haarala's information did not come from town records, which were destroyed in 1850, but from genealogy gathered "from local cemeteries by an interested person." It should also be noted that the register of Cochran's committal to prison in November 1819 gives his age as 38, which would indicate a birth date of 1781. See Commonwealth of Massachusetts, State Prison at Charlestown, "Entries of Convicts [1819]," MaSA. A further search for accurate documentation is obviously needed.

13. Accounts qualifying to a degree as exceptions are Joel M. Marshall's series, and Witness, "Jacob Cochran." In "Two Strange Gods," *Biddeford Daily Journal*, October 12, 1892, an unknown writer tells of an instance in which Cochran is supposed to have informed a follower that by divine revelation he is to exchange his wife for Cochran's. The follower is described as "one of [Cochran's] firm disciples, whose descendants still live in North Saco, and who would not... relish seeing their ancestor's weaknesses in print."

14. Joel M. Marshall, "In State Prison," *Biddeford Daily Journal*, March 13, 1896.

15. A Watchman [Ephraim Stinchfield], *Cochranism Delineated*, 2d ed. (Boston: N. Coverly, 1819), p. 19.

16. Marshall quoted extensively from the journal and letters in his "In State Prison." See also Marshall's letter dated November 22, 1910, which appeared in the *Portland Argus*. Argus Scrapbook, 1:40, Maine Historical Society (hereafter MeHS).

17. York County Supreme Judical Court Records, 1819, MeSA. This collection includes a ledger of "Proceedings and Judgments" and assorted loose documents (indictments, warrants, etc.) for Cochran's preliminary trial in February, as well as his final trial in May.

18. Gamaliel E. Smith, *Report of The Trial of Jacob Cochran* (Kennebunk, Me.: James K. Remich, 1819).

19. Witness, "Jacob Cochran."
20. "Entries of Convicts, [1819]."
21. "Two Strange Gods," and Ridlon, *Saco Valley Settlements*, 269.
22. Witness, "Jacob Cochran."
23. Ridlon, *Saco Valley Settlements*, p. 273.
24. Joel M. Marshall, "Cochrane's Arrest," *Biddeford Daily Journal*, January 31, 1896.
25. Ridlon's contention that Cochran was a teacher is supported by Marshall. For Cochran's military service, see Loring, "Cochran Fanaticism," p. 23, and Marshall, "First." Although no documentary evidence could be found in the National Archives, Washington, D.C., Cochran's statement, "I have traveled in ten states...," as reported in D. M. Graham, "Cochran and Cochranism," *The Life of Clement Phinney* (Dover, N.H.: William Burr Printer, 1851), p. 81, might lend support to the claim for his military service. In 1888 the granddaughter of Cochran's brother Robert denied that Cochran had ever been a teacher or in the Army (see Marshall, "Cochrane's Power"); however, another letter from her to Stephen Mayberry of Cape Elizabeth, dated March 18, 1886, Mayberry Papers, Miscellaneous Box 21, Folder 11, MeHS, contains so much misinformation that she cannot be wholly relied upon as an accurate source.
26. Remich, *History*, p. 268. Remich must have gotten much of his information from his father James, who witnessed Cochran's activities in York County and printed Gamaliel Smith's report of the trial. The fullness of Remich's reporting of events in Fryeburg before Cochran came to York County and his evident acquaintance with Cochran's Fryeburg landlady (see pp. 268–270), also lend credence to his reliability.
27. Ibid.
28. Harrison Otis Smith, "Cochrane-ites," *Ossipee Valley News*, January 1, 1883, describes Cochran as "a man of ready wit and much shrewdness, a fine singer, an elegant dancer, a ready speaker, the compass of his voice [ranging] from the coo of a dove to the roar of a lion...." Loring, "Cochran Fanaticism," p. 26, names Cochran's "attractions as a public speaker... his unparalleled, artful cunning and deep penetration into human nature." Marshall, "Cochrane's Power," describes Cochran's "oratory [to be] conceded by all to be brilliant and sometimes very eloquent." In "Two Strange Gods," Cochran is said to have been "credited with having preached the most remarkable and effective sermons ever heard in his generation." Even setting such hyperbole aside, it is clear that Cochran was a remarkably effective speaker.
29. For an explanation of New Light revivalists see Wish, *Society and Thought*, vol. 1, p. 158, and Whitney R. Cross, *The Burned-Over District*, 2d ed. (New York: Harper & Row, 1965), p. 7. For a full discussion of the evolution of the "New Light Stir," see Marini, *Radical Sects*, pp. 40–59. For more details concerning the revival in southern Maine, see G. A. Burgess and J. T. Ward, *Free Baptist Cyclopedia* (no location: Free Baptist Cyclopedia Company, 1889), p. 357.
30. Marini, *Radical Sects*, p. 83.
31. For a brief history of Clement Phinney's entry into the ministry, see Burgess and Ward, *Cyclopedia*, p. 528. For a description of Cochran's deference to Phinney, see Graham, *Life of Clement Phinney*, p. 81.
32. Witness, "Jacob Cochran."
33. Stinchfield, *Cochranism Delineated*, pp. 7, 9.
34. Joel M. Marshall, "The Cochrane Craze," *Biddeford Daily Journal*, January 10, 1894. See also Benjamin Simpson, Diary, 1781–1849, Dyer Library, Saco, Maine.
35. Marshall, "The Cochrane Craze."
36. Cross, *Burned-Over District*, p. 143.
37. Marini, *Radical Sects*, p. 63.
38. Whitney Cross, analyzing the initial success of the Mormon prophet, Joseph Smith, wrote that "The fundamental condition leading to the new faith was the credulity and spiritual yearning [of the times] which made people anxious to follow a prophet, whoever he might be." Cross, *Burned-Over District*, p. 143.
39. George Folsom, *History of Saco and Biddeford* (Somersworth, N.H.: New Hampshire Publishing Co., reprint of 1830 ed., 1975), pp. 296–297.
40. For a brief history of the Christian Society, see Jonathan Greenleaf, *Sketches of The Ecclesiastical History of The State of Maine* (Portsmouth, N.H.: Harrison Gray, 1811), pp. 292–293. See also Peter Young, *Brief Account of The Life and Experiences of Peter Young* (Portsmouth, N.H.: Beck and Foster, 1817); Mark Fernald, *Life of Elder Mark Fernald* (Newburyport, Mass.: George Moore Payne and D. P. Pike, 1852).
41. For the history of Andrew Sherburne and the struggle of Arundel Baptists against the orthodox church, see Andrew Sherburne, *Memoirs of Andrew Sherburne* (Utica, N.Y.: William Williams, 1828); Joyce Butler, "Andrew Sherburne," *Kennebunkport Scrapbook* (Kennebunk, Me.: Thomas Murphy, 1977), vol. 1, pp. 17–21. In his *Cochranism Delineated*, Ephraim Stinchfield reported a visit to a "considerable society" of Cochranites in Arundel.

42. When Paul Coffin died on June 6, 1821 he was eighty-four. See "Memoir of Rev. Paul Coffin, D.D.," *Collections of the Maine Historical Society*, 1st ser., 4 (1856), 256–257. It is significant that in 1817 Levi Loring of Saco was ordained and appointed Associate Minister by the Buxton Church. See Cyrus Woodman (ed.), *The Records of The Church of Christ in Buxton, Maine* (Cambridge, Mass.: Privately published, 1868), pp. 81–86.

43. The same pattern of varied churchgoing evident in Simpson's diary can be seen in the 1828–1865 diary of Tobias Walker of Kennebunk, MeHS.

44. For Simpson's Revolutionary War service, see Folsom, *History*, p. 287, and Joyce Butler, "Arundel and The War For Independence," *Kennebunkport Scrapbook* (Kennebunk, Me.: Thomas Murphy, 1977), vol. 1, p. 82. For his civil service and occupation, see his diary and "Records of The Town of Saco, 1807–1830," Dyer Library, Saco, Maine.

45. Remich, *History*, p. 274. Affidavits of church membership in the tax records of Saco call the society "The Free Brethren."

46. The "Eye Witness" who wrote about Jacob Cochran in 1839 gave the following biblical references for his doctrines: Acts 2:33, 4:32–37, 8:10, 19:1–6; Matthew 3:11 and 26:19–26; and Revelations 18:4.

47. Ibid.

48. Edward E. Bourne, *History of Wells and Kennebunk* (Portland, Me.: B. Thurston and Company, 1875), p. 634.

49. Joel M. Marshall, "Cochranism," *Biddeford Daily Journal*, March 13, 1892.

50. For descriptions of Cochranite meetings, see Marshall, "Cochrane's Power" and "Cochranism;" Remich, *History*, p. 271; Stinchfield, *Cochranism Delineated*, pp. 4, 6. For footwashing by the Baptists, see Marini, *Radical Sects*, p. 105.

51. Wish, *Society and Thought*, vol. 1, p. 249; Cross, *Burned-Over District*, pp. 173–184; Charles Nordhoff, *The Communistic Societies of The United States* (New York: Dover Publications, reprint of 1875 ed., 1966), p. 131.

52. Marshall, "Cochrane's Power." See also Marshall, "The Cochrane Craze" for a long description of the "rigid discipline connected with ... religious observance."

53. Young, *Brief Account*, p. 13.

54. Joel M. Marshall, "Jacob Cochrane," *Biddeford Daily Journal*, January 16, 1895.

55. For estimates of the size of the Society, see Stephen Mayberry writing about Cochran in the *Saco Union and Journal*, January 5, 1882; Witness, "Jacob Cochran." For Cochran's estimate of the size of his sect, see Stinchfield, *Cochranism Delineated*, p. 13. For the quotation from Moses McDaniel's journal, see Marshall, "Cochrane's Craze."

56. *Minutes of The Cumberland Baptist Association, 1818* (Hallowell, Me.: S. K. Gilman, 1818), p. 11.

57. Tristram Frost Jordan, *The Jordan Memorial* (Boston: David Clapp and Son, 1833).

58. Folsom, *History*, p. 304.

59. Loring, "Cochran Fanaticism," p. 29. Loring contended that Cochran "assailed the institution of Freemasonry with unsparing severity."

60. Letter to the Selectmen of Saco from the Selectmen of Hamburg, New York, July 8, 1829, Dyer Library, Saco, Me.

61. Genealogy of the King Family of Saco, Collection No. 296, Box 4, Folder 16, MeHS.

62. This is only a guess based on the similarity in names and ages of the two young women in court testimony during the summer of 1818. Mary King was attended by Cochran as her doctor, a role he evidently filled for his followers. See Smith, *Report* p. 80.

63. Cross, *Burned-Over District*, pp. 87–89, 177–178.

64. For a complete discussion of this viewpoint, see Louis J. Kern, *An Ordered Love* (Chapel Hill, N.C.: University of North Carolina Press, 1981), pp. 52–60; Cross, *Burned-Over District*, p. 178.

65. John Dennet of Saco, who was not a Cochranite although his wife was, is another example. After Cochran's death, Dennet provided a burial site for him on his farm, and after the removal of Cochran's body to Enfield, N.H., his stone was recut and placed on the grave of Dennet's wife, Sarah, by their son Jacob, who had been named for the prophet. See "More About Cochran," *Biddeford Daily Journal*, October 19, 1892.

66. Marshall, "Jacob Cochrane."

67. Smith, *Report*, and Supreme Judicial Court, Records, 1819.

68. Marshall, "Cochrane's Arrest." Benjamin Simpson's son Ebenezer was among them. See Simpson, Diary, May 21, 1819.

69. For biographies of Wallingford and Holmes, see William Willis, *A History of The Law, The Courts and The Lawyers of Maine* (Portland, Me.: Baily and Noyes, 1863), pp. 252–255, 275–289. Holmes would go on to serve as Maine's first congressman from the new state of Maine.

70. Smith, *Report*, p. 32.

71. Mayberry Papers, MeHS, quoted from an unknown source.

72. Joel M. Marshall, "Bolted from Court," *Biddeford Daily Journal*, February 2, 1896, and Supreme Judicial Court, Records, 1819.

73. Joel M. Marshall, "End of Cochrane," *Biddeford Daily Journal*, November 18, 1896.

74. No firm documentation for Cochran preaching and practicing spiritual wifery has been found, but the weight of secondary evidence seems to leave little doubt that in some form it was part of his teaching and a practice of the Cochranites.

75. Loring, "Cochran Fanaticism," pp. 29–30.

76. Commonwealth of Massachusetts, Governor's Council, Petitions to His Excellency and The Honorable Council of The Commonwealth of Massachusetts, November 20 and 25, 1820; January 8, September 20, and October 8, 1821; January 18, 1822, MaSA. Cochran's second son and fourth child, Edwin, was born March 6, 1819 in Saco. See Simpson, Diary; Marshall, "Arrest," and the Mayberry Papers.

77. Remich, *History*, pp. 274–276; Letter to the Selectmen of Saco....

78. Bureau of Vital Records and Health Statistics, State of New Hampshire, Concord, N.H.

79. Marshall, "End." Today the site of Cochran's grave in Enfield is not known. Jeanette Haarala, the town's historian, in correspondence with Joyce Butler in the spring of 1983, stated that "Jacob Cochran is not buried in Enfield." That he is seems certain, as his birthdate in the town's records was supposedly taken from his gravestone in one of the town's cemeteries. See note 5, above.

80. Witness, "Jacob Cochran."

81. Steward Holbrook, *The Yankee Exodus* (New York: Macmillan, 1950), p. 52.

82. Remich, *History*, p. 276.

83. Ridlon, *Saco Valley Settlements*, p. 281.

84. "Two Strange Gods."

85. Kern, *An Ordered Love*, pp. 158–159.

86. Ibid., p. 142. Apostates from Mormonism referred to the practice of polygamy as "the spiritual wife system." See Foster, *Religion and Sexuality*, pp. 181, 317–318, 159 n.

87. Kern, *An Ordered Love*, p. 55.

88. Joseph Decker of Hollis was one of Cochran's more notable missionaries. See Ridlon, *Saco Valley Settlements*, p. 279. Called "The Massachusetts Prophet," he left his family and became a wandering preacher. See Martin H. Jewett and Olive H. Hannaford, *A History of Hollis, Maine* (Farmington, Me.: Knowlton and McLeary, 1976), p. 41.

89. Letter to the Selectmen of Saco....

Laurel Thatcher Ulrich

CHAPTER 8

MARTHA MOORE BALLARD AND THE MEDICAL CHALLENGE TO MIDWIFERY

Politics, economics, and religion occasioned frequent crises of authority in post-Revolutionary Maine. Another great potential for conflict arose in the practice of obstetrics. Here the tension was between midwives, who derived their knowledge and skills from years of experience and tradition, and the new professionally trained physicians. The potential for conflict is especially interesting to modern historians sensitive to the gender distinctions implied in the terms "physician" and "midwife." Through a close study of the diary of Martha Moore Ballard, a midwife of Hallowell, Laurel Ulrich discovered that the tension between physicians and midwives in that frontier setting was subtle, and outright conflict remarkable for its absence. Although male physicians were attending births in rural Maine as early as 1785 and beginning to challenge the traditional role of midwife, doctors and midwives seem to have co-existed peacefully and cooperatively. Physicians around Hallowell were not yet so arrogant, nor their patients so confident of modern science, as to exclude the services of an experienced, determined midwife. Ulrich's study, therefore, suggests that differing sources of authority, even when sharpened by gender, did not always lead to a crisis or a conflict in this period. Instead there was involved here, if only temporarily, a blending of the learned and practical traditions.

Some time in the afternoon or evening of October 9, 1794, David Sewall of Hallowell sent word to Martha Ballard that his wife was "unwell." There was nothing unusual in the call or in the casual entry in Mrs. Ballard's diary, "I was there all night." In her sixteen years as a midwife, Martha Ballard had lost many nights' sleep attending a woman in labor. This birth would be unusual, however. On October 10, in Mrs. Sewall's chamber, a minor drama in the history of American midwifery unfolded. "They were intimidated," wrote Mrs. Ballard, "& Calld Dr. Page who gave my patient 20 drops of

Laurel Thatcher Ulrich is assistant professor of history at the University of New Hampshire.

52. Medicine chest and bottles, 1790–1810, owned by Dr. Samuel Nye (1777–1826) of Saco. (The York Institute Museum, Saco)

Laudanum which put her into such a stupor her pains (which were regular & promising) in a manner stopt till near night when she pukt & they returned & shee was delivered at 7 hour Evening of a son her first Born."[1]

The three elements in this story—the patient's "intimidation," the doctor's employment of laudanum, and the midwife's annoyance—fit perfectly into the larger history of childbearing in late eighteenth century America. Recent studies have concluded that the transition from traditional midwifery to medical obstetrics began in the northern United States between 1760 and 1820 and that it was a consequence both of new medical technology and of changes in the attitudes of women. Midwives had always been taught to call doctors in medical emergencies, but beginning in the 1760s in urban centers like Philadelphia, New York, and Boston, doctors trained in Edinburgh and London began officiating at normal births, employing forceps to hasten delivery and administering opiates to relieve pain. "By the second decade of the nineteenth century," Jane Donegan has concluded, "northern urban women of means, convinced that the superior training of doctors equipped with instruments meant safer and shorter parturition, hardly ever employed a midwife."[2]

Although traditional midwifery would persist among immigrants and in isolated rural communities to the end of the nineteenth century, the physicians who founded America's first medical societies and colleges were successful in associating medical delivery with scientific progress. By 1820, an influential Boston physician could pronounce the exclusion of women from the practice of obstetrics one of "the first and happiest fruits of improved medical education in America." He argued that a revival of female practice would threaten the safety of Boston's women. "Heretofore, where midwifery has been in the hands of women they have practiced among the poorer and lower classes," he wrote, "the richer and better informed preferring to employ physicians."[3]

Women's historians have argued that male doctors promoted "science" at serious cost to women. Midwives were not only deprived of their occupation but were also shut out of the new medical education. Childbearing women were also hurt as birth became a medical event to be managed by interventionist attendants. Giving up the comforting circle of female support, mothers faced an increasing threat of infection and the possibility of overdoses of anesthesia or damage from forceps, as medical education failed to keep pace with the expansion of the profession. "Only after 1940," Judith Walzer Leavitt has argued, "did medicine begin to achieve a record of safety commensurate with the promises it had held out to women centuries earlier."[4]

Martha Ballard's account of Hannah Sewall's delivery seems to summarize, then, the key themes in the transformation of childbirth in the late eighteenth century: A traditional midwife patiently waiting for the operations of nature was upstaged by an interventionist physician whose opiates promised a frightened young woman relief from pain. A closer look at the participants in this drama reinforces that impression. At 59, Martha Ballard came to Mrs. Sewall's chamber with the authority of her own motherhood as well as with the specialized skills she had acquired in her sixteen years as a midwife. Benjamin Page, on the other hand, was barely 24, still unmarried, fresh from his apprenticeship with Dr. Thomas Kittredge of Andover, Massachusetts. Yet he brought the promise of the new "scientific" obstetrics. In Dr. Kittredge's library he had probably read the works of Dr. William Smellie, the British physician who popularized the new medical obstetrics. Under Kittredge's supervision he may have used the improved forceps Smellie designed.[5]

Hannah Sewall, too, fits the model. Though only 20, she might well have classified herself among the "richer and better informed" of Hallowell women. Married less than a year, she had come to the Kennebec valley from the coastal town of York where her father, Nathaniel Barrell, and her grandfather, Jonathan Sayward, were prominent merchants. Her older sister, Sally (later known as "Madame Wood"), became Maine's first novelist. Although another sister, Ruth, the wife of Moses Sewall of Hallowell, had already delivered four children with the assistance of Martha Ballard, Hannah may have come to the town sympathetic to doctors if not already predisposed toward medical delivery. Another sister, Olive, had recently married Dr. Samuel Emerson of Kennebunk; her younger brother later married the daughter of

Dr. Job Lyman, whose obstetrical forceps are now owned by the Old York Historical Society.⁶

All the elements characterizing the transition to medical obstetrics seem to have been in place by 1794 on the Maine frontier. Yet Hannah Sewall's delivery was only one among 48 that Martha Ballard performed in that year, and only one of the 797 deliveries she recorded in her diary between January 1785 and May 1812.⁷ Seen in this context, Dr. Page's intrusion was a minor annoyance, a bungling effort set right by nature. There was no question in Martha Ballard's mind that she knew more about delivering babies than Ben Page, whom she once described as "that poor unfortunate man in the practice."⁸ Her practice was increasing, not decreasing, in 1794. Only after 1800, when age and frequent illness undermined her strength and when a move to a new farm took her farther away from the river and from major roads, did she sharply curtail her practice.

Martha Ballard's diary gives us a surer sense of the differences between "male" and "female" obstetrics than earlier studies based largely on prescriptive literature and on the lives of medical leaders. In late eighteenth century Hallowell, doctors were not as scientific or midwives as ignorant as older accounts would suggest, nor was there as much friction between the two specialties as more recent literature might lead us to believe. For the most part, medical obstetrics and midwifery coexisted peacefully. Yet there were important differences between men and women practitioners. That doctors were both better paid and less experienced than midwives created a troublesome discrepancy between the promise and the practice of the new medical obstetrics. Ironically, it was not "science" that undermined traditional midwifery but a new appreciation by doctors of the "ordinary" births that had long been managed by women.

Born in Oxford, Massachusetts, in 1735, Martha Moore Ballard emigrated to the Kennebec River country in 1777 with her husband, Ephraim, and five children. The Ballards spent the rest of their lives in Maine, living in four different locations in what would later be the towns of Hallowell and Augusta. Ephraim Ballard was a miller and surveyor. Although by no means a wealthy man, he was a respected citizen who served for a time as selectman of Hallowell.⁹ Martha Ballard was a dutiful and productive housewife, who raised pigs and poultry, cultivated a large garden, and produced both woolen and linen cloth in addition to practicing midwifery and physic. There is no indication that she had anything more than a primary education, though her younger brother, Jonathan, graduated from Harvard College in 1761 and eventually became the minister of the First Church of Rochester, Massachusetts.¹⁰ She later noted that she delivered her first baby in 1778, just after coming to Maine. Although she may have kept some sort of record of deliveries from that point on, her diary begins in 1785, the year she turned fifty. It closes in May 1812, a month before her death at the age of 77.¹¹

53. *View of AUGUSTA County of KENNEBEC in the State of Main,* ca. 1825. Artist unknown.
(Watercolor. The Colby College Museum of Art)

The focus of this chapter is on the first fifteen years of the diary, 1785–1800, the period of Martha Ballard's most active years as a midwife. In 1785, Hallowell was still a frontier town, but it was growing rapidly. In 1797, the section of the town near Fort Western separated from Hallowell, becoming the town of Augusta. The population of Hallowell had been 1,199 in 1790; by 1800, the combined population of the two towns was 2,680.[12]

The categories *doctor* and *midwife* inadequately describe the diversity of medical practice in this eighteenth century town. Hallowell's "doctors" ranged from the eminently visible Dr. Daniel Cony, Justice of the Peace, Representative to the General Court, and founding President of the Kennebec Medical Association, to the anonymous "negro woman doctor" who appears two or three times in the diary. Not until after 1796, when Benjamin Vaughan arrived in Hallowell with an M.D. from Edinburgh, did the area have a college-trained physician.[13] Although most male physicians had served apprenticeships, it would be a serious mistake to read back into this period twentieth century notions of "medical science."

Doctor Cony, for example, had trained with Dr. Samuel Curtis of

Marlborough, Massachusetts, a Harvard graduate, who later practiced in New Hampshire where he published "A Valuable Collection of Recipes" that included, in addition to homespun medical remedies, formulas for removing grease spots, bedbugs, and fleas, and for bleaching straw, mending china, and making red hair black.[14] His work is a striking example of the practicality and disdain for theory that characterized New England medicine, even of the "professional" variety, in the late eighteenth century.[15] In his *American Medical Biography*, published in 1828, Thomas Thacher praised Benjamin Page for his treatment of spotted fever between 1810 and 1816 and acknowledged the "Moral rectitude and public virtue" of Daniel Cony, but he concluded that the District of Maine "possessed little claim to the merit of contributing to the improvement of medical science." Clearly, though there were the beginnings of medical organization in Hallowell before 1800 (Dr. Cony was a member of the Massachusetts Medical Society as early as 1787), there was very little "science," even by contemporary standards.[16]

It is equally inappropriate to distinguish between midwives and doctors, as some writers do, by saying that one group has been concerned with a natural process (birth) and the other with a medical event (illness). Like most early American midwives, Martha Ballard not only delivered babies but also treated the sick.[17] She seems to have specialized in diseases of women and children, though she also treated grown men, especially those suffering from burns, rashes, or frostbite. Mrs. Ballard's patients came to her house seeking salves, pills, syrups, ointments, or simply advice. Forty to seventy times a year she went to them, spending a few hours or several days administering "clisters" (enemas), dressing burns, or bathing inflamed throats. She did not pull teeth, set bones, or let blood (though once she drew blood from a cat and applied it to a man who was suffering from shingles). She cut infant tongues, lanced abscessed breasts, and composed remedies for intestinal worms and the itch. She also dressed and laid out the dead. Martha Ballard was both a midwife and a doctor; significantly, her most frequent term for labor was "illness."[18]

The diary mentions six women—Mrs. Fletcher, Mrs. Hinkley, Mrs. Ingraham, Mrs. Clark, Mrs. Cox, and Mrs. Winslow—often enough or in such a context as to suggest that they also were midwives. Whether they practiced physic is difficult to say, although it is perfectly clear that several local physicians practiced obstetrics. Doctors Cony, Williams, and Hubbard, who were working in Hallowell or nearby towns by 1785, performed deliveries. In fact, Dr. Cony's only known literary contribution to the Massachusetts Medical Society, a one-page paper submitted in 1787, described "a circumstance which I had never before met with" in a delivery that he himself had performed in August of that year. Dr. Page, who arrived in Hallowell in 1791, and Dr. Parker of Pittston, who appears in the diary at about the same time,

IX. *The Signals at Portland Lighthouse,* by Lemuel Moody (1761–1846), 1807. (Watercolor. The Maine Historical Society)

x. Montpelier wallpapers: *a.* "Festoon" border. *b.* Detail of "Festoon" border applied over yellow ground paper. *c.* Mica paper. *d.* Fruit paper. *e.* Chinoiserie (Montpelier, Bureau of Parks and Recreation, Maine Department of Conservation).
f. Lozenge paper.
(Courtesy of The Society for the Preservation of New England Antiquities)

d.

e.

f.

XI. *The Latter Harvest,* by Jonathan Fisher (1768–1847), 1804.
(Oil on canvas. The William A. Farnsworth Library and Museum, Rockland)

xii. *Four Birds,* by Jonathan Fisher, 1820.
(Oil on canvas. The Jonathan Fisher Memorial, Blue Hill)

XIII. *A Morning View of Blue Hill Village,* by Jonathan Fisher, 1824.
(Oil on canvas. The William A. Farnsworth Art Museum and Library, Rockland)

XIV. *Francis O. Watts With Bird,* by John Brewster, Jr. (1766–1854), 1805.
(Oil on canvas. The New York State Historical Association, Cooperstown)

xv. *The Old State House, Augusta,* by Charles Codman (ca. 1800–1842), 1836.
(Oil on canvas. The Maine State Museum)

also delivered babies. Dr. Samuel Colman did not, nor did Dr. Steven Barton of Vassalboro, Martha Ballard's brother-in-law.[19]

Yet Martha Ballard's diary demonstrates that relations between midwives and physicians were more cooperative than competitive. Mrs. Ballard delivered Dr. Colman's children and even attended the doctor himself during an illness; she borrowed medicines from Daniel Cony and he from her; and on various occasions she summoned Drs. Hubbard, Williams, and Cony to her own patients. For the most part, her remedies seem to have been compatible with theirs. When her daughter, Hannah, became delirious about ten days after delivering, Mrs. Ballard sent for Dr. Cony, who simply, as she said, "approved of what I had done—advised me to continue my medisin till it had opperation."[20] In general, her records support the conclusion of Richard Brown that "learned" and "folk" medicine in Massachusetts "were part of the same medical spectrum and overlapped considerably."[21]

After three men were injured when a fieldpiece misfired during militia training on May 31, 1792, Mrs. Ballard was summoned to bathe and dress the burns. Although Doctor Colman also attended the men during the next few days, it was Martha Ballard who "made an ointment" and applied it to Samuel Johnson's "soars" on June 2.[22] Some of the services Mrs. Ballard performed for the sick might today be defined as nursing, but in very few cases does she seem to have operated under a doctor's direction. She prepared her own medicines and apparently determined the best method of treatment. Furthermore, there are many references in the diary to "nurses," or specialists who seem to have been younger than midwives. Martha Ballard usually left her own patients about two hours after delivery in the care of an "after nurse."[23]

In addition to their joint commitment to what Martha Ballard would have called "pukes" and "purges," doctors and midwives had something else in common: the part-time nature of their work. As housewives, the midwives had heavy burdens at home including responsibilities for gardening, food processing, and animal care, but the doctors also divided their interests, none so strikingly as Dr. Steven Barton, who was a carpenter as well as a physician. In June 1774, for example, he charged Jonathan Ballard for "Visits & attendance" to his sick child and then for making a coffin.[24] Daniel Cony, Hallowell's most distinguished physician, was a judge, politician, agriculturist, and land speculator. His varied interests were typical of gentlemen physicians of the period. In 1808 he apologized to the President of the Massachusetts Medical Society for failing to convene a group of doctors in the District of Maine, explaining that "The dispersed situation of your Committee joined with their various avocations has prevented a meeting."[25]

Nor did Hallowell's practitioners claim a certain set of patients as their own. In troublesome cases, nearly everyone with any expertise—

and some without—offered advice. When Martha Ballard's niece, Parthena Pitts, was suffering from a prolonged illness, she got up one morning about an hour after sunrise, as her aunt reported it, and "went out & milkt the last milk from the Cow into her mouth & swallowed it." This peculiar remedy had been "recommended as very Beneficial by Mr. Amos Page."[26] An eighteenth century patient might summon more than one doctor or midwife at once and then employ whomever she chose. Mrs. Parker did not think it amiss to borrow Mrs. Ballard's horse "to go and see the negro woman doctor." Nor did a sense of loyalty to Dr. Colman, who had earlier treated him, prevent Calvin Edson from summoning Dr. Williams as well, or from applying to Martha Ballard for salve.[27] Some of this overlapping may have originated with the healers themselves—one practitioner might understandably consult with another—but even allowing for that, the territorial boundaries seem to have been very loose.

Perhaps the best evidence of Martha Ballard's cooperative relationship with male doctors is her attendance at autopsies. She observed at least three "dissections" between 1794 and 1801, carefully recording the results in her diary. Although none of these cases was obstetrical, two of the subjects were women and the third a small child. At Nabby Andrews' autopsy in September of 1800, Mrs. Ballard reported that twelve doctors and three midwives were present, though she did not give names.[28] That the women were there at all argues that medical practice in frontier Maine was still relatively open; neither professional exclusiveness nor womanly delicacy barred Hallowell's midwives from what was after all an important educational experience. That they were outnumbered four to one by male doctors testifies to the localized nature of their specialty as much as to their minority position in the medical world. The twelve doctors had no doubt gathered from miles around.

Thus Martha Ballard's diary modifies the picture of late eighteenth century midwifery presented in secondary accounts. In Hallowell, relations between doctors and midwives were less antagonistic and the two specialties less separate than we might have supposed. What, then, of the encounter between Martha Ballard and Benjamin Page at the delivery of Hannah Sewall?

Though the Sewall incident was atypical, it does suggest broader differences between men and women practitioners during this period. Recall that in 1794, Benjamin Page was 24 years old, unmarried, fresh from his apprenticeship with Dr. Kittredge of Andover, Massachusetts. Martha Ballard was 59, a mother and grandmother many times over, and at the height of her obstetrical career. The contrast, though stark, was repeated in important ways in the medical community as a whole. Where midwives in eighteenth century Hallowell claimed the authority of experience, physicians carried the aura of learning; where midwives depended on the support of a local community of women, doctors affiliated with a wider society of professionals; where midwives

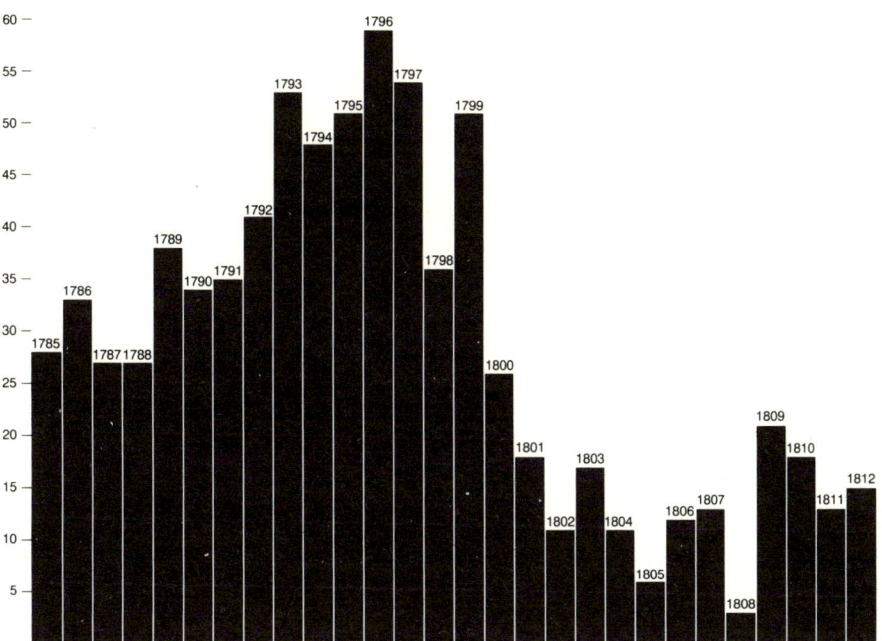

CHART 1. Martha Ballard's Obstetrical Practice (1785–1812)—Number of Deliveries.

primarily turned to their own gardens and kitchens for remedies, doctors had recourse to instruments and to imported drugs with Latin designations.

We must not assume, however, that the practical training of midwives was necessarily less effective or their local reputations less powerful than the learning or the professional affiliations of the physicians. Martha Ballard's diary gives striking evidence to the contrary. By the time of her death in 1812, she had performed 981 deliveries, 797 of which are listed in the diary. The habit of counting deliveries seems to have been common to midwives. In June 1790, Mrs. James Marsh from nearby Vassalboro, called on Martha Moore Ballard. "The Old Lady informs me Shee has extracted 756 children in the coars of her practice," Mrs. Ballard wrote in her diary.[29] Martha Ballard's statistical habit makes it relatively easy to reconstruct her thirty-five-year career. Retrospective entries show that she delivered about thirty babies a year between 1778 and 1785. Chart 1 shows yearly totals for the years 1785–1812. Note the expansion in her career between 1792 and 1800, the very years during which Benjamin Page was attempting to establish his practice.

At the end of the last entry for 1789, Martha Ballard tabulated total Hallowell births and deaths for the years 1785–1790. Although she does not give the source of these figures, they allow us to estimate the scope of her practice in relation to that of her competitors. If we assume that all the births recorded in the diary occurred in Hallowell unless marked otherwise, Mrs. Ballard delivered 64 percent of the babies born in the town during this six-year period.[30] There is no reason to suggest that her share of Hallowell births for the next ten years was any less. Had a single practitioner delivered the 36 percent of Hallowell babies not accounted for in her records, Martha Ballard's eminence would still be unquestionable, yet these births were divided among five physicians and at least six other midwives, as the diary clearly shows.

Many of Martha Ballard's references to her competitors appear as "news" entries in her diary, that is, bits of information received by hearsay. After her daily entry for July 19, 1787, for instance, she turned her page perpendicularly and wrote: "Mrs. Church was dilivered of a son last Tusday marn at 1 Clock & 20 m Doct Coney operator." Below that she added, "Jerymy Baddoks wife the same Night of a dafter, old Mrs. Fletcher performed the ofice of a midwife for her." Other entries come from more direct experience, as on April 26, 1785, when she wrote, "I was Calld at 2 O'Clok to Nathan Tylors wife in Travil found her delivrd of a Dafter Doct Williams operator." Apparently some women, afraid of being caught without any help at all, called more than one attendant.

In 32 of the 481 births to which Martha Ballard was called between 1785 and 1796, some other person performed the delivery, usually because she did not arrive in time. In twelve cases the other attendant was a midwife, in four a physician; in the remaining sixteen, the identity of the assistant is not given. This set of cases may give us a rough estimate of the proportion of deliveries performed by physicians in the period. If we apply the same ratio to all Hallowell births, we might conclude that doctors performed 9 percent of the deliveries in the town and other midwives the remaining 27 percent. Of course, it is entirely possible that those families who did not summon Mrs. Ballard may have called a physician more frequently than those who did summon her. Still, by any numerical measurement, midwifery prevailed over medical delivery in late eighteenth century Hallowell.

Yet the seemingly casual appearances of Drs. Cony, Williams, Parker, and Hubbard at the bedsides of Hallowell women, like the more dramatic incursion of Benjamin Page, undermined a traditional distribution of responsibility. Midwives had always been taught to summon a doctor in an emergency. Dismembering a dead fetus was a necessary skill for a surgeon; knowing when to let blood or to prescribe drugs was a proper role for a physician. In normal deliveries, the quite different talents of a midwife were enough.[31] That even a few Hallowell families could summon *both* a doctor and a midwife to a *normal* delivery, employing whichever attendant arrived first, suggests a remarkable change.

We must consider here the different backgrounds of doctors and midwives. Although medical reformers lamented the haphazard training of New England physicians, most male doctors could make some small claim to "learning." At the least they had mastered prescribed texts and spent a year or two as an apprentice. Dr. Page had attended Phillips-Exeter Academy before apprenticing with Dr. Thomas Kittredge. A hundred years earlier, of course, a literary education would have been enough; many New England ministers doubled as physicians.[32]

For midwives, giving birth themselves was an essential part of the training process; assisting at other women's deliveries was another. A traditional midwife was simply the most skilled member of an assemblage of female neighbors who assisted at each birth. After one delivery, for example, Mrs. Ballard wrote, "my comp[anions] were Old Lady Cox, Pitts, Sister Barton, Moody, Soal, & Witherel." At the Abial Herington house in June 1796, she noted, "there were 22 in number slept under that roof the night."[33] A doctor might be twenty-four years old and unmarried, like Benjamin Page, but only in middle age, and usually only after her own childbearing years were over, could a woman acquire the full stature of a midwife.

Physicians can be located in town records and on tax lists (as well as in Martha Ballard's diary) by the title *Doctor*, which originally was simply a designation for a man of eminent learning. No woman, whether a midwife or a practitioner of physic, can be discovered by title. Hallowell's mysterious black healer might be referred to as a "doctor" or "doctoress," but she is never called *Doctor* Black. If midwives had any sort of distinguishing label in this period, it was probably the word *old*. Mrs. Ballard referred to "Old Mrs. Fletcher," "Old Mrs. Ingraham," and "Old Lady Cox," and when Mrs. Marsh came to visit, she wrote of her as "The Old Lady."[34] In traditional society such terms connoted respect, a respect for expertise acquired by experience rather than through systematic study.

Martha Ballard respected the formal training of Hallowell's physicians. She had obviously been taught, like other midwives, to call a doctor in an emergency. On November 11, 1785, when she arrived at Henry Babcok's house too late for the delivery and found the patient "greatly ingered by some mishap," though Mrs. Smith, who had delivered the baby, did "not allow that shee was sencible of it," Mrs. Ballard summoned Dr. Williams who "prescribed remedies." The inexperienced midwife had undoubtedly caused the injury. Though Martha Ballard felt competent to "inquire into the Cause," she did not attempt to correct it without a physician.

Only once in 797 births, however, did she herself feel incapable of handling a delivery. She described the delivery of Mrs. Prescott on May 19, 1792 in the following manner:

> Her Case was Lingering till 7 pm I removd difuculties & waited for natures opperations till then, when she was more severely atackt with obstructions which alarmed me much I desired Doct Hubard might be sent for which request was complied with but by Divine assistance I performed the oppration, which was blisst with the preservation of the lives off mother and infant the life of the latter I dispard of for some time.

The Medical Challenge to Midwifery

In the margin, she wrote: "the most perelous sien [scene] I Ever past thro in the Cours of my practice blessed be God for his goodness." Her ability to negotiate this "perelous sien" without Doctor Hubbard's assistance may have given Martha Ballard renewed faith in her own abilities, although characteristically she gave the credit to God.

In her obstetrical practice, Martha Ballard was obviously quite capable of managing alone. Still, the unspoken assumption that a man's knowledge was in some sense superior to a woman's experience colored her more ordinary relations with the men. She may have considered Ben Page incompetent, yet most of the time when in the actual presence of a physician she seems to have deferred. In May 1792, for example, she was called to Pittston to see the wife of Peter Grant and wrote, "They had called Doctor Parker before I arived and he seemed to chuse to perform the opperation which took place at 1 h 11 am." Her use of the verb *choose* is telling. On another occasion she and Dr. Page both appeared at a delivery. "I Extracted the child," she reported. "He Chose to close the Loin."[35] There is a silent acknowledgment here of the place of women in the traditional medical hierarchy.

Ironically in at least one respect—the keeping of records—Martha Ballard was a more methodical and progressive practitioner than most male doctors of her time. While medical leaders in early America urged the keeping of journals and commonplace books, few country physicians seem to have done so. Besides Martha Ballard's diary, the only surviving medical document from eighteenth century Hallowell is Daniel Cony's one-page letter to the Massachusetts Medical Society. In some respects, Martha Ballard was herself a product of the medical enlightenment of the eighteenth century. Her willingness to attend autopsies, her meticulous recording of medical and obstetrical detail, her concern with vital records, and her commitment to "facts" in general, all suggest habits of mind not far removed from the best doctors of her age.

Her descriptions are often annoyingly formulaic ("she was not so well as Could be wisht") and her notation of methods exasperatingly obscure ("used means"); yet taken as a whole her records tower above those of most of her male contemporaries.[36] Where one Maine physician wrote, "delivered a dead child" and another scrawled "parturition," Martha Ballard routinely gave the approximate length of labor, the condition of the mother and infant, and sometimes even the weight of the newborn baby. Most entries read simply "safe delivered" or "left mother and infant cleverly," but others indicate specific symptoms and results. While we might have hoped for a more precise description of the "perelous sien" that prompted Martha Ballard to call Dr. Hubbard in May 1792, there is surely no more revealing description of medical obstetrics in the Maine literature than her account of Benjamin Page's administration of laudanum. Had there been a women's equivalent of the Massachusetts Medical Society, this event would surely have merited a one-page paper.

There was no professional association of midwives, of course. Women like Martha Ballard derived their authority from the larger community of women rather than from an exclusive society of professionals. This difference between doctors and midwives was reflected in their fees. Although there are no surviving accounts from Hallowell physicians for the period between 1785–1800, records from other Maine physicians suggest that doctors may have charged from two to three times as much as midwives.[37] Martha Ballard must have been pleased, therefore, when her more affluent patients treated her as they might have treated a doctor. About ten days after the encounter with Dr. Page at the delivery of Hannah Sewall, Mrs. Ballard was called to the home of Chandler Robbins, a Harvard graduate and new resident of the town. "Mrs. Robbins Linguerd till 4 h pm when her illness came on," she wrote, adding, "Doct Parker was Calld but shee did not wish to see him when he Came & he returned home." Then she noted without comment that Mr. Chandler had given her eighteen shillings, three times her usual fee.[38] In Hallowell, the "richer and better informed" might still prefer a midwife.

Considering Martha Ballard's eminence, we can only wonder whether there really was a medical challenge to midwifery in her lifetime. Although the sources clearly indicate the actions that in urban centers supposedly eliminated women from the practice of obstetrics—the development of medical societies, the appearance of physicians at normal deliveries, and the use of instruments and drugs—the results were hardly impressive. Martha Ballard respected the supposedly more specialized skills of the doctors, but she seldom required their help. As an accoucheur, she was more experienced than the doctors, and she was cheaper. Nor did the presence of male physicians have anything to do with her gradual withdrawal from practice after 1800. What we would like to know, of course, is who took up the work she eventually laid down.

Unfortunately, there is no evidence in the diary that she trained a successor, which in itself is a suggestive omission, although any of the many (mostly anonymous) women attendants at Hallowell births may have been preparing informally to succeed her. That the interaction between doctors and midwives continued into the nineteenth century is clear, however. In a diary entry for March 27, 1812, just a few months before her death, Mrs. Ballard wrote:

> I was called at 10 h am Edwd Savage to go and see his wife who was in labor I had a fall on my way but not much hurt found the patient had called two midwives and Doct Ellis before she saw me I found her mind was for Doct Cony he was called and as Providence would have she called on me to assist her I performed the case.

The entry is ambiguous. The fact that Mrs. Savage called three midwives and two doctors shows that traditional midwifery survived into the second decade of the nineteenth century. Yet the form of the entry, the anonymity of the women, and the patient's apparent wavering between Martha Ballard and Daniel Cony suggests that the medical challenge was real.

Without additional evidence we cannot be certain of conditions in Hallowell after the death of Martha Ballard. Her diary allows us to see, with a clarity not provided in other sources, the relative strengths of traditional and medical obstetrics and the probable course of change. Clearly, there would be little potential for a gentleman physician to increase his obstetrical practice as long as he charged as much for delivering one baby as a midwife did for delivering three. In eighteenth century terms, however, the medical consequences of this arrangement were serious, even if every midwife were as sober, experienced, and successful as Martha Moore Ballard.

As long as medical science was itself seen as rather static, something to be acquired primarily through mastery of the writings of ancient authorities, and as long as midwifery was considered a manual art best sustained and transmitted within the community of women, the book learning of the doctors and the practical learning of the midwives could complement one another. In the medical enlightenment of the eighteenth century, medical science became more experimental, more progressive. As a consequence, the lore of the midwives, passed from one generation of women to another, became suspect, while the active practice of obstetrics became more appealing. Historians have given considerable attention to the first consequence but little to the second.

The earliest collection of papers of the Massachusetts Medical Society provides a striking instance of medical disdain for traditional midwifery. In an account of an incident that had occurred sometime in the 1760s, Dr. Edward Augustus Holyoke of Salem told of being called from his bed to visit a newly delivered woman who was dying because the midwife had used such force in extracting the afterbirth that she had disengaged the uterus itself. "But what better can be expected from an Operator utterly destitute of all Knowledge of the Figure, Situation, & Anatomy of the Parts," he concluded.[39] We recall here the "perelous sien" reported by Martha Ballard in which an inexperienced midwife unknowingly damaged her patient.

This situation is a classic confrontation between medical and traditional obstetrics, as seen from the medical side. But suppose the situation were reversed, and the doctor rather than the midwife were the incompetent practitioner. Suppose that wide experience in managing ordinary births rather than formal training in anatomy were the decisive factor. Suppose, in fact, that a young physician fresh from his apprenticeship met an experienced and confident midwife at the bedside of a laboring woman. What then?

We need not go into the diary of Martha Ballard or to secondary accounts by feminist historians to find the answer. Dr. William Smellie's *Collection of Preternatural Cases and Observations in Midwifery* will do quite well. Doctor Smellie, the British physician whose improvements in obstetrical forceps supposedly paved the way for an interventionist and male-dominated practice of obstetrics actually showed genuine respect for the skills of traditional midwives. His works, which Benjamin Page might well have read in the library of his mentor, Dr. Thomas Kittredge, even included an account of a successful caesarean operation performed by an illiterate Scots midwife named Mary Donally.[40] Although Smellie included an occasional anecdote about the stereotypical loquacious and ignorant midwife, far more often he criticized half-educated physicians who foolishly intervened in normal births. In a number of these accounts, midwives come across as more effective practitioners than physicians.[41] Obviously, what Smellie hoped to encourage was the integration of the practical skills of the midwives, who had long managed normal births, and the more specialized training of doctors, who had now acquired improved instruments for use in difficult deliveries. He did not put it in those terms, of course, but the direction of his argument is obvious: Midwives had skills that doctors needed.

The Massachusetts physician who in 1820 wrote *Remarks on the Employment of Females as Practitioners in Midwifery* understood the problem perfectly. "A man must be a universal practitioner in midwifery, before he is qualified for a practitioner in difficult cases," he wrote. That is, a person unfamiliar with normal deliveries could not manage preternatural ones. If midwifery were reintroduced among the upper classes in Boston, he argued, there would be an inevitable decline in the quality of emergency obstetrics because physicians would be denied the day-to-day experience that good medicine required. That midwives might learn to manage difficult as well as normal deliveries was to him simply unthinkable. No woman could pass through the dissecting room and the hospital without losing "those moral qualities of character, which are essential to the office."[42] We can only wonder what he would have thought of Martha Ballard and the other midwives who attended autopsies in late eighteenth century Hallowell.

Seen in this light, Benjamin Page's effort to administer laudanum at the delivery of Hannah Sewall is hardly the ominous foreshadowing of later medical triumphs that it seemed at first glance. Rather, it is yet another example, to be added to those of Smellie, of the limited obstetrical experience of eighteenth century physicians. As long as Martha Ballard continued to dominate the practice of obstetrics in the region, it is difficult to imagine Benjamin Page or any other doctor acquiring the practical expertise that the new medical obstetrics demanded. That was exactly the point: It was not Dr. Page's competence but his incompetence that made it essential for him to practice midwifery.

The history of midwifery in nineteenth century Maine is yet to be written, but the general direction of change can be glimpsed in a document published at Norridgewock in March of 1823 by an association

54. Silk maternity and mourning dress, Maine, owned and last altered by Betsey Rogers Barker (1765–1812). (Old Sturbridge Village photo by Henry E. Peach)

of Somerset County physicians. Following the example of Boston doctors of a generation earlier, these men established fees for various treatments, from "Extirpating tumors" to performing an "Operation for Hare-Lip," each man agreeing not to "under value his own services" nor to "undermine the practice of others" by charging less than the minimum prescribed. The doctors also pledged not to visit a patient previously treated by another physician "unless it shall be the frank and unbiased wish of the party calling him to dismiss the other from further attendance." Significantly, their rates included $4 for attendance "in ordinary Obstetric cases" and $8 "In cases where a Midwife has been first employed."[43]

The Somerset County agreement neatly defines the structural changes that transformed the medical world of Martha Ballard into the medical world with which most of us are familiar. These doctors cared about territorial boundaries in a way that she would have found puzzling. They were also bent on destroying the old system that had allowed midwives to perform "in ordinary cases" while calling doctors in an emergency. By charging twice as much for backup calls as for deliveries, they put extraordinary pressure on midwives as well as on their clients. The expected outcome, we may be sure, was that parturient women would call a doctor first.

Whether the Somerset physicians were successful in their reforms we do not know, yet the long-term direction of change is clear. The expansion of medical obstetrics was part of a larger process through which medicine changed from a learned specialty to a full-time profession.[44] For women the consequences of that shift cannot be overemphasized. Martha Ballard had sustained her practice while simultaneously running a household, supervising textile production, and rearing her youngest children. In her century such a pattern of part-time specialization was not unusual—for men or women. By the middle of the nineteenth century, this condition was no longer so. Doctors were doctors; midwives were also housewives. Ironically, then, the medical enlightenment of the eighteenth century, in teaching physicians to value ordinary midwifery, eventually guaranteed the exclusion of women from its practice. Still denied "learning," women no longer had the advantage of "experience."

None of this could have been foreseen, of course, on that October day in 1794 when Martha Ballard encountered Dr. Page at the delivery of Hannah Sewall. Having delivered forty babies already that year and having made dozens of medical calls, she had reason to feel superior to young Ben Page, "that poor unfortunate man in the practice."

ACKNOWLEDGMENTS

For helpful comments on an earlier version of this chapter, I would like to thank Dr. Marcella Sorg of the University of Maine at Orono,

Professor Sarah McMahon of Bowdoin College, and Professor John Demos and members of the American social history seminar at Brandeis University.

NOTES

1. Diary of Martha Moore Ballard, 1785–1812 (hereafter MMB) in Maine State Library, Augusta, Me. (hereafter MeSL). An eighteenth century English doctor suggested 10–20 drops of laudanum as the appropriate dosage for "weak women" and 12–24 drops for "weak men & midling women." See J. Worth Estes, "John Jones's Mysteries of Opium Reveal'd (1701): Key to Historial Opiates," *Journal of the History of Medicine and Allied Sciences*, 34 (April 1979), 202.

2. Jane B. Donegan, *Women & Men Midwives: Medicine, Morality, and Misogyny in Early America* (Westport, Conn., and London: Greenwood Press, 1978), p. 141. See also Catherine M. Scholten, "On the Importance of the Obstetrick Art: Changing Customs of Childbirth in America, 1769 to 1825," *William & Mary Quarterly*, 34 (July 1977), 426–445.

3. Judy Barrett Litoff, *American Midwives: 1860 to the Present* (Westport, Conn., and London, England: Greenwood Press, 1978), p. 26; A Physician, *Remarks on the employment of females as practitioners in midwifery.* (Boston: Cummings and Hilliard, 1820), pp. 12, 21. Some historians attribute this work to William Channing, the first professor of obstetrics at Harvard Medical School; the Countway Medical Library, Harvard Medical School, Boston (hereafter CML), also lists it under the name of John Ware.

4. Judith Walzer Leavitt, "'Science' Enters the Birthing Room: Obstetrics in America since the Eighteenth Century," *Journal of American History*, 70 (September 1983), 281–304.

5. *Collections of the Maine Historical Society*, 2nd ser., 9 (1898), 428 (hereafter *Coll. MeHS*); Mabel T. Kittredge, *The Kittredge Family in America* (Rutland, Vt.: Tuttle, 1936), p. 34.

6. *Coll. MeHS*, 2nd ser., 7 (1896), 439–440; Doris R. Marston, "A Lady of Maine: Sally Sayward Barrell Keating Wood, 1759–1855" (M.A. thesis, University of New Hampshire, 1970), pp. 84, 110, 207; conversation with Dr. Eldridge Pendleton, Director, Old York Historical Society. Marston says that Dr. Hall Jackson of Portsmouth delivered Sally Keating's first child.

7. Charles Elventon Nash included an abridgement of Martha Ballard's diary in *The History of Augusta*, a book printed in 1904 but not bound and published until 1961. The Nash abridgement, heavily biased toward genealogy, includes only about one-third of the original, though it does suggest the sort of material in it. Except for brief reference to Nash's version in Nancy F. Cott, *The Bonds of Womanhood: 'Woman's Sphere' in New England, 1780–1835* (New Haven and London: Yale University Press, 1977), pp. 19, 29, and in Richard W. Wertz and Dorothy C. Wertz, *Lying-in: A History of Childbirth in America* (New York: Schocken Books, 1977), pp. 9–12, 18, 20, the diary has been unused by historians.

8. MMB, June 14, 1798. In this case, the child Dr. Page delivered was born dead.

9. *Vital Records of Oxford, Massachusetts* (Worcester, Mass.: Franklin P. Rice, 1905), pp. 13, 14, 268; MMB, Oct. 14, 1797; Nash, *History of Augusta*, pp. 235, 301; James W. North, *The History of Augusta, Maine* (Augusta, Me.: Clapp & North, 1870; reprinted, Somersworth, N.H.: New England History Press, 1981), p. 819. Ephraim Ballard was in the top 20 percent of taxpayers of the middle parish of Hallowell in 1794, although his estate was less than 10 percent that of James Howard, the largest taxpayer. See Invoice of rateable property, MeSL.

10. John L. Sibley, *Biographical Sketches of Graduates of Harvard University* and Clifford K. Shipton, *Biographical Sketches of those who attended Harvard College*, 17 vols. (Boston: Massachusetts Historical Society, 1873–1975), vol. 15, pp. 80–82 (hereafter *Sibley's Harvard Graduates*).

11. MMB, January 15, 1796. Because the diary begins on January 1, 1785, with rather cursory entries and gradually takes on a more complex form over the next two or three years, I have assumed that it is complete. There may have been earlier lists of births, however, or even some sort of record kept in an almanac.

12. North, *History of Augusta*, p. 301; *Heads of Families at the First Census of the United States Taken in the year 1790: Maine* (Washington, D.C.: U.S. Government Printing Office, 1908), p. 9; Federal Census, 1800, microfilm.

13. North, *History of Augusta*, pp. 388–389, 836–837. I have not yet been able to identify the "black healer." There were very few nonwhite persons in Hallowell in this period. Martha Ballard occasionally mentions "Beulah" or "black Hitty," but she never mentions the "doctoress" by name.

14. Ibid., pp. 170, 201; *Sibley's Harvard Graduates*, vol. 16, pp. 352–354; vol. 10, pp. 282–284; Samuel Curtis, *A valuable collection of recipes...* (Amherst, N.H.: Elijah Mansur, printer, 1819), pp. 52–54.

15. Eric H. Christianson, "The Medical Practitioners of Massachusetts, 1630–1800: Patterns of Change and Continuity," *Publications of the Colonial Society of Massachusetts*, 57 (1980), 56–67 (hereafter *Pubs. Col. Soc. Ma.*); Joseph Kett, *The Formation of the American Medical Profession: The Role of Institutions, 1760–1860* (New Haven and London: Yale University Press, 1968), pp. 9–14.

16. James Thacher, *American Medical Biography* (Boston: Richardson & Lord, 1828), p. 45. North, *History of Augusta*, p. 170–172; "Documents Illustrative of the Early History of the Massachusetts Medical Society." II: 22, MS, CML; *Massachusetts Register and United States Calendar* (Boston: Manning & Lorring, 1804), p. 43.

17. Douglas Lamar Jones notes the importance of midwives as healers in "Charity, Medical Charity, and Dependency in Eighteenth-Century Essex County, Massachusetts," *Pubs. Col. Soc. Ma.*, 57 (1980), 207–208.

18. MMB, e.g., burns, September 17, 1786; bruises, October 8, 1785; frostbite, November 28, 1786; salves, November 19, 1786; pills, January 17, 1792; syrups, June 5, 1794; ointments, February 18, 1787; clisters, May 25, 1791; dressings, January 28, 1791; bathing throats, September 13, 1787; bleeding cat, October 13, 1786; cutting tongue, February 1, 1786; lancing breast. August 1, 1788; worms, August 3, 1802; itch, March 27, 1786; laying out dead, June 9, 1788; labor as illness, March 31, 1790, February 21, 1791. She also refers to women in labor as "unwell," e.g., April 12, 1791.

19. MMB, Dr. Cony, July 19, 1787, May, 19, 1792, November 4, 1802; Dr. Williams, April 26, 1787; Dr. Hubbard, August 23, 1794; Daniel Cony, "An extraordinary case in Midwifery," read April 1788, in "Documents Illustrative of the Early History of the Massachusetts Medical Society," II: 22, MS, CML; MMB, Dr. Page, November 17, 1793, October 9, 1794, July 5, 1798, July 27, 1799, July 10, 1796; Dr. Parker, October 22, 1794, May 3, 1792.

20. MMB, October 30, 1791, December 13, 1785, September 18, 1786, May 19, 1792, December 10, 1787, March 26, 1787, July 25, 1785; October 27, 1795.

21. Richard D. Brown, "The Healing Arts in Colonial and Revolutionary Massachusetts: The Context for Scientific Medicine," *Pubs. Col. Soc. Ma.*, 57 (1980), 41–42.

22. MMB, May, 31, June 1, June, 2, 1792.

23. Ibid., e.g., September 23, 1790, January 24, 1794.

24. Stephen Barton Account Book, MeSL.

25. Daniel Cony to the President and Counsellors of the Massachusetts Medical Society convened in Boston, June 1808, CML.

26. MMB, July 23, 1794.

27. Ibid., November 9, November 15, 1793, August 12, November 10, 1785.

28. Ibid., September 2, 1794, September 16, 1800, February 4, 1801.

29. Ibid., June 3, 1790.

30. Additional genealogical research to identify her patients may reveal more out-of-town births, although a cross-check of 1790 births with the federal census for that year suggests otherwise. The only births for which names could not be found in the census were either clearly identified as out of town (usually Winthrop) or listed as having occurred in the home of a Hallowell resident. For example, "Magr Stickney's" child was born "at Jacksons."

31. For a typical injunction to send for a doctor in an emergency, see William Salmon [Aristotle], *The Experienced Midwife* (Philadelphia: no publisher, 1799), p. 39.

32. *Coll. MeHS*, 2nd ser., 4 (1893), 428; Brown, "Healing Arts," pp. 37–40; Laurel Thatcher Ulrich, *Good Wives: Image and Reality in the Lives of Women in Northern New England, 1650–1750* (New York: Alfred A. Knopf, 1982), pp. 132–134.

33. MMB, March 5, 1801, June 15, 1796.

34. Ibid., e.g., June 4, 1785, June 18, 1786, May 31, 1785, July 19, 1787.

35. Ibid., May 3, 1792, November 17, 1793.

36. As the frontispiece for a prospective history of Maine medicine, Dr. Jeremiah Barker of Gorham quoted Benjamin Rush's injunction to good record keeping but he concluded that few Maine doctors had taken his advice, "Diseases in the District of Maine," MS, MeHS. In Chapter 2 he praised Dr. Cony and other Lincoln County physicians but lamented their failure to keep "records of extraordinary cases, which occurred in their extensive practice." I have examined, in addition to the Barker notes, the account books of John Swett, York, Maine, 1775–1790 and Josiah Gilman, York, Maine, 1803–1813, Old York Historical Society; and Joseph and George Osgood Accounts, Andover, Massachusetts, 1770–1805 and Daniel Peirce Accounts, Kittery, Maine, 1762–1801, CML.

37. When Martha Ballard was charging six shillings, the physicians cited above were charging from twelve shillings to a pound. Dr. Peirce of Kittery, who performed only about six deliveries in 1792, charged extra for long labors or false alarms: Peirce Account Book,

pp. 4, 14, 18, 19, 24, 36, 42, 54, 72, 228. A fragmentary account shows that between 1804 and 1811, Dr. Page charged one patient six dollars for each of three deliveries, although in 1796 Dr. Moses Appleton of Waterville charged his landlord only two dollars for delivering his wife; William Mathew debtor to Dr. Benjamin Page, February 29, 1804-April 4, 1814, Benjamin Vaughan Pps., MeHS; Diary of Moses Appleton, September 5, 1796, Waterville Historical Society, Waterville, Me. (hereafter WHS).

38. MMB, October 22, 1794.

39. Edward Augustus Holyoke, "Account of an inverted uterus" read July 1, 1784, in "Documents Illustrative of the Early History of the Massachusetts Medical Society," III, MS, CML.

40. William Smellie, *A Collection of Cases Preternatural and Observations in Midwifery*, 3rd ed. (London: no publisher, 1764), vol. 3, pp. 420-421.

41. Ibid., pp. 533-534. A handwritten transcription of lectures by a London physician in the papers of Dr. Moses Appleton of Waterville supports this argument. The English doctor argued that earlier doctors were dangerously interventionist because "all cases were difficult and so bad before they were called in that every one was frightened.... But if they had understood midwifery and what great things nature was capable of doing they would ... seldom have had occasion to act in that manner." (Moses Appleton's notes from Dr. William Hunter's Lectures, 1793, MS, WHS.) I am grateful to Stephanie Hart of Colby College for calling this document and the Somerset physicians' agreement cited below to my attention.

42. *Remarks*, pp. 14, 7, and passim.

43. Articles adopted by Somerset County Physicians, March 23, 1823, MS, WHS.

44. That early efforts at professionalization were strenuously resisted by various nonacademic movements in the nineteenth century is clear. See William G. Rothstein, *American Physicians in the Nineteenth Century* (Baltimore: Johns Hopkins University Press, 1972), pp. 128-138; Kett, *The Formation of the American Medical Profession*, pp. 101-107. On the complexities of professionalism for women, see Virginia G. Drachman, *Hospital with a Heart: Women Doctors and the Paradox of Separatism at the New England Hospital, 1862-1969* (Ithaca, N.Y.: Cornell University Press, 1984).

Charles E. Clark

CHAPTER 9

JAMES SULLIVAN'S HISTORY OF MAINE AND THE ROMANCE OF STATEHOOD

Maine's cultural expression did not evolve from the dramatic clash of conflicting authorities, but from the local adaptation of imported styles and themes that gave expression to local sentiments. In form, therefore, Maine's culture was provincial but neither distinct nor unique, though its content often showed evidence of a growing pride of place. Such was the case with James Sullivan, lawyer, judge, governor, and author of *The History of the District of Maine*. Charles Clark identifies in Sullivan's work two powerful imported intellectual traditions then beginning to merge: the rational and scientific Enlightenment; and intuitive and dynamic romanticism. Together they provided the fundamental assumptions upon which Sullivan based his democratic faith in the republic and its destiny, which included the past, present, and future of Maine with its inevitable progress toward statehood. Quite unconsciously, Sullivan resolved the potential conflict between national and local loyalties by refusing to recognize it.

Henry Adams sensed that the difference between Federalists and Republicans was at least as much emotional as programmatic. "Federalists in the United States," wrote Adams in 1889, "... often attributed to the democratic instinct a visionary quality which they regarded as sentimentality, and charged with many bad consequences." And since the Federalists thought that the "visionary quality" produced such serious consequences for American politics, Adams reasoned, a modern historian might do well to try to study that supposed Republican trait. The trouble with undertaking such a study, however, was a lack of sources. Adams lamented:

> Nothing was more elusive than the spirit of American democracy. Jefferson, the literary representative of the class, spoke chiefly for Virginians, and dreaded so greatly his own reputation as a visionary that he seldom or never uttered his whole thought. Gallatin and Madison were

Charles E. Clark is professor of history at the University of New Hampshire.

still more cautious. The press in no country could give shape to a mental condition so shadowy. The people themselves, although millions in number, could not have expressed their finer instincts if they tried, and might not have recognized them if expressed by others.[1]

Fashions in the writing of history come and go. We have by now passed through at least two periods since Adams's time during which the mere notion of trying to study the "spirit of American democracy" would have been dismissed as pointless. We appear to be entering a period in which social science can coexist, and on rare occasions even merge, with a renewed effort to understand ideas, values, and the patterns of thought and behavior—or "culture," as these patterns are usually called—that mark a particular society of the past.

The movement for Maine statehood was surely part of the democratic impulse that was manifested in so many ways during the period of the Early Republic. Republican culture in general, as distinguished from that of the "democracy" of the Jacksonian presidency, tended to emphasize balance, order, and a restrained rather than exuberant faith in the people's rule and optimism about the future. The politics, social values, literature, religion, and arts of the period between 1783 and 1820 reveal a tension between the rationalism and classicism of the Enlightenment and the mysticism and individualism of the beginnings of American Romanticism. Within the republican consensus, there were the polarities revealed most delightfully and instructively in the correspondence between Thomas Jefferson and John Adams in their old age.[2] Ronald Banks has taught us that on the level of partisan politics, the movement for statehood (at least in the form that won final victory) was a movement of the Jeffersonian or "democratic" end of the republican spectrum of the era.[3]

What was true in politics was also true in thought and feeling. Just at the time when prominent Federalists were leading their second unsuccessful attempt to separate Maine from Massachusetts,[4] there appeared a book-length celebration of the past and future of Maine. It was written by an eloquent Jeffersonian who had left the District twenty years earlier to pursue a career in Massachusetts provincial and state politics. The author was James Sullivan, the Maine-born future governor of Massachusetts who was then serving as first president of the Massachusetts Historical Society, and who in 1795 published *The History of the District of Maine*. This first history of Maine concludes with an assertion of eventual statehood that is based on an imaginative vision of Maine's future. No writer and statesman of the period, unless it was his political idol Thomas Jefferson himself, better deserved the Federalists' pejorative label of "visionary" than James Sullivan.

Unlike the fifty-four-page tract on the subject by Federalist spokesman Daniel Davis published four years earlier,[5] Sullivan does not make a legal, or even a logical, case—despite his background as a lawyer and judge. He even expressed regret as a Massachusetts man that separation would deprive this state "of the advantage of our political acquaintance with so many good and valuable characters."[6] Statehood for Maine as he sees it, however, is inevitable; it will proceed as a matter of course from the logic of history, which has a dynamic of its own. Sullivan's thesis about statehood, along with his other writings, establish him as a leading spokesman for democratic romantic nationalism.

Thus we can study the movement for Maine statehood as, among other things, a *literary* effort. If we use Sullivan's *History* as the main piece of evidence, this phase of that effort emerges as an expression of romanticism. That is because his work is best understood and appreciated as romantic literature rather than as history.[7]

We tend to place American romanticism, as distinct from European romanticism, in the nineteenth century rather than in the eighteenth, usually focusing on the New England Transcendentalists of the 1830s, 1840s and 1850s. Emerson went to England, learned from Carlyle, and came back to celebrate "Nature" and "Self-Reliance." When we consider romanticism in politics, our first thought is of Jacksonian democracy with its adulation of the common man, along with the reform movements that mark the first half of the nineteenth century. In painting, there was the celebration of the American landscape, represented especially in Thomas Cole and the Hudson River School, and in architecture there were both Greek and gothic revivals, each in its own way equally romantic.

Even though all these expressions of American romanticism appear primarily after 1820, romantic tendencies abounded in the pre-1820 culture that we have called "republican." They were present in most of the intellectual activities of Thomas Jefferson, for example, and in the historical writings of his Maine disciple James Sullivan (Illus. 55).

Born April 22, 1744, Sullivan was the fourth son of an Irish immigrant from Limerick. His birthplace was on one or the other side of the Salmon Falls River: either in Somersworth, New Hampshire, or in Berwick, Maine.[8] Whichever it was, he spent most of his boyhood on his father's farm in Berwick. His father was a schoolmaster and linguist. One of his older brothers was John Sullivan, the future Revolutionary War general and later "President," as the chief executive was called for a time, of the new state of New Hampshire. James was trained in the law by his older brother and then practiced law in Biddeford, Maine, where he supplemented his income by selling goods for John Hancock of Boston, one of the richest merchants in America. It was through Hancock's friendship and influence that James Sullivan got into Massachusetts politics.

Sullivan never went to college, although he received honorary degrees from both Harvard and Brown. However, as one of only six lawyers in the district of Maine in the 1760s and early 1770s and as a friend of Hancock, he found himself heavily involved in public life at the beginning of the Revolution. He was a representative to the Massachusetts General Court and delegate to the extralegal Provincial

James Sullivan's 187
History of Maine

55. *James Sullivan* (1744–1809), by John Christian Rauschner (1760–?), 1808.
(Wax. Courtesy of The Society for the Preservation of New England Antiquities)

Congress before Independence. During the Revolutionary War he served in the Massachusetts legislature as judge of admiralty for the Eastern District, and at the age of 32 as a justice of the Supreme Judicial Court of Massachusetts. In 1782, the year before the war's end, he left the bench to serve in the Continental Congress; he then served as judge of the Probate Court for Suffolk County, attorney general of the commonwealth, and finally, in 1807 and 1808, governor of Massachusetts. He died in office in December 1808 at the age of sixty-four. With his friend Jeremy Belknap, author of the superb *History of New-Hampshire*, he was one of the principal founders in 1791 of the Massachusetts Historical Society, which he served for many years as its first president.[9]

Sullivan's public career was by no means without controversy. One of his Boston political enemies in the 1780s bitterly satirized his rustic origins and lack of formal education in a poetic response to what he characterized as an unprincipled and false libel published by Sullivan in the Boston press:

> The dews of education ne'er refined
> Thy MOHAWK manners, and thy rustic mind.
> On thee fair Science never deign'd to smile
> Nor rubb'd thee polish'd with her smoothing file.
> For thee nor Learning rais'd her classic flame,

Rough as the savage wilds from whence you came;
But Cunning, still of knaves the sure defence,
Fill'd with profoundest guile, tho void of sense,
Deep, deep within thee fix'd her fell retreat,
And oil'd each supple thought with dark deceit.

We need to add that Sullivan, if indeed scholars have correctly identified him as the "Zenas" who signed the original attack, apologized to his adversary in print.[10]

Sullivan's *History of the District of Maine* was only the most notable of his published writings. His other major work, published six years after the *History*, was a treatise on his main legal specialty, the apparently unromantic topic of land titles. He also wrote a half-dozen or so other books and pamphlets, including *The Path of Riches*, an attack on the monopolistic tendencies of the Massachusetts Bank and an argument for the substitution of a more limited state bank; a spirited defense of the French Revolution; *Observations upon the Government of the United States of America*, a very clear exposition of American constitutionalism, especially the question of divided sovereignty; a treatise on freedom of the press in opposition to the Sedition Act of the Adams administration; a tract upholding the powers of the laity versus those of the clergy in Congregational churches; and a history of the Penobscot Indians.[11]

Sullivan's publications as well as his public career disclose a mind that naturally took a position consistently on the popular, or "democratic," side of any political or religious issue. Just as he had been an early and fervent patriot during the Revolution, so in later years he became a partisan of Jefferson, with whom he shared more than political assumptions and preferences. He also shared with his hero a view of the progressive improvement of the new nation, based at least as much upon sentiment and faith in the goodness of man and the efficacy of the environment as upon any sort of reasoning that we would call logical. The best expression of this view and this faith is found in his *History*.

The importance of Sullivan's book as a work of history was reduced almost laughably the instant William D. Williamson's infinitely superior *History of the State of Maine* appeared in 1832. In one sense, therefore, Sullivan's book had a life of only thirty-seven years during which it could be taken seriously as history. It is full of factual errors, and is not well documented; the interpretations, while they tell us much of Sullivan and his time, do not help us to understand history.

On the other hand, Sullivan's *History* provides an exceptionally valuable insight into the mind of his time. In the dedicatory address to the governor and legislature of Massachusetts at the front of the book, Sullivan states in as clear language as any of his contemporaries ever did the impulse for writing history and collecting historical documents that was almost an obsession at the end of the American Revolution:

Upon an attentive review of the history of each part of our country, we cannot fail to be convinced, that the genuine seeds of *republicanism*, which have produced our glorious *revolution*, with a rich harvest of civil liberty, were planted by our ancestors, in the soil of America, at a very early date; and that nothing but an unreasonable indulgence of a disposition to avarice, and ambition, groundless jealousies, a criminal supineness in public concerns, or an unpardonable inattention to the modes of education, can ever deprive us, of that elevated prosperity and happiness, to which, under the direction of a good and wise Providence, the principles of civil freedom, well understood, and wisely exerted, have raised our *nation*.[12]

Sullivan intended his history of Maine to further the underlying purpose of the Massachusetts Historical Society, which was to "aid in the completion of a perfect history of United America."[13] He believed that history contains lessons that have "a tendency to prevent evils, and to render mankind more wise and happy,"[14] but beyond the specific lessons of history a spur to virtue and patriotism that comes from contemplating the antiquity and ideal beginnings of a person's country. And beyond even that, according to Sullivan's dedication, history discloses an unfolding of design, a forward movement guided by "a good and wise Providence," by which the favored nation moves inexorably toward a glorious destiny. This is a process to be celebrated as well as understood, and to understand and celebrate it at the state and regional level is the first step toward comprehending the whole of the national destiny.

The main body of Sullivan's text, like Jefferson's *Notes on Virginia* and the third volume of Belknap's *History of New-Hampshire*, begins with a precise description of location and borders.[15] This is a good scientific approach, appropriate to the late eighteenth century, as are the next few paragraphs, which discuss the seasons and the climate. But not far into that discussion, Sullivan pauses to point out the advantages of Maine's cold weather. He admits that the winters may seem "tedious," but thinks it is far better to endure "our northern snow banks" than the "fever and ague, and the other disorders" that are found in places like Virginia and the Carolinas. Then he goes on to generalize:

> However disagreeable the winters of a northern climate may be, yet the northern part of every country is more healthy, than that part which is nearer to the equator: and we know that the human race is increased between the fortieth and fiftieth degrees of latitude, much beyond what it is any where else.

He believed that even by comparison with nearby Massachusetts proper, life in the District was clearly healthier because the birth rate was higher and infant mortality lower. "Besides this," he adds, "an enquirer will be clearly convinced, that there are not so many pulmonic complaints here, as are found in the other parts of New England."[16]

Sullivan backs some of these scientific and quasi-scientific assertions with observations, references to a few published natural philosophers of the day, and in one case statistics from the first federal census. By comparison with the similar writings of Jefferson and Belknap, however, this portion of Sullivan's discussion is remarkable for its *lack* of confirming data and evidence of careful observation. Here, for example, is a sample of Belknap's approach to discussing climatic phenomena in New Hampshire:

> On the seventeenth of February, 1782, an unusual kind of hoar frost was observed. The wind had been northerly on the preceding day, with some appearance of snow. The morning was calm and foggy. The trees and bushes were white with frost, which appeared on the north sides, only, of the twigs and smaller branches; but on the larger limbs and trunks, there was none: Nor was any seen on the houses or on fences, excepting on the sharp edges of boards; but every point of a stick or nail, and every rope and string, which was exposed to the north, was covered. The spiculae were of all lengths, from an inch downward, and about the thickness of a knitting pin. They increased in number and size, for about two hours after the rising of the sun; and in about an hour after this, began to fall, like snow, on the ground; they did not all disappear till two hours after noon.[17]

Belknap devotes a twenty-page chapter to a discussion of the "Effect of the climate and other causes on the human constitution," a topic to which Sullivan gives a bit more than a page. However, Sullivan arrives at far broader conclusions about Maine than his more conservative friend and colleague considers warranted for New Hampshire. Belknap buttresses his cautious conclusions with population tables, tables of baptisms and deaths in selected towns, tables of "casualties"—that is, causes of death—and three pages worth of "Remarkable instances of Longevity."[18]

Nothing of this sort appears in Sullivan's works. His observations are very generalized, aimed far more at establishing Maine's natural advantages to human health than at contributing to the store of knowledge about nature. But the establishment of that proposition, it turns out, is only the first building block in his case for the glorious destiny of Maine. He goes on to develop the ideas that the natural environment of Maine promotes both health and virtue; that although there are few precious metals, there is a great abundance of fish, harbors, timber, and arable land, and that the scarcity of the one and the plenty of the others are both good things. Captain John Smith had argued in much the same way almost two hundred years before. Sullivan put it this way: "The expectations founded on the advantages of mines of gold and silver ore have never failed to produce idleness, profligacy, and dissipation of manners; while commerce, agriculture, and the fisheries necessarily urge people to industry, frugality, prudence, and economy: and have a direct tendency to render man an active, virtuous and respectable creature." He then discusses at length the bad effects of "ease and leisure," ending with the comforting observation that in Maine there is no such thing. "We may conclude," he asserts triumphantly, "that the advantages of the northern part of the continent, exciting to industry and toil, are much superior to those in the south, where wealth is expected, without the toil and labour of the proprietor."[19]

Sullivan's treatment of the Indians—a subject that became another romantic preoccupation once the image of a passing race replaced the dread of imminent danger—serves a twofold rhetorical purpose, neither of which is "scientific."[20] One is to reinforce the point just made about the moral superiority of the northern environment; the other is to justify the European settlement of America.

It is instructive to compare Sullivan's view of the Indians with that of both Belknap and Jefferson. Belknap's rather detailed, though selective, catalogue of anthropological details contains very little by way of moral judgment, though he does object to the continuation of certain Indian superstitions among too many of his contemporary New Hampshiremen. His main purpose is to record, almost without comment, some of the details of the Indians' technology and folkways, with particular emphasis on those that were adopted by, and thus affected, the white culture.[21] Jefferson's answer in *Notes on Virginia* to Francois Marbois's query on "Aborigines" is more comprehensive than Belknap's treatment of the subject in *The History of New-Hampshire*. Of course, the subject itself was a much larger one in Virginia than in New Hampshire. Jefferson attempts to list all the tribes in Virginia—under their respective confederations—with their locations and numbers of warriors at two dates in the seventeenth century. He adds a similar list of remaining eighteenth century Indians in and near the United States. He addresses archaeological discoveries relating to Indian history, and even includes a brief discussion of language in order to prove that the "red men of America are of greater antiquity than those of Asia."[22] So far this is the approach of a scientist, not far different from that of Belknap. In another portion of the *Notes*, however, Jefferson uses anthropological materials to make a point that is not so much scientific as ideological. Responding to the Count de Buffon's aspersions on the American environment, Jefferson shapes his scientific materials to uphold the physical excellence of all species in America compared to those of Europe, including the admirable physical, intellectual, and moral qualities of the American Indian. In other sections, Jefferson makes similar use of scientific materials in order, for example, to argue for the original perfection of creation or to account for what he perceived to be the biological inferiority of the Negro while upholding his equality of rights.[23]

Sullivan, as we might expect, is much closer to Jefferson than to Belknap—except that he slants his historical and anthropological materials to ideology much more than Jefferson does. His ideological need is twofold, and conflicting. In the first place, he must consistently portray the northeast's natural environment as particularly advantageous to human character. But in the second place, he must portray the Indian stage of history as flawed and temporary in order to justify what Francis Jennings has called the "invasion" of America.[24]

The best he is able to come up with on the first count is that "on the whole we are obliged to conclude, that the Savages of North America, are, and always have been, more humane and less cruel than those of the South; or that Spanish writers, in order to excuse the unexampled cruelties of their nation, have deceived the world with tales which had no foundation."[25] He argued that they also dress better and build better houses (a function of the difference in climate), wrap their infants so as to keep their bodies straight rather than disfiguring their skulls, and treat their women better.[26] But there is little indication here of Rousseau's noble savage, the picturesque and wistful image that Cooper also uses to portray the Indian, for example, and of which we catch a glimpse in Jefferson's transcript of the speech of Logan in *Notes on Virginia*.[27] Sullivan was no primitivist. His Indians are handsome, strong, and clever, but the author does not linger over admiration of these characteristics, nor does he hold them up as in any sense meriting the white man's envy. Instead he stresses the lack of ambition, political progress, intellectual achievement, and true religion to which nature apparently has condemned the native inhabitants of North America.[28]

And there is good reason for this portrayal, which appears in the two chapters on his other specialty, land titles.[29] In one of those chapters he discusses titles to American land from European governments. As an obvious consequence of debates over English sovereignty during the Revolution and exposure especially to the ideas of John Locke, Sullivan dismisses all such titles as invalid.[30] In the other chapter he discusses titles granted by the Indians. He concludes that they are equally invalid because neither under Locke's view of natural law nor by their own understanding did the Indians ever possess title to the soil of America—that the Indian deeds are worthless but that the European possession of former Indian hunting grounds is both fair and legal. True enough, the Indians were entitled under natural law to use the land for a time in their own "savage" way, but they had not used it efficiently or with any idea of "a permanent use and improvement of the soil." And now the Indian has "had his day." Worldwide human necessity now compels the improvement of the land of America; it can no longer be used simply for hunting. Therefore the new occupiers have the same right of occupancy as the old ones once had.[31] Sullivan's language in these passages combines a small sense of regret for the passing of the red man with a vigorous assertion that when the common good of mankind demands that the civilized world move into "savage" territory—population pressure seems to be the overriding issue in Sullivan's mind—the older people must give way in accordance with an immutable law of nature. Here are some examples of his rhetoric on this point:

> If the Savages cannot be incorporated with the emigrants, or become civilized as a nation, it will clearly follow, that they will by degrees be

extirpated, and finally cease to exist as a nation. A writer is not obliged to hold himself accountable for the consequences of any of the established principles, upon which this world is projected: whether we see it or not, all are established in wisdom, and will be improved for the highest advantage of the human race collectively. The religion of nature, the light of revelation, and the pages of history, are combined in the proof, that God has ordered that nations shall become extinct, and that others shall take their places.

. . .

His [the Indian's] agonies, at first, seem to demand a tear from the eye of humanity: but when we reflect, that the extinction of his race, and the progress of the arts which give rise to his distressing apprehensions, are for the increase of mankind, and for the promotion of the world's glory and happiness; that five hundred of rational animals may enjoy life in plenty, and comfort, where only one Savage drags out a hungry existence, we shall be pleased with the perspective into futurity.

. . .

There may be an apparent foundation for a charge of advancing a position, that the civilized people may take the land of the Savages when they please.[32]

On the one hand, this argument stems from Locke's concept of the right of property, which seems to have inspired it.[33] On the other, it looks forward to the "manifest destiny" of the nineteenth century, the romantic notion that was used—and taken seriously by most Americans—to justify the conquest of the West. Sullivan's language, too, is the language of romantic nationalism:

The earth was made for man. . . . The exigencies of his nature compel him, by toil, to till the earth for food, and the faculties of his mind, prompting him to an excellency in the art, give a certain indication that he was intended to beautify with dress, and to ornament with architecture, that part of creation which was assigned to him.

He goes on to predict with utter confidence a "progressive improvement" of the world, until the mighty mountains, and the deep and dangerous morasses . . . in their turn become subject to the hand of agriculture, and yield to man a compensation for his labour." The world began as "a rude mass of matter." It will advance finally to "the highest state of elegance to which the noblest refinement of human reason can bring it." Such an evolution, or unfolding, is surely related to the Romantic concept of *Streben*[34]—a striving from "chaos" to "an uninhabited and desolate desert" to "the habitation of beasts, and birds; then the haunts of roaming and unsocial barbarians; then the dwelling of savage tribes; and finally the high cultivated, and beautifully decorated soil of civilized nations."[35]

Sullivan gets to the question of statehood for Maine at the very end of his book. It is a simple prediction, flowing naturally from the assumptions of inevitable progress in much of the rest of the work. Romantics were confident in the inexorable laws of history. Daniel Davis's Federalist tract of 1792 in support of statehood had laid out a succession of hard-headed political and economic arguments: gaining two senators in Congress, permitting more frequent sittings of a Supreme Judicial Court in the District, placing the seat of government in the midst of the people, getting a fair share of federal appointments, reducing the costs of government, and the like. Sullivan's argument, if that is what it is, proceeds by simple assertion.[36]

"This extensive country," writes Sullivan, "is so large and populous, and its situation so peculiar, that it cannot remain long a part of the commonwealth of Massachusetts." Certain difficulties of geography, affecting the choice of a site for the state capital, he feels, will delay the separation temporarily. He concludes:

> But, whenever the people can agree upon and procure a separation, it will give an energy to their public conduct, and a spirit of enterprise to their public exertions, which can never be produced by any other means. Events of such magnitude, generally take place as soon as the nature of things and a proper concurrence of circumstances render it fit and proper. While we lament the prospect of losing a part of our civil society, ... we rejoice in the anticipation of that elevated prosperity, and high degree of importance, to which the District must, from its peculiar advantages, be finally raised.[37]

In stark contrast, John Adams, a Federalist and no romantic, wrote in 1819 that "when there arises in Maine a bold, daring, ardent genius with talents capable of inspiring the people with his own ambition, he will tear off Maine from Massachusetts and leave her in a state below mediocrity in the union."[38] Henry Adams could hardly have done better than cite these words of his great-grandfather to demonstrate the Federalist suspicion of democratic "visionaries."

James Sullivan, however, was more than simply a democrat. The structure of his *History of the District of Maine* begins with the idea of an advantageous natural environment, builds through various precivilized states to "improvement" by civilized society, and looks toward an inevitable state of political dignity and importance—all under the guidance of a beneficent and approving Providence. This description is an adequate summary of the creed of postrevolutionary American nationalism, which Sullivan applied, not even to one of the states but to a confidently proclaimed future state. It was a nationalism powered by a spirit of progress, a faith in the mysterious but inexorable process of history. It was the process, with its inevitable climax, that Sullivan set about reporting in his *History*. His age offered him alternatives to this kind of history writing, but for Sullivan's purpose, "science" was useful only as a handmaiden to romance; when he used it at all in dealing with the larger questions in his book, it was not to help him know, but to help him explain what he already "knew" by inspiration.

Sullivan did not take part in the movement for Maine statehood; he died twelve years before the Missouri Compromise, after spending most of his public career in Boston. But every important political movement needs its underlying rationale, its fundamental assumptions. Sullivan comes as close as anyone whose words survive to articulating the romantic, nationalistic, republican spirit of the age. We look in vain to find Sullivan's name invoked by the democratic leaders who brought the statehood movement to successful fruition, but the spirit that Sullivan expressed in 1795 was the same spirit that a quarter of a century later helped produce the separation of Maine from Massachusetts.

NOTES

1. Henry Adams, *History of the United States During the Administration of Thomas Jefferson*, 2 vols. (New York: A. and C. Boni, 1930), vol. 1, pp. 176–177.

2. Available most conveniently in Lester J. Cappon (ed.), *The Adams-Jefferson Letters: the Complete Correspondence Between Thomas Jefferson and Abigail and John Adams*, 2 vols. (Chapel Hill: University of North Carolina Press, 1959; reprinted New York: Simon and Schuster, 1971). The paperbound 1971 edition contains both volumes.

3. Ronald F. Banks, *Maine Becomes a State: The Movement to Separate Maine from Massachusetts, 1785–1820* (Middletown, Conn.: Wesleyan University Press, 1970).

4. See Banks, *Maine Becomes a State*, pp. 26–40, for the second separation movement.

5. Daniel Davis, *An Address to the Inhabitants of the District of Maine upon the Subject of Their Separation from the Present Government of Massachusetts* (Portland: Thomas Wait, 1791).

6. James Sullivan, *History of the District of Maine* (Boston: I. Thomas and E. T. Andrews, 1795; reprinted Augusta: Maine State Museum, 1970), p. 396.

7. The reader will find a similar, though curtailed argument, in Charles E. Clark, *Maine: A Bicentennial History* (New York: W. W. Norton, 1977), pp. 53–58.

8. Most biographers of Sullivan have placed his birth in Berwick, but Charles P. Whittemore, in a relatively recent biography of James Sullivan's older brother John, *A General of the Revolution, John Sullivan of New Hampshire* (New York: Columbia University Press, 1961), has all the children of John and Margery Sullivan born in Somersworth, New Hampshire, before the family moved across the river to Berwick in 1747 or 1748, p. 2.

9. The standard biographical treatments of James Sullivan are Thomas C. Amory, *Life of James Sullivan with Selections from his Writings*, 2 vols. (Boston: Phillips, Sampson and Co., 1859), and Horace H. Burbank, "James Sullivan," *Collections of the Maine Historical Society*, 3rd ser., I (1904), 322–338. There are also sketches in John L. Sibley, *Biographical Sketches of Graduates of Harvard University* and Clifford K. Shipton, *Biographical Sketches of those who Attended Harvard College*, 17 vols. (Boston: Massachusetts Historical Society, 1873–1975), vol. 15, pp. 299–322, and at the front of the Maine State Museum's 1970 reprint of Sullivan's *History of the District of Maine*.

10. [John Sylvester John Gardiner], *An Epistle to Zenas* (Boston: Peter Edes, 1786?).

11. *The Path of Riches: an Inquiry into the Principles of Stocks and Banks* (Boston: P. Edes for I. Thomas and E. T. Andrews, 1792); *The Altar of Baal Thrown Down: Or, the French Nation Defended Against the Pulpit Slander of David Osgood, A.M., Pastor of the Church in Medford. A Sermon, par Citoyen de Novion* (Boston: From the Chronicle-Press, by Adams & Larkin, 1795); *Strictures on the Rev. Mr. Thatcher's Pamphlet Entitled, Observations upon the State of the Clergy of New-England* (Boston: Benjamin Edes and Sons, 1785); *A Dissertation upon the Constitutional Freedom of the Press in the United States of America* (Boston: David Carlisle for Joseph Nancrede, 1801); *History of Land Titles in Massachusetts* (Boston: I. Thomas and E. T. Andrews for the author, 1801); and "The History of the Penobscot Indians." *Collections of the Massachusetts Historical Society*, 9 (1804), 207–232 (hereafter *Coll. MaHS*).

12. Sullivan, *History*, pp. vi–vii.

13. Ibid., p. iii.   14. Ibid., p. v.

15. See Thomas Jefferson, *Notes on the State of Virginia*, William Peden (ed.) (Chapel Hill: University of North Carolina Press, 1955), pp. 3–4; Jeremy Belknap, *The History of New-Hampshire*, 2nd ed., 3 vols. (Dover, N.H.: O. Crosby and J. Varney, 1812), vol. 3, pp. 9–14; vol. 3 reprinted as vol. 2 in The Sources of Science edition, New York: Johnson Reprint Corp., 1970.

16. Sullivan, *History*, pp. 8–9.

17. Belknap, *New-Hampshire*, vol. 3, pp. 17–18.

18. Ibid., 171–190. Belknap also adds in an appendix a letter from a correspondent purporting to demonstrate an error in his method of making population projections, pp. 344–353. Belknap was more conservative than Sullivan in politics as well as in scholarship; for whatever it may signify, he was a Federalist. See George B. Kirsch, *Jeremy Belknap: A Biography* (New York: Arno Press, 1982), pp. 92–114.

19. Sullivan, *History*, pp. 60–61.

20. For one treatment of the romantic interest in Indians in the Early Republic, see Richard Beale Davis's discussion of the Virginian fascination with Pocahontas in *Intellectual Life in Jefferson's Virginia, 1790–1830* (Chapel Hill: University of North Carolina Press, 1964), pp. 313–319. The discussion includes a proposition that is in harmony with the main argument offered in this chapter: "The birth of the American nation and the beginnings of the triumph of Romanticism as an attitude toward life and art came almost simultaneously. Pride in liberty, nostalgic and sentimental glances at the past, and genuine antiquarianism existed side by side. Each state consciously and unconsciously was intent on finding at least some of its roots in an American rather than a European past."

21. Belknap, *New-Hampshire*, vol. 3, pp. 63–72.

22. Jefferson, *Notes on Virginia*, pp. 92–107.

23. Ibid., pp. 43–65, 137–143.

24. Francis Jennings, *The Invasion of America: Indians, Colonialism, and the Cant of Conquest* (Chapel Hill: University of North Carolina Press for the Institute of Early American History and Culture, 1975).

25. Sullivan, *History*, p. 107.

26. Ibid., pp. 102–103, 106–107.

27. For Logan's speech and Jefferson's commentary, see *Notes on Virginia*, pp. 62–63. Logan (or Tahgahjute) was a Mingo chief whose eloquent remarks to the Earl of Dunmore, governor of Virginia, Jefferson quotes in order to challenge Buffon's contention that the American Indian is mentally as well as physically inferior to the European.

28. Sullivan, *History*, pp. 84–87, 98–100, 104–106. Whereas Jefferson takes great pains to defend the nature and character of the Indian against the aspersions of Buffon, Sullivan actually uses some of the same evidence that Jefferson refutes in order to sustain a case for the Indian's lack of virility. See pp. 80–82, and compare to Jefferson, *Notes on Virginia*, pp. 58–61.

29. Sullivan published separate works on two of the subjects covered extensively in the *History*. One was his history of the Penobscot Indians, *Coll. MaHS*, 9 (1804); the other was *History of Land Titles in Massachusetts*.

30. Sullivan, *History*, pp. 109–111.

31. Ibid., pp. 129–139.

32. Ibid., pp. 138–139.

33. The most relevant passage from Locke's *Two Treatises of Government* would appear to be a portion of paragraph 34 of the Second Treatise: "God gave the world to men in common; but since He gave it them for their benefit, and the greatest conveniences of life they were capable to draw from it, it cannot be supposed He meant it should always remain common and uncultivated. He gave it to the use of the industrious and rational...." [John Locke, *An Essay Concerning the True Original, Extent and End of Civil Government* (1691) in Edwin A. Burtt (ed.), *The English Philosophers from Bacon to Mill* (New York: Random House, 1939), p. 413.] More than a quarter of a century ago, Wilcomb E. Washburn produced a pioneering essay on justifying the European occupation of Indian lands ["The Moral and Legal Justifications for Dispossessing the Indians" in James Morton Smith (ed.), *Seventeenth-Century America: Essays in Colonial History* (Chapel Hill: University of North Carolina Press, 1959), pp. 15–32]. The essay does not discuss any arguments offered at the time of settlement or subsequent to it that are really similar to Sullivan's, but does draw attention to Sir Thomas More's proposition in *Utopia* (1516) that the Utopians had a just cause of war "when any people holdeth a piece of ground void and vacant to no good or profitable use: keeping others from the use and possession of it, which, notwithstanding, by the law of nature, ought thereof to be nourished and relieved." (p. 24.) Sullivan's analysis certainly contains echoes of More and others who professed the right of an occupier to vacant land. However, it is probably more like the rationalizations of John Winthrop, who in 1629 while pondering his move to America, in effect anticipated Locke by reasoning that "because the Indians had not 'subdued' it [the land] by methods recognized in English law, ... [they] therefore had no 'natural' right to it...." (Jennings, *Invasion of America*, p. 135.)

34. For one treatment of *Streben*, see Willson H. Coates and Hayden V. White, *The Ordeal of Liberal Humanism: An Intellectual History of Western Europe* (New York: McGraw-Hill, 1970), vol. 2, pp. 55–58.

35. Sullivan, *History*, pp. 129–131, 135, 139.

36. Banks summarizes Davis's arguments in *Maine Becomes a State*, pp. 29–31.

37. Sullivan, *History*, p. 396. To continue the parallel—and contrast—between Sullivan and Belknap's histories, we note that Belknap concludes his *History of New-Hampshire* with a celebratory paragraph of about the same length as Sullivan's final statement. But instead of anticipating a glorious future in which his state has changed its status or reached a new state of development, Belknap's much quoted conclusion celebrates an existing institution in its ideal form: the well-ordered New England town. "Such a situation," he concludes, "may be

considered as the most favourable to social happiness of any which this world can afford." If Belknap was a visionary, his vision was of a perfected model of a society that he may have sensed already belonged more to the past than to the future. (Belknap, *New-Hampshire*, vol. 3, p. 251.) For some more thoughts on Belknap's history, see Sidney Kaplan, "*The History of New-Hampshire*: Jeremy Belknap as Literary Craftsman," *William and Mary Quarterly*, 21 (January 1964); 18–39; Jere R. Daniell, "Jeremy Belknap and the *History of New-Hampshire*," in Lawrence H. Leder (ed.), *The Colonial Legacy*, vols. III–IV (New York: Harper & Row, 1973), pp. 241–264; Charles E. Clark, "History, Literature, and Belknap's 'Social Happiness,'" *Historical New Hampshire*, 35 (Spring 1980); 1–22.

38. Quoted in Banks, *Maine Becomes a State*, p. 204.

Dorsey R. Kleitz

CHAPTER 10

JONATHAN FISHER'S EMBLEMATIC MIND

No single figure of the Early Republic commanded more scholarly attention in "Maine at Statehood" than the Reverend Jonathan Fisher, the versatile parson of Blue Hill. As Dorsey Kleitz points out in this chapter, Fisher has been attracting a modest following of students ever since Mary Ellen Chase published a biography of the man in 1948. True, Fisher was just a country preacher whose ability to devote so much time to his intellectual and artistic interests had at least something to do with the declining demands of a diminishing parish. Moreover, his contemporaries would probably not have regarded those interests as especially unusual for one of Fisher's training and station. However, the very volume of Fisher's productions in print and paint has made him more accessible than the great majority of his contemporaries to modern students; the content of his imagination and versatility of his talent have proved an irresistible lure. In the rather different hands of Mr. Kleitz and of Richard Moss (Chapter 11), Fisher becomes an especially noteworthy representative of an age and place in transition. Kleitz places the work of Jonathan Fisher in the context of the "emblem" tradition, which evolved during the Renaissance as a means of expressing complex truth in a concise and comprehensive manner. By the eighteenth century, the emblem had become an instrument of popular education. Fisher's *Youth's Primer* and *Scripture Animals* reflect the continuing influence of the tradition of relating illustration to text. Kleitz also provides an "emblematic" reading of two of Fisher's paintings, *Self-Portrait* and *A Morning View of Blue Hill Village*. The latter is so rich in symbolism and so evocative of its time and place as almost to merit the status of the central cultural icon of Maine in the Early Republic. Kleitz's analysis of *Morning View* combines nicely with the interpretations of Richard Moss and David Watters in the two concluding chapters to provide a remarkably full discussion of this most notable work of Maine folk art.

> An emblem is but a silent parable ... Before the
> knowledge of letters, God was known by
> hieroglyphics. And indeed, what are the
> Heavens, the earth, nay every creature, but
> Hieroglyphics and Emblems of his glory?
>
> Preface to Francis Quarles's *Emblemes* (1635)

Dorsey R. Kleitz is a doctoral candidate in English at the University of New Hampshire.

Since the publication of Mary Ellen Chase's biography, *Jonathan Fisher, Maine Parson* (1948), an increasing amount of attention has been paid to this New England original. Most of this interest has focused on Fisher's artwork—his watercolors, oils, and numerous wood engravings—and on his mechanical genius—he designed and built his own house and furniture. The result has been a careful assessment of his life, together with an examination and cataloging of his many accomplishments. Today, Jonathan Fisher is viewed, in Alice Winchester's words, as a "versatile Yankee," a country parson who, possessed of tremendous energy and a consuming sense of the value and purpose of life, epitomizes the best of rural New England in the late eighteenth and early nineteenth centuries.[1] Thinking of Fisher in these general terms is a useful start toward the closer, more specific examination I would like to make. I suggest that Jonathan Fisher can be placed in a particular tradition, which he exemplifies in his literary works, art, and perception and which relates him to the vision and rhetoric of New England. It is the tradition of emblem literature.

Typically, an emblem is a device that instructs and consists of three parts: an engraving or woodcut of some symbolic object, person, or event; a phrase or motto accompanying the illustration; and a poem or prose passage interpreting the scene, often drawing some suitable moral application. An example from Francis Quarles' *Hieroglyphikes* of 1638 (Illus. 56), one of the most notable English emblem books, depicts a candle set on a globe surrounded by flowers. To the left of the flame is the zodiac symbol for Taurus, a spring sign, and to the right, a small peacock, a symbol of vanity. Behind the candle a youth tries to control a rearing horse. The mottos, one in Latin and one in English, tell us, "Your child, May, is youth," and, from Job, "His bones are full of the sinnes of his youth." The last stanza of the poem following clarifies the meaning:

> Proud Blossom, use thy Time; Time's headstrong Horse
> Will post away;
> Trust not the foll'wing day,
> For ev'ry day brings forth a worse:
> Take time at best; Beleeve't, thy daies will fall
> From good to bad; from bad to worst of all.[2]

The use of emblems as allegories and to convey moral meanings began in the sixteenth century in Italy and spread to England. Transplanted to America, the tradition was modified by the colonial interest in the natural world. Cotton Mather's *Winter Meditations* (1693) and John Flavel's *Husbandry Spiritualized* (1709) are examples of Puritan literature that view the natural world metaphorically and show the compatibility of the Book of Scripture and the Book of Nature. Flavel, whose text is without illustration but is organized much like an emblem book, states his position clearly:

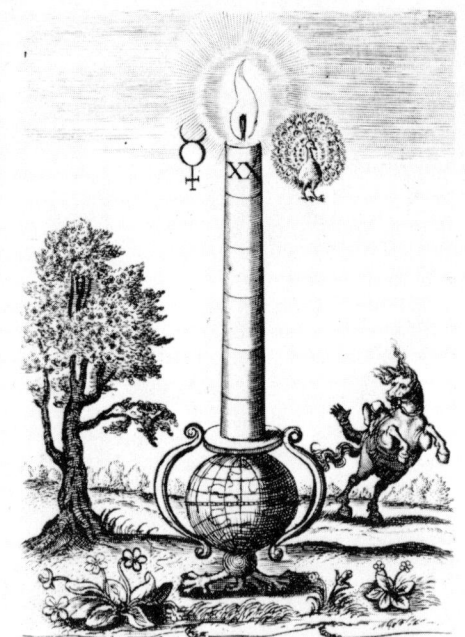

56. "HIEROGLIPH. X.," from *Hieroglyphikes* by Francis Quarles, 1638. (By permission of the Houghton Library, Harvard University)

God hath endowed the creatures with a spiritual as well as fleshly usefulness; they have not only a natural use ... but also a spiritual use, as they bear the figures and similitudes of many sublime and heavenly mysteries. Believe me thou shalt find more in the woods, than in a corner; stones and trees shalt teach thee what thou shalt not hear from a learned doctor.[3]

It is in the context of their Puritan impulse to "read" the Bible in the world, informed by the English emblem tradition, that much of the work of Jonathan Fisher can best be understood.[4]

The greatest popularity of emblem literature came during the Renaissance and can be attributed, at least in part, to the emblem's effectiveness as an instrument for moral and religious teaching. Through an emblem, the explanation of nature, scripture, and history could be oriented in a particular manner. Complex points of doctrine could be framed concisely and comprehensively. As instruction and reference texts, the English emblem books supplied visual, coded parables, which several generations of the English used to interpret the world.[5]

The English emblem tradition underwent an important change with John Bunyan. By the Restoration in 1660, the usually accepted turning point in seventeenth century thought, the best work in the emblem convention had been done. The educated classes directed their attention to the elegance and lucidity of Dryden and left the emblem, with its emphasis on allegory, to the ordinary reader. In England there was no longer a place for emblems in the main course of literature and the emblem book quickly shifted from a serious literary form to a means of instruction primarily for the young. John Bunyan's *A Book For Boys and Girls* characterizes this shift.

Published in 1686 and later, in a radically revised version called *Divine Emblems or Temporal Things Spiritualized, Fitted for the Use of Boys and Girls*, Bunyan's book was extremely popular in eighteenth century England. As an emblem book it differs considerably from earlier Renaissance examples. In keeping with the title, the themes are elementary and developed with little interest in rhetoric. The naive style is well suited to its subject matter, much of which is taken from nature and concerns such animals as moles, spiders, birds, frogs, and ants. Religious topics take up only a small part of the book, most of the poems being secular in content and ethical in application. Bunyan's book thus marks the transition of the emblem book from serious literature to an instrument of popular education aimed at youth. It is broadly in this form that the emblem tradition in literature manifests itself in the United States in the late eighteenth and early nineteenth centuries and appears in the work of Jonathan Fisher.

One of the most influential books printed in early America, *The New England Primer*, includes an emblematic alphabet in which pictures and rhymes complement each other[6] (Illus. 57). This classic text was used throughout New England for over 150 years and provided

57. Emblematic alphabet, from *The New England Primer* (Springfield: 1809).
(By permission of the Houghton Library, Harvard University)

FAITH has a shield
O'er death to wield;

With steady eye
She looks on high.

58. "FAITH," from *Youth's Primer* by Jonathan Fisher (Portland: 1818). (By permission of the Houghton Library, Harvard University)

the model for Jonathan Fisher's first published book, *The Youth's Primer*.

Fisher's *Primer* consists of pairs of short verses arranged in alphabetical order. Accompanying each pair is a woodcut illustrating the theme and a prose explanation, usually religious or moral in content. The use of woodcuts was common in primers, but the three-part structure of woodcut, motto, and interpretation found in Fisher's work was not. The example from the letter "F" in Fisher's *Primer* shows a woman holding a shield marked "Faith," and raising an open book (Illus. 58). Lying on the ground is a skeleton reaching out to her. The verses, "FAITH has a shield / O'er death to wield; // With steady eye / She looks on high," tell us that the skeleton is Death, and introduce us to the prose explanation that urges us to put our faith in the Bible (Faith's open book) and in Christ.

Another example, this one drawing more explicitly from the emblem tradition, is Fisher's treatment of the letter "H" (Illus. 59). Here, a bird is shown flying with a large heart pendant around its neck. Under the bird is a woman on the ground weeping. The verses give us a clue as to what is happening: "Our HEART and love / Should soar above, // While here we lie, / And humbly cry." The prose passage gives us the author's application:

> Though we lie on our faces, in the very lowest posture of reverence, and speak very earnestly to God with our lips, if our hearts and affections do not go forth towards him, our prayers will not be heard.[7]

Our HEART and love | While here we lie,
Should soar above, | And humbly cry.

59. "Our HEART," from *Youth's Primer* by Jonathan Fisher. (By permission of the Houghton Library Harvard University)

The heart was an extremely popular Renaissance emblem motif and was the subject of several emblem books, including Christopher Harvey's *Schola Cordis* (1647) and George Wither's *A Collection of Emblems* (1635). Wither's book contains an example with the moral, "be cautious with your heart" (Illus. 60).[8] While Wither's emblem is secular and addresses an older, educated audience, both he and Fisher are examining the general question of how to direct the heart, and both of them are employing emblems to do this. As in all fully developed emblems, none of the three parts in Fisher's emblem is as effective by itself as they all are together, woven into a whole. Thus the illustration of the Heart cannot successfully stand alone; it needs the verses which, in turn, need the text. This relationship between word and picture is essential to the emblem convention.

Fisher's second book, a collection of his poems entitled *Short Poems, Including a Sketch of the Scriptures to the Book of Ruth, Satan's Great Device . . . and a Few Others on Various Subjects*, contains only two woodcuts, but one of them has a definite emblematic relationship to the poem it illustrates. The poem, on the evils of drunkenness, is called "Satan's Great Device." The author's title refers to drink as the device or method by which Satan traps man, but "device" also has the traditional meaning of a design, as a coat of arms. Here Fisher may intend an ambiguity; Satan's "device," his coat of arms, could be the engraving itself. The cut (Illus. 61) shows a man, apparently drunk, supported by his wife while his son looks on. The motto, actually a stanza printed between the illustration and the main poem, advises:

60. Heart emblem, from *A Collection of Emblems* by George Wither, 1635. (By permission of the Houghton Library, Harvard University)

> See the vile drunkard, how he reels,
> How like a fool he looks and feels;
> Reader, be warned and shun the way,
> Which leads to ruin while you may.[9]

The opening words indicate that the motto was specifically written to complement the cut. The message relies on our seeing the engraving. The cut, then, is not simply "dumb poetry," but adds pictorial strength to the motto. The little boy looking at his father appears to represent the reader as a kind of innocent viewer who sees the drunken man headed toward disaster. The poem, a long, fairly dramatic religious piece with allusions to *Paradise Lost*, tells us that the drunkard's disaster is not only physical, but also spiritual:

> In many a church there's more than one,
> Whose soul by tippling is undone,
> Who yet, the discipline so slack,
> Retains his place, and will not lack
> His full proportion in the wine,
> And thus profanes a holy sign.[10]

In 1819 Jonathan Fisher began seriously to write a natural history of the animals in the Bible, an idea he first had while a student at Harvard. The final result, published in 1834 under the title *Scripture*

See the vile drunkard, how he reels,
How like a fool he looks and feels;
Reader, be warn'd, and shun the way,
Which leads to ruin, while you may.

SATAN'S GREAT DEVICE.

61. "SATAN'S GREAT DEVICE,"
from *Short Poems, Including a Sketch of the Scriptures to the Book of Ruth, Satan's Great Device . . . and a Few Others on Various Subjects* by Jonathan Fisher (Portland: 1827).
(By permission of the Houghton Library, Harvard University)

Animals, or Natural History of the Living Creatures Named in the Bible, Written Especially for Youth, combined the author's lifelong interest in nature and art with his intimate knowledge of the Bible and his concern for training the young. To illustrate his book, Fisher made more than one hundred woodcuts and arranged them in alphabetical order from Adder to Woodcock. A foreword explains that most of the cuts are copied from other engravers and states the book's educational purpose:

> The work is designed especially to assist young people in gaining a knowledge of the natural history of the Bible. . . . At the close of most of the articles I have added something in the way of moralizing or spiritualizing.[11]

From the title page we know that we are involved in emblem literature. The wood engraving shown in Illus. 62 is one of Fisher's finest, depicting a landscape of mountains, forests, and streams—full of wildlife. The accompanying quotation from Psalm 147, "He giveth to the beast his food and to the young ravens which cry," reminds us that the setting is Biblical and that the animals are those mentioned in the Bible. Closely following this motto is a complex engraving containing a flock of birds in the sky, a stag standing by a doe drinking from a stream, a raven bringing food to a nest full of young, and less tranquil,

206 Dorsey R. Kleitz

62. Title page, *Scripture Animals* by
Jonathan Fisher (Portland: 1834).
(By permission of the Houghton Library,
Harvard University)

a lion leaping on its prey. The illustration seems to be a Garden of Eden without man. Without man? A more careful examination reveals the profile of a head neatly set in the branches of the trees in the center of the engraving. The silhouette is cut off by the mountain that dominates the background. The optical effect makes it part of the landscape yet separate from it; in the Garden and outside the Garden. In the Biblical text, this figure is God, the Creator whose image is found everywhere in nature; in Fisher's text, the silhouette is of Jonathan Fisher, the author, whose image is found and understood in his creation, the book. One additional element that locates the Garden and places it firmly in Parson Fisher's care is the identification of the mountain in the cut as Blue Hill, the hill that gave its name to the coastal town in Maine where Fisher spent most of his life as a Congregational minister. *Scripture Animals* can thus be viewed as one large, complex emblem whose illustration and motto are on the title page and whose application is the sum of the emblems contained in the text.

Inside the book, Fisher uses this same three-part structure to organize the information on the different animals. The treatment of the ant, for example, begins with an engraving of the insect (Illus. 63). This is followed by a detailed description of the ant and its habits, by a listing of the places in the Bible where the ant is mentioned, and finally by a poem that draws a moral:

> Go to the Ant, thou sluggard go;
> This very day be wise;
> And spare no pains to have thy gains
> Well stored above the skies.[12]

The verses exhort us to follow the ant's example and provide for the future. They are particularly interesting because they echo John Bunyan's poem "Upon the Ant," in his *Book for Boys and Girls*:

> But since thy God doth bid thee to her go,
> Obey; her ways consider and be wise;
> The ants, they tell thee what thou must do,
> And set the way to life before thine eyes.[13]

Bunyan's concern with the ant is almost the same as Fisher's. For both, the ant is a living emblem of industriousness—a model for man. In its overall intent, tone, and subject matter *Scripture Animals* contains many similarities to Bunyan's book. *A Book For Boys and Girls* was

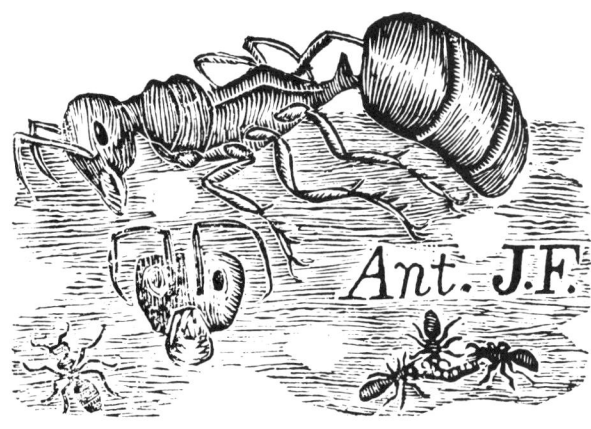

ANT.
[The figure is from nature and magnified.]

63. "ANT," from *Scripture Animals* by Jonathan Fisher.
(By permission of the Houghton Library, Harvard University)

64. "PEACOCK," from *Scripture Animals* by Jonathan Fisher.
(By permission of the Houghton Library, Harvard University)

published in the United States in 1794 with the title, *Divine Emblems*, and so could easily have been known to Fisher.

Several times in the poems in *Scripture Animals* the author directly refers to animals as emblems. The frog is "an emblem of spirits unclean," and about the pigeon he writes:

> We have here an emblem for those who would join
> In dear marriage union to teach them to live
> Most faithfully true and their skill to combine
> To make it their pleasure sweet pleasure to give.[14]

The use of the pigeon as an emblem of constancy appears also in John Wynne's *Choice Emblems* (1790), the first emblem book published in the United States and a book, like *Scripture Animals*, written for youth. *Choice Emblems* frequently uses animals in the emblems. In both Fisher and Wynne the peacock with spread tail illustrates vanity (Illus. 64). The accompanying poems also contain similarities:

> Are witless youth of beauty vain,
> And proud of gaudy dress?
> The noisy peacock, with his train,
> May well their state express.
> (Fisher)[15]

> Behold that silly bird, how proudly vain,
> Of the bright colors of his gaudy train!
> ...
> O son of vanity, be wise in time!
> Apply the moral of this homely rhyme.
> (Wynne)[16]

Both writers explain their illustrations by drawing a parallel between the "gaudy train" of the bird and the "gaudy dress" of youth. This is not to imply Fisher's dependence on Bunyan or Wynne, but to indicate a similarity of approach common to them all, an approach that is fundamentally emblematic and at the same time oriented toward the instruction of young people.

At one point, when discussing Biblical references to the stork, Fisher declares that two women, "with wings like storks," mentioned in Zechariah are an "emblem" of God's judgment of wicked Jews. Here the author extends his emblematic interpretation of Biblical animals to an emblematic interpretation of Biblical characters, something beyond the intended scope of *Scripture Animals* and revealing Fisher's general desire to view the world emblematically.

65. Woodcut from the last page of *Scripture Animals* by Jonathan Fisher.
(By permission of the Houghton Library, Harvard University)

The woodcut on the last page of *Scripture Animals*, depicting a gravestone and the setting sun (Illus. 65), echoes in abbreviated form the final cut in another well-known English emblem book, Geoffrey Whitney's *Choice of Emblems* (1586) (Illus. 66).[17] Fisher's Latin motto, "The sun sets; the shadows gather," while not as direct as Whitney's

66. "Tempus omnia terminat," from the last page of Geoffrey Whitney's *Choice of Emblems,* 1586.
(By permission of the Houghton Library, Harvard University)

Jonathan Fisher's Emblematic Mind   209

"Time ends everything," contains the same closing sentiment. Although it can be viewed simply as a literary convention—the author's leavetaking—it is particularly appropriate for Fisher to end his emblem book with an emblematic woodcut combining word and image. The colonial stone carver commonly engraved emblematic devices on gravestones; it is fitting, then, that Jonathan Fisher use an emblematic engraving of a gravestone to end his book.[18]

Scripture Animals can be viewed as an example of an early nineteenth century American emblem book. In its structure and the relationship of picture to text, it draws heavily from the English emblem tradition, and in its orientation, from John Bunyan's influence on this tradition. In its combination of natural history and religion, and in its mature vitality, however, *Scripture Animals* reflects the attitudes of rural New England in the early nineteenth century.

All the examples of Fisher's use of emblems discussed so far center on his published work, where an illustration is coupled with a specific text. Fisher also employs emblematic methods in his major paintings. Two of them reveal a broadly emblematic world view: his *Self-Portrait* (Illus. 67) and his *A Morning View of Blue Hill Village*. (See Plate XIII).

Jonathan Fisher painted four self-portraits for members of his family: the first in 1824, another in 1825, and two others in 1838. All are almost identical, except that in the later versions the artist paints himself as a bit older, with his features more weathered. In the top half of the portrait we see the head of a middle-aged man staring out at the viewer from a somber interior containing only a coat hanging on the wall. The look on his face is a mixture of determination and curiosity. In the bottom half of the painting is a collection of texts and writing instruments: a letter from New Jersey addressed to "Rev. Jonathan Fisher," an open Bible in Hebrew, a note with Fisher's name and the year on it (the painting's signature), and an inkstand containing a quill pen. The two halves of the work are connected, in part, by Fisher's right arm with a finger of his right hand pointing firmly to a verse in the open Bible. Usually, portraits emphasized the head and the hands, and here the artist takes full advantage of this convention. Compositionally, Fisher's portrait "reads" like an emblem. The viewer's attention is first fixed on the face—the image—and then, following the movement of the painting, on the hand pointing to the Bible—the text. As in most of Fisher's emblematic work, there is a three-part structure: the painting itself, the motto (Fisher's name, identifying the subject), and the explanation (the Biblical text). The top half of the painting is visual, while the bottom half is verbal. The message is instructional. In his self-portrait, Fisher is emblematic of the man in the world (symbolized by the coat on the wall and the letter) who lives by the Bible.

Fisher painted *Morning View* in 1824, the same year as the first self-portrait and roughly ten years before he completed the title page to *Scripture Animals*. Although it appears to be a simple landscape paint-

67. *Self-Portrait,* by Jonathan Fisher, 1824.
(Oil on panel. The Jonathan Fisher Memorial, Blue Hill)

ing, in the context of the self-portrait and the engraving it is more. As with these two works, we can read *Morning View* as Fisher's complex emblemizing of the world around him. Although the only text visible in the painting is the title, date, and the artist's signature in the lower right corner, the work is charged with scripture.

One reading of the painting tells us that we are viewing the progress of rural America in the early nineteenth century. A ship with full sails is arriving in port. The town, while not large, looks prosperous. The road leads by neat houses and fenced fields to a church prominently positioned on the hill across from the viewer. In the foreground, two well-clothed women stand next to a fat horse, behind which a man with a stick is attacking a large snake. Over the first stone wall we see the stumps of the primeval forest cleared and made safe by man. The scene is pastoral, the "dawn" of the nineteenth century.

Another, closer reading tells us that we are viewing Jonathan Fisher's work in Blue Hill, Maine, in 1824. Fisher was the first settled minister in the town and as such was intimately involved in the spiritual growth of the community. The church was built for him, and his house is visible just beyond and to the left of it. Note that the artist arranged his painting so that these two buildings appear above the town where, symbolically, the minister can watch over and guide his people. In part, the well-ordered fields and the town's prosperity attest to Fisher's personal influence in Blue Hill. The chaos of the wilderness has been brought under control; all that remains are a few stumps to remind us of the spiritually dark past. Continuing this reading, the drama taking place in the lower right becomes highly significant. Satan is being driven from the Garden as a new day begins for Christianity. One of the main lines of movement in the painting follows the road up past the church toward the brightening sky. This is the way, through religion and the Reverend Mr. Fisher, that the villagers must go to reach spiritual salvation.

A Morning View of Blue Hill Village is the immediate inspiration for the later title page to *Scripture Animals*. The artist is as ingenious in his painting of the village of Blue Hill as he is in the woodcut with the mountain of Blue Hill. The major difference between these two pieces is the starting point. In the painting the artist begins with a natural setting and spiritualizes it; in the woodcut he begins with a Biblical setting and naturalizes it. While the painting cannot fully sustain the emblematic interpretation the engraving can, the same allegorical faculty was involved in its creation. In both, the natural world has become God's sacred text and Fisher is the translator.

It is tempting to take the short step from Jonathan Fisher to Ralph Waldo Emerson and say that if Fisher had been born a generation later, Nature and Scripture might have been interchangeable for him. True, Fisher was a contemporary of William Ellery Channing, the spiritual father of the Transcendentalists, but to make too much of this would be unfair. Fisher is, after all, first and foremost, a man of the Bible. When his finger stabs at the text in his self-portrait, it is with the supreme confidence that the Bible is the word of God and is, perhaps, as close to God as man can come. For Fisher, fashioning emblems and allegories of the world was a method of seeing God in the world, but never, consciously, a method of transforming nature or man into God. Fisher inherited his method from the English emblemists and Protestant orthodoxy, but he applied it freely, expressing his delight and curiosity in life as he experienced it.

NOTES

1. Mary Ellen Chase, *Jonathan Fisher, Maine Parson, 1768–1847* (New York: Macmillan, 1948); Alice Winchester, *Versatile Yankee, The Art of Jonathan Fisher* (Princeton: Pyne Press, 1973).

2. Francis Quarles, *Hieroglyphikes* (London: Augustine Matthews, 1638; reprinted Menston, England: Scolar Press, 1969), pp. 38–39.

3. John Flavel, *Husbandry Spiritualized* (Elizabethtown, N.J.: Shepard Kollack, 1795), p. 3.

4. There is little evidence that any of the well-known English emblem books reached New England before the eighteenth century. Brief references to the literary works of the English emblemists exist in library catalogs and colonial wills, but our understanding of the role of the emblem in early American literary imagination comes largely from Edward Taylor, whose poetry employs blind emblems. In everyday colonial life, emblematic devices were occasionally used in silversmithing and cabinetmaking, and commonly used in stonecarving, on gravestones. See Alan Howard, "The World as Emblem: Language and Vision in the Poetry of Edward Taylor," *American Literature*, 44 (November 1972), 359–384; Allan Ludwig, *Graven Images: New England Stone Carving and its Symbols, 1650–1815* (Middletown, Conn.: Wesleyan University Press, 1966).

5. The two standard sources for this information are Rosemary Freeman, *English Emblem Books* (New York: Octagon Books, 1966), and Mario Praz, *Studies in Seventeenth Century Imagery*, 2nd ed. (Rome: Edizioni di Storia e Letteratura, 1964).

6. *The New England Primer*, Paul Leicester Ford (ed.) (New York: Dodd, Mead & Co., 1897; reprinted New York: Teachers College, Columbia University, 1962).

7. Jonathan Fisher, *The Youth's Primer, Containing a Series of Short Verses in Alphabetical Order, Each Followed by Religious, Moral, or Historical Observations* (Boston: Samuel T. Armstrong, 1817), p. 19.

8. George Wither, *A Collection of Emblems* (London: Richard Royston, 1635; reprinted Menston, England: Scolar Press, 1968).

9. Jonathan Fisher, *Short Poems: Including a Sketch of the Scriptures to the Book of Ruth . . . and a Few Others on Various Subjects* (Portland, Me.: A. Shirley, 1827), p. 74.

10. Ibid., p. 85.

11. Jonathan Fisher, *Scripture Animals, or the Natural History of the Living Creatures Named in the Bible, Written Especially for Youth* (Portland, Me.: William Hyde, 1833; reprinted New York: Weathervane Books, 1972), p. iv.

12. Ibid., p. 19.

13. John Bunyan, *Divine Emblems* (Philadelphia: Mathew Cary, 1794), p. 83. Besides the Bible, another common source for both Fisher and Bunyan could have been Aesop. The use of animal tales to instruct the young has been well-known since antiquity.

14. Fisher, *Scripture Animals*, p. 220.

15. Ibid., p. 215.

16. John Huddlestone Wynne, *Choice Emblems* (Philadelphia: Joseph Crukshank, 1790), p. 35.

17. Geoffrey Whitney, *Choice of Emblems* (Leyden, 1586; reprinted Menston, England: Scolar Press, 1969), p. 230.

18. For emblematic devices on gravestones, see Ludwig, *Graven Images*.

Richard Moss

CHAPTER 11

JONATHAN FISHER AND THE "UNIVERSE OF BEING"

While Richard Moss, whose imagination was also captured by the Reverend Mr. Fisher, would not deny Dorsey Kleitz's argument that Fisher embodied the old emblematic tradition in his writing and art, Moss places it in the broader, more ancient context of the "Great Chain of Being." Fisher was convinced not only that God had created all things and arranged them in a hierarchy, but also that he had made them all for man's use and edification. Each animal, therefore, possessed a special moral symbolism and served as a particular emblem in this divine order of creation. Moss argues that at the same time, however, the way in which Fisher painted nature was essentially modern in its scientific detachment and attention to detail. Fisher's art, then, is a blending of two distinct approaches—one ancient, the other modern. Moss writes, "Fisher dealt with nature in two ways that are reflected in his art. He sought and found a natural world that could easily be transformed into a cornucopia of symbolic meanings. He also dealt with nature as a detached observer who sought only to see . . . and record." Like Martha Moore Ballard, the midwife of Hallowell, Jonathan Fisher unconsciously spanned a growing gap between a traditional and modern world view.

In 1832 the Reverend Jonathan Fisher stood before his Blue Hill congregation and asked them to ponder the following:

For if the happiness of the animals is not beneath the notice and care of God, surely man ought not to be too proud or too indifferent to notice and to care for them. It is a mark also of the goodness of God that he has provided abundant means by which man's mind may be fed with knowledge. He has raised up from time to time men of understanding, who have written upon interesting subjects, such as insects, birds, and beasts, so that the minds of children and men may be stored with that information and so that their hearts may be interested and enlightened and their happiness refined and greatly exalted.

For these gifts, my dear hearers, man has surely reason to love and to praise God.[1]

These words suggest that perhaps students of American culture have overemphasized the influence of the trackless forests on the American mind. The animals of the forest and farmyard were also everyday in-

Richard Moss is associate professor of history at Colby College.

fluences and Americans never lacked "men of understanding" eager to find meaning and significance in the animals with whom Americans shared their new land.

Indeed, Jonathan Fisher was one of those who sought to enlighten his fellow man. As he spoke the words just quoted, he was also putting the final touches on a most charming and important, soon-to-be-published work: *Scripture Animals: A Natural History of the Living Creatures Named in the Bible*. Begun in 1819 and not finished until 1832, the work was, in Fisher's words, intended "especially to assist young people in gaining knowledge of the natural history of the bible." He confessed that it also contained "something in a way of moralizing, or spiritualizing, that my young readers may be led to practical and useful meditations."[2] In this volume, Fisher translated ancient notions about the very structure of nature into terms that children could understand and absorb. These notions were premodern, but *Scripture Animals* also shows Fisher writing and acting as a modern man with a detached and scientific approach to his subject.

Jonathan Fisher had been Blue Hill's Congregational minister for twenty-four years when he began to work on *Scripture Animals* in 1819.[3] His biography is deceptively simple. Born in 1768 at Braintree, Massachusetts, he was the eldest son of Jonathan and Katharine Fisher. After his father died in the Revolutionary War, his mother was forced to distribute her seven children among willing relatives. Jonathan, at age nine, went to live with his uncle Joseph Avery, a Congregational minister at Holden, Massachusetts. Jonathan possessed a lively intellect; spurred on by his mother, he devoted himself to study and in 1788 was admitted to Harvard. After graduation in 1792, he stayed on in Cambridge and took the Master's degree in 1795. In 1796 he accepted the call from the Congregational Church at Blue Hill where he had preached the two previous summers. These simple facts do not indicate the intensity and versatility of his intellect. During his pastorate at Blue Hill he developed an almost impossibly complex internal intellectual life. In addition to pursuing his continuing interest in religions and philosophical thought, he wrote poetry and studied languages, architecture, and mathematics. On top of all this he drew and painted constantly, creating in his lifetime a huge body of engravings, drawings, and paintings. Finally, he designed and built his own house, an interesting and eccentric example of nineteenth century architecture. The book *Scripture Animals* was only a fraction of the output of this lively mind.

When the book was finished in 1832, Fisher traveled to Boston in a vain effort to find a big-city publisher. Back in Maine he struck a deal with William Hyde of Portland to publish one thousand copies of the work. Fisher purchased 625 himself and probably made a small profit selling them in Blue Hill and the surrounding area. His son-in-law, Captain Jeremiah Stevens, bought 125 copies, testifying to his respect for his father-in-law. Hyde sold the remaining 250 in the Portland area.

The design of the work is quite simple. Proceeding in alphabetical order, Fisher includes an entry for each animal named in the Bible. The entries contain an engraving of the creature, hand-cut by Fisher, and a prose description of the animal followed by an explanation of the biblical passages in which the animal is named. Fisher usually appended a few paragraphs of "moralizing" and almost every entry concludes with one of his own poems that sums up the overriding moral, or point, of the entry. The descriptions are often charming, especially when they are based on first-hand experience with the animal in question. For example, according to Fisher:

> [The grasshopper] is of the Locust kind, and is of several species. That most common in New England, when full grown is one inch and three-fourth in length; its head has some resemblance to that of a sheep without the ears; from the front of it proceed two feelers about half an inch in length; its whole body is covered with a kind of crust, or shell, like a coat of mail, but not as hard as that of the common bug, or beetle; its wings are about an inch in length, covered with a thin, semi-transparent crust. Its abdomen, or part of the body below the waist, consists of seven successive rings, and is terminated with a sort of double spade; it has six legs; the two hindmost when extended are about an inch and a half long, admirably fitted for leaping to a great distance, even without the help of its wings; when its wings are used the distance is increased; and before a strong wind it will sometimes proceed several miles at one flight. Its general color is green, its breast peagreen, its back of a muddy green approaching to black; its hind legs below the middle joints are nearly red. Its mouth is furnished with sharp nippers, with which it preys upon almost all kinds of grass and green herbs. It is said to be furnished with two holes under the wings, through which, by emitting wind it makes its chirping sound.[4]

In describing the animals Parson Fisher made use of years of observation and his astonishingly large collection of ancedotes. A lifelong collector of idle tidbits of information, Fisher laced *Scripture Animals* with stories, often hard to believe, of deer defeating tigers and tortoises living for days with their heads severed from their bodies. Fisher also provided a glimpse into the everyday life of early nineteenth century Maine. While discussing the ox, he showed that frontier life required a person to use virtually everything that came to hand. Even a dead ox had many uses: The hide was used for shoes and harnesses, the bones for buttons and knife handles, the hair was mixed with plaster, the suet made excellent candles, the horn became combs and handles, the feet became neats-foot oil, the blood nourished young fruit trees and served as an ingredient in making the color Prussian blue and the remainder went into the gluepot. Fisher repeated many times that God had made animals for man's use; the ox was but one example.

The book, however, was much more than anecdotes and lessons on the uses of a dead ox. It was a philosophical tract that sought to describe for its young readers the way in which "the universe of being" was built. Parson Fisher had inherited the Puritan piety that could allow no question to go unanswered, that could not tolerate a gap in the portrait of reality. He had to lay the foundation before he set the posts and beams; for nature was very much like a home to him, and he sought to build on bedrock. His truth rested on two old and trusted conceptions: the great chain of being and the notion of divine intervention and providential design. He believed that we could understand Nature and the questions it posed only after accepting the idea that "the universe of being" was arranged like links in a chain planned and crafted by a God who, at His pleasure, intervened. In addition, Fisher also found in nature countless symbols that he used to illustrate and enliven the moral lessons that abound in the book. Animals as symbols, the great chain of being, and divine intervention—all were concepts characteristic of a premodern Christian mind.

The most fundamental idea in *Scripture Animals* was the great chain of being. This ancient concept reached back to Plato and Aristotle.[5] For Fisher it was, no doubt, a commonplace concept. Simply stated, the great chain of being was a way of conceiving nature that held all matter to be organized into an immense, or infinite, number of links, hierarchically arranged from the lowest kind of inert matter up through the various creatures to the human being, who was assumed to be the highest form of natural creature. The chain extended upward from human beings through an array of angels and other supernatural creatures to God. Generally, it was assumed that the links of the chain were very small and that the chain had no gaps. Fisher most clearly revealed his belief in this concept in his poem at the end of the section on whales:

> . . . all this world,
> This universe of being, has its worth;
> Each link above to links beneath is bound,
> And each beneath by those above is held,
> And all existence is a mighty scale
> From to nothing downward, and from man
> In grades ascending to the one supreme.

Parson Fisher used the idea of a great chain of being most often to explain the relationship between creatures. Animals were linked together not only hierarchically, but also because they served each other. The owl, for example, was linked to "a number of small animals and creeping things" for a clear purpose. The owl was provided with food and in the process of feeding, the owl thinned out rodents and other vermin. The purposes of humanity were also served because without the owl's "ravages," rats and other small creatures might "so abound, as greatly to annoy us, and bring a famine upon us." Animals were also linked because they resembled each other. For example, "the Ourang Outang" [sic] seems to be the first link in the descending chain of gradation below human." This resemblance, Fisher stated, created "unpleasant feelings" in human beings because the ape suggested "something monstrous, or deformed of the human species." The parson argued that these feelings are misguided; the ape was really evidence of "the wonderful wisdom of God, who has left no vacancy in His works, but has made the chain perfect from "the living atom, which sports in the dew drop, to the highest archangel."[6]

68. "LOUSE," from *Scripture Animals* by Jonathan Fisher, 1834.
(By permission of the Houghton Library, Harvard University)

Even the most bothersome creatures were evidence of the chain's perfection. Fisher saw even the louse (Illus. 68) as playing an important role in "the scale of being." God had created this apparently loathsome insect as an instrument to torment the "indolent and filthy." Even when the clean and industrious were infested, as Fisher admitted they occasionally were, this was also a good thing; it stimulated the victim to greater cleanliness and industry. Thus Fisher concluded that the louse "is one link of the almost infinitely progressive scale of being, the entire removal of which would leave a vacancy, which could not possibly be so well filled in any other way." Fisher argued that human beings are served by the louse because the louse functions to keep people cleaner and therefore more moral and industrious.

Where might Fisher have come by his belief in the idea of a great chain of being? New England Puritans of the seventeenth century, as Perry Miller has shown, insisted that God had created the universe as a great chain of orders and types of being. This plenitude served God and, secondarily, humanity in various ways according to a divine plan. Undoubtedly, this Puritan notion became part of New England everyday wisdom. However, it could not have endured into the nineteenth century without the support of eighteenth century biological thought, which made the great chain of being one of its most fundamental concepts.[7] Fisher probably encountered the idea in numerous places as he went through Harvard and as his reading about nature expanded after he went to Blue Hill. Certainly, one source was John Locke. On March 4, 1790, Fisher recorded in his journal that he paid three dollars for a copy of "Lock's [sic] essays in calf" (an extraordinary sum because of his poverty during college). In *An Essay Concerning Human Understanding,* Locke gave the conception one of its most succinct statements:

> In all the visible corporeal world we see no chasms or gaps. All quite down from us the descent is by easy steps, and a continued series that in each remove differ very little one from the other.... There are some brutes that seem to have as much reason and knowledge as some that are called men; and the animal and vegetable kingdoms are so nearly joined, that if you take the lowest and most inorganic parts of matter, we shall find everywhere that the several species are linked together, and differ but in almost insensible degrees.[8]

In the end, however, there is no reason to believe that Locke's writings influenced Fisher any more than countless other writers, notably Alexander Pope and Joseph Addison, whom he also read. Like most large ideas, the great chain of being passed from generation to generation, not in the work of a single writer, but as part of a highly generalized cultural heritage.

The great chain of being was a very helpful principle for Fisher, but it could not explain all of nature. The chain had to have a creator and Fisher consistently attributed the wondrous linkages found in nature to God. Furthermore, the idea of a great chain could explain only some of the events that took place in the natural world. To explain change in nature, Fisher evoked a deity that actively intervened to achieve special purposes. Thus Fisher saw natural phenomena, such as floods, earthquakes, and droughts, not so much as causes but as means to an end:

> The Creator of the world has all the laws of nature perfectly under his control, and can dispose of them as he pleases. In some cases, according to the adjustment of his great plan a people may become wicked in just such time and place, that the laws of nature in their common, [not miraculous] operation, may bring destruction upon them. At other times by a special, or miraculous interposition he may increase, or diminish the power of the operation of the laws of nature, so as either to bestow blessings, or to inflict judgments...."[9]

Fisher used the ideas of divine providence and intervention countless times in *Scripture Animals*. For example, he evoked the concept of divine intervention to explain the existence of Negroes and their enslavement. For the most part, Fisher simply recounted the story of the curse placed on Canaan. Because Canaan's father, Ham, had looked upon the drunken and immodestly exposed figure of Noah, Canaan and his descendants "were destined to be for long ages subjected to bondage." However, this was one case in which Fisher was unsure of himself. He would very much have liked to explain the existence of Negroes and their enslavement using the biblical account, but he was also familiar with the naturalistic explanation that placed the emphasis on climate:

> Whether the color and features of the Negro are wholly the effect of climate, as some suppose, or whether they were a mark of distinction put upon the race of Ham by a special providence of God, to be a memorial of the divine displeasure against immodesty, are, in my mind, questions not easy to be resolved. If it be admitted that their complexion and wooly hair, are altogether the effect of climate, I must believe that it was through a superintending providence of God that they received their lot in a part of the world so much calculated to fit them to be servants, in fulfillment of the ancient prediction.

Having disposed of that thorny problem, Fisher concluded that we should not worry too much about it. The lesson he sought to teach concerned the original "iniquity of Ham, in his immodest conduct." He urged his young readers to "cultivate modesty, and due respect for our superiors...." Concerning Negro slavery, Fisher counseled his young audience "to labor to christianize and civilize the Africans, and to be the means of their abandoning all those evil manners, which now bring them into servitude."[10]

Fisher's convictions that God had planned the natural world and that He exercised constant control over it found another important use in Fisher's philosophy. He used these beliefs to resolve the age-old problem of evil. Throughout the book he posed this problem in different ways. After acknowledging that the history of human beings has been "a somewhat gloomy picture," characterized by "slaughtered multitudes" who often have died "by the hands of those of the same flesh and blood with themselves," he asked, "How can this be consistent with the supposed benevolence of the Creator?" His answer depended on the existence of a divine plan that human beings, in their fallen state, were too addled to understand. Fisher had faith that "the misery of the fallen world" was but "a small dark spot" set in the universe "to set off by contrast an immensity of moral beauty" that dominated the whole of creation.

Fisher asked much the same question about animal life: "Why do animals devour one another? Why is one species food for another?" In this case he argued that God has established the most utilitarian system that provided the greatest good:

> As there must be a dissolution [death], as well as a generation of insects, that they may not overwhelm the earth; and it is probable that the suffering of an animal, that does not anticipate its death, may be even less when suddenly destroyed than when removed by a lingering natural death; and seeing that many more species and individuals may subsist and experience enjoyment, by reason of feeding of some upon others, it appears to be very wise and benevolent in God to ordain that one class in many cases should feed upon other classes.

However, Fisher did not believe that this providential order was a mechanical system that operated unchanged over eons. He clearly believed that God's plan was progressive and that it was aimed at paradise. Those in "the lower world" had reason "to believe that we have not yet seen the brighter side of the divine administration of nature."

God had long been endeavoring to show human beings the effects of sin, the degree of human depravity, and the necessity of grace. When God finished this massive job, "the pride of all mere human endeavors to reform the world may be brought low ... and this world for a long season will be a blooming paradise." Violence and death would be eliminated, the earth would produce an abundance beyond calculation, and "cheerfulness will sit on every brow; tears will give place to smiles" and human beings would be "to a high degree happy." Finally, the Parson assured his young readers that God would employ "many of the rising generation to bring forward ... this golden age."[11] Although Fisher touched on the idea that the millennium was coming, he never developed it fully. He implied that it would come at God's bidding and that the human will alone was insufficient to reform the great evils of man.

Since Fisher had such certain faith in the existence of a divine plan of nature, it is not surprising that he should find some creatures invested with great symbolic meaning, as did premodern people. He finds the bee and the ant, for example, to be symbols not only of industry and far-sightedness—both working diligently and storing up wealth for the future—but also of the centrality of the family as a unit of production. The lion for Fisher was a symbol of the "divine Saviour ... in respect to his strength to subdue all enemies under him ... and in respect to the awful majesty in which he will appear to the wicked in the day of judgement." The poems that concluded the section on each animal often used the animal discussed as the representation of a virtue. For example, the bee inspired Fisher to advise:

> Hence learn, my youthful friends, to weigh,
> and fix the worth of every day;
> In life's fair prime your stores increase,
> That hoary age may pass in peace.

Fisher was also more than capable of impressing his own values onto the system of symbolic meanings that he attributed to God's creatures. For years he had wished to own a horse, but his small income and natural frugality had prevented him from buying one. In his mind, the horse had become one of nature's most wondrous creations. The horse is "noble," "generous," and "brave," built "to impress us by his swiftness, to charm us by the gracefulness of his shape."[12]

The snake (under various names such as "Serpent," "Viper," and "Adder") carried a complex symbolic load. In the "Viper" Fisher found a symbol for the scorner and infidel who taught "destructive doctrines." He saw the viper's venom as analogous to false doctrines of any kind that undermine true Christian principles. Fisher used the snake in this way as a symbol in the shorthand code he devised and used in most of his writing. In this code the coiled snake was employed as a pictograph for the word "against," suggesting that the snake represented the opponent, or an opposer, of virtue and Christianity. In the section on the adder, Fisher compared the venom of this reptile to liquor. He warned his readers that "strong drink, received intemperately may be compared to the stinging of an Adder, because like poison its intoxicating influence is diffused through the whole system." Fisher also believed that "Serpents" represented something much more fundamental than false doctrines or intemperance. After noting that few, if any, people can repress the unpleasant feelings of terror and disgust when they come upon a snake, Fisher concluded that:

> These feelings toward Serpents is the result of a divine constitution, the object of which is to keep in remembrance the instrument, used by the prince of devils, in tempting our first parents to eat of the forbidden fruit. The great, and ever abiding enmity is between the spiritual seed of the woman, and the devil himself; but these want not the traces of a corresponding enmity between man and the literal Serpent.[13]

The tradition of investing animals with precise, God-given symbolic meanings clearly influenced Fisher's painting. The parson's most famous painting, *A Morning View of Blue Hill Village* (see Plate XIII), provides the clearest evidence of this tendency to use animals as symbols in his paintings. The painting depicts the village as it appeared in 1824. In the foreground Fisher painted what appears to be a very strange scene: A man with a stick is chasing a snake away from the sleeping village and, the figures in the foreground. These figures, two women and a horse, suggest that Fisher was injecting his own symbols into the painting. In driving the snake away from the village, he is symbolically driving off intemperance and false doctrines; in driving the serpent away from the horse, he is protecting his favorite animal, one that he invested with great virtue and usefulness; and in keeping the snake from the two women, who oddly are turned away from the action, he is symbolically breaking the supposed connection between woman and the Edenic snake. The village itself is cut off from this scene by a long stone wall that neatly bisects the painting, creating in effect, two paintings. For Fisher, it seems, the community was a symbol of virtue that was always threatened at its borders by evil. Looked at this way, his painting of Blue Hill becomes a complex representation of his perception of the world.

The views he expressed in *Scripture Animals* also help us to see more deeply into some of Fisher's other paintings. His love of the horse is clearly present in his portrait of a noble black horse, which he painted in 1800. His oil painting of four birds (see Plate XII), upon close inspection, represents his view that animal life is inextricably linked like a chain. The work shows four birds (a King-Wood-Pecker, Golden Crowned Woodpecker, Slate-colored Snow-Bird and a Seeder) in a somewhat artificially rendered natural setting. Among the birds, Fisher placed four different types of insects: a moth, three spiders on an invisible web, and two different types of flies. It seems reasonable to suggest that Fisher was trying to depict his conception of nature, characterized by a divine plan in which God provided a bounty of insects and the birds to keep their numbers in check. In many of his paintings and drawings, Fisher clearly worked from models provided by others. In fact, *Scripture Animals* might provide the best example of Fisher as a simple copyist. The woodcuts in the book were, as Fisher admitted on the very first page, copied from other books, and very few of them were original. But it seems that in some of his original works, he attempted to instill meanings that had occurred to him as he observed and pondered nature. His art is much more than that of a backwoods craftsman struggling to improve his technique; it is also the product of a thinker who drew his inspiration from nature and gave that inspiration life on his canvas.[14]

Scripture Animals is the sort of book that allows us to see the basic ideas that a New England minister used in understanding nature. Parson Fisher saw nature as a complex chain, with each link related to the others in the context of a divine plan. He explained extraordinary events as the special providence of God working out his intentions for human beings and nature. The world around Jonathan Fisher abounded in meaning: The animals were symbols of virtues and vices, the feeding of one animal upon another was evidence of God's plan, and in all this Fisher saw some evidence that God was slowly improving the earth. Keith Thomas, in his remarkable book, *Man and the Natural World: A History of the Modern Sensibility*, identified the conviction that animals had religious or symbolic meaning as a traditional viewpoint, which slowly gave way to a "revolution in perception" in the late eighteenth and early nineteenth centuries. Long, deeply rooted tradition held that nature was "redolent with human analogy and symbolic meaning, and sensitive to man's behaviour. . . ." But by the mid-nineteenth century this view was being replaced by one that saw nature as "a detached natural scene, to be viewed and studied by the observer from the outside, as if by peering through a window, in the secure knowledge that the objects of contemplation inhabited a separate realm offering no omens or signs, without human meaning or significance."[15] The development of a modern view of nature was, of course, vastly more complex than this. Yet Thomas makes a convincing case that this revolution was central to the transformation of a premodern view of nature into a modern scientific conception of the natural world.

Surprisingly, Fisher with his deep traditionalism, also illustrated this more modern attitude in *Scripture Animals*. Beneath the expressed purpose of the book, which was to use animals as topics for "useful meditations," lurked a second Jonathan Fisher who merely wished to observe animals without translating the observations into useful lessons. This second Jonathan Fisher made numerous appearances in the text. He always attempted to include an accurate physical description of the animal he is discussing with the description of its symbolic and material uses. The description of the grasshopper cited earlier is an example, as is his portrait of the "Cock-Pigeon:"

Its length from the crown of the head to the end of the tail thirteen inches, height, as it naturally stands, eight inches. Its head is a shade between purple and ash-color; its neck changeable from purple to crimson; the part of the back towards the head ash-color, inclining to purple; lower down inclining to blue, then to purple again towards the tail, The shoulder of the wing light purple, inclining to slate color; thence to the large feathers, and next large feathers purple, inclining to ash-color; quill feathers, and next large feathers, dark slate, with a very narrow edge of white; upper tail-feathers the same; under tail-feathers, the half towards the point, white. The throat is white, the breast purple, the belly nearly white, the legs flesh color, the beak and claws black.

This triumph of observation and description, with its clipped tone of scientific objectivity, stands in stark contrast to his discussion of the symbolic qualities of animals. On several occasions in *Scripture Animals*, Fisher actually recounted some of his encounters with nature. For example, in the section on the spider, he provided a woodcut of a large female spider, which "was drawn from life, August 12, 1826, while on the center of her wheel-net." Soon after making the drawing, he found "a cod in the shape of a pear, of the size of a lady's thimble . . ." hanging on the web. The covering on the egg cod was "as strong as common silk stuff," but he managed to remove it along with another cod "the size of a large pea" that contained the eggs laid by mother spider. A few days later he visited the same spider web where he found yet another egg cod which he left alone. To this point in his tale he is the scientist providing us with dated, detailed, and detached observations. For a moment, however, the desire to find symbolic meaning in his observations reasserted itself; after noticing the quick appearance of the second egg cod he noted, "I could not but admire the wonderful instinct, which the benevolent Creator has given to all his creatures to preserve their kind." In the very next paragraph, however, Fisher became again the detached observer recounting a meeting with "a Wheel-net Spider" that took place "on the 20th of August, 1825." The parson was "amused" on that day to watch the spider demolish his old web and create a new one. On that occasion he found no lessons in the work of the spider, only the pleasure of watching. In no other section of the book do the desires to find symbolic meanings and to merely observe blend so clearly and pleasantly.

Just as Fisher's habit of finding symbolic meaning in animals influenced his art work, so too did the habit of observing nature from a detached point of view. In most of his art, Fisher was devoted to creating accurate renderings of plants and animals. The best examples of this work are in a leather-bound folio at the Jonathan Fisher House in Blue Hill. This folio contains a number of watercolors of flowers and animals ranging from the St. Jago monkey to the larkspur (Illus. 69). The watercolors were all signed and dated; some were done as early as 1795, other in the 1840s. The names of the subjects were given in a number of languages and in many cases were accompanied by long

Jonathan Fisher and the "Universe of Being"

69. *Larkspur,* by Jonathan Fisher, 1810. (Watercolor. The Jonathan Fisher Memorial, Blue Hill)

scientific descriptions. While Fisher copied many of his works, some of the best—such as his painting of the garden pea—he drew from life. The lion in this collection, oddly enough, was also drawn from life; during one of his trips to Boston, Fisher paid fifty cents to see a lion that had recently been captured in Africa.[16] This work is in sharp contrast to paintings such as *A Morning View of Blue Hill Village*. (See Plate XIII.) The painting of the village with the figures in the foreground has a clear symbolic intention. The work in the folio has no such intention; Fisher's purpose is to create as accurate a re-creation of the natural object as possible. It seems apparent that Jonathan Fisher dealt with nature in two ways that are reflected in his art. He sought and found a natural world that could easily be transformed into a cornucopia of symbolic meanings. He also dealt with nature as a detached observer who sought only to see, in the simplest sense of the word, and record.

It is the blending of these two approaches in *Scripture Animals* that gives it real significance. As Keith Thomas has noted, the conviction that animals had symbolic meaning for human beings "remained an article of faith for many Victorian country folk, but it no longer had the support of intellectuals; for the educated were now coming to believe the natural world had its own independent existence and was to be perceived accordingly."[17] Fisher spanned this growing gap; he was both a simple religious man—one of the "Victorian country folk," using the animals of the Bible for his own purposes—and a scientist of sorts, conceding to nature its own existence, which he could not manipulate for human purposes. Jonathan Fisher was a rare example of an author and artist who blended these two perspectives in his work.

NOTES

1. Quoted in Mary Ellen Chase, *Jonathan Fisher: Maine Parson 1768–1847* (New York: Macmillan, 1948), pp. 121–122.

2. Jonathan Fisher, *Scripture Animals: A Natural History of the Living Creatures Named in the Bible* (1834; reprint Princeton, N.J.: Pyne Press, 1972, with a preface by Mary Ellen Chase), p. iv.

3. For a lively account of Fisher's life, see Chase, *Jonathan Fisher*.

4. Fisher, *Scripture Animals*, pp. 127–128.

5. For a detailed history of the great chain of being concept, see Arthur O. Lovejoy, *The Great Chain of Being: A Study of the History of an Idea* (Cambridge, Mass.: Harvard University Press, 1942).

6. Fisher, *Scripture Animals*, pp. 21–22.

7. See Perry Miller, *The New England Mind: The Seventeenth Century* (New York: Macmillan, 1939), pp. 207–238; Lovejoy, *The Great Chain*, Chapters VI–VIII.

8. John Locke, *An Essay Concerning Human Understanding*, John W. Yolton (ed.), 2 vols. (New York: Dutton, 1972), vol. 1, pp. 47–48.

9. Fisher, *Scripture Animals*, p. 226.

10. Ibid., pp. 325–327. Fisher justified discussing humankind by defining the human being as a scriptural animal and devoting an appendix to the subject.

11. Ibid., pp. 340–348.   12. Ibid., p. 145.   13. Ibid., p. 320.

14. See, for example, Alice Winchester, *Versatile Yankee: The Art of Jonathan Fisher 1768–1847* (Princeton, N.J.: Pyne Press, 1973). This work is the best introduction to Fisher as artist.

15. Keith Thomas, *Man and the Natural World: A History of the Modern Sensibility* (New York: Pantheon Books, 1983), p. 89.

16. The best selection of this work appears in Winchester, *Versatile Yankee*. See also Alice Winchester, "Rediscovery: Parson Jonathan Fisher," *Art in America* (November-December, 1970), 92–99.

17. Thomas, *Man and the Natural World*, p. 91.

Jonathan Fisher and the "Universe of Being"

David H. Watters

CHAPTER 12

MAINE AT STATEHOOD
The Search for a National Style

The Revolution initiated a debate among Americans over several esthetic issues: the subject and style suitable to the arts in a new republic, the authority of classical and European culture, and the authority of the classes that had traditionally supported the arts. David Watters, a specialist in the literature and material culture of early New England, argues that the issues of style debated on a national level were resolved in Maine through works that expressed the shared values of the elite and the common people. While acknowledging Maine's many examples of direct cultural transfer from Boston, Philadelphia, and Europe, Watters uses examples of gravestone carving, poetry, and painting to demonstrate how Maine artists adapted the neoclassical forms of the elite culture to express the republican ideals of the region and the nation.

The progress of the arts in America from 1783 to 1820 is a key index to the political and social conflicts of the era, and Maine's statehood in 1820 coincided with the emergence of a consensus on the role of the arts in America. Indeed, the period exhibits what Emory Elliott calls a "crisis of culture," during which American myths and metaphors, developed by politicians and artists alike, helped to contain revolutionary anarchy.[1] Nearly everyone agreed that the arts, like education, could enlighten and pacify the settlers of the frontier, but not everyone agreed about the place in a republic of European aristocratic traditions, especially the newly popular neoclassical style.[2] Americans hoped to borrow from Europe those esthetic principles that promoted harmony, virtue, and learning, while avoiding the elitism and decadence of its society. By 1820 an emerging national style bridged conflicting political and esthetic ideals by modifying European images to reflect republican ideals. The celebrants of Maine's statehood who gathered in Portland's Union Hall were well aware of the use of the arts to symbolize, if not to effect, social and political change: "In front of the orchestra our national armorial an eagle lately killed in this neighborhood spread its capacious wings, bearing on his breast a brilliant star, significance of the addition now made to our national

David H. Watters is associate professor of English at the University of New Hampshire.

constellation."³ As this image reveals, the period's arts mix high-style and emerging local forms, reflecting a compromise between those who favored neoclassical style—with its appeal to authority in matters artistic and moral—and those who favored vernacular forms—often reflecting the egalitarian spirit of the frontier.

Shortly after Independence, Noah Webster set the nationalistic terms of esthetic debate by printing a literary declaration of independence from England:

> This country must in some future time, be as distinguished by the superiority of her literary improvements, as she is already by the liberality of her civil and ecclesiastical constitutions. Europe is grown old in folly, corruption and tyranny—in that country laws are perverted, manners are licentious, literature is declining and human nature debased. For America in her infancy to adopt the present maxims of the old world, would be to stamp the wrinkles of decrepid age upon the bloom of youth and to plant the seeds of decay in a vigorous constitution.⁴

Webster placed esthetics and politics under moral philosophy: He believed that aristocracy and its arts were based on decadent moral grounds. Similarly, Timothy Dwight, the president of Yale and a distinguished poet and theologian, saw a "glorious contrast" between England and America; the Englishman was "a dy'd serpent, tinselled outside, painted tomb, foul harlot, a fribble dwindled from a man," but Americans were "sunny geniuses, Phoenixes divine, plain, frank and practical."⁵

It proved easier after the Revolution to criticize European arts and morals, however, than to propose indigenous alternatives. America could boast little literature—and less art; what was produced was usually in imitation of Georgian, neoclassical models. Poetry and painting were patterned after classical and renaissance examples, as interpreted by enlightened minds in London and Paris. In England epic poetry and historical painting were the pinnacle of the arts because they reminded people of the great moments of history and those who had taken part, who were to be emulated; the arts encouraged reason, social harmony, and piety. As Washington Irving complained in 1819, such preferences left little space for new-world art:

> [America has] the sublime and beautiful of natural scenery. But Europe held forth all the charms of storied and poetical association. There were to be seen the masterpieces of art, the refinements of highly cultivated society, the quaint peculiarities of ancient and local custom. My native country was full of youthful promise; Europe was rich in the accumulated treasures of age.⁶

The problem in Maine and elsewhere was twofold. An appropriate subject for American art, reflecting the ideals of the Republic, had to be found. And this subject had to be presented in a style that would lead to moral elevation, a style that would prevent degeneration either into wildness or aristocratic luxury.

Generally speaking, in the District and in Massachusetts proper, those who saw a need for strong central authority in government to balance the forces of disunion and growth on the frontier favored neoclassical learning and the arts to foster a natural elite and to elevate by example the morals of society.[7] In Maine the strongest support of neoclassical style was found in the older settlements, often Federalist in political sentiment, such as Kittery, Wells, Paris Hill, Bath, Blue Hill, Portland/Falmouth, and Yarmouth. Citizens patronized Boston architects and painters, and Boston, Salem, and Plymouth gravestone carvers, importing items of taste and style in the neoclassical manner to the Maine frontier. After the Revolution, however, such stylistic taste—that is, an allegiance to authority and tradition—became a convenient target of those who resented the wealthy proprietors. This is not to say that the forces for and against separation can be neatly divided along esthetic and class lines. People who came to Maine as squatters built Federal-style houses when they could afford them; Federalists such as John Gardiner, who saw the danger of mobocracy if the best citizens did not rule, supported separation from Massachusetts in the belief that it would foster the growth of the District's own aristocracy to lead the new state politically, morally, and culturally.

During the 1790s in Maine, debate over esthetics appeared often in writings on the place of political and religious authority in a republican society. Abraham Cummings of North Yarmouth wrote that even the best of constitutions can be ruined by wicked rulers and by factions. Cummings used the language of biblical prophecy, as had so many New England ministers before him, to warn of the destabilizing effects of liberty:

> The false doctrines of *liberty and equality*, which have contaminated millions of mankind, have certainly a most pernicious influence in society, and are introductory to all those horrid scenes of insurrection and anarchy, distress of nations and perplexity, which must fulfill the prophetic scripture in the last days.[8]

In Cummings' view, the best government was one to be instituted by Christ in the millennium, so Christ's ministers in this world deserved the respect of society.[9] The style of Cummings' discourse, based in biblical prophecy, is as important as its substance, for his language springs from a tradition of sectarian discord.

In an important shift, those ministers who abandoned the language of millennial fervor employed more secular metaphors to argue that social happiness depends on religious authority. Henry Cumings occupied a middle ground in the conflict between the religion of reason and the religion of revelation. In an ordination sermon preached in Falmouth in 1799, this minister from Billerica, Massachusetts, argued that the secular values of democracy alone cannot nurture human moral development:

> Detached from religion, what are truth and fidelity, honor and honesty, friendship and patriotism, benevolence and philanthropy, but sounds of

uncertain meaning, or empty boasts of ill-designing and insidious hypocrisy? Such excellent qualities and noble virtues can never be cultivated to an advantage, in the fields of irreligion, where they will lie exposed to the perpetual chilling blasts of infidelity and atheism, which will effectually prevent their growth. Religion is their proper soil, and they flourish best under the cultivation of christianity, and the genial beams of the *Sun of righteousness*.[10]

The opponents of these ministers could also raise the issue of style to counter their authority. James Sullivan, the early historian of Maine, called certain members of the clergy Tories in disguise who favor tyranny and aristocratic luxury. He claimed that they would "place the Altar of the Lord, at the foot of the Throne of Tyranny; and who would offer their adoration to vice and folly, when they found these in the glittering robes of wealth, or in the splendid garb of power."[11] Sullivan rhetorically associates ministerial authority with royalty and wealth, and not incidentally, the style of dress that goes with them.

Ministerial authority declined noticeably after the Revolution. Emory Elliott has argued that this decline left a vacuum in moral and artistic leadership. As Elliott sees it, authors and artists hoped that they could take over the leadership role previously held by the clergy.[12] In *The Monthly Anthology and Boston Review*, published from 1803 to 1811 in Boston, District readers could find a full debate over the role of the arts in society. In the *Anthology*, the role of the classic is hotly debated; the editors were equally afraid of aristocratic decadence and the "common" culture that would attend mass rule. For John Thornton Kirkland, "If those enjoyments that flow from literature and taste are not emulated, we shall be exposed to that enervating and debasing luxury, the object of which is sensual indulgence, its immediate effect, vice, and its ultimate issue, publick degradation and ruin."[13] The goal is a republic led by the best minds who could find in the classics "first principles in morals and politicks," for "a great mind is like some august temple, the slow work of labor and genius."[14] As in architecture, so in morals: The learned author would be a monument to tradition and a model for emulation. Occasionally, the innovating spirit of the democratic frontier found a place in the *Anthology*. Edmund Trowbridge Dana believed the influence of the ancients on the dynamic, though youthfully naive, American to be bad:

> Inferiority to antiquity, that scarecrow of moderns, like others of the brotherhood of frightful demeanor, is a mere imposition of stubble and straw; and it will be discovered, when children have courage from reflection, that it is rather erected to frighten praise from our neighbours than facilitate by caution the advancement of mind.[15]

Without an aristocratic patronage, artists in both Boston and Maine faced the challenge of producing art that would appeal to the tastes of the people while preserving the values of the classics. Public taste might improve with exposure to classical architecture, high-style painting, and literature, but the public would not accept traditional arbiters of taste in the ministry or the elite. Certainly America could not escape the popularity of the European neoclassical style of the eighteenth and early nineteenth centuries, spurred by discoveries at Herculaneum and Pompeii, but Americans did find astonishing ways to adapt such designs to American values.

While many American writers and artists, such as Washington Irving, lamented their removal from the sources of classical design and correct taste, this distance proved to be a strength as well as a weakness. Americans could choose those aspects of neoclassical style that could be modified to reflect democratic values. For example, Thomas Jefferson used the Roman temple at Nimes, dedicated to pagan deities, as a model for the Virginia statehouse, a building dedicated to democracy. After Independence, many Americans wanted to revive the democracy of ancient Greece and the Roman republic. Especially with the death in 1799 of Washington, that American Cincinnatus who laid down the plow to save his nation, neoclassical ornaments became closely associated with people and objects that represented American democracy. In the outpouring of mourning that followed Washington's death, numerous prints, samplers, poems, sermons, and even milk pitchers depicted his tomb as a small temple flanked by weeping willows. Such imagery in classical, pagan tradition, may seem appropriate for immortalizing Washington (and for the few great people of Maine), but similar images also grace thousands of gravestones for the nearly anonymous multitudes of Americans. Because of Maine's distance from the style centers of the new nation, which themselves were removed from European esthetic centers, neoclassical imagery was often transformed by democratic, local taste, with little regard to correctness of design.[16]

Tombstones are one of the best records of changes in style because they were relatively inexpensive and were portable; new designs could gain wide exposure in a relatively short period of time. For people living in uncertain economic and political times—and faced with the trauma of death—memorialization reaffirmed family roots in the older settlements of New England. Gravestones were imported from the Foster and Lamson shops of Boston, from the Maxcy shop of Salem, and from shops in southeastern Massachusetts, the old bounds of the Plymouth colony. In towns ravaged by Indian attack and later besieged by the British, there is an unusually large number of surviving markers. The Indian Fighter's Burying Ground of North Yarmouth is a fine example of the use of gravestones to recommit settlers to land that their ancestors fought and died for. Some epitaphs call attention to death as a metaphor for the uncertainty of settlement on the frontier; Mrs. Bassett's epitaph in North Yarmouth reads, "How strange, my God, who reigns on high! / That I should come so far to die, / and leave my friends where I was bred, / To lay my bones with strangers' dead" (c. 1750?).[17] But most epitaphs use traditional phrases to emphasize cultural continuity, and especially large and elegant stones were erected for the first settlers of a town, such as Lemuel Jackson, Jr., of Paris Hill. Classical urn and willow designs may have appealed to these settlers precisely because they evoked history and permanence in a place that had little of either.

The regional stonecarving traditions of New England produced an astonishing variety of designs, often boldly displaying sectarian values. The most popular forms—death's heads and winged cherubs—were flexible, if not ambiguous, messages of religious and social values.[18] As religious sentiment changed, so too could the interpretation of symbols. Thus the death's head of the seventeenth century, with its origins in the *memento mori* ("remember to die," i.e., a reminder of the certainty of death) tradition favored by Calvinists, survived in many parts of New England late in the eighteenth century after the original force of Calvinism had waned. Where that symbol once called attention to the terrors of death and the futility of mourning in the face of predestination, in the late eighteenth century Anglicans and Presbyterians alike could use the death's head as a symbol of sentimental piety and the efficacy of mourning, as celebrated by the Graveyard School of poets.

Perhaps the best example of a multipurpose symbol is the cherub, a design with roots deep in pagan and Judeo-Christian tradition. Abraham Cummings of North Yarmouth devoted an entire treatise to the symbol, and he begins by listing the many interpretations of the image, each reflecting a different critical and doctrinal position:

> By various expositors they are made to signify either the four covenants; or all the creatures; or the four cardinal virtues, justice, wisdom, fortitude and temperance; or four faculties in the soul, rational, irascible, concupiscible and conscience; or the four chief passions, joy, grief, hope and fear; the four monarchies, the four elements, the four evangelists, or those who are more complete and perfect in the church.[19]

Cummings rejected all these interpretations and promoted his own concept of a rational, benevolent Christianity. The four cherubim in the Jewish Temple were thus "emblematical of the divine Trinity in union with holy and happy men;" after death, "Not only the church in general, but every individual of that body will manifest this union, and shine divinely glorious with these four faces."[20] The elegantly bewigged cherub on a stone for William Titcomb of Falmouth (Illus. 70a) represents a child who is happy in heaven because he was a member of a holy and culturally refined family on earth. Cummings's religious doctrine, which stressed piety as a benevolent social force the end of which is happiness, is inseparable from the esthetic preference for elegant cherubs favored by the culturally elite in Boston and Newport since the early eighteenth century. Not far from the Titcomb stone is an effigy design with roots in Plymouth County, Massachusetts vernacular tradition (Illus. 70b). Cut by Noah Pratt of Freeport, this image recalls fervent anticipation of saintly rule in a millennial kingdom.[21] Certainly this is a sectarian view in conflict with that of Cummings,

70. Tombstones: *a.* William Titcomb, Falmouth, 1806. *b.* Mrs. Anna Pote, Falmouth, 1781. *c.* Mrs. Mary Freeman, Portland, 1785. *d.* Brigadier General Francis Osgood, Portland, 1817.

but in Maine design preference marking sectarian boundaries was not so clearly established as it was in other parts of New England.

The ambiguity of these images may be a reason for their wide acceptance in Maine, and it explains the popularity of neoclassical tombstone design that swept aside vernacular forms by 1820. The great advantage of the urn and willow design was that it could not be identified with an existing sectarian movement in New England, nor could it be identified with a particular region. This foreign style was "safe" in religious content; moreover, it resolved the conflict between classical traditions associated with aristocracy and indigenous styles associated with democracy. The elegantly designed urns and willows denoted

c.

d.

taste and refinement, but they also recalled the origins of democracy in classical times. Finally, they supported the new ideology of the Republic, which claimed that the common person might aspire to immortality by skill and hard work.

In Portland's Eastern Burying Ground a group of extremely important stones demonstrates the process whereby these new design elements were assimilated with local Christian traditions. As secular writers, such as Philip Freneau and Joel Barlow, adopted religious rhetoric to describe the "rising glory" of America, so stonecarvers used neoclassical designs from pagan mythology to show secularized Christian values. Mrs. Mary Freeman's earthly elegance, style and refinement of taste—her "mortal part"—is indeed celebrated by the presence of pillars, urn, and willow. However, the epitaph reminds us to see these designs as metaphors for the elegance of her "immortal part," fashioned by "Christ's power" (Illus. 70c). The carver had placed the cherub within the urn to cement the association of earthly refinement, taste, and religious piety, so we see her as "holy and happy," to use Cummings's phrase.

The most striking example of this identification of values is the stone for Brigadier General Francis Osgood, 1817, Portland (Illus. 70d). Here the tympanum design, in which cherub head becomes urn and urn becomes cherub is highly effective in communicating the merging of secular and Christian values. In many ways, the classical tradition evokes a vision of order, balance, and reason inconsistent with a Christian vision of a fallen world. In these images, death is both a social concern, inspiring mourning for the community's loss of mother, father, minister, or sea captain, and a religious concern, inspiring contemplation of the Christian piety of the successful citizen. The epitaphs often combine Christian resignation with a kind of community boosterism in praise of the departed. This stone exhibits Osgood's wealth and taste and argues that he was an aristocrat of piety and taste to be emulated. These designs obviously appealed to the common people of Maine, who bought countless cheap, mass-produced stones with urn designs and who produced embroidered mourning pictures with neoclassical designs. An art critic in 1800 in Paris or London might laugh at these provincial examples that incorrectly mix styles; yet their originality is entirely appropriate and pleasing.

These gravestone designs show how esthetics reflect ideological compromises. In adapting aristocratic and authority-based neoclassical styles to a democratic setting, Americans created genuinely popular designs. In the literature and painting of Maine in the early national period, the issues of style were compounded by debate over the appropriate subject for American arts. American writers and artists generally agreed with eighteenth century English theories that the arts should present an idealized picture of human virtue, as it resided in the aristocratic mind, and a general view of the natural world that reveals God's benevolent Providence and the beneficial effects of human wisdom. As Washington Irving noted, the American wilderness and its earnest though mediocre inhabitants were the most immediate subject for American artists, but these subjects were unsuited to a grand and ideal treatment. In the early 1800s, few Americans embraced the primitivism of Rousseau or knew of the natural overlaid with the scientific rationalism of Charles Wilson Peale and Thomas Jefferson. The wilderness must be civilized, since the frontier presents examples of social degradation. Timothy Dwight discovers that the Maine squatters build no churches or schools, and the land seems, consequently, to be less fertile than that of villages exhibiting the "New England plan."[22]

Enlightenment traditions of poetry and painting celebrate the aristocrat whose estate shows nature tamed by art. Given the conditions of the American frontier, most poetry of the period offers "prospects" of future fertility; the so-called Connecticut Wits of the 1790s imitate Pope, Cowper, Thomson, and others to voice their hopes for the American land. Critics have offered many explanations for the failure of these poets schooled in neoclassical verse to establish an indigenous poetic tradition of the American landscape in these years.[23] It may simply be that the rhetorical conventions of the picturesque and the sublime are unsuited to the daily grubwork of transforming forest to farm. It has been suggested that the popularity of oratory overwhelmed poetry with rhetoric. At the time critics suggested that American wits were overwhelmed by "sophisticated and decadent models of poetry from England...."[24]

"The Village," written about Fryeburg by Enoch Lincoln, is a good example of the failure of local poets to capture the essence of Maine's landscape. A pale shadow of the poetry of Goldsmith and Cowper, the poem traces the development of nature and human nature from wilderness to civilization. The Indians are true children of the wilderness: "Such is the savage, such is Nature's child, / Where'er we look, unsocial, fierce, and wild."[25] But white society has tamed the Saco River to make it useful and beautiful: "When, joining hand in hand, what charm imparts / The potent touch of labour and the Arts." Lincoln looks forward to the time when all the land will be tamed by the mind in the abstract terms preferred by Augustan writers:

> Hence too, in this, our dear Columbias clime,
> Blooming as spring, and durable as time,
> The stately three of science and of art
> Shall wave luxuriant over every part.

So much for prophecy; when Lincoln descends from Parnassus to describe Maine, he attempts to elevate an American tree to the level of the sublime:

> Fair Maple! honors purer far are thine
> Than Venus' Myrtle yields or Bacchus' vine;
> Minerva's Olive, consecrated tree,
> Deserves not half the homage due to thee.[26]

For whatever reason, such poetry had little appeal for the people cutting and tapping maple trees. In painting, however, Americans quickly transformed European styles of presenting human beings in nature to create a style that became popular throughout New England. It is this American style that John Brewster, Jr., brought with such success to Maine.

By the late eighteenth century, American painters were well aware of the conventional method of portraying a gentleman on his estate. The subject was accompanied by accessories, such as books, papers and pen, or sword or gun, which served as emblems of the powers of the human mind; the landscape forming the background depicted the results of cultivation by this cultivated mind. Ralph Earl of Massachusetts was one of the first American painters with roots in the country tradition and limner technique to adopt this formula when he studied art in England during the Revolution.[27] A typical portrait from his English period, *Man with a Gun* (1784), presents an aristocrat with his gun and hunting dogs in a parklike setting. The landscape is abstract, with no local reference, as if to assert the universal principles by which nature and the reasoning mind function. This aristocratic formula is significantly altered by Earl when he returns to America in 1785. First, he strips away aristocratic portrait conventions to depict in a realistic fashion those whose position in society is based on their character, intelligence and hard work, not inherited privilege. Second, whether in a window or in a prospect behind the subject, Earl paints realistic landscapes of the house or village connected with the person's life. The effect is stunning, for what had been an aristocratic convention now serves to celebrate republican virtues that ensure a profitable and moral development of the land.

Earl's masterpiece, *Chief Justice and Mrs. Oliver Ellsworth* (Illus. 71), contains all the signs of the benefits of wise leadership by a natural aristocracy with, in this case, strong Federalist leanings. The couple is surrounded by books. Mr. Ellsworth holds a copy of the Federal Constitution, symbolic of the active role he played in shaping the new nation. Mrs. Ellsworth, by extending one hand toward the document, shows her position as a partner to her husband's vision. The couple flanks a window that frames a view of their home in the distance. The house is in the Georgian style and is surrounded by a fence painted white, a style of fencing associated with the gentry in America, and a boundary that emphasizes the rule of law. The painting is organized formally by a series of telescoping frames, which are metaphors for the mutually supporting institutions of marriage and the law; such institutions arise from the character of the people, and they contribute to the order and prosperity of the landscape. It should be noted that realistic landscape painting in and of itself was still rare during the period, since the view of nature was mediated by human presence, but Earl's work was an important step in that direction.

Ralph Earl was the founder of the Connecticut School of painters, which included John Brewster, Jr.[28] Brewster was born deaf and dumb in Hampton, Connecticut, in 1766. He was a bright boy who received instruction in painting and drawing in the Earl style from the minister-painter Joseph Steward. An example of his Connecticut style is *Mr. James Eldredge* (Illus. 72a) and *Mrs. James Eldredge (Lucy Gallup)* (Illus. 72b). There is what has to be called an American directness of observation, even when the overall composition is European. The pen in Mr. Eldredge's hand represents the authority of the educated mind, which extends its influence into the world beyond the home, as indicated by the prospect in the window to which his hand leads. Mrs. Eldredge cultivates the morals of the home, as represented by the Bible

71. *Chief Justice Oliver Ellsworth and his wife, Abigail Wolcott,* by Ralph Earl (1751–1801), 1792.
(Oil on canvas. Wadsworth Atheneum, Hartford. Gift of Ellsworth Heirs)

at her side and the enclosed garden behind her. Here in painted form is an affirmation of the role of women in the "domestic sphere." While Brewster does not have the skill, nor perhaps the inclination, to paint detailed landscape backgrounds, his directness of observation and limner technique show his affirmation of vernacular American traditions.

In about 1796, John Brewster, Jr., brought this style to Maine where he moved when his younger brother, Royal, married Dorcas Coffin of Buxton, Maine. Brewster painted in Maine, with trips to Salem, Newburyport, and Connecticut until his death in 1854 at age 88. In 1796 he began a series of ten remarkable paintings for the Cutts family of Saco. His portraits capture the human potential of Maine: its merchants, sea captains, lawyers, farmers, and their wives and their children. Each subject is in a traditional pose of authority, or in a compo-

72. *a. Mr. James Eldredge,* by John Brewster, Jr. (1766–1854), 1795. (Oil on canvas. Collection The Connecticut Historical Society)

sition borrowed from an aristocratic tradition, to show that authority does spring from republican accomplishments. In *James Prince and His Son William Henry Prince,* father and son flank a glass bookcase filling the space that usually holds a village scene (Illus. 73). The composition implies that knowledge is the window to the world, an impression reinforced by the pen in Mr. Prince's hand and the letter in William's. The children of the Republic first need education and the arts, and they can then turn to improving the land.

Brewster's paintings of Maine children in the early years of the nineteenth century utilize traditional poses, but their sheer numbers, compositional details, and monumental size reflect a new emphasis on childhood in the developing nuclear family. As Karin Calvert notes, "Art portrayed the new freedom accorded children and a new fondness for, or at least acceptance of, childish behavior."[29] Brewster's young boys often hold birds, indicating active natures, and the girls hold books, symbolizing the domestic and feminine. His *Francis O. Watts*

72. b. *Mrs. James Eldredge* (Lucy Gallup), by John Brewster, Jr., 1795. (Oil on canvas. Collection The Connecticut Historical Society)

With Bird of 1805 presents this two-year-old citizen of Kennebunkport in a loose frock against a brightening prospect, which mirrors the bright future of this child and his generation in Maine. (See Plate XIV.)

Brewster's paintings bring to Maine a compositional form that emphasizes the importance of education, piety, and the arts to the leading families of the state and in the successful encouragement of these qualities through local institutions. It is in the Reverend Jonathan Fisher that we find in one person a full vision of a cultural style that will ensure harmonious, republican development of the frontier. Jonathan Fisher is a perfect representative of Maine at statehood because he embodies a mixture of Yankee tradition and classical and Christian learning.[30] Born in Braintree, Massachusetts, in 1768 and educated in Divinity at Harvard, he was a man with one foot in the colonial past of Calvinist and classical tradition and one foot in the frontier society of nineteenth century Maine. Fisher's was a life of incredible activity. He ran a large farm, had eight children, engaged in various craft ac-

73. *James Prince and William Henry Prince,* by John Brewster, Jr., 1801. (Oil on canvas. The Historical Society of Old Newbury, Newburyport)

tivities (including the manufacture of thousands of hats), wrote books, painted, attended to church and missionary activities, preached 3,000 sermons, helped found Blue Hill Academy, and preached against slavery, intemperance, and separation from Massachusetts. His reputation today, however, rests on his paintings, which show his awareness of American conventions for presenting the local scene.

At first he seems a man of paradox. An old-fashioned Congregational minister, he had the Socratic injunction "Know Thyself" carved in a book on his tombstone. A man who deeply studied the mysteries of God's will in nature, he was also an accomplished mathematician. He revealed an early mechanical genius by teaching himself how to make clocks, but he showed his early piety by beginning a life-long spiritual diary with the poem:

> But my hard heart is prone to sin.
> What deep pollution reigns within!
> Meanwhile I tread with awful speed
> Those ways which to destruction lead.

Fisher had prepared himself for entry into Harvard in 1788 by studying classical and Christian texts:

> Having finished the select Orations of Cicero and the Aeneads of Virgil, having studied all three first Evangelists and a part of the book of

Acts in the Greek Testament, and being a good measure recovered from the whooping-cough, I rode this day to Cambridge and offered myself for admission to the college.[31]

This passage reveals much about his way of thinking: He combines notice of his intellectual accomplishments with remarks about the trials of disease and other practical matters. Fisher fully participated in the evolving social and esthetic order of his time, and he almost single-handedly put this order into effect by fostering the growth of Blue Hill, Maine, on the "New England plan." He combined a fundamental Christian belief in God's controlling Providence with an appreciation for social order based on education and for prosperity based on pious behavior and Yankee ingenuity.

At college, Fisher studied religion and mathematics, wrote poetry, and learned to draw, paint, and cut wood engravings. Fisher saw no conflict in these pursuits. His early nature studies of the common flora of Massachusetts were guided by the belief that the book of Nature confirms the spiritual truths revealed in Scripture. As God's creation is based on principles of order, so mathematics and the physical sciences foster an appreciation of the divine plan, not skepticism of it.

Jonathan Fisher accepted a call to the village of Blue Hill in 1795, where he remained until his death in 1847. He ministered to a growing flock, and also to residents of the frontier on arduous missionary journeys on foot into the Maine woods. He knew the wilderness and the enterprising seacoast towns, and in his writing and painting we can trace a growing awareness of the American landscape as a fit subject for literature and art. Fisher's frontier experience of the "low state of religion in general found throughout this unchartered region,"[32] convinced him of the need for the improvement of society through religion and education. He did find some pious souls, whom he mentions in *The Youth's Primer* (1817), but he was struck by the dreadful ignorance and drunkenness of the people. His concern is expressed in his work to found Blue Hill Academy in 1803. The Academy surely echoed Fisher's opinions in 1806 when it asked for financial support, for "in so doing they will find their reward in beholding their tender offspring possessing that degree of literature as will, by Divine Assistance, make them a peculiar comfort to themselves and a blessing to the rising generation."[33] Jonathan Fisher helped forge the American belief in education as a means not only for social, but also for moral and spiritual improvement, and in Blue Hill and other towns, the schoolhouse joined the church as a prominent feature of the built landscape of Maine.

Fisher's greatest contribution to the development of a national style is in his works on nature. Here Fisher shows his remarkable ability to see in the particular features of the American scene a landscape blessed by God. In his poem recalling a voyage from Blue Hill to Salem in 1809, he employs an ancient Christian trope by comparing his physical voyage to a spiritual one:

> Shipmates, adieu! We part, perhaps to meet
> On earth no more; be this our future prize:
> Through faith in Christ, to find a calm retreat,
> Each in the Salem of the blissful skies!

Fisher renews the hopes of the founders of New England who associated the landscape of Israel and New England with Heaven, but he breaks with tradition by cataloging the very real discomforts of a New England voyage: "By many an insect in our berths beset; / ... Now comes the sickening swell, the vessel rolls, / The head and back are pained, the stomach heaves."[34] Fisher's notebooks contain further indications that nature does not need to be merely a part of other worldly meditations. He notes, on April 2, 1827, that "the frogs now begin to sing on the edge of the evening," and in July he decides that fireflies are "an astonishing revelation of God's generous plan for the delight of his children upon the earth."[35]

Mary Ellen Chase suggests in her biography of Fisher that the observation and recording of natural phenomenon in his painting and in his book, *Scripture Animals*, satisfied three basic needs.[36] First, he could indulge his delight in the American landscape; second, he could instruct youth; and third, he could glorify God. In *The Latter Harvest* (see Plate XI), Fisher presents an emblem of the way he has come to see the American landscape. Here are very American vegetables lovingly realized in paint and inviting an appreciation of the bounty of the land. The fruits reveal God's goodness, but the accompanying Bible text and the title of the work, are prophetic: The harvest anticipates the realization of God's plan to restore the earth to an eden of plenty. As the Bible verse painted by Fisher expresses it,

Thou crownest the year with thy goodness; and thy paths drop fatness.
They drop upon the pastures of the wilderness: and the little hills rejoice on every side.
The pastures are clothed with flocks; the valleys also are covered with corn; they shout for joy, they also sing.

(Ps. 65:11–13)

Fisher's own harvest of souls in Blue Hill and the town's success in transforming the wilderness into a garden must have provided Fisher with satisfaction, and perhaps with inspiration for his painting.

Fisher's most interesting paintings represent the successful blending of American and European styles. It is not merely coincidental that he began his *Self-Portrait* and *A Morning View of Blue Hill Village* in the same year, 1824. (See Illus. 67 and Plate XIII.) They are companion pieces, recalling the Earl-Brewster formula, which emphasized the connection of human wisdom and piety with the American landscape. The portrait is direct, forceful, unadorned, and rather bold in its composition, which identifies Jonathan Fisher as a man of this world; Fisher avoids the traditional portrait pose of a minister with hand on Bible or covering the heart. The painting of Blue Hill shows the product of his mind. It is a "prospect" piece painted in morning, promising the dawn of a new era in Maine. Fisher implies that the American scene deserves the attention once reserved for classical and biblical texts. All the elements of the prosperous and, it is hoped, pious town built on the "New England plan" are present: church, school, parsonage, merchants, farmers, and sailors. In these works, Fisher allies himself with those Americans who have found a national style that preserves the essential esthetic vision of bettering society through art while celebrating the distinctly common, democratic forms of American life. In terms of the development of local culture, Maine was fortunate to be somewhat removed from the dominance of urban style centers, for the works of artists such as Brewster and Fisher, the poetry of Enoch Lincoln, and the distinctive gravestone designs could find local patrons. Moreover, it is the work of these artists that now lends distinction to the culture of Maine at statehood.

NOTES

1. Emory Elliott, *Revolutionary Writers: Literature and Authority in the New Republic, 1775–1810* (New York: Oxford University Press, 1982), Chapter 1.

2. The best single study of the place of the arts in America, 1763–1789, is Kenneth Silverman's *A Cultural History of the American Revolution: Painting, Music, Literature, and the Theatre in the Colonies and the United States from the Treaty of Paris to the Inauguration of George Washington* (New York: Thomas Y. Crowell, 1976). For views of the influence of the Enlightenment and neoclassical style in America, see Henry F. May, *The Enlightenment in America* (New York: Oxford University Press, 1976); Henry Steele Commager, *The Empire of Reason: How Europe Imagined and America Realized the Englightenment* (Garden City, N.Y.: Anchor Press, 1977); Bernard Bailyn, *The Ideological Origins of the American Revolution* (Cambridge, Mass.: Harvard University Press, 1967); Richard M. Grummere, *The American Colonial Mind and the Classical Tradition: Essays in Comparative Culture* (Cambridge, Mass.: Harvard University Press, 1963).

3. Quoted in Ronald F. Banks, *Maine Becomes a State: The Movement to Separate Maine from Massachusetts, 1785–1820* (Middletown, Conn.: Wesleyan University Press, 1970, reprinted Somersworth, N.H.: New Hampshire Publishing Co., 1973), p. 3.

4. Noah Webster, *A Grammatical Institute of the English Language . . .* (Hartford, Conn.: Hudson and Goodwin, undated [1783]), p. 14.

5. Quoted in Kenneth Silverman, *Timothy Dwight* (New York: Twayne Publishers, 1969), pp. 47–48.

6. Washington Irving, *The Sketch Book of Geoffrey Crayon, Gent.* (New York: New American Library, 1961), p. 14.

7. This paragraph applies to the arts the conclusions of the first chapters of Banks, *Maine Becomes a State*.

8. Abraham Cummings, *The Present Times Perilous. A Sermon, Preached at Sullivan, on the National Fast, April 25, 1799* (Castine, Me.: David J. Waters, 1799), p. 13. For the religious controversies of the period, see Stephen A. Marini, *Radical Sects of Revolutionary New England* (Cambridge, Mass.: Harvard University Press, 1982).

9. Abraham Cummings, *A Dissertation on the Introduction and Glory of the Millennium. To Which is Prefixed, A Discourse on the Two Witnesses* (Boston: Manning and Loring, 1797), p. 114.

10. Henry Cumings, *A Sermon, Preached on the 9th Day of October, 1799 at the Ordination of the Rev. Caleb Bradley* (Portland, Me.: E. A. Jenks, 1799), p. 22.

11. [James Sullivan], *The Altar of Baal Thrown Down: Or, The French Nation Defended, Against the Pulpit Slander of David Osgood, A.M.* (Boston: Adams and Larkin, 1795), p. 30.

12. Elliott, *Revolutionary Writers*, p. 16.

13. Quoted in Lewis P. Simpson (ed.), *The Federalist Literary Mind. The Monthly Anthology, and Boston Review* (Baton Rouge: Louisiana State University Press, 1962), p. 144.

14. Ibid., pp. 49, 79.   15. Ibid., p. 209.

16. Richard Grummere notes a similar literary use of classical imagery in *The American Colonial Mind*, p. viii.

17. Recorded in Augustus W. Corliss (ed.), *Old Times ... of North Yarmouth, Maine* (1877–1884; reprinted, Somersworth, N.H.: New Hampshire Publishing Co., 1977), p. 1045. The epitaph is not dated.

18. For New England gravestone iconography, see Allan I. Ludwig, *Graven Images: New England Stonecarving and Its Symbols, 1650–1815* (Middletown, Conn.: Wesleyan University Press, 1966); David H. Watters, *"With Bodilie Eyes:" Eschatological Themes in Puritan Literature and Gravestone Art* (Ann Arbor: UMI Research Press, 1981).

19. Abraham Cummings, *Contemplations on the Cherubim: Wherein is Considered the Use and Design of those Sacred Symbols* (Boston: John Eliot, Jr., 1812), p. 9.

20. Ibid., p. 17.

21. Peter Benes, *The Masks of Orthodoxy: Folk Gravestone Carving in Plymouth County, Massachusetts, 1689–1805* (Amherst: University of Massachusetts Press, 1977), pp. 142–147.

22. Timothy Dwight, *Travels in New England and New York*, Barbara Miller Solomon (ed.), 4 vols. (Cambridge, Mass.: Harvard University Press, 1969), vol. 2, pp. 160–162.

23. See Leon Howard, *The Connecticut Wits* (Chicago: University of Chicago Press, 1943); Gordon E. Bigelow, *Rhetoric and American Poetry of the Early National Period*, University of Florida Monographs, 4 (Gainesville: University of Florida Press, 1960); Grummere, *The American Colonial Mind*; Elliott, *Revolutionary Writers*.

24. Bigelow, *Rhetoric*, p. 39.

25. [Enoch Lincoln], *The Village; a Poem. With an Appendix* (Portland, Me.: Edward Little and Co., 1816), p. 16.

26. Ibid., pp. 21, 74, 22.

27. See Laurence B. Goodrich, *Ralph Earl: Recorder for an Era* (Albany, N.Y.: State University of New York, 1967); Silverman, *A Cultural History*, pp. 591–592.

28. See Nina Fletcher Little, "John Brewster, Jr., 1766–1854: Deaf-Mute Portrait Painter of Connecticut and Maine," *Connecticut Historical Society Bulletin* 25 (1960), 97–129.

29. Karin Calvert, "Children in American Family Portraiture, 1670–1810," *William and Mary Quarterly* 39 (January 1982), 112. Two important works on the idea of the child, the woman's sphere, and the family in this period are Bernard W. Wishy, *The Child in the Republic: The Dawn of Modern American Child Nurture* (Philadelphia: University of Pennsylvania Press, 1968) and Linda Kerber, *Women of the Republic: Intellect and Ideology in Revolutionary America* (Chapel Hill, N.C.: University of North Carolina Press, 1980).

30. The best treatment of Fisher's life is by Mary Ellen Chase, *Jonathan Fisher, Maine Parson, 1768–1847* (New York: Macmillan, 1948). See also *The Arts and Crafts of the Versatile Parson Jonathan Fisher 1768–1847* (Rockland, Me.: William A. Farnsworth Library and Art Museum, 1967); Alice Winchester, "Jonathan Fisher," in *American Folk Painters of Three Centuries* (New York: Hudson Hills Press, 1980), pp. 82–87.

31. Quoted in Chase, *Jonathan Fisher*, pp. 14, 16–17.

32. Ibid., p. 177.   33. Ibid., p. 103.   34. Ibid., p. 184.
35. Ibid., p. 144.   36. Ibid., p. 233.

INDEX

INDEX

Note: t = table; bold refers to black-and-white illustrations. Color plates I–VIII follow p. 106; plates IX–XV follow p. 170. State is named only for towns outside Maine.

Acadians, 35–37
Adams, Henry, 184–85, 194
Adams, John, 185, 194
Adams, Samuel, 102, 124
Addison, Joseph, 219
Aesop's fables, 213 n.13
Agriculture: Acadian, 35; and centralization of village, 29; and land development, 13–25; salt marsh, 14, 24 n.6
Albion, *see* Fairfax
Alfred, 45, 56; Bussell's plan of, plate V
Allegory, and the emblem, 199
Allen, William, 59 n.14
Alna, 46
American Builder's Companion, The (Benjamin), 29
American Medical Biography (Thacher), 170
Andrews, Nabby, 172
Androscoggin River valley, development of, 129
Anesthesia, 167
Anglicans, *see* Episcopal church
Animals: in fables, 213 n.13; scriptural, as emblems, 204–10
Animals, domestic: cows, 18; hogs, 18; horses, 18 (as symbol in Fisher's art, 222); oxen, 18; sheep, 18, 20
Ant, in Fisher's *Scripture Animals,* **207**, 221
Anti-Federalists, 84, 93, 94, 133, 141. *See also* Democratic-Republicans
Ape, in Fisher's *Scripture Animals,* 217–18
Appleton, Moses, 183 n.37
Architecture: colonial vernacular, 29; country estate, 66–67 (*see also* Montpelier); county, public, 44–49; domestic, built out from one-room cabin, 17; Federal neoclassical, 29–31, 56–57; Georgian, 29, 30; Gothic Revival, **57,** 57–58, 186; Greek Revival, 31, 51, 186; interior furnishing, 35, **69,** 70–79, **73–79** passim, 81 n.33; of meeting houses (*see* Meeting houses); Montpelier (Thomaston), 64–69; in Portland, 51–54; Shaker, 37, 38
Aristocratic tradition, and neoclassical style, 228, 229
Aristotle, 217
Arminian theology, 124, 131, 143
Arts and esthetics, 9–10; and authorship, 231–33, 235; European, criticism of, 229; gravestone carving, 232–36; moral authority and, 228–31; music, 10; painting, 237–41; poetry, 237, 242–44. *See also* Style
Arundel, *see* Kennebunkport
Asbury, Francis, 133
Ashton, Isaac, 78; demi-lune table by, **78**
Atonement, substitutionary, 124; and universal salvation, 132 (*see also* Universalism)
Augusta, 45, 169; anonymous watercolor of, **169**

Author, and post-Revolutionary style, 231–33, 235
Authority: esthetic, 228–29; ministerial, 231; responses to, 11 (*see also* Resistance)
Autopsies, 172
Avery, Joseph, 215
Ayer, James, 33

Backus, Isaac, 140
Badlam, Stephen, 81 n.37
Bailyn, Bernard, 119
Ballard, Ephraim, 168, 181 n.9
Ballard, Hannah, 171
Ballard, Jonathan, 171
Ballard, Martha Moore, 11, 168–69; assists at deliveries, 174, 175–76; career profile, 172–74, 173 t; cooperative relationship with male doctors, 172–73; fee charged by, 177; non-obstetric treatment by, 170; record-keeping by, 176, 178, 181 n.11; at Sewall childbed, 165–66
Bangor, 14, 48–49
Banks, Ronald, xvii, 95, 96, 125, 136, 185
Baptists, 132, 133, 154, 156, 157. *See also* Freewill Baptists; Separate Baptists
Baring, Alexander, 66, 69
Barker, Benjamin, 182 n.36
Barlow, Anson, James, and William, 113
Barlow, Joel, 235
Barlow, Nathaniel: arrested and imprisoned, 113; early years, 106–8; vision of, 102–3, 111; "white Indian" resistance, 103–4
Barlow, Obed, 106–8
Barnes, John, 132
Barrell, Joseph, 66, 67
Barrell, Nathaniel, 167
Barrell, Olive, 167
Barrell, Sally ("Madame Wood"), 167, 181 n.6
Barrels, 43–44, **44**
Bartlett, Jonathan, 116 n.21
Barton, Steven, 171
Bath, 39, 54, 230
Beaver Hill (now Freedom), 104, 112
Bee, in Fisher's *Scripture Animals,* 221
Belcher, Supply, 10
Belfast, 6, 39
Believers, Society of, *see* Shakers
Belknap, Jeremy, 187, 190, 193 n.18, 196–97 n.37
Benjamin, Asher, 29; meeting house design, **30**
Bentley, William, 66
Berry, John, 158
Bertault, George, 70
Bethel, 14, 32–34; proprietors' map of, **33**
Betterment Act of 1808, 140
Bible: animals as emblems, 204–10; as own emblem, 210, 212. *See also* Scripture
Biddeford, 45

249

250 Index

Biddeford Daily Journal, 152
Biddeford Weekly Journal, 152
Bill of Rights, U.S., 141
Billy Hans (Codman), **54**
Bingham, William, 66, 69
"Black regiment" of New England clerics, 124
Blackburn, Joseph, 77
Blacks, 181 n.13; in Fisher's *Scripture Animals,* 219–20; Hallowell healing-woman, 169, 172, 175, 181 n.13; in Jefferson's *Notes on Virginia,* 191
Blue Hill, 32, 34, 42, 206–7, 211–12, 215, 222, 224, 230, 243
Blue Hill Academy, 242, 243
Blunt, John S., *The Launching of the Washington,* plate VIII
Bond, Eunice and Abigail, 158
Book for Boys and Girls, A (Bunyan), 201, 207–8
Boston Tea Party, 155
Boston, Maine gravestones from, 230, 232
Bowdoin, James, 94
Bowdoin College, 40, 95, 127, 140
Bowdoin College Campus, The (Brown), plate VII
Box pews, sale of, 48
Boxer captured by *Enterprise* off Monhegan, 54
Brackett, Daniel, 103–4, 105
Bradbury, Wyman, 60 n.41
Bragg, Stephen, 107
Breed, Nathan, 107
Brewster, John, Jr., 10, 237, 238–41; Eldredge portraits, **240, 241**, *Francis O. Watts With Bird,* 241–42, plate XIV; Prince double protrait, **242**; Samuel Deane portrait, **121**
Brewster, Royal, 239
Brick-making, 66
Brigadier General Samuel Waldo (attr. to Feke), **77,** 77–78
Brooks, Edward, 126
Brooks, Noah, 65
Brown, John G., painting of Bowdoin College, plate VII
Brown, Richard, 171
Brunswick, 4, 39–42; 1828 map, **42**; 1780 and 1802 maps, **40**
Bucksport, 14, 39
Bulfinch, Charles, 8, 10, 30, 48, 51, 55; design for Maine state house, Plate XV; Pleasant Hill (Charlestown, Mass.), 66–67, **67**; proposal for Boston theater, 67–68; U.S. Capitol, 51
Bunyan, John, 201, 207, 209
Burned-Over District, The (Cross), 157
Burr, Aaron, Sr., 130
Bussell, Joshua, *A Plan of Alfred, Maine,* plate V
Buxton, 146, 154

Caesarian section, 179
Caldwell, Bill, 161 n.5
Calvert, Karin, 240
Cambridge, 20
Camden, 39
Capitol buildings, 8, 10; Maine, Codman's painting of, plate XV; United States, 51; Virginia, 232
Carding mills, 42
Carleton, Osgood, maps of the District of Maine: 1795, **ii**; 1798 (detail), **27**
Carlyle, Thomas, 186
Castine, 45, 47, **47**, 54, 56, **85**; occupied by British, 6, 84, 87
Catholics, 56–57, 120, 120 t
Chain of being, 217–19

Chandler, John, 7, 113
Changes in the Land, (Cronon), 13
Channing, William Ellery, 212
Chaplin, Jeremiah, 140
Charles I, 90
Charters: Gorges', for the Province of Maine, 90; of Massachusetts, 1691, 83
Chase, Mary Ellen, 199, 244
Chase, Stephen, 106
Chauncy, Charles, 122
Cherubim, as symbol, 233–36
Chestnut Street Theatre (Philadelphia), 67
Chief Justice Oliver Ellsworth and his Wife, Abigail Wolcott (Earl), 238, **239**
Children, instruction of, 201–2, 203, 204–10, 213 n.13, 214
China, *see* Harlem
China ware, 75, **75**
Choice Emblems (Wynne), 208–9
Choice of Emblems, A (Whitney), **209**, 209–10
Christ Church (Gardiner), 57
Christian Society (Christ-ians), 118, 120 t, 134, 142, 143, 154–55
Churches: Christ Episcopal (Gardiner), 57; St. Patrick's (Newcastle), 56. *See also* Meeting houses
Clapboard mill, 41
Clark, Abigail, 158
Clark, Isaac, 55
Clark, Mrs. (midwife), 170
Classical statuary, 70–71
Clay, Daniel, 116 n.21
Climate, Maine, 189
Cochran, Jacob, 11, 160–61 n.1; appeals to women, 149, 157–58; arrested, 157; begins ministry, 154–55; draws followers from organized churches, 156–57; early years, 149, 152–53, 161 n.12, 162 n.25; gravesite, 164 n.79; imprisoned, 151, 158, 159; meeting observed by Betsy Foss, 1817, 146; in nude tableau vivant, 150, 157; resurrects "Sister Mercy," 150–51; theology of, 155–56; trial and conviction, 148, 151–52, 158
"Cochran Delusion, the" (Ridlon), 149
Cochranism, 148–53, 154–60, 161 n.5
Cochranism Delineated (Stinchfield), **147,** 152
Codd, Nicholas, 56–57
Codman, Charles, 54, 60 n.54; *Billy Hans,* 54; *Old State House, Augusta,* plate XV
Coffin, Dorcas, 239
Coffin, Nathaniel, 46
Coffin, Paul, 69, 154, 163 n.42
Colby, Benjamin, 101 t
Cole, Thomas, 186
Collection of Emblems, A (Wither), 203, **204**
Collection of Preternatural Cases . . . (Smellie), 178–79
Colman, Samuel, 171
Columbage, en (Acadian log house style), 36–37
Communal living, 156
Complete Anti-Federalist, The (Storing), 141
Concord, 20
Congregationalism, 48, 119–21, 120 t, 154; decline in number of ordinands, 128; growth in, by county, 134, 135 t, 137 t
Connecticut Wits, 237
Constitution: Federal, 4, 92, 93–94, 133; state, 91
Continental Congress, 83–84, 187
Conventions, separatist, 50, 88, 91–92, 125
Cony, Daniel, 169–70, 171, 174, 176, 177
Cookbooks, 23

Coopers, 43–44, **44**
Copley, John Singleton, 77
Corinth, 14
Cosmopolitanism, in ministerial style, 121–22, 123–25
Cottrill, Matthew, 56–57
Country Builder's Assistant, The (Benjamin), 29, 68; meeting house design from, **30**
County seats, plans and architecture of, 44–49
Courthouse architecture: Cumberland Co. (1816), 46, **46**, 51; Lincoln Co., **46**, 46–47; Somerset Co., **49**
Cox, Mrs. (midwife), 170, 175
Cox, William, 74, 76; armchair by, **74**
Creditors, merchant, 100, 101, 108, 113. *See also* Debt
Cronon, William, 13
Crop diversification, 19
Cross, Whitney, 157, 162 n.38
Culture: expressions of, Maine, 8–10; localised versus cosmopolitan, 129. *See also* Arts and esthetics; Style
Cumberland Baptist Association, 157
Cumberland County, 15, 134, 135 t, 137 t, 138 t; courthouse of 1816, 46, **46**, 51; population, 129 t
Cumberland Gazette, 93. *See also* *Falmouth Gazette*
Cumings, Henry, 230–31
Cummings, Abraham, 230, 233
Curtis, Samuel, 169–70
Cushing, Tileston, 46
Cushing (town), 32
Cutts, Richard, 7
Cutts, Thomas, 39

Dana, Edmund Trowbridge, 231
Davis, Daniel, 185, 193
Davis, James, 105
Deane, Samuel, 50–51, 88, 96, **121**, 121–22, 123–25, 127, 128
Deane, Sarah Dwight and (Deacon) Samuel, 121
Dearborn, Henry, 7
Death's heads, 233
Debt, settlers', 100, 101, 107, 108. *See also* Creditors
Decker, Joseph, 164 n.88
Deforestation, 16–17, 23. *See also* Land: clearing
Democratic values, neoclassicism modified to reflect, 232, 235
Democratic-Republicans, 4, 6–8, 97, 118, 136, 138. *See also* Anti-Federalists
Dennet, Jacob, 163 n.65
Dennet, John, 159, 163 n.65
Dennet, Sally, 158, 163 n.65
Denny Soccabeson (artist unknown), plate III
Depression, commercial, 1808, 54
Derby, Elias Hasket, 51, 81 n.33
District of Maine, 2, 84. *See also* Maine
Divine Emblems, (Bunyan), 201, 207–8
Donally, Mary, 179
Donegan, Jane, 166
Draft animals, 15, 18
Drake, Edwin S., 78
Dresden, 46
Droving, 14, 16, 24 n.7
Drunkenness, Fisher on, 204, **205**, 222. *See also* Taverns
Dunton, Ebenezer, 68, 70
"Durham Dancers" (charismatics of Durham, N.H.), 126

Dwight, Timothy, 40, 49, 52, 236

Eagle, as emblem of Maine statehood, 228
Earl, Ralph, 238; portrait of the Ellsworths, **239**
Eastern Argus, 140
Eastern Burying Ground (Portland), 235
Eastport, 6
Eaton, Cyrus, 65
Ecclesiastical law, 7. *See also* Ministerial tax
Eden: Fisher's Blue Hill as, 206–7; tableaux-vivants depicting, 150, 157, 159–60. *See also* Paradise
Edson, Calvin, 172
Education: Blue Hill Academy, 242, 243; Bowdoin College, 40, 95, 127, 140; Harvard College, 120–26 passim, 168, 170, 177, 215, 241, 242–43; Maine Literary and Theological Institute at Waterville, 140; and medical professionalization, 167, 171, 179–80, 183 n.44; neoclassical, and the moral society, 230; Yale, Maine ministers prepared at, 120; of young children (*see* Children, instruction of)
Edwards, Jonathan, 122
Ejectment suits, 101
Elden, Gideon, 146
Eldredge, James, portrait of, 238, 239, **240**
Election, theological, 124, 143
Elliott, Emory, 228, 231
Ellis, Dr. (Hallowell), 177
Ellsworth, Oliver, and Abigail Wolcott, Earl's painting of, 238, **239**
Ellsworth (town), 47
Ely, Samuel, 94, 102, 105
Embargo of 1807, 41, 50, 51, 52, 54, 101. *See also* Non-intercourse Act
Emblems, rhetoric of, 199–212, 213 n.4, 228; in portrait painting, 238–39, 240. *See also* Symbolism
Emerson, Ralph Waldo, 186, 212
Emerson, Samuel, 167
Energy: and pioneer diet, 23; from burning wood (*see* Fuel wood)
Enfield, N.H., 37, 149, 156, 164 n.79
Enterprise (brig), 54
Episcopal church, 120, 120 t; and Gothic revival, 57
Epitaphs, 232
"Essay Concerning Human Understanding, An" (Locke), 219
Evangelism, 118, 138–40, 156
Evil, 220
Exchange, extralocal, 29
Exeter, 20

Fairfax (now Albion), 102, 103, 112
"Faith" emblem, in Fisher's Youth's Primer, **202**
Falmouth (now Portland), 6, **47**, 50, 96, 230; First Parish of, 122, 123–35; Seymour's 1786 pencil drawing, **50**. *See also* Portland
Falmouth Gazette, 88, **89**, 90, 93
Farmington, 14, 16
Fashion, *see* Style
Federalists, 6, 93, 124, 125, 127, 133, 134, 140, 184, 230
Fees, medical, 182–83 n.37; Somerset County agreement, 179–80; midwife's, 177
Feke, Robert: Waldo portrait, **77**, 77
Fencing, 18, 19, 20, 69
Ferme ornee, 65, 66, 79
Fernald, Mark, 154
Fessenden, Samuel, 140

Fires, 6, 16–17, 18, 19, 24 n.9, 50, 51
First Church of Boston, 122, 130
First Church of Rochester, Mass., 168
First Parish Meeting House (Brunswick), 40
Fisher, Jonathan, 10, 34, 199, 200, 241–45; early years, 215; emblematic shorthand, 221; *Four Birds,* 222–23, plate XII; *Larkspur,* 225; *The Latter Harvest,* 244, plate XI; *A Morning View of Blue Hill Village,* 10, 34, 42, **43**, 222, 226, 244–45, plate XIII; as natural historian, 14, 215–18, 223–27; parents of, 215; as poet, 216, 217, 242–44; *Scripture Animals,* 204–10, **206–9** passim, 215–22, **218**, 223–24, 244; *Self-Portrait,* **211**, 244; *Short Poems,* 203–4, **205**; silhouette self-portrait in *Scripture Animals* title page, **206**, 206–7; *Youth's Primer,* **202**, 202–3, **203**, 243
Flagg, Gershom, 46
Flavel, John, 199–200
Fletcher, Mrs. (midwife), 170, 174, 175
Fletcher, Nathaniel, 154
Flooding, 17, 20
Flucker, Lucy, 62, 73
Flucker, Thomas, 62; Copley's portrait of, 77, 82 n.39
Fodder, 14, 15
Food, 23
Forceps, obstetrical, 166, 167, 168
Forest-related activities on a Maine farm, 21 t
Foss, Betsy, 146
Foster (Boston stonecarvers), 232
Four Birds (Fisher), 222–23, plate XII
Fowler, Henry Thatcher, 65
Foxcroft, Thomas, 130, 132, 133–34
Francis O. Watts With Bird (Brewster), 240–41, plate XIV
Free will, 124, 131, 143
Freedom, 113. *See also* Beaver Hill
Freeman, Mary, 235–36; tombstone of, **235**
Freeman, Nathan, 131
Freemasonry, 157
"Freetown" (Fairfax), 107
Freewill Baptists, 118, 120, 120 t, 130–55 passim; growth of, by county, 134, 135 t, 137 t
French and Indian War, 121
Frenchman's Bay, 87
French-speaking settlers, 35–37
Freneau, Philip, 235
Friends, Religious Society of, *see* Quakers
Friendship (schooner), 78
Fries Rebellion, 4
Frog, in Fisher's *Scripture Animals,* 208
"From Revolution to Statehood, Maine Towns, Maine People" traveling exhibit, xviii
Frontier, 11, 14, 20, 129
Frost, William, 45
Frothingham, Benjamin, 76, 79, 81 n.37; bedstead by, **76**
Fryeburg, 14, 16, 45, 56, 153, 237
Fuel wood, 17, 18, 19, 20, 22–23
Fulling, 41, 42, 43, 60 n.30
Furnishing, interior, 35; of Montpelier, **69**, 70–79, **73–79** passim, 81 n.33

Gallatin, Albert, 184–85
Gallup, Lucy (Mrs. James Eldredge): portrait of, 238–39, **241**
Gardiner, John, 230
Gardiner (town), 41, 57
Garrison houses, 36
General Court (Mass. legislature), 83, 84–85, 87, 94, 95, 187

General Henry Knox (Stuart), **63**
Gilman, Nicholas and Mary Thing, 126
Gilman, Tristram, 126–28, 132
Gleason, John, 80 n.2
Gloucester, Mass., 132
Gookin, William Stoodley, *View of Saco Falls,* plate VI
Gore, Samuel, 81 n.37
Gorges, Ferdinando, 90
Gorham, William, 88
Gothic Revival, architectural, **57**, 57–58, 186
Gouldsborough, 87
Granger, Daniel, 151, 157
Grant, Moses, 71, 81 n.37, 176
Grasshopper, in Fisher's *Scripture Animals,* 216
Gravestones: as emblems, 209–10; style in, 230, 232–36, **234**, **235**
Graveyard School of poets, 233
Great Awakening, 122, 126, 148. *See also* New Light Stir
Great chain of being, 217–19
Great Fire of 1866 (Portland), 51
Greek Revival, architecture, 31, 51, 186
Greely, Jacob, 116 n.21
Greenleaf, Jonathan, 154
Greenleaf, Moses, 10, 15, 96
Gristmills, 14, 38, 39, 41, 66

"Half-shire" towns, 44–45
Hallowell, 55–56, 169; Milbert's ca.-1820 view of, **56**
Ham, son of Noah, 219, 220
Hamburg, N.Y., 159, 160
Hamilton, William, 80 n.10
Hamlin, Cyrus and Hannibal, 47
Hancock, John, 85, 86, 186
Hancock County, 47, 102, 134, 135 t, 137 t, 138 t; population, 129 t
Hannah Waldo Flucker (Blackburn), 77, 82 n.39
Hans, Billy, 54, 60 n.54; Codman's portrait of, **54**
Hanson, William, 18
Hapgood Carding Mill, So. Waterford, **43**
Harding, Chester, portrait of Moses Mason, **33**
Hardy, Jeremiah Pearson, 35; portrait of Sarah Molasses, plate IV
Harlem (now China), 107
Harmony of Maine (Belcher), 10
Hartford Convention, 6
Harvard College, 120, 121, 126, 168, 170, 177, 215, 241, 242–43; opposition to New Lights at, 122, 123
Harvey, Christopher, 203
Harvey, John, 105
Hasey, Isaac, 17–23
Hathaway house (Paris Hill), 28
Hay, 14, 15
Healing: medical (*see* Medicine; Obstetrics; Public health); spiritual, 156
Heart as emblem, 202–4, **203**, **204**
Heimert, Alan, 119
Herculaneum, 232
Hieroglyphikes (Quarles), 199, **200**
Hill, Eliza, 158
Hinkley, Mrs. (midwife), 170
History of New-Hampshire (Belknap), 187, 189, 196–97 n.37
History of the District of Maine (Sullivan), 10, 185, 188–95
History of the State of Maine (Williamson), 188
Hodgdon, Samuel, 77
Holmes, John, 7, 158
Holyoke, Edward Augustus, 178

"Hopkinsians," 48
Hubbard, Dr. (Hallowell), 170, 171, 175, 176
Hudson River School, 186
Humanism, Enlightenment, 124
Husbandry Spiritualized (Flavel), 199–200
Husbands, Herman, 105
Hyde, William, 215–16
Hypnotism, 153

Ilsley, Enoch, 88, 96
Indian disguises, settler protests in, *see* "White Indians"
Indian Fighter's Burying Ground (North Yarmouth), 232
Indian Island, 34
Indians, 2, 4, 34–35; deter British incursions, 84, 87; in Enoch Lincoln's "The Village," 237; in Jefferson's *Notes on Virginia*, 191, 192, 196n.28; in Sullivan's *History*, 191–93
Industrialization, rural, 38–42. *See also* Gristmills; Sawmills; Textile Manufacturing
Industriousness, 207, 221
Inflation, monetary, 128
Ingraham, Joseph Holt, 51
Ingraham, Mrs. (midwife), 170, 175
Interior furnishings: of Montpelier (Thomaston), **69,** 70–79, **73–79** passim
Intervention: divine, and slavery, 219–20; obstetrical, 183n.41
Irving, Washington, 229, 232, 236
Isaac, Rhys, 119, 138

Jackson, Andrew, 6
Jackson, Hall, 181n.6
Jackson, Henry, 68
Jackson, Lemuel, Jr., 233
James Prince and William Henry Prince (Brewster), 240, **242**
Jarvis, Samuel Forman, 56
Jefferson, Thomas, 6, 71, 185, 186, 191, 192, 196n.28, 232
Jeffersonians, 6, 143. *See also* Democratic-Republicans
Jennings, Francis, 192
Johnson, Bradbury, 39; design for Pepperellborough (Saco) meeting house, **39**
Johnson, Moses, 37
Johnson, Samuel, 171
Jonathan Fisher, Maine Parson (Chase), 199
Jonathan Fisher House (Blue Hill), 224
Jones, William, 105
Jonesborough, 87
Jordan, Ichabod, 157
Jordan, Rishworth, 157
Joseph Anthony and Company (Philadelphia), 81n.33

Kavanaugh, James, 56–57
Kendall, Edward Augustus, 108
Kennebec County, 45, 129, 134, 135t, 136, 137t, 138t; population, 129t
Kennebec Purchase, 136: map, plate I
Kennebec River valley, development of, 129, 136
Kennebeck Proprietors, 101, 102, 113, 136
Kennebunk, 45, 56, 154
Kennebunkport, 56, 154
Kentucky, 2
Kern, Louis J., 159–60
Kimball, John, Sr. and Jr., 51
King, Cyrus, 157
King, Mary, 157, 158, 163n.62. *See also* "Sister Mercy"

King, William, 7, 50, 111, 138; commissions Gothic Revival cottage, **57,** 57–58; Stuart portrait of, **139**
Kirker, Harold, 67
Kirkland, John Thornton, 231
Kittery, 42, 230
Kittredge, Thomas, 167, 179
Knox, Henry, 34, 58n.9, 62, **63,** 64, 65, 91; estate inventories, 73, 74, 75, 78; as land proprietor, 91, 102 (*see also* Waldo Patent); and Montpelier, 68, 69–70
Knox, Lucy Flucker, *see* Flucker, Lucy
Kossuth, 20

Lamson (Boston stonecarvers), 232
Land: clearing, 17 (*see also* Deforestation; Slash-and-burn agriculture); intervales, 14; proprietors, 4, 100–101, 106, 130, 136, 137–38, 230; speculation in, 2; titles, 192 (*see also* Property rights); use, and agricultural development, 13–25
Land transfer fees, 94
Langley, Batty, 56
Larkspur (Fisher), **225**
Latter Harvest, The (Fisher), 244, plate XI
Laudanum, 166, 181n.1
Launching of the Washington, The (Blunt), plate VIII
Law, Maine: ecclesiastical, 7; civil, 45. *See also* Taxes
Leavitt, Judith Walzer, 167
Lebanon, 14, 17–23
Lee, Jesse, 132
Lee, Mother Ann, 131
Legislature, Massachusetts, *see* General Court
Lewis, Lathrop, 140
Lexington, 20
Life expectancy, mariners', versus landsmen's, 54
Lime burning, 23, 43, 66
Lincoln, Enoch, 48, 237
Lincoln and Kennebec Bank building (Wiscasset), 46
Lincoln County (now Knox County), 45, 46, 134, 135t, 136, 137t, 138t; courthouse (built 1824–25), **46;** martial law declared, 85; population, 129t; subdivided, 94
Lion, 226
Litchfield, 112
Livestock, 18–19
Locke, John, 192, 193, 196n.33, 218–19
Log houses, **36,** 36–37, 48–49, 59n.14, 60n.41
Logan's speech, in *Notes on Virginia*, 192
Logging, 19, 21–22
Longfellow, Stephen, 88, 96
Lord, Nathaniel, 130
Loring, Amasa, 158, 161n.5
Loring, Levi, 163n.42
Lotteries, land, 15
Louisiana Purchase, 6
Louse, in Fisher's *Scripture Animals*, **218**
Lovell, 14
Lumbering, 16, 19, 41, 49, 66
Lyman, Job, 168

Machias, 14, 87, 92, 94
Madawaska Territory, 35–37; farmlots along St. John River, **35**
Madison, Dorothy ("Dolly"), 7
Madison, James, 184–85
Madrid, 20
Maine: architecture, 29–61; backcountry settlers, 100–2; cultural expressions, 9–10 (*see also* Arts

and esthetics; Painting; Poetry; Style); dependent on Massachusetts during Revolution, 1–2; emergence of post-Revolutionary cultural style in, 228–45; geology, 24n.6; land development and agriculture, 13–25; laws, 7, 45; legislative representation in General Court of Mass., 83, 94, 119; maps of the District, ii, **27**; population growth, 2, **3, 5**, 14–15, 15t, 22–23, 88, 90, 96, 129, 129t, 135t, 136, 137t, 138t; religious dissent in, 118–19, 128–43; separatist movement, **9**, 44, 48, 50, 83–97, 125, 230; statehood, 2, 7–8, 88, 91–92, 186, 193–94, 228; town plans (*see* Town plans); in War of 1812, 6, 7, 35, 50, 54, 97, 134

"Maine at Statehood: The Forgotten Years," Maine Humanities Council project, xvii

Maine Becomes a State (Banks), xvii

Maine Fire and Marine Insurance Company building, 52

Maine Historical Society, xviii

Maine Humanities Council, xvii–xviii

"Maine in the Early Republic" symposium, xviii

Maine Literary and Theological Institute at Waterville, 140

Maine Marine Fire and Insurance Company (Parris, architect), **52**

"Maine Towns, Maine People" traveling exhibit, xviii

Man and the Natural World (Thomas), 223

Man with a Gun (Earl), 238

Map of the District of Maine, A, (Carleton): 1795 version, **ii**; detail from 1798 version, **27**

Maple, 22; apostrophe to, 237

Marble quarrying, 44

Marbois, Francois, 191

Marden, Stephen, 116

Marsh, Mrs. James, 173, 175

Marshall, Joel M., 152, 153, 158

Martial law imposed in Lincoln County, 85

Mason, Moses, 32–34; portrait by Harding, **33**

Massachusetts: charter of 1691, 1; ecclesiastical law, 7; fails to defend District of Maine, 6, 7 (*see also* Neutrality); legislature (*see* General Court); navy sunk, 84; western, separatism in, 92–93, 94, 95

Massachusetts Bank, 188

Massachusetts Hall (Brunswick), 40

Massachusetts Historical Society, 185, 187, 189

Massachusetts Medical Society, 170, 171, 178

Mather, Cotton, 199

Maxcy (Salem stonecarvers), 232

McDaniel, Moses, 152, 157

McIntire, Samuel, 51

McLellan, Stephen and Hugh, 51

Medicine: learned versus folk, 171; as practiced by midwives, 171; professionalization of, 179–80, 183n.44. *See also* Obstetrics; Public Health

Meeting houses, 28, 120, 128; Asher Benjamin's design for, **30**; Brunswick's First Parish, 40; Hallowell's Old South, 55; Norridgewock, 48, **49**; Paris Hill Baptist, **28**, 47; Pepperellborough (now Saco), 39, **39**; Sabbathday Lake Shakers', 37, **37**

Melcher, Aaron, 40

Melcher, Samuel, III, 40, 42; weathervane by, **xix**

Merchant creditors, 100, 108, 113

Methodism, 48, 118, 132–43 passim; growth of, by county, 134, 135t, 137

Mica, 71

Midwifery, 165–80

Milbert, Jacques Gerard, *View of Hallowell,* **56**

Millenial Laws, Shaker, 38

Millenialism, 105, 112, 113, 114, 230, 233. *See also* Visions

Miller, Perry, 218

Mills, *see* Gristmills; Industrialization; Sawmills; Textile manufacturing

Mining, 43–44

Ministerial taxes, 7, 130, 132

Ministry, 120–21; cosmopolitan style, 121–22, 123–25; decline in number of Congregational ordinands, 128; New Light, 125–28

Miracles, 156

Miramichi fire (1820), 24n.9

Missouri Compromise, 8, 97

Mollasses, Sarah, 35, plate IV

Monmouth, 133

Monthly Anthology and Boston Review, The, 231

Montpelier (Thomaston), 64, **64**, 66–69; floor plan, **68**; interior furnishings, **69**, 70–79, **73–79** passim; wallpaper, 70, **71**, 71–73, **72**, 81n.29, plate X

Moody, Lemuel, 52; *The Signals of Portland Lighthouse,* plate IX

Moody, Samuel, 122

Mooney, William, 70

Moore, Jonathan, 168

Moral authority and esthetics, 228–31. *See also* Religion: and esthetics

More, Thomas, 196n.33

Mormonism, 148, 159–60, 162n.38

Morning View of Blue Hill Village, A (Fisher), 10, 34, 42, 210–12, 222, 226, 244–45, plate XIII; detail, **43**

Morton, Perez, James Swan's house design for, 66

Moseley, Elisha, 13

Moses Mason (Harding), **33**

Mr. James Eldredge (Brewster), 238–39, **240**

Mrs. James Eldredge (Brewster), 238–39, **241**

Murray, John, 132

Music, 10

Mysticism, and resistance, 103–6

Narraguagus, 87

Nash, Charles Elventon, 181n.7

Nash Cooperage, Waldoboro, **43**

Natural history, 14, 215–18, 223–27, 244

Nature and scripture, compatibility of, 199–200, 209, 212, 218, 219, 220–21, 223

Negroes, *see* Blacks

"Negro woman doctor" of Hallowell, 169, 172, 175, 181n.13

Neoclassicism, Federal, 29–31; Georgian, 228, 229; and interior statuary, 70–71; modified to reflect democratic values, 232, 235. *See also* Greek Revival

Neutrality, and the separation movement, in Revolutionary War, 84–87

New Birth, *see* Regeneration, spiritual

New Durham, N.H., 131

New England Conference, Methodist (1802), 133

New England Farmer, The (Deane), 51, 124

New England Primer, The, **201**, 201–2

New Gloucester, 37, 44, 140; New Light Stir at, 130–34

New Lebanon, N.Y. (now Mt. Lebanon), 37

New Light Particular Baptists, 130

New Light Stir: 118, 129–30; and political dissent, 133, 136, 138–43. *See also* Great Awakening

New Orleans, battle of, 6

Newcastle, 56

Newfield, 43
Nimes, Roman temple at, as model for Virginia statehouse, 232
Non-intercourse Act, for foreign trade: Jeffersonian, 6. *See also* Embargo of 1807.
Non-intercourse Act of 1790, regarding Indian relations, 4
Norridgewock, 48; county courthouse and meeting house, **49**
North Carolina, Regulation of 1768–1772, 105
North Yarmouth, 16, 92, 132, 232
Norway, 14
Notes on Virginia (Jefferson), 189, 191, 192
Noyes, John Humphrey, 160
Nursing, 171
Nutrition, 23
Nylander, Richard C., 81 n.29

Observations upon the Government of the United States of America (Sullivan), 188
Obstetrics, 165–80, 183 n.41
Old Lights, 122, 142
Old South Meeting House (Hallowell), 55
Old State House, Augusta, The (Codman), plate XV
Old Town, 14, 34–35
Oneida (N.Y.) Perfectionists, 148, 160
Opiates, 166
Orchards, 18, 19
Ordered Love, An (Kern), 159–60
Osgood, Francis, tombstone of, **235**
Otis, Harrison Gray, 65
Ourang Outan, in Fisher's *Scripture Animals*, 217–18
Owl, in Fisher's *Scripture Animals*, 217
Oxford and Cumberland Canal, 33
Oxford County, 15, 44–45, 129, 134, 135 t, 137 t, 138 t; jail, 47; population, 129 t

Page, Amos, 172
Page, Benjamin, 165–66, 168, 170, 172, 176, 179; fees, 183 n.37; medical training of, 167, 174–75
Paine, Lemuel, 112
Painting, 237–41; emblems of portraiture, 238–39, 240; historical, 229; Hudson River School, 186; portrait, 77–78, 82 n.39, 238–39, 240 (*see also individual subjects*)
Palermo, 106, 116 n.21
Paradise, 220–21. *See also* Eden
Paradise Lost (Milton), 204
Paris, 14, 16
Paris Hill, 28, 45, 47–48, 56, 230, 233; Hathaway House overmantel painting, plate II
Parker, Dr. (Pittston), 170, 176, 177
Parris, Albion K., 48
Parris, Alexander, 10, 51–52; design for Maine Marine Fire and Insurance Company, **52**; design for Portland Bank, **53**
Parsonages, 120, 128
Parsonsfield, 56
Passamaquoddy Indians, 34–35
Path of Riches, The (Sullivan), 188
Patricktown (now Somerville), 102
Pattee, Ezekiel, 106
Peacock as emblem, **208**, 208–9
Pearce, Joseph, 132
Pearl ash, 22
Peirce, Dr. (Kittery), 182 n.37
Penobscot (now Castine), *see* Castine
Penobscot County, 48–49, 129, 134, 135 t, 137 t, 138 t; population, 129 t
Penobscot Indians, 34, 35

Penobscot River valley, development of, 129
Pepperrell, William, 39
Pepperellborough (now Saco) meeting house (Johnson, architect), 39, **39**
Perfectionists, Oneidan, 148, 160
Phinney, Clement, 153
Piety, as benevolent social force, 233
Pigeon, in Fisher's *Scripture Animals,* 208, 223–24
Pitts, Parthena, 172
Plan, divine, 218, 219, 220–21, 223
Plan of Alfred, Maine, A (Bussell), plate V
Plato, 217
Pleasant Hill (Charlestown, Mass.), 66, 67
Plymouth, Mass., 112, 230
Plymouth Company, *see* Kennebeck Proprietors
Poetry: epic, 229; epitaph, 232; Fisher's emblematic, 216, 217, 242–44; Graveyard School, 233; neoclassical, Maine, 237
Poland, 132
Polygamy, 159. *See also* Spiritual wifery
Pompeii, 232
Poor, Jonathan, 33
Pope, Alexander, 219
Population, Maine, growth of, 2, **3**, **5**, 14–15, 15 t, 22–23, 88, 90, 96, 129, 129 t, 135 t, 136, 137 t, 138 t
Porter, Rufus, 33
Portland, 6, 92, 96, 230; architecture, 49–54; harbor, Moody's painting of, plate IX. *See also* Falmouth
Portland Bank, 54; Parris's design for, 52, **53**
Portland Convention for Independence, 50
Portland Observatory, 52, 54
Portraiture, at Montepelier, 77–78, 82 n.39. *See also individual subjects*
Portsmouth Naval Shipyard (Kittery), 42, plate VIII
Potash, 22
Pote, Anna, tombstone of, **234**
Pote, Elisha, 131
Potter, James, 127, 132
Pownalborough (now Wiscasset), *see* Wiscasset
Preble, William Pitt, 7
Predestination, 124, 143
Prentiss, Appleton, 71; billhead of, **73**
Presbyterians, 120, 120 t
Prince, James and William Henry, Brewster's portrait of, **242**
Privateers, 54
Property rights, 192, 193, 196 n.33
Proprietors, 4, 100–101, 106, 130, 136, 137–38, 230
Protest, violent, 4. *See also* Resistance
Providence, divine, and natural order, *see* Nature and scripture
Provincial Congress, 186–87
Public health, 189. *See also* Life expectancy; Obstetrics
Purges, 171
Puritanism, and emblematic world-view, 199, 200, 209, 212, 218, 219, 220–21, 223

Quakers, 119–20, 120 t, 139, 142
Quarles, Francis, *Hieroglyphikes,* 199, **200**
Quebec style farmstead, 35–37
Quincy Market (Parris), 51

Radicalism: in Massachusetts (*see* Shays' Rebellion); religious (*see* Religion: dissenting); separatist, in Maine, 95, 96
Randel, Benjamin, 131, 132
Record-keeping, medical, 176, 178, 181 n.11

Regeneration, spiritual, 122, 141, 142
Regulation of 1768–1772 (North Carolina), 105
Religion: and architecture (see Gothic Revival; Meeting houses; Millenial Laws); Cochranism, 148–53, 154–60, 161 n.5; discriminatory taxation of nonconformists, 7; dissenting, 50, 118–19, 129–43; esthetics and, 38, 57, 230–31. See also individual sects
Relly, James, 132
Remarks on the Employment of Females as Practitioners in Midwifery, 179
Remich, Daniel, 152–53
Remich, James, 159, 162 n.26
Republicans, 184, 185. See also Democratic-Republicans
Resistance, 4, 117 n.40; "White Indian," 101, 103–5, 105, 106, 112–13
Reverend Samuel Deane (Brewster), **121**
Revivals, 132, 153–54, 156. See also Great Awakening; New Light Stir; Second Great Awakening
Revolutionary War: Castine occupied by British, 84, 87; debates on English sovereignty during, 192; disrupts education of divinity students, 128; Knox employs fellow veterans of, 81 n.37; logic of, used to defend separation, 86–87, 88, 90–91; Mass. navy sunk, 84; neutrality movement in Eastern Maine, 84–87; Portland burned (1775), 51; religious dissent fostered by, 154; veterans given land warrants, 15; western Mass. counties isolated from, 95
Ridlon, Gideon T., 149–51, 159
Road building, 29, 30, 94–95
Robbins, Chandler, 177
Robinson, Moses, 103–4
Rogers, John, 122
Romanticism, American, 185, 186, 193, 196 n.20
Ruggles, Thomas, 57
Rush, Benjamin, 182 n.36

Sabbathday Lake Shaker meeting house, **37**
Saco, 39, 153, 154; Gookin's *View of Saco Falls,* plate VI; Pepperellborough meeting house, **39**
Saco Iron Works Corporation, 39
Saco River valley, development of, 129
St. John River valley, settlement of, 35
St. Patrick's Church (Newcastle), 56
St. Paul's Cathedral (Bulfinch), 51
Salem, (Maine), 20
Salem, Mass., 230, 232, 243, 244
Salt marsh agriculture, 14, 24 n.6
Sands, David, 129
Sarah Molasses (Hardy), plate IV
"Satan's Great Device" (Fisher), 203–4
Savage, Edward, 177
Sawmills, 14, 40–41, 66
Scarborough, 16, 92, 154
Schola Cordis (Harvey), 203
Scott, Donald, 120
Scripture: emblems of, in Fisher's *Morning View of Blue Hill Village,* 210–11; and nature, compatability of, 199–200, 209, 212, 218, 219, 220–21, 223
Scripture Animals (Fisher), 204–10, **206–9, 218,** 244
Searsport, 39
Second Great Awakening, 126, 133, 134, 148
Sedition Act, Sullivan's treatise against, 188
Separate Baptists, 118, 120, 120 t, 130–43 passim; growth of, by county, 134, 135 t, 137
Separate Congregationalists, 122–23, 130. See also Separate Baptists

Separatist movement, 44, 48, 50, 83–97, 125, 230; broadside of, **9;** conventions, 50, 88, 91–92, 125; election results, 138 t; and religious dissent, 133, 136, 138–43
Serpent, as symbol in Fisher's art, 221–22
Settlement patterns, Maine, 2, **3, 5,** 14–15, 15 t; Acadian French, 35–37; Indian, 34–35; in new agriculture communities, 32–34; river valley development, post-Revolutionary, 129
Sewall, David, 165
Sewall, Hannah, 165–66, 167, 179
Sewall, Moses, 55, 167
Sewall, Ruth Barrell, 167
Seymour, John, Jr., drawing of Falmouth (now Portland), **50**
Shakers, 37–38, 118, 120 t, 130–56 passim; Sabbathday Lake Meeting House, **37**
Shannon, Richard Cutts, 157
Shaw, Francis, Jr., 85, 86, 96
Shaw, Samuel, 75
Shays' Rebellion, 4, 91, 92–93, 95, 125, 133
Sherburne, Andrew, 154
Sherman, Aaron, 57
Shipbuilding, 16, 24 n.6, 41, 42, **43,** 44, 66
Shipping, 4, 49
Shire towns, plans and architecture of, 44–49, 56
Short Poems (Fisher), 203–4, **205**
Shurtleff, James, 108–12, 113, 116 n.28
Signals of Portland, Lighthouse, The (Moody), plate IX
Simpson, Benjamin, 154–55, 157
Simpson, George and Ebenezer, 155
Simpson, Henry, 70
"Sister Mercy" revived by Cochran, 150–51
Skowhegan, 14
Slash-and-burn agriculture, 16–17, 18, 19, 21, 24 n.9
Slavery, 8, 97, 219–20
Smellie, William, 167, 178–79
Smith, Elias, 134, 154, 159
Smith, Gamaliel E., 152, 159
Smith, Hezekiah, 130
Smith, John, 16th-c. description of New England by, 190
Smith, Joseph, 162 n.38
Smith, Rowland, 55
Smith, Thomas, 88, 122, 123, 125
Snake, as symbol in Fisher's art, 221–22
Soccabeson, Denny, 35, plate III
"Society of Free Brethren and Sisters" (Cochranites), 155, 159, 160
Society of Friends, see Quakers
Society of the Cincinnati, 75
Somerset County, 48, 129, 134, 135 t, 136, 137 t, 138 t; courthouse, **49;** physicians' fee agreement, 179–80; population, 129 t
Somerville, 102
Soul effigies, gravestone, 233, **234,** 235
South Waterford, Hapgood Carding Mill, **43**
Southeast View of Fort George, A (Jones), **85**
Sovereignty, English, 192
Speculators in land, 2. See also Proprietors
Spider, in Fisher's *Scripture Animals,* 224
Spiritual wifery, 156, 157, 159, 160
Squatters, 7, 100–107 passim, 113, 137–38, 236
Statehood: Kentucky and Tennessee, 2; Maine, 2, 7–8, 186, 193–94, 228
Statehood conventions, Maine, see Conventions, separatist
Statistical Surveys (Greenleaf), 10
Statuary, neoclassical, 70–71
Stephenson, Abigail Colcord, 152

Stinchfield, Ephraim, 152, 157
Stone, Joseph, 131
Stonecarving, New England traditions of, 232–33
Stone fences, 18, 20
Storing, Herbert F., 141
Streben, 193
Strict Congregationalists, 122–23, 130. *See also* Separate Baptists
Stuart, Gilbert, 10; *General Henry Knox,* **63**; *William King,* **139**
Sturbridge, Mass., 30; comparative maps of town center, **31**
Style: architectural, 8, 10, 29; emergence of, in post-Revolutionary Maine, 228–45; ministerial, 121–28; and status, 79; in tombstone art, 232–36, **234, 235**
Substance of a Late Remarkable Dream, The (Shurtleff), 108–11
Sudbury Canada, *see* Bethel
Sullivan, James, 10, 40–41, 96, 113, 185, 231; birthplace, 195 n.8; *History of the District of Maine,* 185, 188–95; portrait of, **187**; youth and public career of, 186–88
Sullivan, John, 186
Surveying, 18, 113
Swan, James, 67
Symbolism, Fisher's, 221–22. *See also* Emblems

Tableaux-vivants, Edenic, 150, 157, 159–60
Taverns, 29, 39
Taxes: abatements of, 94; church, and dissenters, 7, 120, 130, 132; Samuel Deane fulminates against, 125
Tennent, Gilbert, 122
Tennessee, 2
Textile manufacturing, 4, 41, **43**
Thacher, Thomas, 170
Thatcher, Lucy Flucker Knox, 64, 82 n.39
Thomas Flucker (Copley), 77, 82 n.39
Thomas, Keith, 223, 226
Thomaston, 43–44, 65, 66
Thompson, Conn., 30
Thompson, Deborah, 48
Thompson, Samuel, 88, 93, 94, 95, 97
Timber lands, 19. *See also* Lumbering; Woodlots
Titcomb, Benjamin, Jr., 50; portrait of, **51**
Titcomb, William, gravestone of, 233, **234**
Toleration Act of 1811, 140
Tombstones: as emblem, 209–10; style in, 230, 232–36, **234, 235**
Topsfield, 15, 20
Topsham, 4, 39–42, 45; 1828 map, **42**; 1780 and 1802 maps, **40**
Torrey, Priscilla, 116 n.28
Town and Country Builders Assistant, Ye (Benjamin?), 68. *See also Country Builder's Assistant*
Town plans, 26–29, 30–31, 32; Acadian, 35; Brunswick, **40, 42**; and county seats, 44–49; and rural industrialization, 39–42; Shaker, 37–38; Sturbridge, Mass., **31**; Topsham, **40, 42**
Treaty of Paris, 1, 2
Tree: beech, 22; birch, 22; elm, 22; hackmatack, 22; hemlock, 23; hornbeam, 22; larch (juniper), 22; oak, 16, 22; pine, 14, 22; spruce, 23
Turner, Benjamin and David, 116 n.21
Tyng, Eleazar, 122

Unitarians, Deane as precursor to, 124
United Society of Believers, *see* Shakers
Unity, 112
Universalism, 118, 120 t, 130–49 passim

Urn/willow motif, on gravestones, 234–35, **235,** 236
Utopia (More), 196 n.33

"Valuable Collection of Recipes, A" (Curtis), 170
Vaughan, Benjamin, 55, 169
Vaughan, Charles, 55
Veterans, Revolutionary War: employed by Knox, 81 n.37; land warrants, 15
View of Hallowell (Milbert), 55, **56**
View of Paris Hill, A (from L. Hathaway house, artist unknown), plate II
View of Saco Falls (Gookin), plate VI
"Village, The" (Lincoln), 237
Village centers, 26, 28–29, 32
Violent protest, 4. *See also* Resistance
Virginia, religious dissent in, 138–39
Virtue, promoted by Maine climate, 190–91
Visions: Barlow's, 102–3, 111; Shurtleff's, 108–11
Vose, Thomas, 81 n.37
Voyage trope, 243–44

Wadsworth, Peleg, 88
Wait, Thomas B., 20, 50, 88, 93, 96, 97
Waldo, Hannah, 62; Blackburn's portrait of, 77, 82 n.39
Waldo, Samuel, 62; portrait of, **77,** 77–78
Waldoboro, 41; Nash's Cooperage, 43, **43**
Waldo County, 102
Waldo Patent, 62; resistance in, 106
Wallingford, George, 158
Wallpaper, at Montpelier, 70, **71,** 71–73, **72,** 81 n.29, plate X
Ware, John, 48
War of 1812, 6, 7, 35, 50, 54, 97, 134
Warren (Maine), 45
Warren, R.I., Baptist Association, 130
Washington, George, and neoclassical mourning ornaments, 232
Washington (frigate), 42; launching of, plate VIII
Washington County, 94, 134, 135 t, 138 t; population, 129 t
Washington Plantation, *see* Newfield
Water power, 14, 40–41
Waterboro, 45
Waterford, 56
Watts, Francis O., portrait of, 240–41, plate XIV
Webster, Noah, 229
Webster-Ashburton Treaty, 35
Wedgwood, Josiah, 72
Weld, 20
Wells, 154, 230
Wesley, John, 142
Whiskey Rebellion, 4, 105
"White Indians," resistance by, 101, 103–5, 105, 106, 112–13
Whitefield, George, 122, 123, 131, 158
Whitney, Geoffrey, **209,** 209–10
Whittemore, Charles P., 195 n.8
Whitwell, Benjamin, 107
Widgery, William, 88, 94, 95
Wiggins, Bradstreet, 108
Willard, Simon, 74
William King (Stuart), **139**
Williams, Dr. (Hallowell), 170, 171, 172, 174, 175
Williamson, William D., 16, 26, 58 n.7, 188
Wilson, Harold, 13–14
Wilton, 14
Winchester, Alice, 199
Winslow, Mrs. (midwife), 170
Winter Meditations (Mather), 199

Index 257

Winthrop, John, 196n.33
Winthrop (town), 41
Wiscasset, 45, 46, 54, 56, 57
Wither, George, 203, **204**
Wolcott, Abigail, and Oliver Ellsworth, Earl's painting of, 238, **239**
Wolves, 20
Wood, Gordon, 119
"Wood, Madame" (Sally Barrell), 167, 181n.6
Wood, *see* Deforestation; Forest-related activities; Fuel wood; Logging; Lumbering; Tree
Woodlands, the (suburban Philadelphia estate), 80n.10
Woodlots, 17. *See also* Fuel wood; Timber lands

Wright, Conrad, 124
Wynne, John, 208–9

XYZ Affair, 127

Yale, Maine ministers prepared at, 120
Yarmouth, 230
York, 31, 41, 45–46, 92
York County, 15, 45, 134, 135t, 137t, 138t; population, 129t
Yorktown, battle of, 2
Young, Peter, 154, 156
Youth's Primer, The (Fisher), **202**, 202–3, **203**, 243

PHOTOGRAPHIC ACKNOWLEDGMENTS

J. David Bohl: Illustrations 24, 27, 34, 38, 39, 40, 41, 42, 45, 47, 48, 49, 52, 67, 70; Plates III, IV, VI, VIII, IX, X, XII
Tom Jones: Illustration 2
Abe Morell: Plate II
Henry E. Peach: Illustrations 17, 19, 54